D1117484

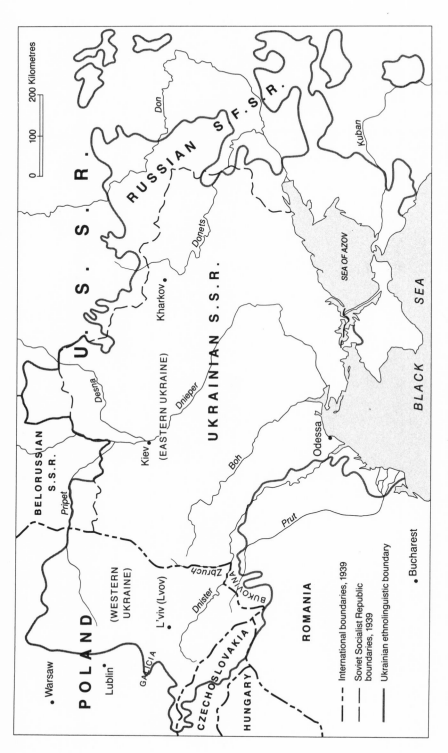

Map by Geoffrey Matthews

Old Wounds

Jews, Ukrainians and the Hunt for Nazi War Criminals in Canada

Harold Troper
and
Morton Weinfeld

University of
North Carolina Press
Chapel Hill and London

Preface © 1989 by Harold Troper and Morton Weinfeld
All rights reserved

First published in the United States in 1989
by the University of North Carolina Press

Originally published in Canada in 1988
by Viking, a division of the Penguin Group
© 1988 by Harold Troper and Morton Weinfeld

The paper in this book meets the guidelines for permanence and durability of the Committee on Production Guidelines for Book Longevity of the Council on Library Resources.

Printed in the United States of America

93   92   91   90   89   5   4   3   2   1

Library of Congress Cataloging-in-Publication Data

Troper, Harold Martin, 1942–
    Old wounds : Jews, Ukrainians and the hunt for Nazi war criminals
in Canada / Harold Troper and Morton Weinfeld.
      p. cm.
    "Originally published in Canada in 1988 by Viking, a division of
the Penguin Group"—T.p. verso.
    Bibliography: p.
    Includes index.
    ISBN 0-8078-1852-6 (alk. paper)
    1. Jews—Canada—Politics and government. 2. Ukrainians—Canada—Politics
and government. 3. War criminals—Canada. 4. Canada—Ethnic relations.
I. Weinfeld, M. (Morton) II. Title.
F1035.J5T76   1989   88-40535
323.1'1924'071—dc19   CIP

Passages from the following are used by permission:

Heike, Wolf-Dietrih, "History of the Ukrainian Division 'Galicia'," ms. p. 97. Translated by Andrij Wynnyckyj. The manuscript has now been reedited and published as Wolf-Dietrih Heike, *The Ukrainian Division 'Galicia': A Memoir*, Shevchenko Scientific Society (Toronto), 1988. Edited by Yury Boshyk.

Kostash, Myrna, *All of Baba's Children*, Hurtig Publishers Ltd. (Edmonton), 1977, p. 214.

Paris, Erna, *Jews*, © 1980. Used by permission of Macmillan of Canada, a Division of Canada Publishing Corporation, pp. 153–54.

Lupul, Manoly, ed., *Visible Symbols: Cultural Expression Among Canada's Ukrainians*, Canadian Institute of Ukrainian Studies, University of Alberta (Edmonton), 1984, p. 187, pp. 154–55.

Riasnovsky, Alexander V., and Barnes Riznik, eds., *Generalizations in Historical Writing*, University of Pennsylvania Press (Philadelphia), 1963, p. 134.

Deschênes, Jules, *The Sword and the Scales*, Butterworths (Scarborough), 1979, p. 189.

To our families

H.T., M.W.

Contents

Preface

On April 18, 1988, an Israeli court declared a Cleveland motor mechanic guilty of war crimes and crimes against humanity. The court was satisfied that John Demjanjuk was the notorious Ivan the Terrible who operated the gas chambers at the Treblinka death camp, where more than a million Jews and other innocent victims of Nazi terror were systematically murdered. This Ukrainian immigrant, who came to the United States in 1952, becomes only the second person in Israel's history to be sentenced to death. The other was Adolf Eichmann.

Treblinka, the factory of death in which Demjanjuk committed his crimes, was completed in 1942. But in the bitter autumn of that year, Treblinka was still unknown to the Allies. Their focus was on the Nazi war machine then both successfully shoring up its victories in western Europe and smashing eastward into the Soviet Union. It seemed all of Europe would soon be under the Nazi heel. If there were a single ray of hope, it was that the United States had finally entered the war, its industrial and military power now committed to a total defeat of the common enemy.

The promise of eventual Allied victory could hardly have been cold comfort to those crammed into the boxcars that pulled into Sobibor, Chelmno, Majdanek, Belzac, Auschwitz and Treblinka. In these man-made outposts of hell, the Nazis and those who joined them as foot soldiers in the Holocaust were writing a new chapter in the already tragic saga of human bestiality.

But during 1942, even as Allied concern was focused on the battlefield, evidence of Nazi atrocities continued to mount. The Allies responded with promises — not of rescue today but of justice tomorrow. There would be a "fearful retribution," promised Franklin Roosevelt. The Nazi murder of "scores of innocent hostages" would not go unpunished. No less forceful, Winston Churchill added his own pledge: "Retribution for these crimes must henceforth take its place among the major purposes of the war." Civilized society, he asserted, would demand that the Nazi acts of wanton savagery be accounted for.

But, for both the Nazis and their victims, the death camps were the end of a long process during which the democracies had at no time offered refuge to those who faced death. When offered the Jews, the democracies turned their backs. If they did not care before, why should they suddenly make a show of caring now? Perhaps the warnings were designed more for Allied domestic consumption than they were for the Nazis and their collaborators. In any event, the Nazis were not listening. They were fixed on their murderous course and were not about to be deterred, at least not by words with so hollow a ring. To be credible the words would need to be backed up by the possibility of action, and that appeared most unlikely. The Nazis were then winning the war.

Nor were Allied promises of retribution backed by preparatory action. Although a United Nations War Crimes Commission was announced in the autumn of 1942, it was not given a clear mandate, a credible budget, technical assistance or practical authority to plan any post-war initiatives against Nazis then drawing a circle of death around conquered Europe. During the next three years, those caught in the circle could only pray for rescue through Allied victory. For millions of Nazi victims, this victory, in 1945, would come too late.

What became of Allied promises of a post-war accounting? Very little. Action taken against war criminals can hardly be judged sufficient when measured against the monstrosity of the crimes committed. Why was this the case? Even had the Allies' post-war resolve to deal with the war criminals been firm — and there is reason to conclude it was not always so — problems in applying Western standards of justice were monumental. The legal structure for international war crimes trials was largely unknown and untested. The problems of agreeing on law, jurisdiction, logistics, research, and the appeals processes, to name only a few, were incredibly difficult while much of continental Europe lay in rubble. Perhaps the most telling truth was that, in the end, justice simply was not a priority. Indeed, the post-war world barely stopped to take account of the terrible night of Nazi mass murder. Weary of war, yet confronted by a deterioration in international relations, the world community was fixed on other problems.

Events were moving quickly. Barely had the rumble of war grown still before the grand alliance that had so recently crushed the Nazis was itself in ruins. With the exception of the high-profile Nuremberg Trials, Soviet and Western authorities could not or would not cooperate on further joint war crimes trials. Both sides rejected cooperation on even such basic elements as a justice program. Mutual mistrust crippled almost all transfers of accused criminals or exchanges of evidence and witnesses between Soviet and Western-controlled jurisdictions. Sporadic war crimes trial initiatives by the Western Allies were difficult, few and often ill prepared.

What is more, as the Soviet ally was being redefined as a dangerous enemy, the German enemy was being rehabilitated into an ally. Western energy was directed not at punishment of the old Nazi enemy but at assuring that a reconstructed West German state would be a stalwart of the emerging Western alliance. Important advocates of German reconstruction argued that trials of Nazi criminals and their collaborators were counterproductive. It was time for a new beginning. Whatever their faults, the Nazis were anti-Communists, and Communism was now the clear threat. Before long, some leaders who had so recently administered Nazi Germany would be called upon to ensure a smoothly operating transition to the new democratic Germany.

As the victorious Allies turned their attention to virtually everything but punishing Nazi war criminals, no group must have been more surprised than the Nazi war criminals themselves. Many were not about to second guess whether or not the Allies would eventually get around to them. Instead, they scrambled to remove themselves as far as possible from Allied hands. Some of those involved in the mass murder of millions were secreted out of harm's way along the "Rat Line," a well-marked and well-maintained route organized to rescue Nazis from the clutches of the Allies and give them new homes and identities. Others, particularly those non-Germans who collaborated with the Nazis and played a hands-on role in the mass murder of Jews, Gypsies and others, quietly melted in with post-war displaced persons awaiting resettlement in the West.

When the United States, like Canada, decided to open its doors to displaced persons, it had to cope with domestic fears that any program of wholesale Displaced Person (DP) immigration would be dominated by Jewish arrivals — Holocaust survivors. Accordingly, the United States Congress approved legislation giving preference to non-Jews, especially Balts and *Volksdeutsche*, who refused post-war repatriation back to their countries of legal origin, countries now behind the iron curtain. While this legislation specifically prohibited the entry of Nazis into the United States, slipshod security checks, more intent on barring suspected leftists than on keeping out Nazis, may well have made it easier for Nazi war criminals and collaborators to get into the United States than it was for their victims.

Throughout the 1950s and 1960s, occasional revelations that Nazi war criminals were living in the United States brought virtually no government response. This inattention was not caused by the government's lack of legal options. Any entry of Nazis into the United States was clearly illegal until 1952 when the DP legislation ended. Even after that date American immigration legislation branded Nazis and Nazi collaborators an undesirable class of immigrant. But almost nothing was done. Why? Admittedly, overworked government immigration investigators could not give equal priority to all immigration-abuse cases. And with little public outrage and no encouragement from superiors to track down suspected war criminals, Nazi cases were seldom marked urgent. Those few cases initiated against alleged Nazi war criminals were ill prepared and complicated by a reluctance of federal authorities to reach outside American borders for evidence, especially if the effort meant dealing with Soviet authorities.

But pressure for action was building. To some, particularly American Jewry, the fact that even one Nazi war criminal should have found safe haven in the United States was intolerable. By the early 1970s influential representatives of the B'nai Brith's Anti-Defamation League and the Jewish War Veterans put their lobbying strength behind the growing chorus of those demanding action. All that seemed to be lacking now was political will.

Before long the cause was taken up by Congressman Joshua Eilberg and, more importantly, Congresswoman Elizabeth Holtzman. Incensed at the apparent lack of commitment among federal immigration authorities, Eilberg and Holtzman put their political weight behind the campaign for effective legal action. In 1978, after repeated prodding and several false starts, the Justice Department assumed jurisdiction for dealing with alleged Nazi war criminals in the United States. In turn the Justice Department organized an Office of Special Investigation (osi) and gave it the mandate and resources necessary to begin a housecleaning of Nazi war criminals living in the United States. Furthermore, on the initiative of Congresswoman Holtzman, the Immigration Act was specifically amended to call for the deportation from the United States of any person who had participated in wartime persecution of anyone "because of race, religion, national origin or political opinion."

The basic legal procedure for initiating legal proceedings against suspected war criminals was clear enough. If a Nazi war criminal had entered the United States, he or she could only have done so by lying about wartime activities. If entry was illegal, then any subsequent American naturalization proceeding was also illegal. If the osi could gather evidence to show that an alleged war criminal had knowingly lied or otherwise concealed relevant information about wartime activities, proceedings could be initiated first to strip that person of American citizenship and then to have him or her deported. If deportation would not guarantee that the alleged war criminal would ever face the bar of justice, at least it affirmed an

American determination not knowingly to be a haven for war criminals.

The procedure looks simpler than it has actually proven to be. Even with the cooperation of other countries — including countries behind the iron curtain — regarding the collection of documentary evidence and the availability of eye witnesses, federal authorities have proceeded with caution. The process of denaturalization and deportation is not taken lightly. No government wants to make mistakes, and research often takes years. Legal proceedings are slow, often cumbersome, and with the likelihood of appeals, cases can drag on for years. What is more, the biological clock keeps on ticking. It is increasingly apparent that no more than a handful of accused Nazi war criminals will ever face loss of American citizenship and deportation. Most will die peacefully in their beds, their American beds.

But the United States can use another legal route to rid itself of these unwelcome guests. The American legal system is able to cooperate with countries seeking the extradition of accused Nazi war criminals in order to put them on trial. It did so in the case of John Demjanjuk, for example, who was turned over to Israel and eventually found guilty of war crimes and crimes against humanity.

These legal proceedings have not gone without their controversial spin-offs. On occasion they have inflamed inter-ethnic tensions. For some ethnic communities, especially eastern Europeans rallying to the defense of one of their own, the issue is not about ridding America of a war criminal. It is about defending their community's good name. Whereas Jews see the OSI program as long overdue, eastern Europeans and others see it as a wholesale witchhunt directed against their communities. For them, the Soviet Union is forever in the shadows attempting to manipulate a war criminal scare. No group has been more forceful in its protest than the Ukrainian American community. Consequently, in the United States, as in Canada, the gulf between the organized Ukrainian community and the Jewish community over this issue has ripped open old wounds and set off a fireworks of political lobbying.

One suspects that a behind-the-scenes look at this lobbying in Canada and the United States would reveal parallels in tactics and dilemmas. Both national societies are ones in which ethnic lobbies are still regarded as somehow "suspect." For all the proliferation of ethnic and racial organizations and accompanying hoopla about the value of ethnic diversity, a cloud hangs over ethnic political activity. It seems vaguely disloyal, smacking of dual allegiance.

Accordingly, partisans on the war criminal issue, like partisans for any interest group, are quick to cloak their advocacy in the rhetoric of national interest. Their cause mirrors cherished values and fundamental ideals of freedom and justice. To Jewish groups, the pursuit of war criminals underscores America's fidelity to law, justice and public morality. Ukrainian and other eastern European groups warn against violations of due process. They also caution against group slander and letting down American vigilance in the face of Soviet subterfuge.

Thus inter-ethnic conflict seems unavoidable and, in liberal democracies like Canada and the United States, such conflict complicates the always difficult task of accommodating diverse groups within a political framework whose original intent was to link individuals and the state. Social reality tramples political theory. How can it be otherwise? Acting on their rights to associate freely and to petition government for redress of grievances, citizens do not give a wit about theory. If their activities strain the pluralist character of the society and conflict with one another, then that is the price of democratic freedom. No one should assume that politics in pluralist democracies is simple.

If the Ukrainian and Jewish communities have collided over the problem of war criminals, the points of impact have been different in the United States and in Canada. In the United States, the two groups collided after the 1978 Holtzman Amendment and after the osi gave legal and administrative force to the purge of accused Nazi war criminals from America. Not so in Canada; there the groups locked horns in 1985 when the government initiated a public policy debate over what course of action, if any, was open to rid Canada of Nazi war criminals. In the United States, the Ukrainian community reacted against legislation already in place. In Canada, it attempted to influence the introduction of legislation — and succeeded.

The Jewish and Ukrainian communities of Canada and the United States themselves also differ. In both societies the Jewish community is reckoned as a major player in the game of ethnic politics, but the Ukrainian community enjoys a much greater status within the Canadian ethnic mosaic than it does in the United States. According to the 1980 U.S. census, approximately 730,000 Americans claimed some or all Ukrainian ancestry. Canada's figures are roughly the same, but the U.S. population is about ten times that of Canada. Thus the Canadian Ukrainian community is proportionately about ten times the size of its American counterpart.

In addition, in the United States, Ukrainians comprise a relatively small ethnic group when compared with other Euro-ethnic groups like Italians, Irish, Poles and, of course, Jews, who alone number more than five million. Ukrainian Americans have a relatively low profile and are but a drop in the American political bucket. In Canada, by contrast, Ukrainians comprise one of the largest ethnic groups, white or nonwhite. According to the Canadian census, they outnumber the Jewish community by more than two to one. Ukrainian Canadians are also a well-organized, cohesive group and certainly a dominant force in Canadian ethnic politics.

Part of the Ukrainian Canadian clout results from patterns of regional concentration. In the United States, Ukrainians are scattered throughout the northeastern and central industrial states, where they form a small, almost negligible proportion of the population. Although almost half of those who claim Ukrainian ancestry are concentrated in the mid-Atlantic states, they have nothing to compare with the clout of Ukrainians in the western Canadian provinces, where 70 percent of Canada's Ukrainians live and comprise a major voting block.

Ironically, given comparable group sizes, the Ukrainian American community has a proportionately larger post-war migration, about 80,000 as compared with Canada's estimated 33,000. But if the representation of a Ukrainian DP generation among Ukrainian Americans is larger, it is also more dispersed across major American urban centres of the northeastern and central states. The Canadian post-war immigrants are, by contrast, centred in Toronto and Montreal rather than in the Canadian west. As a result Ukrainian DP politics, often nationalist and anti-Communist, is more intense in Canada than in the United States.

In both countries, however, Ukrainians have experienced a steady weakening of community bonds as one generation gives way to the next. The outlook for maintaining their community is brighter in Canada, in part because of the community's relative size and concentration. Moreover, Ukrainian Canadians enjoy a more advantageous socioeconomic position. According to an analysis of the 1970 U.S. census, Ukrainian American males seem unable to translate their above-average educational credentials into comparable professions and incomes.

Population size, regional concentration and substantial economic mobility have given Ukrainian Canadians a secure power base in the Canadian political system. They have been prominent in federal and provincial governance both as elected officials and as public servants. In contrast, American Ukrainians have very little representation and influence in the legislative or executive branches.

In some ways, comparing the Jewish communities in Canada and the United States yields inverse conclusions. American Jews outnumber Canadian Jews 5 million to 300,000. In addition, American Jews are more integrated into the fabric of American political life both as elected officials and as members of organizations that lobby the American polity. Conversely, Canadian Jews are "more Jewish" than their American counterparts. In Canada, one hears more Yiddish and Hebrew. Canadian Jews also have a lower rate of intermarriage, are less likely to be religiously Reform, are more likely to be Orthodox, contribute proportionately more to Jewish charities and, most important, have a higher proportion of Holocaust survivors as part of their community.

One explanation for these differences lies in the immigration sequence. The foundations of Canadian Jewry were laid almost a century after those of the United States. Even today proportionately more Canadian Jews are likely to be foreign-born, whether Holocaust survivors or more recent arrivals from North Africa, Israel or the Soviet Union, than are American Jews. This difference might explain both the strengthened Canadian Jewish identity and the lower levels of political integration.

The other explanation has to do with the posture of Canada toward its ethnic minorities. Canada is portrayed as a mosaic, a society that actively encourages its ethnic groups to retain their heritage, while the United States is seen as a melting pot, holding out to ethnic groups the option of Americanization. On the surface these differences prove more apparent than real. Both societies continue to see pronounced slippage in ethnic identification among second and subsequent generations. Both have also seen historic racism and paternalism directed at immigrant and racial or ethnic minorities.

But the mosaic-versus-melting-pot distinction is pronounced at the levels of public political rhetoric and legislation. The recognition of group differences is embedded in the fabric of Canadian society dating back to the recognition of equal status for English and French languages and the equal protection of Catholic and Protestant education in the legal compact that organized the Canadian state well over one hundred years ago. The new Canadian Constitution and its important Charter of Rights and Freedoms also recognizes in official form the multicultural nature of Canadian society. This recognizion is backed up by federal and provincial agencies and by financial assistance to ethnic minorities, which enables them to survive and flourish. Nothing nearly comparable exists in the Constitution of the United States or in American governance.

Ironically, the greater identity of Canadian ethnic groups and the constitutional recognition of the legitimacy of ethnic group life have not yet translated into a corresponding degree of political clout. It is in America that the conception of the ethnic vote, notably in major urban centres, is a recognized feature of the political landscape. But Canada is catching up. Ethnic political muscle will increasingly be a force to reckon with. Ethnic lobbying on the issue of Nazi war criminals stands as a testament to this shift.

In the United States, Jewish lobbying on the issue of war criminals and the subsequent Holtzman initiatives met little effective Ukrainian opposition. In Canada, the large-scale Ukrainian presence, mobilized and increasingly self-confident, proved able to ethnicize the war criminal issue to such an extent that it commanded the attention of Canadian politicians. In spite of all their protests, as during the Demjanjuk hearings, the Ukrainian American lobby and its allies proved unable to close down the OSI or to blunt its thrust. In Canada, however, the Ukrainian lobby has had a major impact in shaping the course of government response to the Nazi war criminal problem.

In both the United States and Canada we are witnessing the coming together of strong ethnic attachments and increased political sophistication and mobilization. In the past, these two traits varied inversely with one another. In both societies, this may decreasingly be the case. The United States has a long tradition of ethnic politics at the local, state and federal levels. The current ethnic revival, much ballyhooed, may serve to energize the ethnic dimension of American politics along both racial and ethnocultural lines. The politicization of ethnic life and the ethnicization of politics proceeds apace in both the United States and Canada, if by different routes. In both North American societies, similarities, if not overlapping tactics, dilemmas and challenges for democratic and effective governance, remain. So, unfortunately, do too many Nazi war criminals who have yet to account for their crimes.

Acknowledgments

The actual writing of *Old Wounds* was the easiest part of our enterprise. Initially we set our sights no higher than producing a scholarly article. But as we developed a research plan, collected data, evaluated and organized the information, we realized a book might be possible. As our project expanded, we kept reassuring each other there would be a publisher interested in our final work. But we were never really alone. Our labour was made much easier by the assistance and encouragement of colleagues and friends of this enterprise. Without them this book would be far weaker and our efforts less rewarding.

We are especially grateful to those who demonstrated trust in our scholarship by allowing us unrestricted access to important collections of documentation. The cooperation of John Gregorovich (Ukrainian Civil Liberties Commission), Milton Harris, Jack Silverstone and Alan Rose (Canadian Jewish Congress), and Frank Dimant and Ellen Kachuck (B'nai Brith) is much appreciated. Others also eased our access to manuscript material. We remain indepted to Myron Momryk and Lawrence Tapper (National Archives of Canada), Judy Nefsky (Canadian Jewish Archives), Lillian Petroff (Multicultural History Society of Ontario) and Myroslav Yurkevich (Canadian Institute of Ukrainian Studies), and Rabbi Gunther Plaut, Dr Trudy Rosenberg, Nadia Diakun and Michael Kubyk.

More than ninety individuals granted us interviews in connection with this study. We went to them for information and sometimes returned again and again for clarification. Most responded with patience, candour and valuable insight unavailable to us in the written documentation. A few individuals requested anonymity and others that portions of their comments be kept confidential. Every effort has been made to respect these requests.

Our research load was lightened by the assistance of Karen Indig, Luigi Pennacchio, Bob Hromadiuk and Lorne Sirota.

Converting our draft chapters into readable form and demonstrating unending calm as we wrestled with deadlines and revisions were Lynda Bastien, Margaret Brennan, Margie Fedak, Eleanor LaFay and Beulah Worrell. At various steps along the way, others were there with assistance and encouragement, everything from facilitating our interviews to hearing out our ideas, from checking parts of our manuscript to explaining the vagaries of the law. We acknowledge our debt to Barry Arbus, Borys Balan, Yury Boshyk, Jean Burnet, Paula Draper, Nester Gula, Robert Harney, Gershon Hundert, Morris Ilyniak, Bohdan Krawchenko, David Levine, Cyril Levitt, Sol Littman, Victor Malarek, Robert Magocsi, David Matas, Richard Menkis, Blake Murray, Kenneth Narvey, Howard Palmer, E. Christopher Olsen, Manuel Prutschi, Bernard Shapiro, Danylo Husar Struk, Emanuel Weiner, Sharon Wolfe, Judy Young and David Zussman.

Seed money for this project came from Social Science and Humanities Research Council funds administered by both McGill University and the Ontario Institute for Studies in Education. Funding for the research and manuscript preparation was granted through the Berman Fund, the Montreal Jewish Community Foundation and Multiculturalism Canada. Without this generous assistance, our work might never have been completed.

We remain indebted to Bev Slopen, who understood the potential of our project, and to Morton Mint and his team at Penguin for their unending support. We are especially grateful to David Kilgour, whose suggestions were nearly always right even if his taste in restaurants leaves much to be desired, to Aaron Milrad for his wise and balanced counsel, to Mary Adachi for her careful editing and to Iris Skeoch, Noona Barlow and Patricia Cooper for easing the final stages of our work.

Preparation of the American edition of this book would not have been possible without the enthusiasm of Lewis Bateman at the University of North Carolina Press and support from other press staff members, especially Suzanne Bell, David Perry and Amy Schutz.

No words can adequately express our gratitude to our families, Eydie, Carla and Sarah Troper and Phyllis, David, Rebecca and newborn Joanna Weinfeld. Their love and emotional support were a constant comfort.

As we indicate in these acknowledgments, scholarship is inevitably a collegial enterprise. We thank all those mentioned above and others we may have omitted. They are, of course, not responsible for our own interpretations. Any remaining errors, while inadvertant, are the fault of the other guy.

Harold Troper, Toronto
Morton Weinfeld, Montreal
1988

Introduction

Zalman Is Coming
with the Key

Judge Jules Deschênes was adamant. He had brought his Commission of Inquiry on War Criminals in Canada to Winnipeg for only one day of public hearings.[1] He wanted to hear submissions about individual war criminals living in Canada — nothing else. But when the session opened on the morning of May 22, 1985, Deschênes knew that several of those wishing to give testimony would speak either out of the pain of Holocaust memories they carried with them through every waking hour or of fears that the Commission's effort, in and of itself, posed a direct threat to their ethnic community. Before the first submission was presented, Deschênes warned all those in attendance that his inquiry was "not set up to start the Second World War all over again." With members for both Ukrainian and Jewish communities scheduled to give testimony, Deschênes continued, "This Commission is not directed at any group of people of any ethnic origin whatsoever, and is not, therefore, to be used as a kind of platform where old wounds would be re-opened."

But re-opened they were. Two speakers, a Jew and a Ukrainian, did not get to finish their presentations. A Jewish survivor and former concentration camp victim began his submission by disclaiming any intention of group slander. Rather than "point an accusing finger," he demanded, "we have to seek justice. There are good and bad elements in every community." What he wanted was to place his personal record of wartime suffering in Ukraine on the record. He was cut off.

He was followed by a spokesman for one Ukrainian group, identified as a former concentration camp inmate, who launched into a protest against the media for wholesale attacks on Ukrainians. He too was cut off.

Judge Deschênes was no more prepared to hear a survivor detail pained memories of the Holocaust than he was to hear a Ukrainian defend his community's good name. In turn, Deschênes demanded to know from each of them what evidence would be presented which had direct bearing on individual war criminals then living in Canada. The Ukrainian had none and indeed believed there was none. He was thanked and dismissed. Informed that a list of alleged war criminals would be submitted to the Commissioner later, Judge Deschênes also thanked and dismissed the Jewish speaker.

Both men, clinging to a deeply felt sense of victimization, scarred by memories of wartime Europe, confronted one another in the lobby outside the hearing room. The tension between the two was almost electric. According to the press, the Jew tapped a finger on the Ukrainian's chest and asserted, "You know, here in your heart, there are war criminals here [in Canada]." The Ukrainian shook his head.[2]

Ukrainian-Jewish relations in Canada have been tense for decades. The two communities and their leaders have eyed one another across a gulf of mistrust so vast that few have attempted to bridge it. But acknowledging the existence of inter-ethnic tension is one thing; explaining how this state of affairs came to be is quite another. Indeed, finding the roots of this tension reminds one of the traveller who got lost and asked a local farmer for directions. The farmer scratched his head for a time, then replied, "Start somewhere else. You can't get there from here."

That's not good enough. If we are to ever understand, we must begin *here*. The *here* in Canadian Jewish-Ukrainian relations is the period following the Deschênes Commission.

The issue of war criminals, the pressures which led up to the Deschênes Commission and the forces at work within the Ukrainian and Jewish communities are the foci of this book. Yet the origins of Jewish-Ukrainian mistrust, so evident during the Deschênes enquiry, begin well outside of Canada and well before the tragic events of World War II examined by Judge Deschênes. They tumble out of a Ukraine of several centuries ago where the structure of Jewish-Ukrainian relations was forged. They drag in their wake a litany of historical wrongs both Ukrainians and Jews feel they have endured at the hands of the other — a litany of wrongs not forgotten with the passage of time.[3]

But there remains little agreement on a single historical narrative. For if Canada's Jewish and Ukrainian communities share a common geographic origin in eastern Europe, they do not share a common historical memory. Both groups have confronted the same forces of history. But in the process whereby experience becomes memory and the memories of many converge to become communal historical understanding, both Ukrainians and Jews have inherited very different and distinct understandings of the past and the role played by the other in that past.

Intrinsic to the survival of national or ethnic groups is this sense of shared historical experience, real or imagined.[4] American historian David Potter wrestled with the question of the place of history and historical myth in the creation of group consciousness. He argues

> . . . nations have always relied upon a certain amount of carefully cultivated mythology to reinforce the unity of their people. Their success in fostering a belief in a common identity has often been an essential part of the process of forging the identity itself; the belief has operated as a kind of self-fulfilling prophecy. If the members of a population are sufficiently persuaded that they have cause to be a unified group, the conviction may unify them, and thus may produce the nationalism which it appears to reflect.[5]

But it is incorrect to see mythology and history as an-
tithetical. Historian Lester Stephens tries to separate
myth from history by arguing that history must "stand
the test of scrutiny," while myth "generally can be neither proven nor disproven in any empirical sense because it is a personal, a private image." But, Stephens
allows, myth is fact to those who believe. Myth is
"valid for its subscriber; hence, it is not a 'myth' but
truth to him. It becomes myth, that is, fable, only after
he has ceased to accept it."[6]

This view may seem too rigid. History, or rather that
chronicle of events and interpretation selected from the
past which constitutes the history of a society or group
— its so-called proximate history — may well take on
mythic proportions. Nor need it be a fiction, a fable, to
take on mythic proportions. To understand this, one
must also understand how the past is selected, interpreted and used in bonding communities together.

The scholar, for all his or her academic training, is
part of this process whether exploring a nation-state
like Canada, or the separate and often distinct character of ethnic communities. As the thoughtful scholar
knows full well, interpretation grows out of continual
dialogue between the researcher and his or her sources,
between the mind of the scholar and the interpretive
weight given a particular set of facts. Historian E.H.
Carr notes, quite correctly, "facts of history cannot be
purely objective, since they become facts of history in
virtue of the significance attached them by the
historian."[7] So interpretation is a dynamic, shifting according to the evidence examined and the questions
asked of that evidence. What research reveals depends
on where one digs for evidence, and where one digs depends on questions one wants answered.

Scholars are human beings; they do not come to their
studies *tabula rasa*. Whether in a national or ethnic context, they are engaged in their craft with all the scholarly dispassion and neutrality demanded of it, but also
approach their subject carrying the cultural baggage of
the community with which they identify.[8] In seeking to

probe the past, for example, there may not be — nor need there be — a divorce between the historian's craft and the sense of shared community past which is common to group members. Rather, each historian begins the restrospective analysis with an appreciation of the layered framework of historical understanding defining the group. This is seldom an issue, nor need it be. However, it can and does crop up. For example, Canadian historians of Ukrainian or Jewish descent, like all Canadians, share equally in the common historical legacy of Canada. Their common understanding, however, may well diverge when these same historians begin to explore the respective experiences of Jews and Ukrainians. But this does not disqualify their conclusions. On the contrary, their analysis may be richer, their conclusions clearer, because of an immediacy to their study's focus. Differing interpretations of past events do not mean that scholars juggle data. Rather, the selection, definition and analysis of problems and data are filtered through different perspectives.

A perspective is not the property of the researcher. It is the cultural inheritance of the community — national or ethnic. And for community, history is not neutral or without purpose. It is the shared heritage of past events. It encourages group members to find common cause and reinforce loyalties. It bonds individuals to the group and gives the group a sense of continuity with the past and a shared stake in the future. It is built into our culture, its rituals and celebrations.

Easter festivities at St Demetrius Ukrainian Catholic Church in suburban north-west Toronto would not be complete without the participation of the children's choir. Their playful songs of praise and celebration are intermingled with Ukrainian folk songs recalling Easter in the Old World. One particularly joyous song harks back to the air of anticipation that excited the small Ukrainian peasant village of a bygone era as Easter Sunday finally arrived. The entire community, the song recalls, gathered expectantly outside their church, awaiting not their priest but Zalman the Jew. Zalman, who finally arrives in a grand coach, his wife bedecked in all her finery, brings with him the key to the village church. With due ceremony he unlocks the door and the faithful quickly file in to begin Easter prayers.[9]

This Easter song about Zalman with the key, still so much a part of current Ukrainian Easter celebrations, echoes across generations of Ukrainian-Jewish relations. The lyrics speak not just of a festive morning but also of the complex relationships that developed between Ukrainians and Jews through centuries of contact.

Zalman's tale must be considered on two separate but interrelated levels. Zalman is both a composite of Jewish historical figures spanning hundreds of years and, at the same time, a stock character in much Ukrainian folk tradition which gives Jews a special place.

Zalman, the historical actor, enters onto the Ukrainian stage in the late sixteenth and early seventeenth century as the Jewish population of Ukraine grew rapidly. Forced out of Germany by both persecution and lack of economic opportunities, many Jews had already made their way eastward into Poland in the twelfth and thirteenth centuries, and from there into Ukraine in the sixteenth and seventeenth centuries. Ukraine, destined to be fought over and divided by competing conquerors for centuries to come, was then incorporated into the powerful and expanding Polish-Lithuanian Commonwealth. But as the territory we now call Ukraine fell under Polish domination, the vast majority of Ukrainian peasants remained far removed from their Polish rulers. The Ukrainians were largely eastern Christians, adherents of the Orthodox or Uniate (Greek Catholic) faiths as opposed to the Roman Catholicism of the Poles. Most Ukrainians were also resentful of Polish pressure on them to become Catholics and accept the spiritual authority of the Pope in spite of guarantees that if they did so, their distinctive Orthodox liturgy would remain intact.[10]

Polish control of Ukraine went beyond intrusion into the spiritual realm. Polish authority was solidified through an alliance with the Ukrainian nobility, many of whom became Polonized and even converted to Catholicism. Through such social amalgamation, Polish aristocratic feudal control over large tracts of Ukrainian lands was strengthened. The expansion of Polish rule into Ukraine also unleashed an era of social and economic change. A surge in trade and commerce opened opportunities for newly arrived Jewish artisans, craftsmen, innkeepers, traders and merchants riding on the coat-tails of Polish expansion. Cash-starved but development-minded Polish and Ukrainian nobles turned to Jewish financiers. Landlords employed Jewish estate managers and tax-collectors to ensure an orderly flow of capital or goods from their subject Ukrainian peasants. Over time some Jews acquired subsidiary leaseholdings from absentee landowners. But whether serving as employees of Polish or Polonized Ukrainian noblemen or as leaseholders to absentee nobles, many Jews came to represent the cutting edge of Polish economic and territorial control in Ukraine. Indeed, in some areas Ukrainians were as likely, if not more likely, to have contact with Jewish agents of Polish rule as they were with their actual Polish rulers.

Zalman, who arrived with the church key in hand on Easter Sunday morning, was such a Jewish agent. By unlocking the church door and allowing devotions to proceed on this holiest of days in the Christian calendar, he acknowledged that villagers had dutifully paid their annual taxes. If taxes remained in arrears, the church door might have remained locked. It was not uncommon for individual Jews like Zalman to have been employed as the intermediaries or mediators between the Catholic Polish nobility and the Orthodox and Uniate Ukrainian peasantry. Acting under the authority of wealthy nobles who held land title to whole villages including the local Orthodox church, some Jews not only filled an important economic niche but gradu-

ally developed their own sub-class, a separate estate
distinct from both nobility and peasants.

If the Jewish middleman role was often profitable it
was also not without its potential for pain. Acting as
agents of Polish control, Jews were soon identified with
that control. The security of their positions was increasingly dependent on the goodwill of the Poles and, of
course, the continuity of Polish rule. To the degree that
there was growing Ukrainian hostility to Polish feudal
authority or resentment at the growing intrusion of the
Catholic Church, the resulting hostility was also directed against the personification of Polish rule — the
Jew. Would the Jew who crucified Christ for a fistful of
silver not crucify the Ukrainian peasantry for the same
reward? When Ukrainian disquiet erupted into armed
rebellion, the Jew was an obvious target.

As historian of Polish Jewry Bernard Weinryb explains, Jews were identified by the peasants as being a
tool of the exploiter — the nobility, the landlord and
the tax collector. Although historical evidence remains
scanty, it was once widely rumoured and incorporated
into folklore that Jews like Zalman, who allegedly held
the key to the local church on the vast estates under
their managerial control, abused their position by
squeezing payment out of the faithful for every event
that took place in the village church.

That there were Jewish agents of Polish rule, as represented by Zalman, is historically debated. The nature
of their impact on the Ukrainian peasantry still must be
explored in detail. So must many other elements of the
Ukrainian-Jewish relationship. Indeed, as historian Michael Stanislawski explains, the historiography of
Ukraine, and of Jewish-Ukrainian relations in particular, is very thin when compared to the historiography
available on many other areas of Europe. That which is
readily available today in English, the only possible language of Ukrainian-Jewish dialogue in North America,
is thinner still. Furthermore, Stanislawski points out
that in the paucity of existing historical research, that
which does exist has largely been shaped on one side by

the latter-day debate among scholars as to the legitimacy and veracity of the Ukrainian national cause and, on the other, by a search for the roots of anti-Jewish sentiment which made the Holocaust possible.[11] Those few scholars who have approached the history of Ukrainian-Jewish relations in the Old World, a subject political scientists Howard Aster and Peter Potichnyj have termed "an intellectual minefield," have seldom ventured far from one or the other of these two frameworks.[12] This does not necessarily make their historical analysis invalid. But if the historiography is scant and derivative of quite separate historical traditions, it does little to break down the often prejudicial image many Ukrainians and Jews have developed of one another over generations of contact. Historical scholarship is thus less important on the current stage of Ukrainian-Jewish relations than one might wish.

Consequently, in this case, Zalman is an important symbolic image. A product of complex yet underexplored historical events, he has been transformed into a mythological caricature of the Jew, as compelling in its simplicity as it can be destructive of the truth. The same mythologizing process has informed Jewish notions of Ukrainians or, just as likely today, an undifferentiated image of the eastern European. In the absence of intergroup dialogue each community has remained secure in the solitude of its own home truths; in the absence of definitive scholarship each has taken comfort in the repetition of its own storied past, its own interpretation of historical facts. Whatever past grievances each community can lay at the feet of the other, the absence of any common understanding of the past or realistic vision of one another has too often given intergroup contact, even in the New World, the appearance of border skirmishes in uncharted territory.

The four-hundred-year relationship of Ukrainians and Jews in Ukraine, from Zalman to World War II, is marked by decades of normal and peaceful symbiotic relationships between groups inhabiting common territory. But it is also marked by historical scars, which more often than not dominate the historical memory of each group and therefore still hamper efforts at dialogue. It is not the purpose of this book to survey the whole of that complex history — historians of Ukraine have barely scratched the surface of the work that must be done — nor is it to evaluate the varying historical interpretations and works which now exist.

Rather, this book is about the intersection of ethnicity and public policy in Canada today. The former taps into deeply held, almost primordial passions and identities. The latter brings us into the sober worlds of law and governance. Blending the two, as we shall see, is not always easy. Our goal has been to study the way in which Old World conflicts — tensions in Ukrainian-Jewish relations — have been transplanted into the New. Ethnicity, as identity and as culture, cannot truly exist without history. Where separate versions of history talk past each other, or worse, compete, the result is conflict. That conflict becomes a major dilemma of policy making in a society like Canada, which is multicultural both in ethnic diversity and in ideological commitment.

While the problem of war criminals in Canada threads its way through our study, this book is not primarily about Nazi war criminals, real or alleged, in Canada or elsewhere. Neither is it a legal primer, reviewing the arguments and counter-arguments concerning possible legal remedies available to address the issue of war criminals.[13]

Nevertheless, we do acknowledge the importance of the war-criminal issue to Jewish-Ukrainian relations. Accordingly, we trace the background to the recent Deschênes Commission and analyse the actions, both overt and behind the scenes, of major Jewish and Ukrainian organizations, and the federal government. There will be some readers who may decry our emphasis on the ethnic dimension. They will assert that the war-criminal issue was not, and ought not to have become, an ethnic one. But this assertion blurs a painful reality. Among many of the players, notably among many Ukrainian Canadians, that is just what it became. Our task is to understand why this should be the case and what this means to Ukrainian Canadians, Jews, the government and the larger Canadian civic culture.

There may also be those who question the authors' motives in undertaking this study. It is right they should do so. After all, both authors are Jewish and have personal connections to the organized Jewish communities of Toronto and Montreal. But is this a problem? Do our Jewish backgrounds constitute a possible "bias" in a presumably objective study of Ukrainian-Jewish conflict? We do not deny this possibility. Indeed, we regularly grappled with it, attempting to be fair and impartial. We have tried to let the evidence speak for itself, wherever possible, avoiding editorial comment. At the same time we have tried not to overcompensate, nor to make a fetish out of rigid even-handedness. That would run the risk of emasculating our analysis. Readers can judge the matter for themselves, and those feeling we have allowed the fact of our background to tilt our presentation in one direction or another will no doubt let us know.[14]

Finally, we have no way of knowing what effect, if any, this book will have on the tenor of Ukrainian-Jewish relations in the post-Deschênes era. Privately, we share the objective of promoting cultural harmony among all cultural groups in Canada and hope that historical antipathies can be overcome in the New World. This is a difficult task; as we shall argue, the historical slate is rarely wiped clean. Indeed, we are not indifferent to the emotions and conflicts we describe. "But an attitude of moral indifference," wrote the great German sociologist Max Weber, "has no connection with scientific 'objectivity.' " Accordingly, our purpose in this study is not reconciliation but understanding.[15]

Old
Wounds

Chapter 1

The Old World

An historian recently noted that Ukraine is "one terrible piece of real estate."[1] For almost a millennium it has been ripped apart by competing imperial dynasties — Polish, Lithuanian, Russian, Austro-Hungarian, German, Soviet — each seeking to submit the rich farm lands of Ukraine, a bread basket of Europe, to its own rule. With each successive wave of conquerors have come new destruction and suffering.

The area Ukrainian Canadians today regard as their ancestral homeland, the ethnographic Ukraine, is composed largely of a vast fertile plain covering almost a quarter million square miles. This Ukrainian homeland is cradled north of the Black Sea in an arch bordered by other peoples, notably Poles, Russians, Belorussians and Rumanians. With few natural barriers to the outside and a river system that has allowed for the easy flow of goods out and invaders in, Ukraine has a continuing history of economic exploitation and political upheaval.

The presence of Jews in Ukraine dates back to the seventh century. But it would be another seven centuries before Jews emerged in force on the Ukrainian stage. Descendants of Yiddish-speaking immigrants from German lands in central Europe who in the twelfth century had escaped eastward into Poland to avoid pogroms and other persecutions associated with the Crusades joined in the Polish expansion into Ukrainian lands in the late sixteenth and seventeenth centuries. As they had done in Poland, many Jews who moved into Polish-controlled Ukraine carved out an important economic niche for themselves, especially in towns and cities. Historian Shmuel Ettinger notes that for four hundred years important Jews were "servants and advisors to kings and rulers in financial and commercial matters, money lenders and middlemen, merchants and artisans, sometimes physicians and scholars." But there was a price to pay in isolation from the majority populace. As Ettinger notes, "The more the Jews became detached from agriculture, navigation and government service the smaller was their foothold in the surrounding Christian society."[2]

As a separate estate, and a non-Christian one at that, Jews inadvertently became tied up in exacerbated religious tensions between the ruling Poles and the Ukrainian peasantry. Attempts by Roman Catholic Poles to solidify control over Ukrainian lands included undermining the power of the Orthodox church which then commanded the overwhelming allegiance of the peasant faithful. But even as Ukrainians rallied in defence of their church, they saw their Roman Catholic rulers raise Jews, non-Christians identified with the crucifixion of Christ, to positions of power and influence.

In larger towns, where many Jews tended to settle, they often found themselves in competition with established local Ukrainian artisans faithful to the Orthodox rite. Historian Frank Sysyn argues that the Orthodox church was too distracted by the threat of Roman Catholicism and even Protestantism to spare much worry for Jews who did not proselytize among their neighbours. Nevertheless, Sysyn allows, the local Orthodox population, seething with discontent and increasingly restive, could not help but resent the degree of freedom allowed Jews but denied the Orthodox.[3]

With their church under attack, their lands controlled by foreigners, many of their nobility seduced away by promises of a share in Polish rule, resentment among Ukrainian peasants grew. In 1648 a revolt set Ukraine aflame. Bohdan Khmelnytsky was not an obvious candidate to lead an uprising. Not a natural man of the people, he was born to an aristocratic Orthodox military family. His first loyalty had always been to the gentry class and the status quo. But according to popular history, when his petition for redress of a family grievance was dismissed by the Polish authorities, Khmelnytsky assembled a military force. The Poles struck first, but in May 1648 Khmelnytsky emerged victorious and his success unleashed the pent-up anti-Polish hostility of the Ukrainian peasantry. In the violence that followed, Polish landlords, Ukrainians who served the Poles, Roman Catholic clergy and, of course, Jews were attacked. Reports of the uprising claim it was a practice of Khmelnytsky's followers "to hang on Greek Orthodox churches a pig, a rabbi and a Catholic priest."[4]

Through the ebb and flow of the revolt, Jewish casualties mounted. "During the months of May to November 1648," historian Paul Magocsi notes, "Jewish chroniclers estimated that 300 Jewish communities with 100,000 Jews were destroyed, which amounts to two-thirds of the Jewish population of Ukrainian territory."[5]

Jewish history ranks the bloodletting of the Khmelnytsky era as second only to that of the Holocaust. Although it is allowed that Khmelnytsky's immediate control of the far-flung revolt was limited, the *Encyclopedia Judaica* notes the Ukrainian leader was dubbed " 'Chmiel the Wicked,' one of . . . the initiators of the terrible 1648–49 massacres."[6]

But Khmelnytsky cuts a very different figure in Ukrainian historical narrative. His was a rebellion against foreign domination and he the champion of Ukrainian national awakening. As a nationalist leader, he "succeeded in uniting most of the Ukraine under his control and in ruling the area as if it were an independent state." As a result, "his . . . state provided an inexhaustible source of inspiration for future generations of Ukrainians, many of whom strove to restore what they considered to be the independence of the Ukraine under Khmel'nyts'kyi."[7]

But what is said of attacks on Jews? If they are not denied, neither are they stressed in the Ukrainian narrative. Accounts of Jewish devastation come largely from contemporary Jewish chroniclers, notably Nathan

Hannover, who, it is suggested, may have exaggerated the number of Jewish dead and the ferocity of the attacks, and underestimated the corresponding suffering inflicted on Catholic clergy and Polish landowners. Indeed, according to historian Stefan Possony, Khmelnytsky "went after the Ukrainians who were serving the Poles, just as much as he went after the Jews who were part of the enemy's establishment." Of course, he allowed, "substantial numbers of Jews affiliated with the Polish regime were killed," but this must be seen in the context of the times.

> The Polish nobility was using the Jews as estate managers and tax collectors, and in a unique and provocative arrangement even as custodians of Ukrainian Orthodox churches and monasteries. No wonder, the Kozaks [Ukrainians] regarded the Jews as enemies.

As to the accuracy of sources describing the attacks on Jews, Possony has his doubts. Certainly, he holds, there is reason to question the degree to which Jews were singled out for attack.

> In brief, the Khmelnytsky case is a poor foundation for a general indictment of Ukrainians as anti-semites, especially since under the regime of Ivan Mazepa, who became *hetman* [ruler] in 1696, the Jews and Ukrainians were again on good terms. Indeed if the stories about Khmelnytsky are only half accurate, there should have been no Jews left in Ukraine.[8]

If Khmelnytsky and his seventeenth-century uprising are not part of the history known by most North Americans, they remain part of the proximate history of both Ukrainians and Jews. And for some Ukrainians and Jews the legacy of inherited mistrust continues — Jews were exploiters of the Ukrainian people, forever allied with those suppressing the Ukrainian national cause;

Ukrainians were anti-Semites needing little or no encouragement to turn on peaceful Jewish men, women and children in a frenzy of blood lust. Khmelnytsky was either a visionary Ukrainian nationalist or a blackguard pogromist.

It is impossible in only a few pages to do justice to the complex relationship between Jews and Ukrainians across the centuries following the Khmelnytsky uprising. Suffice to say that for centuries relations oscillated along a continuum from mutual tolerance and respect to hostility and open violence. And always there were third parties — foreign rulers coveting the land, exploiting the peasants, suppressing the Ukrainian language and culture, and employing Jews as intermediaries in dealing with the Ukrainian population and sometimes using Jews as scapegoats to deflect Ukrainian peasant anger at social and economic exploitation.

On the eve of World War I nationalists were far from their goal of an independent and united Ukraine. Their lands were subdivided between soon-to-be warring empires. The Russian Empire claimed sovereignty to that area east of the Zbruch River and the ailing Austro-Hungarian Empire claimed the area to the west. When war exploded in 1914 neither of these two lumbering imperial giants could know that each would be a casualty of the European conflagration. The Russian Revolution in 1917 overthrew the last of the tsars, while defeat at the side of Germany the following year led to the dismemberment of the vast Austro-Hungarian Empire.

In the chaos of these massive post–World War I political upheavals, the hopes of nationalists throughout eastern Europe soared. But in Ukraine these hopes were to be dashed. The overthrow of the tsar in 1917 left an administrative and power vacuum in eastern Ukraine which opposing political forces attempted to fill. For the next three and half years, from March 1917 to October 1920, to the east of the Zbruch River a Ukrainian National Republic struggled to survive. To the west, the collapse of Austro-Hungary encouraged local Ukrainians to declare their own Western Ukrainian Republic and seek international recognition. The two fledgling states hammered out a nominal pan-Ukrainian federation, but in an era of civil war, foreign invasions and peasant upheavals, true unity eluded them. So did lasting international recognition.

If the Ukrainian national cause had trouble showing a united face to the outside world, it was also severely divided within. Factional wrangling, an inability to devise a unifying economic policy and a failure to win the loyalty of important ethnic minority communities, including Poles, ethnic Germans and, of course, the largely urban Jews, weakened the fragile national cause. As a result, control of the new regime, especially in the east, was so weak and disorganized that it stretched credibility to think of a Ukrainian state exercising actual authority over all the territory claimed, let alone commanding the allegiance of the entire population. In the end the nationalist experiment in the east collapsed as the Red Army moved in to secure for the new Soviet regime those parts of Ukraine previously ruled by imperial Russia.

In western Ukraine, especially in the former Austrian province of Galicia, Ukrainians were able to form a government and army, but they were unable to withstand the stronger military forces of a restored Polish state. More importantly, Ukrainian nationalists, whether from the east or west, failed to convince the victorious World War I allies that Ukrainian national aspirations should be rewarded with statehood. As the victors carved up the spoils of the old Austro-Hungarian Empire into a series of independent states, in part along ethnographic boundaries, the Ukrainian homeland was parcelled out to emergent Polish, Czechoslovakian and expanded Rumanian states. The dream of a united Ukrainian homeland was snuffed out. The struggling Ukrainian state was no more.[9]

The failure of a strong and unified pan-Ukrainian national homeland to rise from the ashes of the Russian and Austro-Hungarian imperial collapse still awakens a sense of historical injustice among many Ukrainians in Canada. But some take solace in the fact that a flowering of national self-expression in Ukraine and an assertion of independence, no matter how fleeting, did take place. Like Khmelnytsky in an earlier era, eastern Ukrainian leader Symon Petlura stands as the personification of Ukrainian political aspirations and national continuity in the post–World War I era. Yet, the memory of that same Petlura evokes a very different image for Jews. Under Petlura's short-lived government in eastern Ukraine, Jews suffered a series of pogroms which, many Jews believe, if Petlura did not openly sanction neither did he choose to stop.

Petlura's treatment of the Jews is anything but clear even after almost seventy years. Many Jews, like other ethnic minorities within the Ukrainian National Republic carved out of previously Russian-controlled territory, at first reserved judgment on the new Ukrainian political order. An old Yiddish expression holds that, "*Me torn nisht betn of anyen kayser*": one should not hope for a new ruler." He might prove worse than the one you have. If the previous Russian imperial regime had not been friendly to Jewish needs, what guarantee was there that the new Ukrainian one would be any better?

But the new Ukrainian regime, realizing they would need the support of ethnic minorities, especially those in urban centres, reached out to Jews. Guarantees were made as to the legitimate rights of minorities. Jews were granted personal-cultural autonomy; seats were set aside for Jews in a national assembly, the Central Rada; the public service was opened to Jews. Yiddish was declared an official language and money printed bilingually in Ukrainian and Yiddish. Jewish education was encouraged and Jewish cultural life promised a new golden era.[10]

Whether these moves would have brought revolutionary change or were cynically designed to court Jewish support is interesting but, in the end, a side issue. The promise of equality could not be delivered. The Ukrainian Central Rada, for all its fine words, was never able to exercise control over its own hinterland. Even as the government issued policies, laws and edicts, anarchy and civil strife dominated the countryside. Spontaneous peasant uprisings often turned on Jews. A wave of pogroms swept eastern Ukraine. Troops ostensibly loyal to Petlura's central government did not protect Jews. They often joined in the pogroms. In his classic study, Simon Dubnow estimates that between 1918 and 1921 more than 1,200 pogroms swept away 60,000 Jewish lives.[11]

Historians debate whether or not Petlura and his government personally countenanced these attacks or could have done more to prevent them. In spite of pious statements and promises to the contrary, did Petlura and his advisers tolerate or turn a blind eye to the murder of Jews, because to do otherwise would alienate the central government still further from the Ukrainian peasantry and semi-autonomous military forces? Were others, the invading Poles or Russians, responsible? Whatever the truth, the virtually unchecked epidemic of pogroms in the period of Ukrainian sovereignty ensured that among Jews, Petlura, like Khmelnytsky before him, would become synonymous with both Ukrainian nationalism and unbridled anti-Semitism. Hence, Jewish memories of Ukrainian independence are filled with images of children denounced as Christ killers, violence in the streets, looting of Jewish homes, bullies and thugs intimidating innocent Jews and finally violent pogroms. Among Ukrainians, however, Petlura is recalled as a dedicated and liberal Ukrainian political leader. In spite of sincere efforts by the central government to win their loyalty, many Ukrainians believed Jews were at best indifferent to the Ukrainian national awakening, at worst actively sympathetic to the Bolsheviks who dispatched the Red Army to trample the struggling Ukrainian state. It was a Jew who in 1926 assassinated Petlura in his Paris political exile.[12]

Thus, Jewish and Ukrainian visions of Petlura stand separate from one another. It is as if the mutual trauma of the Khmelnytsky era of almost three hundred years earlier was merely updated to the twentieth century.[13] Jews in particular link the pogroms of the Petlura era back in time to Khmelnytsky and, equally important, forward to the Holocaust.

Many Ukrainians see no such continuity. What is more, if the attacks on Jews during the short-lived Petlura government were regrettable, some might argue that to the degree that Ukrainians were involved, they were provoked, if not by Soviets, then by the Jews themselves. Jews were allied to the oppressors. To rise up against the oppressor was to rise up against Jews. And Jews, rather than embrace the welcome offered by the Petlura government, were instead attracted by the Communist enemy. Is there any doubt then, some might ask, that Jews were largely architects of their own fate?

The wholesale linkage of Jews with Communism does not end with the crushing of the Ukrainian National Republic and the absorption of eastern Ukraine into the Soviet Union. Once they took over, the Communists needed middle management, policy planners and enforcers in Ukraine to consolidate their power. Among others, they turned to better-educated and, in some cases, sympathetic Jews. As a result, Ukrainian historical narrative lays much of the responsibility and the resultant suffering inflicted on the Ukrainian people at the Jewish door. Jews were seen by some as the agents of foreign domination and, in 1932–1933, the foot-soldiers of famine.

When the Soviets consolidated power in eastern Ukraine in 1921, they promised farms to landless peasants. But instead of the carrot of land reform they delivered the stick of forced collectivization of land. By the 1930s collective farms dominated Ukrainian agriculture. Peasants were compelled to work state property, meeting fixed production quotas, and allowed only the little that was left for distribution among members.

But the dream of land ownership was not easily set aside. Many peasants resisted collectivization. Resentment grew worse as unrealistically high grain quotas set in far-off Moscow and a severe drought in 1931 made quotas almost impossible to fill. Peasants organized boycotts of grain deliveries to terminals. In Moscow, party planners saw food deliveries shrink and their hopes of mammoth Soviet industrialization fed by Ukrainian grain production begin to evaporate. Unwilling to compromise and unable to grasp the peasants' plight, the military and an accompanying army of party faithful were dispatched to Ukraine and to other areas where similar quota shortfalls were encountered. They forcibly removed all grain and other food stuffs necessary to fill the quota. A terrible food shortage in the winter of 1932 had become a full-blown famine by the spring of 1933. The elderly, the sick and the very young died first. But before the famine ended, slow death by starvation swept the land. Soviet officials, convinced peasants were still hoarding grain, refused to send aid. Millions died. During the harsh winter the dead were so numerous that it became impossible to properly dispose of the bodies. In some areas they were piled like cords of wood to await the spring thaw and burial. Estimates of the dead run as high as seven million or approximately a quarter of the total Ukrainian population.[14]

Historians still disagree as to whether the famine was primarily engineered by the Soviets as a means to starve out the last vestiges of Ukrainian nationalism or as a systematic program to end peasant resistance to collectivization in Ukraine and several other areas in the Soviet Union.[15] Jews in rural Ukraine and those encouraged onto the land in order to promote the secular "proletarianization" of an urban Jewish majority, suffered side-by-side with their non-Jewish neighbours. But, for some Ukrainians, Jews were less victims than villains. The famine was not an act of nature but of men, and many of those men were Jews. One Soviet official of Jewish origin, Lazar Kaganovich, played a particularly key role. Indeed, the general openness of the Soviet Communist structure of the 1920s and early 1930s to those of Jewish descent and their higher profile in Ukraine underscores a Ukrainian sense of historical wrong at the hands of Jews. Today, the famine has emerged as a focal point of modern Ukrainian history not unlike the Holocaust for Jews.

Nothing, however, so exacerbates the distance between Ukrainian and Jewish communities in Canada today as their respective understandings of events during World War II — especially the Holocaust. The skeletal history of the Holocaust is seared into the collective consciousness of the Jewish community. Six million Jewish men, women and children were systematically murdered, approximately four million of them from Ukraine and Poland. With them was erased a centuries-old Jewish cultural heritage. There is no doubt that Germany carries the lion's share of guilt for the Holocaust. Nazis planned, organized and executed it. The fate of European Jewry was sealed by the Germans' might and their unbending determination to let nothing stand in the way of the genetic eradication of Jews.

What of complicity of others in the Nazi grand design? The Nazis set no easy task for themselves, but both Nazis and European Jewry learned mass murder would be much easier in areas where the Nazis secured the acquiescence, support or even active participation of local populations. The Holocaust was a labour-intensive industry. The systematic disposal of millions of people and their property during wartime required workers and contractors dedicated to genocide or profit, sometimes both. That the Nazi slaughter of Jews and other "undesirables" was so effective in so short a period of time stands as eloquent testament to the fact there was seldom a shortage of hands willing to aid the Nazis.[16]

Time has only hardened the Jewish conviction that wilful collaboration with the Nazis in destroying Jewry was nowhere more widespread than in Ukraine. As such, Ukrainian collaboration is identified as the last chapter in a centuries-old history of unrelenting anti-Semitism. For many Jews, the measure of Ukrainian co-operation is that an estimated 90 percent of Ukrainian Jewry was eventually murdered. Only those who somehow escaped eastward into Soviet-held territory or hid through the long night of Nazi terror emerged alive at the end of the war. Many of those who did survive, it is believed, did so not because of their non-Jewish neighbours but in spite of them. What began with Khmelnytsky ended at Babi Yar and Treblinka.

Ukrainian historical memory of the Holocaust is far different. Destruction of Ukrainian Jewry is acknowledged, and few would deny that individual Ukrainians collaborated in the final solution. But wholesale participation is denied. Indeed, the very notion of wilful cooperation implies choice, and the Ukrainian recounting of wartime events denies this was even possible, let alone welcome. Occupied by repressive foreign armies, unable to defend themselves, Ukrainians were the victims of oppression and terror, not their instrument. Admittedly, some renegades and criminals tried to ingratiate themselves with the Nazis and participated in anti-Jewish action. But why, some ask, must they be regarded as more representative of the Ukrainian people than were the *Kapos* (Jewish campguards), *Judenrate* (local Jewish councils dealing with the Nazis) and ghetto police who also served the Nazi machine representative of the Jewish people?[17]

If general Jewish and Ukrainian narratives are almost diametrically at odds with one another, so are their respective understandings of details.[18] For most Canadians the outbreak of war in Europe in September 1939 conjures up images of Nazi troops rolling across the German frontier into Poland, crushing Polish military resistance in about three weeks. It is far less known that it was not the Germans who invaded the largely Ukrainian-populated areas of eastern Poland in 1939. In the months before he unleashed his armies against Poland, Hitler sought to pacify and neutralize the Soviet Union, Poland's eastern neighbour. He did not wish to widen the planned battle by courting conflict with the Soviets, then fearful of losing their Polish buffer with Germany. Meanwhile, Stalin, concerned that the west-

ern democracies would like nothing more than to em-
broil Germany and the Soviet Union in a mutually ruin-
ous war, also hoped to buy time to prepare for the
eventuality of war with Hitler. As a result, less than a
month before Germany's invasion of Poland, the two
previously sworn enemies signed the Ribbentrop-Molo-
tov non-aggression pact. A secret clause in the treaty
provided that should war break out between Germany
and Poland, the Soviets would shift their own frontier
westward to annex much of western Ukraine which previously had been Polish territory. As a result, two
weeks after Germany invaded Poland from the west in
September 1939, Soviet troops marched into western
Ukraine from the east. They brought with them Soviet
government and economic organization and ruthless
suppression of anti-Soviet resistance.

Given a choice between a Nazi onslaught with its
promise of anti-Jewish terror and the ruthless Soviet
take-over, most Jews had little hesitation in welcoming
Soviet rule. They might not fare any better than their
neighbours, but they would at least fare no worse.
Equality of misery was obviously preferable to Nazi
barbarism. Of course, under Soviet rule Jewish merchants and businessmen, like their Polish and Ukrainian
counterparts, would suffer as would Jewish religious
life. Political life was also restricted. But the small co-
hort of those who had previously been closet Communists, both Jews and non-Jews, had their day. Many
served their new Soviet masters well, and some used
new-found power to take revenge for years of anti-
Communist political repression.

For most western Ukrainians, however, Soviet rule
was not the lesser of two evils. It was the only evil. Soviet rule began with a short period of quiet during
which the Soviets solidified their rule. It was quickly
followed by a nightmare of arrests and deportations of
Ukrainian religious and nationalist leaders, municipal
officials and professionals to forced labour in Siberia
and Kazakhstan. Estimates of deportations run as high

as one and a half million in less than two years. Many
were never heard from again.[19]

Some of those Ukrainians who feared arrest fled
westward into Nazi-controlled former Poland. Here
under a watchful and generally supportive Nazi hand,
two separate and often warring factions of the underground and militant Organization of Ukrainian Nationalists (OUN) organized for the day they would liberate
their homeland — with Nazi backing.[20] Indeed, the faction led by Stepan Bandera (OUN-B) organized its ca-
dres into two small military units code-named *Roland*
and *Nachtigall* and successfully negotiated their attach-
ment to the German army. The Nazis also pulled together a Ukrainian militia from among Ukrainians in
German-held territory.

In April 1941 the OUN-B held a congress at Cracow in
Nazi-occupied Poland. A significant resolution was
adopted which, in part, *condemned* the Soviet occupiers
of Ukraine for igniting anti-Jewish sentiment. "Muscovite-Bolshevik government exploits the anti-Jewish sen-
timents of the Ukrainian masses in order to divert their
attention from the real perpetrators of their misfortune
in order to unite them, in time of upheaval, against the
Jews." But this did not absolve Jews from responsibility. On the contrary. "In the USSR," the resolution began, "the Jews are the most faithful supporters of the
ruling Bolshevik regime and the vanguard of Muscovite
imperialism in Ukraine." It ended with a call to action.
"The Organization of Ukrainian Nationalists combats
the Jews as the prop of the Muscovite-Bolshevik regime
and simultaneously educates the masses to the fact that
the principal enemy is Moscow." The Jewish-Commu-
nist link was made. To attack Jews was to attack the
Soviet Union. Anti-Semitism was as one with anti-Communism.

Interestingly, historian Philip Friedman downplays
the resolution's thrust. The resolution, he points out,
does condemn pogroms "since such actions only play
into the hands of Moscow." Furthermore, the "equa-
tion of 'Jew-Bolsheviks' " was "a classic Nazi formula."

Since the OUN was then closely watched by their Nazi hosts, the resolution's tone may have been obligatory.[21]

Historian Taras Hunczak, on the other hand, does not see the resolution as a token to the OUN's Nazi allies. He argues that it reflects a popular Ukrainian perception "of Jews as agents of Bolshevism." Thus Ukrainian violence against Jews was not so much a product of instigation as a "response to a situation," a lashing out against Soviet rule.[22]

On June 22, 1941, a month after the OUN-B congress, Operation Barbarossa began — the Nazi attack on the Soviet Union. The Germans swept through Ukraine with Ukrainian nationalists hard on their heels. As the Soviets retreated Jews faced not just the advancing Nazi *Einsatzgruppen* or strike commandos — special Nazi killing squads — but the explosive hatred of their neighbours unleashed with a passion that would shock even the Nazis. In July 1941 some fifty-eight pogroms left as many as 24,000 Jews dead in western Ukraine.

Historians debate who is responsible for the pogroms. Aharon Weiss condemns "the traditional anti-semitism spread among various layers of the Ukrainian population," together with "the fostering of the Nazi ideology by the Ukrainian extremists — especially the OUN."[23] Others say this was not the case, or not the whole case. Never denying that the pogroms took place or that the Germans found ready allies, it is argued that Ukrainian participation, such as it was, erupted among "criminal factions" attempting to ingratiate themselves with their new Nazi masters. Ihor Kamenetsky claims that the pogroms took place not because of Ukrainian grievances but in spite of them. The Germans, he insists, were very unsuccessful in instigating Ukrainian attacks on Jews.[24] Bohdan Krawchenko correctly warns against the error of labelling everything that happened in Ukraine as Ukrainian. The Nazis had more than just Ukrainians to call on for assistance. There were Poles and *Volksdeutsche*, those of German descent living in Ukraine. What is more, he states, Ukrainian collaboration was held in check by the Nazis, who demanded

Ukrainian subjugation, not co-operation.[25] If the Nazi invasion was the occasion for a series of pogroms, others claim they were instigated by non-Ukrainians, including Soviet agents left behind to create instability, by non-Ukrainian minorities and perhaps even by Jews who would collaborate in their own destruction whether as ghetto police or in *Judenrate*.[26]

If historians debate who collaborated in the final solution, and to what degree,[27] it is agreed that most Ukrainian nationalists and, indeed, much of the Ukrainian populace of Soviet-occupied western Ukraine (1939–1941) at first welcomed the Nazis as liberators from the Soviets, heralding a new dawn of Ukrainian independence. They were to be disappointed. On entering L'viv (Lvov) on June 30, 1941, in the dust of the German advance, the OUN proclaimed an independent Ukrainian state allied with the Nazis.[28] An immediate outpouring of Ukrainian pride and cultural activity was short-lived. No sooner did the Nazis have their own administrative structure in place than Ukrainian independence was stamped out. The leaders of the nationalist cause, irrespective of faction or previous pledges of loyalty, were arrested, many sent off to concentration camps.

Ukraine was carved up into different administrative zones, its manpower and resources ruthlessly exploited as the Nazis saw fit.[29] Eastern Ukraine, closest to the front, fared worst. The final solution ground mercilessly onward. In the valley of Babi Yar just outside of Kiev, Jews quickly learned the meaning of Nazi rule. In September 1941, a week after the Nazis overran the city, an estimated 70,000 Jews were herded into the ravine, stripped naked and slaughtered. To this day Babi Yar remains synonymous for Jews with the wanton bloodlust of the Nazis and their supporters.

But Babi Yar was not free from the sight of mass murder once the Jews had been massacred. For the next two years, it continued as the killing ground for perhaps a million more of those in any way identified as enemies of Nazi rule. This included many Ukrainians.

In the Nazi racial hierarchy, Ukrainians, a Slavic people, ranked only slightly higher than Jews. In the Nazi thousand-year Reich, Ukrainians might have been consigned to the same end as the Jews.

To the north and west, in what before 1939 had been Polish-controlled western Ukraine, the local population — except the Jews — fared somewhat better. But if Nazi occupation was milder, it was still brutal.[30]

Thus Ukrainians now had two equal enemies — Nazis and Soviets. In the summer of 1942 an underground Ukrainian Insurgent Army (UPA) crystallized largely out of the ranks of Bandera's supporters. The Nazis were then in control, but the UPA did not forget the ruthlessness of the previous Soviet occupation. Historian Lev Shankovsky notes that the UPA did not intend to struggle against the Nazis only to have eventual victory snatched away by the return of Soviet authorities. The UPA's goal was an independent Ukraine.[31]

But what of the UPA and the Jews? Here again the historical water is muddy with controversy. Philip Friedman notes that the UPA crusade to "liberate" Ukraine from "foreign elements" included liberation from Jews. Accordingly, UPA hatred of the Nazis did not preclude some UPA units co-operating with the Nazis by handing over Jews or murdering Jews themselves. But, he notes, the UPA also made use of individual Jews. Jewish doctors, dentists and artisans were pressed into UPA units and disposed of when their services were no longer necessary.[32]

But others tell a different story, of the UPA gladly accepting Jewish volunteers and protecting Jews and of Jews who credit their survival to the luck of linking up with a UPA unit.[33]

Debate may continue on the role of the UPA in either saving or slaughtering Jews, but there is little doubt as to the almost saintly role of Ukrainian (Greek) Catholic Metropolitan Andrei Sheptytsky. Sheptytsky, Archbishop of L'viv and head of the church, was widely known as being sympathetic to the Jews. He was, nevertheless, reportedly distressed by the high-profile roles of Jews during the period of Soviet control after 1939, and he at first joined those welcoming the German invasion as a harbinger of better times. But his enthusiasm was short-lived. His distress grew at the continued suffering of the Jews and the role of his people in that suffering. When immediate post-invasion pogroms did not so much subside as turn into a systematic program of genocidal murder — a program in which some Ukrainians took a hands-on role — Sheptytsky protested. The elderly metropolitan wrote directly to ss commander Heinrich Himmler in the winter of 1942 demanding an end to the final solution and, equally important to him, an end to the use of Ukrainian militia and police in anti-Jewish action. His letter elicited a sharp rebuke, but Sheptytsky persisted even though the death penalty was threatened those who gave comfort to Jews. In November 1942 he issued a pastoral letter to be read in all churches under his authority. It condemned murder. Although Jews were not specifically mentioned, his intent was crystal clear.

We can never know how many Ukrainians were moved by Sheptytsky's appeal. Certainly the church set an example. With Sheptytsky's tacit approval, his church hid a number of Jews throughout western Ukraine, 150 Jews alone in and around his L'viv headquarters. Perhaps some of his parishioners were among those brave but precious few "righteous gentiles" who risked an automatic death penalty for themselves and their families by harbouring a Jew under their roof.

The towering humanity of Sheptytsky remains an inspiration today. But did he represent the spirit of his flock or, with few exceptions, did he stand in sharp contrast to it? Certainly he spoke out against the slaughter of the Jews, he covertly hid them and, most emphatically, he demanded an end to Nazi use of Ukrainians in the final solution. But how widespread was this Ukrainian participation, its circumstances, the extent to which it was countenanced or even encouraged by other influential Ukrainian spokesmen remains to be fully examined.[34]

Sheptytsky's humanity when it came to the Jews did not prevent his endorsing a Nazi scheme to organize a Waffen ss unit from Ukrainian volunteers in late 1943.

From its inception in 1922 the ss was envisioned as being of the purest German "blood." During the war it operated somewhat separately from the regular German army, the *Wehrmacht*, and the oath of loyalty to Hitler and the Nazi state which each ss recruit recited was unambiguous in its sworn hatred of the Jews. The ss was consigned responsibility for the eradication of "undesirables" from the Third Reich. But during the war, even as the mass murder of Jews and others was in progress, other duties, including modified combat duties, were assigned the ss, putting a drain on its resources. Pressed for manpower the combat-ready ss units, the Waffen ss, had to adjust admission criteria so as to admit "near Aryans" and *Volksdeutsche* from conquered northern and western European countries. After the Nazi defeat at Stalingrad in late January 1943, the shortfall in personnel became critical. Although it violated Nazi standards of racial purity, Heinrich Himmler approved recruitment of non-Aryan units for the Waffen ss. What role these post-Stalingrad organized units were to have in the ongoing Holocaust, whether they were envisioned as cannon fodder for the faltering German military machine or as back-up for the hard-pressed and racially pure ss units and *Wehrmacht* are points of historical discussion.[35]

Just how drastic was the Waffen ss shortfall in manpower can be seen by Himmler's readiness to enlist a full division from among western Ukrainians who otherwise ranked as sub-human in the Nazi racial hierarchy. A special allowance was even given the unit, allowing it to have its own clergy and a promise that it would be used in combat only against the Soviets advancing from the east.

Of course other Ukrainian units had already served with the Nazis in one capacity or another. The *Nachtigall* and *Roland*, as loyal to the Ukrainian national cause as to the Nazis, had marched with German troops. Its leaders had a fractious relationship with German authorities and, as a result, most were never fully trusted and some were imprisoned. They would eventually be redirected into the Ukrainian Waffen ss division.[36]

And, as Sheptytsky's condemnation of Ukrainian participation in anti-Jewish atrocities underscores, there were uniformed Ukrainians also serving the Nazis in various other quasi-military capacities, including the final solution and special actions against civilians. It is likely that some were Ukrainians plucked from among Soviet prisoners of war and promised life over almost certain death by starvation and exposure in POW camps if they would "volunteer" to serve a new master. Others may have gladly signed up as members of the auxiliary police, or other Nazi-led units. But there is no doubt that some Ukrainians, like collaborators elsewhere, helped in the round-up and transport of Jews to concentration camps, that Ukrainians served at the concentration camps and perhaps in the destruction of the Warsaw Ghetto. Once again, the question of whether these Ukrainians were the cutting edge of widespread pro-Nazi and anti-Semitic Ukrainian sentiment, as many Jews believe, or anti-social individuals, criminal types and street hooligans common to all peoples, as some Ukrainians have argued, remains to be resolved.

But in the spring of 1943 German authorities, with Ukrainian assistance, began to recruit a Waffen ss division in previously Polish-governed Ukraine. While the division's name went through a series of changes, it is most commonly called the Galicia Division or, among Ukrainians, the Halychyna Division. The name aside, why would Ukrainian youth volunteer for the unit? And why would community elders encourage the recruitment campaign?

The UPA initially denounced formation of the Division in part because it might drain away its UPA recruits. Certainly, the Nazis would have welcomed this side benefit of organizing the unit. But the UPA did not hold sway. Other Ukrainian leaders supported the Division. Historian John Armstrong says of the Ukrainian leaders that, "much as they hated the Nazis and little as they hoped for real help from them, they feared the Communists still more." As German defeat loomed ever nearer, the threat of again falling under Soviet control grew. If the Ukrainian people could resist the Soviet onslaught with a properly trained military arm, perhaps, some thought, they could legitimize a claim to independence.[37]

Historian Myroslav Yurkevich adds that once the Nazis had decided on a Ukrainian ss division, they were prepared to organize it by force if necessary. They were already carting Ukrainian youth off to forced labour in Germany. What would stop them from pressing young men into uniform? Nothing. As noted, it was hoped that by co-operating in recruitment, it might be possible "to influence . . . [the Division] character and defend the interests of the soldiers." And, Yurkevich notes, several concessions were won — Ukrainian chaplains, a promise not to use the Division against the western allies (a condition "not seriously infringed"), a continuing role in checking soldiers' welfare for the Ukrainian recruitment committee.[38]

There proved no shortage of recruits. Within weeks 82,000 men came forward of whom 13,000 were assigned to the three divisional regiments which made up the Galicia Division. Some of the other volunteers were streamed into several ss police units trained for "antipartisan activities" against the underground in Poland and elsewhere. The 13,000-man Galicia Division was sent to Germany for training. In May 1944 Himmler addressed the Division's officers, mostly Germans, on the threat of Bolsheviks and Jews but avoided his usual attack on "sub-human Slavs." Shortly thereafter, the Division was dispatched to the eastern front.

In mid-July it faced a vastly superior and seasoned Red Army force advancing on L'viv. At the Battle of Brody the Division was decimated by mechanized Soviet units and superior firepower. Of the 13,000 men who entered the battle, only 3,000 withdrew in battle-ready condition.[39] The survivors of the Brody defeat who did not desert, fall prisoner to the Soviets or join the UPA were reassembled, and another 8,000 of the original Ukrainian volunteers first dispatched to police units were integrated into the Division. Additional Ukrainian recruits drifted into the Division. Eventually it was brought back to full strength.[40]

As Nazi fortunes crumbled on all sides, the Division was dispatched to help put down partisan-led uprisings in Slovakia and Yugoslavia and then transferred to Austria where, fearing Soviet encirclement, it surrendered to the British. After being moved to a prisoner-of-war camp at Rimini in Italy, members of the unit underwent pro forma interrogation by Allied investigators, including Soviets. As no evidence of criminal action was uncovered, none were held on criminal charges. And once they refused repatriation to now Soviet-controlled Ukraine, the Galicia Division became a British headache, and eventually all members were shipped to England.

In retrospect, the Division did not live up to the hopes of Ukrainian leaders — it did not become the focal point for Ukrainian resistance to the Soviet advance on western Ukraine. Neither did it have a glorious record of service to the Nazis. But it was still part of the SS, albeit the Waffen SS. Each recruit did swear an oath of personal loyalty to Hitler, not to the Ukrainian national cause. The Division was assigned to anti-partisan activities and, after the Battle of Brody, absorbed Ukrainians in Nazi uniform who had served elsewhere. Did it take part in what might be defined as war crimes or crimes against humanity? No evidence has been brought forward to prove this. Does evidence exist to show that individuals committed crimes against innocent civilians, including Jews, before they joined the Division? If so, none has been made public.

Among some Jews, however, suspicion persists. In anticipation of crushing Nazi defeat, might not the Division have made a good cover for Ukrainian collaborators retreating with the Nazis? Certainly, after the

Battle of Brody, Ukrainians retreating westward with the Germans found their way into Divisional ranks. A German member of the Division's staff chronicled these confusing last months of the war.

There was no lack of Ukrainian soldiers [to rebuild the Division after Brody]. New recruits arrived on schedule. However, now there was a marked difference. Initially, all our recruits came straight from civilian life. Now they were mostly ablebodied men from among the Ukrainian refugees fleeing the Red Army. Ostensibly, they joined up voluntarily, but actually, they did it from force of circumstances. No one was actually pressed into military service, but once they came to the Division, they had to obey military rules and could not avoid punishment if they went back on their decision. In terms of quality of people, this time was not as good as the first. All volunteers were immediately dispatched to the reserve-training regiment for battle training.[41]

With the Nazi collapse and the final surrender of Germany in May 1945, Europe barely paused to take stock. Too much was happening. The Soviet sphere of influence shifted westward. Ukraine, in 1939 divided between Soviet and Polish authority, was now united but as a Soviet republic within the Soviet Union. Ukrainian nationalism, suppressed at home, was forced into exile. The Galicia Division members who refused to go home were soon joined by tens of thousands of other Ukrainians who were outside Ukraine at war's end and equally unwilling to return to Soviet rule. They collected in Displaced Persons camps in Allied-occupied Germany and Austria, avoiding relocation back to now-Soviet Ukraine and dreaming of an independent homeland.[42]

Eastern European Jewry had virtually ceased to exist. In Poland and Ukraine barely 10 percent of what was once the greatest seat of diaspora Jewish life survived

the Holocaust. Most of those had found temporary
sanctuary behind Soviet lines. After the war many of
the tattered remnant returned to their former homes
hoping to locate a wife or husband, a child or friend
who had also somehow managed to survive. Most found
they were alone and unwelcome. If homes still stood,
they were likely occupied by local residents reluctant to
give up what was now "theirs." Driven by hostility and
loneliness, many moved westward into Jewish Displaced
Persons camps in western-occupied Germany and
Austria. With grief at their loss and a deep conviction
that their old neighbours shared responsibility for their
plight, Jewish survivors, like Ukrainian Displaced Persons, waited.[43]

Chapter 2

In the New World

Many of the Ukrainian DPS and Jewish Holocaust survivors, fresh from their searing European experiences,
would find their way to Canada. There they would discover thriving Ukrainian and Jewish communities established by earlier generations of immigrants; together
they helped shape the communities of today. The contemporary Canadian context — the build-up of both
groups through waves of immigration, the social and
cultural characteristics of Canadian Jews and Ukrainians, and the structure of their communal organizations
— sets the immediate backdrop to our story.

Despite obvious differences in the New World environment, certain patterns were transplanted. Social segregation and mutual distrust had become a way of life
for many Jews and Ukrainians in Ukraine; when both
groups joined the stream of post-war immigrants to
Canada, this tradition was reinforced by geography.

In fact, ever since Jews and Ukrainians had begun to
settle in substantial numbers in Canada in the late nineteenth century, contact between the two groups had
been rare. A regional settlement pattern in Canada reinforced older patterns of social separation. Jews
congregated in the major metropolitan centres of eastern Canada while Ukrainians, predominantly rural,
made new homes in the prairie west. Several major exceptions to this isolation were to be found in the west,
notably in Winnipeg's now legendary immigrant north
end and in Ukrainian farm settlements where Jewish
shopkeepers or pedlars were part of the social landscape. Author Myrna Kostash recounts the early struggle of a Ukrainian Co-op in the Alberta prairie town of

Vegreville. The competition was the ubiquitous "Jewish merchant":

> The pressure was on the Ukrainian-Canadian consumers to identify the merchant's cause as their own: what's good for Babiuk's Red and White Store — or, for that matter, what's good for the Co-op — is good for you too. In the early 1900s the Vegreville Co-op [Ukrainian-managed] printed slogans on the paper shopping bags.
>
> *Sviy do svoho*
> *Ne idit' bil 'she do chuzhoho.*
> *V Russkim shtori vse kupuyte,*
> *I chuzhentsiv ne huduyt.*

(Rough translation: Let's stick together/Stop going to the foreigner's (i.e. non-Ukrainians)/Do all your shopping at the Ukrainian store/Let the foreign bastards starve.)

> Trouble was, in the case of this Co-op at least, the consumer didn't necessarily always feel treated with consideration. Very often the prices were higher than the competitor's but to go across the street to the "Jew's" was regarded as an act of bad faith.[1]

Perhaps it would have been unrealistic to expect Old-World conflicts to disappear in the new Canadian setting. Author Erna Paris recounts a telling episode involving the Jewish pioneer farm colony of Edenbridge, Saskatchewan:

> In the early years there had been little if any anti-Semitism. Co-operation was vital among those pioneering on the cold flats of Saskatchewan and, although prejudice remained a reality, it was in no one's best interests to act on it. But the old-country antipathies between Jews and Ukrainians had been transported across half a world — they had lived

together in the Ukraine and emigrated together to the Canadian Prairies — and, when life settled into an easier pattern, old irritations occasionally erupted into new conflicts. In 1924 several locals occupied the north-enders' International Hall and Free Library and broke the windows. The farmers of Edenbridge felt intimidated; they were afraid to start an open quarrel. So one day, when the Hall was empty, they simply carried it to a new location, closer to the centre of the colony, where it continued to serve as a place for Hebrew instruction, a library, and a meeting-hall.[2]

These episodes of anti-Semitic friction paled in frequency and intensity compared to Jewish memories of anti-Semitism in the old country. Canada was not Ukraine, and especially not eastern Ukraine with its long history of violent anti-Jewish outbursts. What is more, for many Ukrainian farm families, dealing with Jewish merchants, doctors or lawyers perpetuated an Old World tradition with which they were familiar and comfortable.[3]

Another occasional meeting-place for the two groups was on the political left, in the east as well as out west. For some, like the United Jewish People's Order (UJPO), or the Ukrainian Labour Farm Temple Association, Erna Paris recalls, personal ties could be fused with ideological solidarity.

During the summer vacation when the children weren't in school, the UJPO operated summer camps where the process of left-wing education continued. Camp Naivelt (New World) just a few miles outside Toronto housed the adults in a series of small cottages and the children (called Red Campers) in tents. Occasionally, campers from the equivalent left-wing Ukrainian camp came over to perform Kozatska dancing in a spirit of internationalism; camp songs were anti-racist ("Jim Crow Blues"), the Russian Internationale, and freedom

songs of all origins, including the rousing
"Freiheit."[4]

Aside from these few, often stylized interactions, formal contact remained rare. And yet, there were and are
in Canada emerging similarities between Jews and
Ukrainians: similarities of political and cultural interest,
of aspirations, of shared values, of communal structures. To be sure, the "two solitudes" metaphor still
describes relationships between Canada's Jews and
Ukrainians, with the possible exception of life in
Winnipeg.[5] But by the 1980s these convergences and
ties were becoming more significant than Old World
differences. Ironically, it is these new similarities which,
in part, tend to exacerbate friction today.

As strands within the Canadian multicultural fabric,
Ukrainians and Jews are older, well-organized, white,
middle-class communities. No other ethnic groups demonstrate more sophistication in the ins and outs of ethnic politics. They share some identical concerns. Each
has struggled to overcome vestiges of discrimination
while maximizing integration and individual participation in Canadian life. Yet both groups also put a pre-
mium on cultural and ethnic survival whatever the
seductions of assimilation. Indeed, since both groups
have now "made it" in Canada, the concerns of group
leaders are more and more focused on ethnic identity
and survival. But persisting insecurities lead to regular
taking of the collective pulse. In addition, both groups
share a concern about the fate of far-off motherlands —
Ukraine and Israel — and their respective diasporas.
Events, whether domestic or foreign, are often measured for their impact on the group. Is it good for
Jews? It is good for Ukrainians?

Neither community emerged, overnight, full blown, on
the Canadian scene. Both the Ukrainian and Jewish
communities in Canada have been built up through successive waves of immigration, arriving for the most part
in similar time periods. Within both groups, internal di-

visions reflect differences in the demographic and cultural backgrounds of the various waves. As a result both groups are a patchwork of different places of origin, motives for emigration, social-class composition, ideological baggage and global regional variations in pattern of settlement.

The first wave of Ukrainian migration to Canada took place between 1896 and 1914.[6] The reasons seem simple enough. Canada had a vast expanse of land in the west crying out for settlers for development and as a bulwark against possible American encroachment. Ukrainians, then primarily a farming people, thirsted for land. This thirst could not be satisfied in Ukraine, with its still semi-feudal conditions, over-population and general impoverishment. Class oppression, poverty, foreign domination and compulsory military service added to the push towards Canada.

Why Canada? Clifford Sifton, Prime Minister Wilfrid Laurier's minister of the interior at the turn of the century, was unable to meet this surging demand for agriculturalists from among traditional British and northern European sources. He thus opened the door to central and eastern European mass migration. Dr Josef Oleskow (Oleskiw) of L'viv, a Ukrainian philanthropist and agronomist, toured Canada in 1895. He returned to Ukraine with an official Canadian government endorsement and a drive to mobilize Ukrainian emigrants and assist them in their passage. The marriage of convenience — between Canadian western development and Ukrainian impoverishment — worked. About 170,000 Ukrainians, the legendary stalwart peasants in sheepskin coats, emigrated to Canada from 1896 to 1914.[7] They joined those of other ethnic origins making Canada, especially the Canadian west, their new home.

Counting ethnic groups is always a tricky business, even though Canadian census data, in comparison to American census sources, are a demographer's dream. A case in point is the figure for the total Ukrainian-origin population in Canada. In 1921, despite the fact that 170,000 Ukrainians had immigrated between 1896–1914, the census counted only about 107,000 in Canada.[8] Given the fact that many Ukrainian farm families were large, where were the missing Ukrainians?

One explanation lies in the sex ratio of the immigrants. For many of the years of peak migration to Canada, the ratio of adult males to females was in the order of 3:1 or even 4:1.[9] Thus many of the Ukrainian immigrants may have remained unmarried, not reproducing in the next generation. It is also commonly understood that large numbers of immigrants to Canada moved south to the United States, using Canada as a back door to an idealized America where streets were said to be paved with gold.

Another explanation is that in 1921 many Ukrainians may still have been counted as Austrian, Polish or Russian, or simply as Galicians, depending on who controlled the chunks of Ukraine out of which individuals came at the time of their immigration. By 1931, the census count of Ukrainians had doubled to 225,000, while the Austrian numbers declined from 108,000 to 49,000. Thus as the news of the final destruction of the Austro-Hungarian Empire sank in after 1921, and as people may have better understood the intent of the ethnic-origin question, Ukrainian Canadians may have switched their census designations from Austrian to Ukrainian. The resurgence of Ukrainian nationalism after 1918, and the short-lived Ukrainian National Republic, no doubt also stirred Ukrainian pride.

While the terrain and climate of the prairies reminded many Ukrainian immigrants of the wheat-producing areas of Ukraine, it was not home, not yet. Ukrainian homesteaders and labourers encountered a full measure of discrimination and snobbish hostility. Many, perhaps most, of the immigrants were illiterate in any language, let alone English. In 1908 Galicia, the western Ukrainian area of origin of many immigrants, over four and a half million of the seven and a half million residents were illiterate.[10]

World War I brought unexpected hardship to Canada's Ukrainian immigrants, adding to the normal

problems of economic adjustment and slow accultura-
tion. During the war, thousands of Ukrainian immigrants from areas of Ukraine now controlled by the
Austro-Hungarian enemy were suddenly suspect. Those
who had not been naturalized at least fifteen years earlier were disenfranchised. Approximately 6,000 Austro-
Hungarians, most of whom were Ukrainians, were ripped away from their families and interned in large
camps in the mountains. Even those who dutifully regis-
tered suffered economic hardship and, suspected as possible subversives, remained under police surveillance.
For some Canadians of Ukrainian descent, this episode
remains a historic wrong similar in kind to the forced
evacuation of Japanese Canadians during World War
II.[11]

The first-wave immigrants were concerned with keeping body and soul together. Ukrainian churches provided an oasis of spiritual warmth and social and
communal organization. They also fostered a sense of
continuing Ukrainian identity and cultural education.
Tied to the land, unfamiliar with the language and cus-
toms of Canada, the first generation lived an insular,
simple, hardworking life.

Jewish immigration to Canada likewise occurred in
waves.[12] The first of several ripples stretched from the
mid-eighteenth century to the mid-nineteenth century.
In the main they comprised Jews of Sephardic origin,
immigrating via England. They founded Canada's oldest
synagogue, the Spanish and Portuguese Synagogue of
Montreal. Another ripple in the mid-nineteenth century
consisted of German and central European or Ashkenazi Jews, who also settled primarily in Montreal. A
much smaller community was established in Toronto as
well. Compared to later Jewish arrivals, these earlier
settlers were a relatively educated, urban, affluent
group involved in commerce. They laid the foundations
for a network of Jewish communal and self-help organizations.

The first major wave of Jewish migration began in
the late 1880s and consisted primarily of Jews from

eastern Europe. These Jews were motivated to move by crippling poverty brought about by overpopulation and increased competition in certain economic sectors from recently enfranchised serfs and other eastern Europeans. But what helped turn a large economic migration into a population upheaval was the onset of violent pogroms, beginning in 1881, and again in the 1890s and 1903.

Unlike the Ukrainians who went west, the vast majority of Jewish immigrants joined existing communities in major cities of Quebec, and later of Ontario. Only a small number moved to the west, primarily to urban Winnipeg. Peak years of this immigration were 1905 to 1915. But immigration, often of first-degree relatives of those already in Canada, continued at a steady if reduced rate of 3,000 to 4,000 a year until the Depression, when Canada's immigration doors were shut tight.

By 1901, there were in all of Canada about 17,000 Jews, increasing to 75,000 by 1911, and 126,000 by 1921. In 1921, 76 percent of Jews lived in urban Quebec and Ontario, and this percentage increased over the years.

Most Jewish immigrants were skilled or semi-skilled working-class people. Few had been or wished to remain farmers or farm labourers; many had worked in urban factories or as artisans, petty traders and merchants in small towns in rural eastern Europe. Almost all the men, if not the women, were literate in Yiddish and some in Hebrew. Most spoke and not a few were literate in one or more of Polish, German, Russian or Ukrainian. Many were strongly committed to political ideologies. The first two decades of the twentieth century were turbulent years of ideological debate as Europe's Jews struggled to discover answers to the perplexing "Jewish question." Nor was this debate reserved for the elite. It involved Jews of all classes and backgrounds. Thus socialists, Bundists, Yiddishists, territoralists, anarchists, Orthodox, assimilationists, Zionists of every political stripe and others could be found among Canadian Jewish immigrants.

Contrary to popular impression, the early wave of Jewish immigration was not strongly devout or religiously observant. Rabbinic leaders in eastern Europe generally stayed behind, fearing the corrosive impact on the observant of the much-discussed materialism and secularism of North America. Many counselled their followers to do the same. As a result, many of the communal leaders of the Jewish masses in Canada were resolutely secular. Ironically, many leaders of secular political groups also remained in Europe. They sought solutions to Jewish issues in domestic European reform or revolution, not in overseas migration. Canadian Jewish leaders kept one eye cocked on events in the Old World even as they focused the other on the possibilities of the new.

Thus both the Ukrainian and Jewish communities were established in the pre–World War II era of mass migration. But if they came at the same time and shared common eastern European roots, their Canadian experiences were very different. Ukrainians primarily worked the land in the west. Jews worked in petty trade in the east, as shopkeepers or pedlars and as skilled workers in industries such as clothing, leather and fur. The Jewish masses brought with them, and to a certain extent found in the Canadian Jewish community, a deep tradition of elaborate communal organization, voluntarism, philanthropy, and self-help. The Ukrainian immigrants, of largely peasant background, had to struggle to develop these organizations and structures. Many of these functions were assumed by the church, but not without difficulty. Key Ukrainian religious leaders, like their Jewish counterparts, were reluctant to leave the old country, and Ukrainian lay leadership in rural Canada was slow to crystallize.

The Ukrainians of the first migration brought to Canada a rich culture which was essentially non-literate, folkloric, defined by religious experience and tied to the land. The Jewish mass migration, by contrast, brought a culture which was urban and literate in both Hebrew, the language of prayers and the liturgy, and Yiddish,

the language of daily life, of culture, newspapers, theatre and political debate.

The second great wave of Ukrainian migration to
Canada arrived in the interwar period, 1918–1939. Of
an estimated 68,000–70,000 Ukrainians, nearly 56,000
arrived between 1926–1930.[13] Many of these immigrants
came to Canada like the first wave, seeking economic
opportunity. But their historical baggage was different.
A fair number had military experience. Some had
fought for Ukrainian independence or had forged their
national consciousness through the battle for the short-
lived Ukrainian National Republic and Western Ukrainian Republic. Thus they were politically aware, attuned
to ideological controversies which animated life in
Ukraine and eastern Europe. These immigrants, who
included adherents of nationalism and socialism in their
various shadings, were more urbanized and more educated than those arriving before World War I, and less
likely to work the land.

To many of this second wave, the first-wave Ukrainians and, more particularly, their children may have
seemed too Canadian, or simply too assimilated. But all
would soon be swept up in the political debates which
exploded in the community. The ideological and organizational foundations of left-wing Ukrainian life were
laid before World War I. But the years of the 1920s
and especially the depression years of the 1930s were an
era of intense rivalry between various pro- and anti-Soviet factions, fuelled by the new immigration. The
proper attitude towards Ukraine and the new Soviet experiment became a defining issue of cultural and social
life dividing not just the community but families as
well. Thus there were strong similarities between the
second wave of Ukrainian mass immigration and the
pre–World War I Jewish wave. Each was marked by
tensions with those who had arrived earlier and who
seemed more assimilated. Both groups were predominantly non-agricultural, with a strong working-class and

urban element. Both were awash in internal debate on questions of political, national and cultural importance.

Both the Ukrainian and Jewish communities in Canada absorbed substantial numbers of immigrants in the post–World War II period. Many of these were Displaced Persons, refugees from the horrors and the uncompromising insecurity of post-war Europe. An estimated 44,000 Jews arrived in Canada from 1945 to 1954, the vast majority of these survivors of the Holocaust from many European countries, but in the main from Poland and the Soviet Union, including Ukraine, and especially eastern Ukraine. These Holocaust survivors generally arrived as impoverished immigrants. Some had skilled trades, and relatively few had higher education of any sort, though in this they would not have differed from the Canadian host population. Like the earlier Jewish immigrants, they spoke either Yiddish or, for a minority, the languages of their European countries of origin.

These survivors had to cope with a dual burden. One was the struggle facing any impoverished immigrant, unfamiliar with English or French, in adapting to a new society. The other was the special trauma associated with the Holocaust — the destruction of family and friends, the disruption of career or educational aspirations and, understandably enough, related psychological or physical problems.[14] Many joined or formed *Landsmanschaften*, the Jewish fraternal or mutual-aid organizations of members from specific locations in eastern Europe.

The survivors slowly became established and began to sink roots in the community. When they had arrived they had been DPs, dependent on the existing Jewish community. With the passage of time and the new importance accorded the Holocaust in Jewish self-understanding, the survivors emerged from the shadows and assumed the role of conscience of the Jewish community on matters relating to the Holocaust and anti-Semitism. And the experience of the Holocaust was never far from mind. They formed associations of survivors of specific concentration camps, as well as general organizations of Holocaust survivors.[15] Now in major urban centres there are also associations of children of survivors, dedicated to perpetuating the memory of the Holocaust.

The Ukrainian third wave, which arrived after 1945, shares many similarities with the Jewish survivor immigration, though neither group might appreciate the comparison. From 1945 to 1952 inclusive, close to 33,000 Ukrainians arrived in Canada. They were joined later by other Ukrainian immigrants. But this post-war or third wave was primarily drawn from among the ranks of DPs. A substantial number of them had higher education and had worked in professions. Some had proudly played military or paramilitary roles during the war, fighting the Soviets, the Nazis or both. Among them were members of the SS Galicia Division. Others, accused by the Nazis of the offence of Ukrainian nationalism, had been imprisoned in labour or concentration camps, or carted off to farms or factories in manpower-short Germany. Unlike earlier Ukrainian immigrant waves, largely from western Ukraine, the third wave was drawn from all areas of Ukraine. They have been termed a "united" Ukrainian immigration.[16]

As in the case of the inter-war Ukrainian migration, the third wave also brought an ideological fervour and nationalist commitment far greater than that which awaited them in Canada. They had fought and bled for Ukraine. Their national and ideological passions were stoked in the DP camps of Germany and Austria. Once in Canada they reinvigorated the communal tie to, and concern for, Ukraine. For the majority of these immigrants, there grew a strong and singular ideological mission — militant anti-Communism combined with a strong commitment to Ukrainian nationalism and the survival of Ukrainian culture. Some still focused on the possibility of a liberated, independent Ukraine, but the majority oriented themselves to maximizing the rights of Ukrainians now living under Soviet rule, supporting dissidents and religious leaders, and advocating a generally hardline anti-Communist foreign policy in Canada.

The third-wave migration continued the population drift of Ukrainians away from rural areas into cities and, as well, the redirection of communal politics into Ontario and Quebec. Growth has been particularly rapid in Toronto, which in many ways emerged as the centre of organized Ukrainian life in Canada and indeed of the international Ukrainian diaspora. The national headquarters of the Ukrainian Canadian Committee (UCC), the umbrella organization of all but the far-left Ukrainian groups, has remained in Winnipeg where it was first organized, but population, power and political leadership have increasingly shifted eastward to Toronto or westward to Edmonton.

In this sense, recent demographic trends may be acting to break down some of the geographic basis for the segregation between Jewish and Ukrainian life. For Jews, the centre of organizational life has shifted from Montreal to Toronto. For Ukrainians, the shift, while not nearly so great, has also made Toronto a major Ukrainian centre. But as both communities have gained strength in Toronto, they have remained, even there, largely separate.

Today the Ukrainian population in Canada is more than double that of Jews. In 1981, there were 264,000 Canadians who identified themselves as Jewish only, and an additional 30,000 who identified themselves as partly Jewish. For Ukrainians, the comparable figures were 530,000, and 216,000. The larger proportion of Ukrainians with partial Ukrainian origin, compared to the Jews, reflects the fact that Ukrainians have intermarried far more often than have Jews. This is not surprising. Jews are both a religious and an ethnic group. They therefore face a double barrier regarding intermarriage. Ukrainians, however, may well marry someone of a different ethnic origin who yet shares a common Christian faith, either within a Ukrainian church or in some other Christian denomination.[17]

Both Ukrainians and Jews can be considered "old" groups, in that the majority of the members are Canadian born. In 1981 Ukrainians were almost 90 percent Canadian born, the highest for any non-French or non-English immigrant-origin group in Canada. For Jews, the figure was only 66 percent, reflecting more recent waves of immigration from North Africa, Hungary, Poland, the Soviet Union and Israel.[18] But even that figure was higher than the Canadian-born percentages for other ethnic groups, such as 54 percent for Italians, 27 percent for Chinese and 26 percent for Portuguese.

The Ukrainian-Canadian population, already larger than the Jewish, is also likely to grow more rapidly. Among Jews there is a higher proportion of older people and a lower proportion of young people than among Ukrainians. In addition, Jews have perhaps the lowest fertility rate of any group in Canada. American Jewish fertility is now estimated at *below* what is necessary for population maintenance; Canadian Jews are not far behind. Higher Ukrainian fertility may also be associated with the still significant minority of Ukrainians living in rural areas, where traditional religious values are strong.

Many Ukrainian Canadians are likely to claim Ukrainian as both a mother tongue, which is the language first learned and still understood, and as language of home use. Indeed, given that only one of every ten Canadian Ukrainians is actually foreign born, the tenacity with which families encourage Ukrainian language use is remarkable. For Jews, only 13 percent claim Yiddish or Hebrew as their mother tongue and 4 percent speak it at home. For Ukrainians, the figures are 37 percent and 12 percent respectively.

But it is important to note that both these measures may tend to understate the degree of ethnic-language knowledge and use, for both Ukrainians and Jews. Many Ukrainians, for example, may have a passive knowledge of the language, or some words, phrases or songs of symbolic importance used at festivals, religious occasions and the like. This kind of knowledge may well be far short of fluency or complete literacy, but it is important. It bonds people to the language and to the community. This knowledge can come from community schools or churches, language lessons or from interaction with parents or grandparents. This nurturing role of the ethnic language is not picked up by the census questions, since the census does not take an inventory of all the languages Canadians know or use, let alone the structure of language use. For example, in a 1975 study of ethnic-language knowledge and use in five major Canadian cities, only one Ukrainian in ten said they had no knowledge of their ancestral language. Over one-third claimed they used their Ukrainian "daily" and only 12 percent replied that they "never or rarely" used the language.[19]

A similar pattern exists for the use of Yiddish among Jews, as it would for most other ethnic languages in Canada. In other words, language loyalty is much stronger than would be indicated by census data alone. And yet, there is no doubt that over time and passing generations, the ethnic languages, especially Yiddish, are declining in knowledge and use. For Jews, a complicating factor is that as Yiddish declines, Hebrew has increased both because of its role as the language of prayers and holidays, and because of the impact of Hebrew-speaking Israel on modern Jewish culture. Roughly half of Canadian Jewish children today receive some form of intensive instruction in Hebrew, whether at full-time day schools or afternoon schools.[20] This is a higher proportion than can be estimated among Ukrainian Canadians.[21]

The groups continue to differ in their geographic distribution in Canada, despite population growth in Toronto. Roughly 99 percent of Canadian Jews live in urban areas, and 92 percent live in cities with populations of over 500,000. The comparable figures for Ukrainians are 76 percent and 44 percent. Indeed, 77 percent of Canadian Jews live in Montreal, Toronto and Vancouver, compared to only 20 percent of Ukrainians. Put another way, 84 percent of Canadian

Jews live in the provinces of Ontario and Quebec, while 70 percent of Ukrainian Canadians still live in western Canada, even though most post-1945 third-wave Ukrainian immigrants settled in Ontario or Quebec.[22] Demographically as well as culturally, the third-wave Ukrainians form a "community within a community."

Jewish-Ukrainian differences in the pattern of regional distribution are related to other sorts of differences between the two groups. Jews have "made it" in Canada. They are more highly represented than Ukrainians in those top occupational categories called "managerial and administrative, technical and scientific," by a ratio of two to one. This is due in large part to the differences in education between the two groups. In 1981 fully 41 percent of Jews report at least some university education, compared to 17 percent for Ukrainians. These educational and occupational differences, along with regional and urban-rural differences, explain why, according to 1981 census data, Jewish average incomes are much higher than Ukrainian.

Jews, more so than Ukrainians, have begun to penetrate the top ranks of the Canadian social-economic elite. Families such as the Bronfmans, the Reichmanns and the Belzbergs are not only personally wealthy but have control over large pools of capital. Interestingly, these three families, and others like them, have retained their ties and commitments to Jewish life, though expressed in markedly different ways. While there are many wealthy Ukrainian Canadians, there are relatively few multi-millionaires, and none have that kind of financial clout. A 1986 edition of *Toronto Life* magazine identified what it considered the fifty most influential people in Toronto. Almost one in four was Jewish. None was or appeared to be of Ukrainian origin.[23]

But it is worth noting that both Jews and Ukrainians earn above the Canadian average income. According to one study, in 1981 Jews earned roughly $6,200 above the Canadian average income, compared to $800 above for Ukrainians. This marked a dramatic improvement for Ukrainians, whose average income in 1971 was $640 below the Canadian average.[24]

What sense can we make of this? The 1981 census figures tell us that both these groups are not being victimized economically through discrimination. This does not mean, of course, that in the past these groups were not clearly victimized, or that some Canadians do not still hold negative attitudes about these groups. Far from it.[25] But it does suggest that if there are negative feelings about these groups, they do not affect income. The 1981 census figures suggest that people who are Jewish or Ukrainian are probably not paid less for the same work, are usually not denied promotions or career opportunities, and are not shut out of all networks of professional and occupational contacts because of their ethnic origin. All in all, that is pretty good news. Other groups in Canada, such as blacks or Asian groups, still struggle against a racial discrimination that is far more pernicious.[26]

Money, however, tells only part of the story of social acceptance. Another way to measure ethnic status is through a group's perception of how the majority sees them. Still another is by evaluating members' accounts of their own experiences of discrimination. Here a 1978–79 study, if somewhat dated, reveals an interesting story. The survey sampled eight ethnic groups in Toronto, including 344 Jews and 345 Ukrainians, chosen more or less randomly.[27]

The study found that 92 percent of Ukrainians but only 78 percent of Jews saw themselves accepted as neighbours "very or somewhat easily." For acceptance as would-be family members the figures were 85 percent for Ukrainians and only 42 percent for Jews — the latter reflecting the complications felt about interfaith marriage as well as perceived anti-Semitism. Moreover, for a group with such objectively high occupational levels and income, 17 percent of Jews still claimed that discrimination against them was a "very or somewhat serious" problem, and 12 percent reported having experienced discrimination when trying to get a job. For

Ukrainians the comparable figures were much lower, 4 percent and 7 percent respectively. Overall, then, in spite of differences, only a small minority of both Jews and Ukrainians reported much discrimination, and what they experienced does not seem to have held them back — certainly not when compared to Toronto's visible minorities.

Having largely overcome the problems of historical discrimination and immigrant adaptation in Canada, the organized collective lives of both the Jewish and Ukrainian communities now centre mainly on the goals of enhanced survival of group culture and political concern for the welfare of a homeland — Israel and Ukraine respectively.

The majority of Canadian Jews and Ukrainian Canadians share a similar ancestral place of origin: eastern Europe. Common features of the Slavic experience and environment can be found in eastern European Jewish culture and vice versa. The *shtetl*, the cradle of so much of eastern European Jewish folklore, was nestled within a Slavic, often Ukrainian environment. Ashkenazi Jewish and Israeli music and dance remain to this day strongly influenced by the folk culture of Christian eastern Europe — there is nothing intrinsically Jewish or Israeli about the hora danced at every Jewish celebration. Foods such as blintzes or nalysnyky, stuffed cabbage or holubtsi are common in both Slavic/Ukrainian and Jewish cuisine.

Both Jews and Ukrainians are also peoples with deep historical memory, and one of the ongoing characteristics of Jewish-Ukrainian dialogue is that both Jews and Ukrainians perceive themselves as victims and the other as a dominant or superior entity. Thus Ukrainians understand their history as a centuries-long effort to achieve independence and freedom in Ukraine, struggling gallantly but unsuccessfully against tsarist Russian, Austro-Hungarian, Polish, Nazi and Soviet domination, and they see the continuing oppression of their nationality and religion by the Soviet regime today.

Ukrainian agony in the Canadian diaspora is epitomized by the famine of 1931–32. Many Ukrainians feel that this greatest of their modern national catastrophes has tended to be ignored in subsequent history and historiography. It has not touched the consciousness of nations as have other twentieth-century tragedies, such as the Holocaust of European Jewry, the Armenian massacres of 1915 or the auto-genocidal tragedy of Cambodia. It is as if the world does not heed the Ukrainian cry of anguish. Jews, not Ukrainians, are considered the quintessential victims of modern times.[28]

For some Canadian Jews, on the other hand, Ukrainians still appear as a collective representation of evil. Thus when confronted, albeit infrequently, by Ukrainian sorrows, Jews find it hard to feel sympathy for those who they feel have been their persecutors. Added to this uneasy sense of the Ukrainian as heir to a pogromist tradition is a cultural prejudice which pictures the Ukrainian as simple peasant — both in the old country and in Canada.[29]

For some Ukrainian-Canadians, Jews appear in their historical legacy as alien, subversive and corrupting elements in Ukraine. Thus, and this comes as a shock to most Jews, Ukrainian historical images describe Jews as being in league with Ukraine's oppressors. Ukrainians in Canada certainly recognize and sympathize with the horrors of the systematic mass murder engineered by the Nazis on their victims. There are few, if any, "Holocaust revisionists" among the Ukrainians, denying that the Holocaust took place. After all, many Ukrainian Canadians, or their relatives, were there as it was happening. Indeed, like other eastern European nations, they can point to the large numbers of Ukrainians — leftists, anti-Fascists, Soviet army conscripts, clerics, nationalists, and average peasant folk — who were enslaved, incarcerated, or murdered by the Nazis, alongside Jews. But some claim Jews now have one advantage which soothes the historical trauma of the Holocaust. The Jews have an independent homeland,

Israel, while Ukraine is still unfree. The Ukrainian diaspora remains dispossesed.

For Jews, the creation of the State of Israel in 1948 and the 1967 Arab-Israeli war finished the process of separating the notions of old country and homeland. These are now two distinct entities. The old country is the place from which parents or grandparents emigrated or fled — a world of poverty, oppression and finally mass murder. By the third generation, many Canadian Jews would be hard pressed to recall, or to locate on a map, the precise town or even province of their ancestors.

After the trauma of the Holocaust, most of which took place on eastern European soil, interest in the old country is usually expressed by Jews only when it comes to the "rescue" of those few Jews who remain there. Few Jews wallow in nostalgia for the eastern Europe of the non-Jews. Theirs were two different worlds. Even towns or cities were pronounced differently; Lviv for the Ukrainians, Lvov, Lwów or Lemberg for the Jews, more often influenced by Russian, Polish or Yiddish forms.

For Ukrainians, of course, the old country and the homeland are one. Ukraine was — is — their ancestral home, waiting to be freed from the yoke of Soviet domination. The care and concern which Jews lavish on Israel, Ukrainian nationalists similarly lavish on Ukraine, or rather, on Ukrainian dissidents, religious leaders and ordinary citizens chafing under the Soviet regime. Third- or fourth-generation Ukrainian Canadians — like their Jewish counterparts — may no longer recall the names and location of ancestral villages; few, if any, would leave Canada and return to an independent Ukraine, any more than Jewish Canadians have moved to Israel. But for many Ukrainian Canadians, Ukraine still serves as a vital rallying point for identity in the diaspora.

With some irony, the rebirth of a Jewish state in Israel serves as a model for stalwart Ukrainian nationalists. They cling to the hope that the Soviet Empire will yet collapse, and a free and truly independent Ukraine will emerge from the rubble.

In Canada today, history and homeland continue to play major roles for both groups as they — or specifically their leaders and major organizations — wage the struggle for group survival. They provide the emotional and intellectual glue that joins the members of each group as they organize to shape its future. And organized they are. If the Jewish community in Canada can be considered to have the most developed polity — a set of community organizations which link leaders to group members in common cause to achieve the goals or objectives of the group — then Ukrainian Canadians are second.

Many Canadian ethnic groups are, in a certain sense, self-governing polities. Daniel Elazar, an American political scientist, has fleshed out the idea of the ethnic polity, using American Jews as an example. As Elazar describes it, the Jewish polity represents the set of institutions supported mainly by voluntary charitable contributions and fees raised within the Jewish community. Together this structure defines organized Jewish life. In his view, the central tasks of the organized community are threefold. It serves as a defence of the group against actual or potential threats to its security. It encourages education and other activities designed to promote group culture and survival from generation to generation. Lastly, it offers social services which enhance the quality of group members' lives.[30]

The Jewish polity flourishes in North America. Indeed it is the ethnic polity par excellence. Jewish life has a long tradition of self-regulation and autonomy in the diaspora. Through the centuries Jewish communities had developed a network of communal organizations such as burial societies, orphanages, poorhouses, rabbinic courts and schools to look after the needs of the community, including the less fortunate. This tradition, rooted in both biblical injunctions and old-country realities, was quickly adapted and entrenched in the New World.

The Jewish polity in the Old World was responsible not only for the self-governance of the community but also for dealing with the external state authorities. This usually involved intercession with the ruling government to mitigate some harsh edict directed at Jews, often with a bribe or the rendering of some economic service. Such were the constraints of minority status.

With the migration of Jews to North America, the continuation of the same degree of Old World formal communal autonomy raised problems. After all, Canada and the United States were societies dedicated, at least officially, to the principles of equal citizenship and equal treatment under the law. Jews could vote and run for office, could usually expect fair treatment in the courts, and had access to all state-run services. Moreover, some Jews were apprehensive about the charge of dual loyalty, of setting up "a state within a state." They were afraid that somehow loyalty to Canada could be called into question by excessive commitment to Jewish communal institutions.

None of these fears prevented Jews — and other immigrant groups — from setting up an extensive array of voluntary organizations. After all, the right to freedom of association was enshrined in Canadian common law well before its entrenchment as an article of the Charter of Rights and Freedoms of the new Canadian Constitution. But the surrounding society was an open, even beckoning one. Minority-group members had a smorgasbord of options available to express their identity. Ethnic organizational life was but one option among many. In an earlier age, Jewish communities in the old country had used excommunication to keep dissenters, such as Spinoza, in line. Such an extreme form of punishment could only work in a predominantly closed Orthodox Jewish community. Such was not the world of North America.

Moreover, Jews quickly realized that in North America affiliation with ethnic organizations was not associated with inferior legal status. The Jewish polity in North America came to be modelled and structured like the myriad of other voluntary organizations which typify modern life. It was sustained by, and helped sustain, Jewish identity in the New World.[31]

This has also been the case for Ukrainian Canadians. True, they did not bring with them from Ukraine the same history of traditional use of self-help organizations, and its corollary in communal fund-raising. Inasmuch as authentic, autonomous Ukrainian institutions might be seen as a nationalist threat to Polish, Russian or Austrian control, they were suppressed. Only in western Ukraine did churches and later populist organized co-operatives and reading rooms offer the local populace an avenue of national self-expression.

The Ukrainian diaspora is of more recent vintage. Their historic oppression came from outsiders controlling Ukraine, not as insecure minorities in exile. But in Canada, Ukrainians quickly seized on formal organizations as a vehicle for reconstructing ethnic communal and national life.

Today, both the Jewish and Ukrainian communities are among the most "institutionally complete" ethnic communities in the country.[32] They boast a myriad of ethnic organizations and institutions of different types and objectives. An institutionally complete ethnic community can parallel the state, offering a cradle-to-grave cocoon for interested group members. Ethnic schools, newspapers and community festivals can punctuate life's rhythms, and the elderly can live out their final years in special old-age homes that capture the cultural ambience in which they feel most comfortable.

But institutional completeness does not mean communal uniformity. Both communities have been marked with intra-communal tensions or conflict. Some of this has been ideological. Jewish organizations have split on standard left-right social issues, on Zionism and the degree of support for Israeli policy and on religious issues.

These ideological disputes are also mirrored among Ukrainian organizations. Left-right rivalries are now somewhat muted as the Ukrainian community, like the Jewish, has become overwhelmingly anti-Communist. Pro-Soviet factions are a tiny and increasingly aged minority. Yet even the nationalists have bickered among themselves about strategy, tactics and policies to be adopted *vis-à-vis* the Soviet regime and the struggle for human rights and cultural freedom in Ukraine. They also differ about how much energy to focus on Ukraine versus more local Canadian issues. For many Ukrainians, particularly in western Canada and among third and fourth generations, a constant focus on the homeland, and certainly hopes for a liberated Ukraine, seems misdirected. It deflects from the real task of building Ukrainian life in Canada and of contributing to Canadian society. Similarly, at the 1986 Canadian Jewish Congress triennial plenary session, Rabbi Gunther Plaut called for greater external involvement on the part of Canadian Jews in the affairs and needs of other groups. It was time, he argued, to move beyond an almost exclusive focus on Jewish concerns and Jewish victimization.[33]

If Jewish and Ukrainian organizations in Canada have as a rule kept their distance, they have at various times played coalition politics. They have supported each other's claims as well as the claims of other minority groups in a *quid pro quo* relationship *vis-à-vis* the government.

Thus in Alberta, Jews fell in behind Ukrainians in lobbying the government to secure government funding for private schools. Both Jewish and Ukrainian organizations have supported the Japanese-Canadian claim for redress for lost properties and damages from their forced relocation during World War II. But at times, Jewish-Ukrainian co-operation has been uneasy. A case in point involves the overlapping issues of Soviet Jewry and the struggle for cultural and religious freedoms in Ukraine. Jews have tended to emphasize the right to religious self-expression and the option of emigration for Soviet Jews. Ukrainians have tended to stress enhanced freedom in Ukraine through more decentralization, if not independence, and lessening of Communist ideology and freer exercise of religion. This would necessitate a greater modification, if not dismembering, of the Soviet centralized state; Jewish objectives leave the Soviet state and its ideological particularities intact.

Each of these ethnic polities has other similar sources of internal tension. One, typically Canadian, has to do with regionalism and the size of the country. The Jewish polity has for some time been marked by the rivalry between Montreal and Toronto as centres of power. In recent years the action has shifted steadily from the former to the latter. But the Toronto–Montreal rivalry has only exacerbated resentful claims from the smaller Jewish communities in the Maritimes, western Canada and even other areas in Ontario that they have been systematically neglected by the two dominant metropolitan centres.

Similar complaints resonate through the Ukrainian community as well. Tension has emerged between the older centres of Ukrainian power in the west, notably Winnipeg and Edmonton, and the newer, more urbanized, more third-wave and in many ways more nationalist community in Toronto. As Ukrainians become urbanized, some may worry about the declining strength of rural, traditional life.

In Canada today, both Jewish and Ukrainian communities are enthusiastic celebrants of the multicultural ideal. Both are criss-crossed with a network of newspapers, bulletins and publications serving as an important communications link binding each community together. In numbers of periodicals and their circulation, Jewish and Ukrainian publications of all types rank ahead of any others on a per-capita basis. But looking at recent data for Toronto, we can see that Jews tend to be more committed readers of the ethnic press, extending well into the third generation. Almost none of the third-generation Ukrainians in Toronto read the ethnic press, as compared to over one-half of third-generation Jews.[34]

Within the Jewish community, one publication, the English-language weekly *Canadian Jewish News* has emerged as the dominant newspaper for Ontario and Quebec. A few key newspapers also dominate in most Jewish centres in western Canada. For Ukrainians, there is a greater variety of newspapers, in English and Ukrainian, each holding its own place in the political and religious spectrum. No one publication has assumed a dominant role. Some Ukrainian leaders regard the *Canadian Jewish News* as a model of an ethnic newspaper, for its wide-ranging coverage, its sophistication, advertising support and unifying effect.[35] But one must not mistake a single newspaper for a single world view. Jews no less than Ukrainians are a fractious community.

Apart from ideological disputes, ethnic polities are also typified by internal turf struggles. The more established a community, the more important these struggles between rival organizations may become. In the Canadian Jewish polity, the dominant organizational groups are the Canadian Jewish Congress, the B'nai Brith and the local welfare federations.

The Canadian Jewish Congress, founded in 1919, has been called the "parliament of Canadian Jewry." Modelled on the British Board of Jewish Deputies, it is an umbrella "organization of other organizations," each with a voting voice in Congress in proportion to its membership strength. Triennial conventions are held in which contestants run for the various leadership positions. Some races are won by acclamation, but at times campaigning for delegate votes has been quite intense. Congress sees itself and is seen by others as the main interlocutor of Jewish interests before the federal and, through regional arms, provincial governments. It takes an active role in preparation of briefs and lobbying. With elaborate offices in Montreal and Toronto and smaller offices in other centres of Jewish population, it boasts a large professional staff, as well as lay members serving on committees and the executive. The latter set policy, the former execute it.

Over the past decades the power and authority of Congress have eroded somewhat. This has been largely because Congress does not directly control the community purse strings. It is Jewish welfare federations which administer the local welfare, social, educational and cultural agencies of Jewish communities. The federations dispose of millions of dollars annually, collected through a community-wide appeal. Some of the funds donated are sent to Israel; the remainder, roughly 50 percent, are spent on local charitable needs. This funding pool also covers the budget of Congress. The concerns of the federations are generally local. But they have acquired a professional aura in the community, because of their close alliance with the state, both federal and provincial, in the provision of services and in their reliance on certified professionals, usually social workers, to staff agencies.[36]

Congress has been criticized by some as being too "establishment" in its orientation, or in other words, not being militant enough in pursuing Jewish interests. This charge is retrospectively levelled against Congress for its actions before and during World War II. Communal leaders, past and present, have been accused of toadying to the state power, selling out the community in the process. "Quiet diplomacy" has had a bad press in the post-Holocaust era. Some Jews feel that this same timidity has marked the action of contemporary Jewish leaders on matters such as the emigration of Soviet Jewry, the plight of Ethiopian Jewry, the prosecution of Nazi war criminals and the fight against anti-Semitism. Thus splinter groups have occasionally sprung up with more militant postures on these issues. In the case of one, the Student Struggle for Soviet Jewry, which emerged in the late 1960s, Congress eventually succeeded in integrating the group into the formal Congress structure. But others, such as the Canadian Association for Ethiopian Jewry, the Jewish Defence League, the Canadian Holocaust Remembrance Association or the Canadian branch of the Simon Wiesenthal Center, remain outside the Congress fold. Some have employed establishment-bashing as a useful tool for fundraising.

The B'nai Brith is Canadian Jewry's largest membership organization. Set up as the Canadian chapter of an international fraternal organization, it is active in both local good works and issues of broader significance. Once closely allied to Congress, the B'nai Brith, often taking on a populist posture, now charts its own course and openly competes for prestige in the Jewish organizational world. Its Anti-Defamation League, in the United States, and League for Human Rights, in Canada, are active lobbyists for civil rights and justice for all minority groups.

The dominant organization of the Ukrainian polity today is the Ukrainian Canadian Committee (UCC), which is roughly analogous to the Canadian Jewish Congress. But unlike Congress, which runs on the basis of majority rule, the UCC works on the basis of unanimity. This tends to give each constituent part an equal voice and, of course, a zealously guarded power of veto. Since unity is hard to achieve on many issues, avoidance of controversial issues is common. The UCC, compared to Congress, is weak, underfunded and without a large staff of its own, rather like a parliament with no public service. It has in the past been a useful debating society but, in reality, remains weaker than the sum of its parts.

Formed initially in 1940, on the initiative of the Canadian government, this Ukrainian umbrella organization banded together key non-Communist Ukrainian groups to ensure Ukrainian-Canadian fidelity to the burgeoning war effort, and to act as a counterbalance to the then powerful organizations of the Ukrainian left. Five founding organizations were involved: the Ukrainian Catholic Brotherhood, the Ukrainian National Federation, the Ukrainian Self-Reliance League (Orthodox), the Ukrainian Workers' League, and the United Hetman Organization. The UCC holds periodic national congresses, at which time executives are chosen. Today, the UCC brings together the mainstream organizations within the Ukrainian-Canadian community other than those that are pro-Soviet and pro-Communist, which are, in any event, dwindling in size and influence.[37] It is still plagued by an unwillingness of member organizations to relinquish funds, authority or prestige to the central organization. Yet, like Congress, it too is recognized by the external world of the media and politicians as speaking for the community, lobbying on its behalf.

Oddly, little scholarly attention has been focused on the actual strength or social importance of ethnic polities. Most political scientists who have studied the processes of government in Canada, with particular emphasis on lobbies, pressure groups or interest groups, have ignored the role of ethnic or religious groups. Others have tended to rate them as relatively unimportant or ineffective, compared to other lobbying groups such as business organizations, unions, consumer groups or women's groups.[38] To political analysts, and perhaps to politicians themselves, these ethnic lobbyists seem little more than a side-show in the Canadian political game. Yet as the Canadian state, politicians and senior civil servants change in composition to reflect more adequately the ethnic make-up of the Canadian population, this too will change. As minorities become more entrenched in the middle class, they will find financial means and competent personnel to promote their interests. Perhaps the ideological stamp of a federal multicultural policy will also help elevate ethnic leaders from bit players to major actors.[39]

Certainly, there is a proliferation of ethnic organizations and a large ethnic press. Ethnic lobbying is growing. Much of it is financed, ironically, through federal or provincial government grants. Briefs and letters are written to government. Meetings are held with politicians and senior civil servants. In Canada, Jews and Ukrainians lead the way in actively pursuing political action.

Jews are seen as perhaps the epitome of a well-organized and effective ethnic lobby. But ironically, their actual record is a mixture of victories, partial gains and defeats. When it mattered most, on the eve of the Ho-

locaust, Jews were unable to pry open the doors that
Canada had shut tight in the face of German Jewish
refugees in the 1930s.[40] The Clark government's Jerusalem fiasco of 1979, in which the Tories backtracked on
their promise to move the Canadian embassy in Israel
from Tel Aviv to Jerusalem, brought on a backlash
against the Jewish lobby. Moreover, throughout the
post-war period, the same vaunted Jewish lobby was effective neither in barring Canadian entry to Nazis and
suspected war criminals, nor in persuading the government to adopt a systematic effort to root them out. The
strength of the Jewish lobby has been exaggerated in
the past as it is today.[41]

The point is that no ethnic lobby — whether Jews, or
Japanese Canadians seeking redress, or native peoples
demanding constitutional guarantees of self-govern-
ment, or Ukrainians pressing for a hardening of Canadian policy on the Soviet Union — will ever be fully
satisfied or win all its battles. In this, ethnic groups are
no different from any other interest groups in Canada.

A high level of organizational development is only
one factor which contributes to the political clout of an
ethnic group. Large voting blocs concentrated in key
electoral districts are also important. Urban Jewish voters in select ridings of Toronto and Montreal and
Ukrainian voters concentrated in ridings throughout the
prairie provinces can play crucial roles in a tight election. Ethnic leaders with ties to political parties, as well
as elected politicians representing "ethnic" ridings, are
well-placed brokers in the give and take of ethnic politics. But these brokers must also know when and how
to compromise. Knowing he or she can never provide
everything a community wants or deliver up every seat
a political party is hoping for, the ethnic broker must
know how to make both sides settle for half a loaf.

What is ironic is that this type of ethnic organizational activity may expand just as members of a group
are assimilating themselves to the dominant Canadian
culture. Indeed, some forms of assimilation are abso-
lutely required in order to play the game of ethnic poli-

tics. Groups must be prepared to analyse government policies; write briefs; mobilize resources and people; meet and work with politicians, the media and other interest groups; organize meetings; distribute and produce literature; write letters to editors; sponsor major events; undertake fund-raising drives; join political parties and other organizations. *Shtreimels* (fur-lined hats worn by Hassidic Jews), feathered head-dresses, dashikis and Cossack boots must give way to three-piece suits and attaché cases. Thus, when ethnic leaders confront the state, ethnic particularity is set aside so ethnic interests can be asserted.

To what degree are members of a group aware of this type of activity by their ethnic organizations? Are their leaders generals without troops? Do group members feel lobbying is effective and worthwhile? The 1978–79 survey of ethnic groups in Toronto sheds some light here. For Jews, 89 percent knew of ethnic organizations, and 67 percent indicated they were now or had been members, compared to 57 percent and 51 percent for Ukrainians. Moreover, 49 percent of the Jews said they knew their leaders personally, and 31 percent claimed frequent or occasional contact with them. The corresponding percentages for Ukrainians were 34 percent and 25 percent. Jews also tend to feel that politicians take their leaders seriously, and that their leaders have enough contacts, to a greater extent than do Ukrainians.[42] All of these survey findings confirm widespread impressionistic assessments of the two communities. As perceived by the members of the respective ethnic groups and outsiders, the Jewish polity is thought to be better organized than the Ukrainian. But — and this is key — both groups are still more active and better organized than any other ethnic communities in Canada.

Jews and Ukrainians, like other minorities, are sensitive to cleavages within their respective groups. In the 1978–79 survey, Jews identified the major cleavages as those between rich and poor and between religious streams — Orthodox, Conservative and Reform groupings. Less visible but not unrecognized were divisions between political groups and between groups originally from different areas. For Ukrainians, the major perceived cleavage was between left and right factions of the Ukrainian camp, and shadings throughout the Ukrainian nationalist spectrum. Jews were more fractious than Ukrainians, and both more so than other groups. This is not surprising. A long history of greater intra-communal conflict would naturally spawn more organizations — and vice-versa.

The Toronto survey also provides some revealing data about the quality of ethnic life today for Jews and Ukrainians living in Canada's largest ethnic metropolis.[43]

Overall, the survivalist imperative seems strongest for Jewish respondents; Ukrainians are second only to Jews. This pattern holds for a host of measures. Indeed, according to an ethnic-identity scale devised by Toronto sociologist Wsevolod Isajiw, in the second generation — those with immigrant parents — 55 percent of the Jews and 28 percent of the Ukrainians score "high." But in the third generation, Jews are up to 60 percent and Ukrainians down to 4 percent.

Opposition to intermarriage, one of the greatest threats to the future of a minority group, is greater among Jews than among Ukrainians.[44] Yet an interesting deviation from this general pattern, in the case of Ukrainians, is that almost half still feel obliged to support the group's needs and causes. While lower than the corresponding two-thirds of third-generation Jews, the Ukrainian figure is still much higher than we might expect, given the lower Ukrainian scores on other measures of identification. It is again much higher than for other groups. This suggests there is a tough kernel of ethnic pride and identity lingering strongly in third-generation Ukrainians.

But this exception aside, slippage among third-generation Ukrainians is far greater than among Jews. The political spinoff is telling. The higher levels of assimilation reduce the effective numerical advantages enjoyed by the Ukrainian polity. Thus there are probably an approximately equal number of Jews and Ukrainians in Canada highly committed to defending group interests, even though the census tells us there are more than twice as many Canadians of Ukrainian ancestry as Jews.

There is a dramatic gulf between the generally fervent nationalistic and highly identified post-war immigrant Ukrainians and their children — both deeply affected by the events of World War II and the immediate post-war period — and third- or fourth-generation Ukrainian Canadians. The latter are a more western Canadian, more assimilated, more intermarried group. They have less knowledge of current community politics or facility in the Ukrainian language.

Only one in ten Ukrainian Canadians is foreign-born, and the foreign-born are aging; new immigrants are not flooding in from Ukraine; Canadian-born Ukrainians are increasingly integrated into the surrounding civic culture. Ukrainian community leaders, as well as younger activists, are fully aware of these facts, and their dire implications for the future. What are the tools available to Ukrainian Canadians to strengthen Ukrainian consciousness and identity? What, if anything, can be learned from the Jewish model of intergenerational survival in North America?

While both the Jewish and Ukrainian polities in Canada are well developed and boast many organizations, the Jewish strength is perhaps nowhere as formidable as in the area of fundraising. Like the idea of communal responsibility, the imperative of philanthropy — of voluntary taxation — was nurtured by Jews through the ages. To the uninitiated, the scope of Jewish giving can seem superhuman. For example, the Jewish community of Montreal in 1986 raised twenty-nine million dollars for its main community-wide fundraising drive from a community of just over 90,000. In addition, there are scores of other campaigns launched during any year on behalf of Israeli universities or other charities, local Jewish schools and institutions, Israel Bond drives and more. These amounts exclude donations to charities to which Jews contribute alongside other Canadians and to synagogues, fees for services such as school tuition or YMHA memberships.

How do they do it? Why do they do it? Part of the answer lies in the commitment of a core of extremely wealthy Jews. A rough rule of thumb is that 80 percent of the total contributions comes from 5 percent of the givers. Within that 5 percent, a handful of families, from the Bronfmans on down, contribute between one-quarter and one-third of the total. But in addition, the Jewish polity boasts a highly sophisticated fundraising apparatus employing experienced professionals and effective, forceful techniques of persuasion.

The story is told of an emergency meeting of wealthy givers convened by Seagram owner Samuel Bronfman on the eve of the 1967 Arab-Israeli War. One of the donors wrote a cheque for a quarter of a million dollars. "Mr Sam" looked at it, then tore it up disdainfully. "Get serious," he said. He expected more, and he got it. Whether the story is true or not is unimportant. What matters is that nobody familiar with Jewish fundraising has trouble believing it.[45]

Ukrainian Canadians do not yet boast a comparable fundraising machinery. Ukrainian economic mobility has come through success in agriculture, the professions, higher education and small business. As a result, the community has yet to produce many wealthy business families ready and able to make comparable contributions. Nor is charitable giving as firmly entrenched within the Ukrainian tradition. Thus the disparities between Jewish fundraising and Ukrainian efforts are pronounced. Consider the case of ethnic schooling in Manitoba.

The German supplementary and private schools received $1.7 million from community sources; the Ukrainian supplementary schools received only $231,000 from the same sources. This translates into a per capita expenditure of $13.72 for each German and $2.02 for each Ukrainian living in the

province. Although the differences are most revealing, a comparison with the Jewish community is
even more startling. In 1978–9 the support for Jewish schools was almost $2 million, with a per-capita
expenditure of $106.36 by 18,764 Jews for 1,765
students.[46]

Or to take another example, the national office of the
Canadian Jewish Congress in Montreal, including Quebec region, employs thirteen professionals and twenty
support staff, in a modern four-storey office building
named after the late Samuel Bronfman. By comparison,
the main national office of the UCC is housed in a drab
building well past its prime, in downtown Winnipeg.
Professional and support staff, modern office methods,
technical staff, legalistic know-how and statistical planning are little in evidence. What is true for national
Jewish and Ukrainian organizations more or less holds
for their local constituent groups as well. Commitment
to the Ukrainian cause is not yet translated into funding
of a polished community infrastructure. This makes the
high levels of identity and communal activism among
Ukrainian Canadians all the more remarkable.
The imperatives of Jewish giving and communal involvement are continually reinforced by the unfolding
drama of Jewish history. Jewish scholars have argued
that the two decisive events shaping Jewish consciousness in the twentieth century are the Holocaust and the
creation of the State of Israel. Indeed, Israel and the
Holocaust continue to play dominant roles in Jewish
self-definition.[47] Many Canadian Jews visit Israel or receive visits from Israeli friends or relatives.
But Israel is more than a place to visit. As a symbol,
it is intertwined inextricably with the Holocaust. It is
the triumph of resilience and hope over chaos and despair. The Holocaust, more so in the 1980s than earlier,
is integrated into western historical experience. It
thrusts itself onto the centre stage of cultural, political
and intellectual concerns of the west. Now rather than
Jews reminding the world of the Holocaust, the world

reminds Jews. Any Canadian Jew reading the front page of his or her daily newspaper has his or her Jewishness reinforced. There are stories dealing with Israel and the Middle East conflict, as well as stories about Keegstra or Zundel in Canada, or Mengele, Barbie and Demjanjuk abroad. Reagan's visit to a German cemetery with SS graves in Bitburg, like Waldheim's visit with the Pope, becomes headline news. Canada's refugee policy regarding Jews during the Holocaust is repeatedly invoked to condemn current policy changes. New-found interest in the Holocaust on the part of writers and other artists also makes for a heightened consciousness. Visits to museum exhibits of the treasures of the decimated Jewish community of Prague, or going to see film marathons like *Shoah* become secular pilgrimages. Against this background, the pursuit of alleged Nazi war criminals in Canada and elsewhere reinforces a strong component of Jewish identity.

For Ukrainian Canadians, Ukraine at present cannot serve, in practical terms, the psychological and sociological roles Israel does for North American Jews. Ukrainian Canadians do not have the same luxury of unrestricted exchange of visits with family or friends in Ukraine. Ukraine does not enjoy the independence of Israel, nor does it participate in energizing Ukrainian diaspora life as does Israel for world Jewry. Nor, as yet, have the travails of Ukraine or Ukrainians in this century, such as the famine, captured attention to the same extent as the Jewish Holocaust, perhaps because in the very homeland of Ukrainians, such subjects are often still suppressed by the Soviet regime. One cannot know how the current policy of *glasnost* will change this, if at all.

For some time, Ukrainian-Canadian scholars and communal leaders have been struggling with the task of analysing and strengthening contemporary Ukrainian identity in Canada.[48] The importance of symbols, whether in material artefacts, rituals or ideas, has been central to this effort. And the symbolic role of Ukrainians as victims may have an important part to play in this struggle. But Ukrainians are not just victims of a local tyranny. Their history of victimization must, like the Holocaust, be incorporated into the large historical narrative of western society. Robert Conquest's scholarly study of the famine and a recent film depicting its devastation are steps in this direction.[49] Certainly the Ukrainian legacy of sorrow is a long and profound one. But, as one Ukrainian observer noted, Ukrainians, like others, feel that their history of suffering, unlike the Holocaust, has been ignored by the western world.

> Ukrainian dancers for the Queen are fine, but millions churned into mud for fertilizer following an artificially induced and orchestrated famine do not dance for the Queen; they are silent. Until very recently they had no place in language. Images of perogies are acceptable, images of pysanky and colourful costumes are magnificent, but thousands, hands tied behind their backs with chicken wire, shot in the nape of the neck with .22 calibre pistols are too grisly to contemplate. Vinnytsia, Mordovia, Kolyma — these are past history and not of this social formation. And what of children left to freeze and starve on the Canadian prairies because some immigration official feared the possibility of contagious diseases that did not exist? What of internment camps for the bohunks? The question is not of one oppressed and suffering people, but of the generalized oppression and torment of people. We are shown Auschwitz; we are shown Buchenwald. We are not shown Kolyma; we are not shown Mordovia; we do not hear millions of Armenians; we do not see the smallpox imported on trade-blankets for native Indians. We are not told of the whole truth.[50]

Both Jews and Ukrainians are increasingly turning to ceremony and ritual to mark their respective tragedies: statues, commemorative events, books and films abound. But Jews have a head start. The past ten years have seen an outpouring of books both scholarly and popular, film treatments of all types, university courses, seminars and discussions, and Presidential Commissions focused on the Holocaust. Elie Wiesel, its chronicler, has won the Nobel Peace Prize. In fact, some Jewish critics might suggest that this consciousness raising may go too far, crossing the bounds of good taste, and that the memory of the martyred Jews of the Holocaust may be invoked too readily by Jewish or Israeli political leaders. Reputations and careers are being built on the ashes of the six million. This potential for debasement of the Jewish tragedy is captured in the gruesome quip "There's no business like 'Shoah' business." And in what Ukrainians see as a cruel irony, when it comes to the Holocaust, Ukrainians have been cast, through media coverage and war-crimes investigations, as persecutors rather than as the victims they often were and largely perceive themselves to be.

Thus, once again, the Holocaust casts its long shadow over contacts between Ukrainians and Jews in Canada, making institutional relations difficult. Undoubtedly, contacts between individual Ukrainians and Jews will increase as both communities share the same urban landscape, middle-class professional values and aspirations in an ever more open Canadian society. But will this bridge the distance between the corporate Ukrainian polity and its Jewish counterpart in Canada? This is hard to know. Each community wears its own jacket of moral self-righteousness. Each retains a deeply pained conviction of having been maligned, victimized and repressed partly at the hands of the other.

Some might argue this is all in the past and thousands of miles from Canada's shores; it should be set aside, forgotten. But it isn't. In 1985 Jewish-Ukrainian tensions exploded into the headlines during the course of Judge Deschênes's Commission of Inquiry on War Criminals. But the lighted fuse of conflict stretches back forty years into the turbulent post-war period as Jewish and Ukrainian community organizations in Canada responded to the homelessness of kith and kin in the Displaced Persons camps of Europe.

Chapter 3

Two Solitudes: The Legacy of the War

As hundreds of thousands of DPs waited in camps across Europe, ethnic communities across Canada began to lobby for the admission of their brethren to the country — and Ukrainians and Jews were no exception. In many ways, their lobbying efforts paralleled each other. Both Jewish and Ukrainian campaigns swung into action shortly following the war and both were at first ignored by Mackenzie King's Liberal government.[1]

Tough anti-immigration restrictions imposed during the Depression remained intact. Moreover, government planners, fearing that the end of massive wartime spending would derail a fragile post-war Canadian economy, showed no sympathy whatever for the admission of job-hungry immigrants from Europe. Jobs for demobilized Canadian servicemen would come first. If immigrant labour was needed, most would agree, it should be met by admitting immigrants in a descending order of ethnic preference. Most desirable were those from Britain and the United States, followed by northern and western Europeans, central and eastern Europeans and finally Jews, Asians and blacks.

But if Canadian Ukrainian and Jewish communities had suffered this sort of racial humiliation in the pre-war years, they were unwilling to endure it in the post-war. Both communities had sent large numbers of their children off to fight for Canada. Both communities harboured a deep sense of the suffering endured by their brethren in wartime Europe, and both had relatives languishing in the DP camps of Europe. Both communities

64

galvanized in an effort to relieve their suffering and to lobby for their admission into Canada.

There was little or no contact between the two community campaigns. Nevertheless, their collective input began to be felt as fears of post-war economic backslide into depression subsided in the face of sustained economic strength. The buoyancy of the Canadian economy, a surprise to many economic planners, was so strong that by late 1946, little more than a year after the war's end, labour-intensive Canadian industries joined ethnic leaders in clamouring for immigration reform. The DP camps of Europe promised labour in abundance.

Ukrainians, popularly pictured as simple farm folk, non-disruptive, non-competitive, ever docile and prepared to do rural labour, seemed ideal for those manpower-short sectors of the Canadian economy in need of manual labour. Strangely enough, this stereotype, which today must be seen as negative, actually gave them an advantage over Jews in winning admission to Canada.

Jews were identified as urban in the popular mind of a country that still felt the proper place of immigrants was in rural areas; they were seen as cosmopolitan, perhaps tainted by leftist ideologies, in a country secure in its narrow parochialism; they were seen as aggressively competitive by a community that would truck no "foreign" challenge to its artisans or small-business entrepreneurs. Added to all this were the smouldering embers of ancient religious prejudice and perhaps even suggestions among some that the Jews of Europe must have been guilty of something to make Germans single them out for genocide. The result was to make the Jewish DP as undesirable in the public mind as the Jewish refugee had been in pre-war and war years. In an October 1946 Gallup Poll, Jews were chosen as the least desirable of potential European immigrant groups seeking admission to Canada.[2]

Among Ukrainian Canadians, there grew a fear that Ukrainians in Displaced Persons camps would be forci-

bly repatriated to the Soviet Union. Canada, like its
western allies, originally felt the post-war refugee crisis
would be short-lived. If refugees could simply be
shuffled back to their countries of origin, the refugee
problem would soon resolve itself. But almost a million
persons from the Soviet Union and Soviet-controlled
territory refused to go home in spite of allied encouragement and Soviet insistence. This clouded post-war
Soviet-Western relations and complicated social, economic and political stability in Europe. Canada continued to favour voluntary repatriation but rejected
compulsion. However, opposition to forced repatriation
was one thing, readiness to take these recalcitrant DPs
into Canada was quite another.

In time, however, continuing labour shortages in
Canada, a shortfall in immigration from Britain and
western Europe and growing domestic sympathy for the
anti-Soviet stance of many DPs offered the Ukrainian-
Canadian lobby the opening it needed. When removal
of DPs to Canada was finally authorized in late 1947,
Ukrainians immediately joined the stream of those
moving to new homes in Canada.[3]

But why did Ukrainian DPs want to come to Canada?
Nobody wanted to stay in the camps, and return to a
now-Soviet Ukraine was out of the question. Other options were limited. Canada opened its doors. It has
been argued that migration to Canada was encouraged
by Ukrainian nationalist leaders in the politically
charged DP camps of Europe. Perhaps they saw resettlement in Canada as an opportunity to regroup and re-
coup strength for the protracted struggle for a national
homeland which still lay ahead.[4]

The Ukrainian DPs allowed into Canada before 1950
did not include members of the Galicia Division. The
first official word Ottawa received about the Division
probably did not come from the Ukrainian-Canadian
lobby. It may have come in early 1947 from a Canadian
attached to the Allied Refugee Screening Commission
in Europe, charged with judging the eligibility of applicants for official refugee status. He visited a Division

camp in Italy supervised by the British. With the aid of a translator appointed from among the few English-speaking Ukrainian personnel, he interviewed a selection of officers and enlisted men in an effort to determine the Division's history, organization and post-war disposition. His impression was favourable. "They strike us," he reported to Ottawa "all as being a decent, simple minded sort of people."

> The national emblem of the Ukraine, in the form of a trident, is freely displayed all over camp, and the inmates clearly regard themselves as a homogeneous unit, unconnected either with Russia or Poland, and do not seem conscious of having done anything wrong.

The camp, he continued, had been security screened by both the British and the Soviets. The Russians had also tried to encourage the wholesale repatriation of the Division to the Soviet Union. They failed. The Division, he concluded, was unfortunately ineligible for DP status. Those who had volunteered their services or given aid and comfort to the enemy were expressly prohibited refugee status.

Nevertheless, dismissing the Division as simple quislings was unjust. He argued for taking "into account their motives for having volunteered their services to the enemy." These, he said, included helping family stave off the deteriorating social and economic conditions in Ukraine and a desire "to have a smack at the Russians, whom they always refer to as 'Bolsheviks.' "

> They probably were not, and certainly do not now seem to be at heart pro-German, and the fact they did give aid and comfort to Germans can fairly be considered to have been incidental and not fundamental.

If official DP status, with its assumed protection against forced repatriation to the Soviet Union, proved out of the question, then the Canadian officer hoped the British would "have them removed lock stock and barrel from Italy" to someplace where the Soviets could not get at them. This is exactly what the British did. They moved most of the Division to England.

Efforts by the Ukrainian-Canadian community to bring the Division to Canada began in October 1947. Gordon Bohdan Panchuk, director of Ukrainian-Canadian post-war relief efforts, informed Ottawa that at the request of the British his organization, the Central Ukrainian Relief Bureau, was accepting responsibility for the day-to-day needs of the Division members in Britain. But Panchuk did more than just care for the Division's needs in Britain. He requested they be allowed to settle in Canada. He explained that they had cleared British security checks; Division members had joined the German war effort only to defend their homeland against the Russians.[5]

The request was refused. Members of the German armed forces were specifically prohibited entry into Canada under Subsection (b) of the security prohibitions which expressly demanded "Not Clear for Security" be stamped on immigration applications from all "members of SS or German Wehrmacht found to bear mark of SS Blood Group (Non German)."[6]

For three years the government stood fast in the face of lobbying efforts involving several MPs representing heavily Ukrainian ridings.[7] In the spring of 1950, however, the Liberal cabinet, now under the leadership of Louis St Laurent, again expanded admissible immigration categories by removing existing prohibitions against *Volksdeutche*, non-German citizens of ethnic German origin, and those who had acquired German citizenship after the war began. Although Division members did not qualify under either of these changes, it was further agreed in Cabinet that subsection (b) be waived to permit Division members in Britain to resettle in Canada.[8]

In June 1950, two weeks after Cabinet approval, John Decore, Liberal member of parliament for Vegreville, Alberta, rose in the House with a question for

Immigration Minister Walter Harris. "I was wondering," the prominent backbencher began, "whether the minister was in a position to make a statement with reference to the possible admission of a certain Ukrainian group now in the United Kingdom and who formerly went under the name of 'division Halychina' [sic]?"

With the House listening in unusual silence, Decore gave members a thumbnail sketch of the group's history, much of it, as it turned out, incorrect. The Division, Decore explained, was organized "on Soviet territory" during the war as a core group around which "other military units" could coalesce to battle for an independent Ukraine. Without mentioning that the Division was a Waffen ss unit organized by the Nazis from plentiful Ukrainian volunteers, Decore noted, almost in passing, "In the turmoil this military division found itself under German jurisdiction." Lest this be seen as a problem, he reassured the House that Division members "detested the Nazis as they hated the communists . . ." With Canadian combat units then under fire in Korea and memories of World War II still fresh, Decore pictured the Division, then assembled in England, as hapless victims of tyranny. He concluded, "A lot of them are anxious to reach the shores of Canada and to settle here. I am sure they would make desirable citizens if they come into this country."

As Decore took his seat, Harris rose in reply. It was likely that Decore's question was prearranged. The minister promptly announced a policy departure for which Decore could assume partial credit in his heavily Ukrainian home riding. The minister assured the House the Division had the history outlined. "We have investigated not individuals but the group as a whole, and we are quite prepared to accept them provided they come within the ordinary rules with respect to immigrants; that is, they might be agricultural workers, settlers, and the like."[9]

If the minister hoped his announcement would slip by without controversy, he was sadly mistaken. The Montreal *Gazette* jumped on it as "Easily the most sensational immigration change announced by the minister." However much the government might want to overlook the past, the *Gazette* pointed out, the Division had been not only an active Nazi military formation but an SS unit at that.[10]

Jewish leaders were also shocked. Louis Rosenberg, Polish-born demographer and research director of the Canadian Jewish Congress, sounded the alarm. In an angry memorandum to Saul Hayes, Congress's executive director, Rosenberg attacked the admission of the SS Division as an outrage. He stated, incorrectly, that charges of "massacre and torture" had been laid against the Division. He was correct, however, in noting the " 'Halychyna Division' were not conscripted by the Germans or taken into forced labour by them but volunteered to serve in the German Armed Forces against Russia which was a member of the Allied Forces fighting Germany." For Canadian Jewry, still mourning the loss of millions of their brethren, the admission to Canada of any who served the Nazis was bad enough. That the Galicia Division was an SS Division which had seen active duty made matters even worse.

But did any of the Division members to be admitted to Canada have blood on their hands? The minister's reassurance to Parliament that his authorities had "investigated not individuals but the group as a whole" was not good enough. Rosenberg protested that any investigation should be public and allow for presentation of evidence against the Division or specific members of it.[11]

Anticipating the need for hard evidence, Rosenberg, a scholar in his own right, appealed to Jewish research centres in the United States and Europe for data which might allow Congress to "make strong representations to the Canadian government against the admission of such elements to Canada."[12] But gathering evidence was going to be time consuming. Some Jews berated the Canadian Jewish leaders for their seeming caution. "How," demanded a Toronto Jewish druggist," can Canadian Jewry remain silent . . . Not one Nazi or Nazi collaborator should be allowed into Canada. Immediate action is needed."[13]

The same cry came from the far left. The *Canadian Jewish Weekly*, a pro-Soviet paper in Toronto, published a front-page editorial entitled, "Keep Out Nazi Thugs, Admit Their Victims!"[14] The same call was echoed by the Ukrainian-Canadian left, only too pleased to attack the Division, its anti-Soviet Ukrainian supporters in Canada and the Canadian government as soft on "Fascists." The Association of United Ukrainian Canadians protested to the Minister of Immigration. *"All of them* [Division members] *were volunteers* who responded to the call of the 'Fuehrer' to come and defend the 'Greater Germany' and the 'New Order' when Germany was on its last legs."[15]

Although pressure on Congress to mount public demonstrations grew, Canadian Jewish Congress leaders remained convinced that hard evidence of wrongdoing, not heated protest by the Jewish community, was the best weapon to forestall the Division's entry to Canada. On the last day of June, the Canadian Jewish Congress received what information the World Jewish Congress could muster on the Galicia Division. It was not much. The World Jewish Congress research office conceded they "could find no documentary evidence concerning their participation in anti-Jewish action in Galicia or elsewhere." Nevertheless, it notified Congress "the Nuremberg Military Tribunal declared the ss a criminal organization." This included the Waffen ss of which the Galicia Division was a part. "Since the Halychyna [Galicia] Division was a voluntary organization," the World Jewish Congress continued, "all members must be considered members of a criminal organization."[16]

Although the World Jewish Congress had not delivered the smoking gun, evidence of actual Division participation in war crimes, few doubted the evidence was out there. But, Rosenberg counselled Hayes, even without hard evidence, the World Jewish Congress had given Congress grounds for demanding that Division members be excluded from Canada.[17]

Early in July 1950, three weeks after ministerial permission for admission of the Division was announced, the Canadian Jewish Congress dispatched a formal protest to Ottawa. A telegram over the signature of Samuel Bronfman, National President of the Canadian Jewish Congress, expressed "deep concern" at any welcome accorded recognized criminals who, according to a Jewish Telegraphic Agency report, "participated in the Nazi extermination of Jews in German occupied territories."[18] Bronfman especially decried any entry of ss volunteers into Canada without individual screening. If government would not immediately reverse its decision to admit the unit's members into Canada, then at least it could grant time, time to gather evidence of the Division's complicity in war crimes and, if possible, the hands-on role of individual Division members in Nazi atrocities.[19]

In an effort to still controversy, the Minister of Immigration was conciliatory. He agreed that individual visa approval would be delayed "for a reasonable time." This would allow Congress a period of grace to gather and present evidence. In the meantime, administrative arrangements for the Division's processing by Canadian immigration authorities would continue.[20]

Congress gave the government's reply wide circulation, perhaps in part to reassure Canadian Jewry that their leaders were on top of the issue and, in part, to keep the government from reneging on its promised delay.[21] But if the government's reply was conciliatory, it was also disappointing. It made the Canadian Jewish Congress responsible for gathering evidence. It did not volunteer government resources to further investigate the Division's record. The Canadian Jewish Congress was on its own.

All agreed it would have been easier to stop the admission decision before it was made; reversing it was far more difficult. The government's move had taken Congress leaders by surprise. They had been so preoccupied by problems of Jewish refugee resettlement in Canada and the uncertain survival of the fledgling Jewish state, they had paid little or no attention to Ukrainian political lobbying on behalf of the admission of Ukrainian Displaced Persons or Division members.

Nevertheless, the government's readiness to withhold visas to Division members following Congress's protest gave Jewish leaders one "opportunity to furnish [the authorities] with pertinent materials sustaining the allegations . . ."[22] The scramble to find incriminating evidence was on again. Requests for information went out to a series of Jewish organizations in the United States and Europe and, through the Jewish Telegraphic Agency, to American Jewish newspapers.[23] Many Jewish papers picked up on the story and ran articles attacking the Canadian government's admission decision. The widely read and influential New York Yiddish daily, *The Forward*, exploded in hysteria. "As part of the Nazi army," *The Forward* charged, "the Galician Division of Ukrainians marched with Gestapo units from town to town through Nazi-occupied Ukraine and drove thousands of Jews to their destruction."

In many cities they compelled Jews to march to the outskirts of the town and dig their own mass graves. In other towns they participated in the mass murder of Jews in horrible ways . . . The Jews in Canada are naturally uneasy. Everybody knows that the members of this Hitler Division were Hitlerites. Everyone knows that this Ukrainian Division was a part of the Gestapo army. Everyone knows the text of the oath which each member took, under which he obligated himself to destroy Jews. What further evidence is necessary?[24]

Unfortunately for Congress, it was not emotionally charged rhetoric the government wanted. It was evidence — evidence of hands-on Division participation in war crimes and, equally important, the names of Division members who had personally committed crimes. Rosenberg, charged with gathering the needed documentation, found the going rough. He hoped to assemble a massive convincing dossier. He was forced instead to piece together a case from small scraps of material that came his way. A press reference to the SS oath taken by Division members to "fight Jews" set off a search for a photostatic copy of the original wording.[25] The American Jewish Committee came up with a memorandum listing key individuals known to have collaborated with the Nazis in Poland and Ukraine and the text of a published "apologia" for the Division prepared by the Ukrainian Congress Committee of America, itself described as an ultra-nationalist organization. The text put the best possible face on the Division's inception and record, but it allowed that Division members were volunteers. In addition, it identified the Division as an integral part of the Nazi SS organization. These two points — that the Division was both a volunteer and an SS unit — were key elements in the Jewish case for exclusion.[26]

Rosenberg also unsuccessfully plodded through the index to the twenty-two-volume proceedings of the Nuremberg Trials, hoping for a reference to the Division.[27] He found none. But if he could not tie the Division to the Nuremberg Trials, perhaps he could tie the Nuremberg Trials to the Division. Efforts were made to contact both Justice Jackson, chief American judge at the trials, and the American prosecutor, Brigadier General Telford Taylor, in hopes of eliciting from each a statement that the Tribunal's declaration as criminal all "those persons who were officially accepted as members of the S.S." extended to members of the Division. Although neither replied personally, Rosenberg did establish that the Tribunal and the Allied Control Council for Germany worked under the principle "that knowledge of these criminal activities was sufficiently general to justify declaring that the S.S. was a criminal organization." On this basis all members of the Waffen SS, including the Galicia Division, would be denied admission to the United States.[28]

Rosenberg pulled together what he could find for consideration by Canadian immigration authorities.

Adding to bits and pieces relating directly to the ss or the Division, he included several affidavits taken from Holocaust survivors recently arrived in Montreal who accused Ukrainians of participating in Nazi atrocities. Rosenberg also forwarded assessments of Ukrainian complicity drawn from the Jewish press, two articles from Ukrainian sources which, although firm in their declaration of the Division's innocence of war crimes, affirmed the Galicia Division's integration within the ss and the unit's voluntary membership. He also included several Allied documents attaching criminality to the entire ss. Only too aware that he had failed to find evidence linking the Division or any of its members to specific war crimes, Rosenberg sent the package to Ottawa in early August 1950. He hoped it would be enough to further delay the visa process if not derail it entirely.[29]

The government was not impressed. After six weeks the Minister of Immigration informed Congress leaders that the government's own "further" but unspecified investigation left him confident "screening facilities are adequate" to assure that the Division members admitted to Canada would be free of any war-crimes association. Accordingly he saw no reasons for further delay. The minister reminded Congress officials that he had originally agreed "to delay approval of applications for a reasonable time and this has been done." While he would entertain any additional information on specific individuals that Congress might supply, the minister intended "to give approval to applications on hand and to continue the screening process of any applications received in the future."[30]

Congress had failed. Its argument for exclusion was predicated on the assumption that as part of the ss, an organization declared criminal by Allied authorities, and composed entirely of members who voluntarily joined the unit, the Galicia Division and all its members should be denied entry to Canada. The government dismissed these arguments. Cabinet had already short-circuited the Congress argument by lifting its subsection (b) security prohibition against ss members in this instance. In the absence of specific information linking individual immigration applicants to specific crimes, the government was determined to press on with admissions. The Jewish community could do nothing beyond lodging protest and hoping that incriminating evidence might still turn up.[31]

In one last-ditch effort to uncover the kind of evidence against specific individuals the government demanded, Congress again turned to its sister agencies in the United States and abroad.[32] From Simon Wiesenthal's newly formed Documentation Center in Vienna came an analysis of Ukrainian complicity in the Nazi destruction of eastern European Jewry and warnings that Ukrainian DP camps were infested with war criminals.[33] But Wiesenthal included no names — no incontrovertible evidence. An American Jewish Congress report was also received. It reviewed the history of Ukraine during the war but did not link the Division to specific criminal acts, let alone offer up the names of individuals who could be tied to such acts.

> Strictly speaking, this information does not pertain to the Galician Division which was organized, as most reports indicate, in 1943, at a time when the mass extermination of Jews in Poland and Galicia was substantially complete. But there are reasons to believe that the division might have been recruited mostly among these militia men and guards [who participated in the genocide]. A general survey of the background and activities of the Ukrainian extremist movement, its collaboration with the Germans, and of the activities of the militia is in order.[34]

The assessments from Wiesenthal and the American Jewish Congress yielded no names and no evidence. From here and there a few names were pulled together. Several names were gleaned from a pamphlet published by the left-wing Association of United Ukrainian Canadians, then waging its own separate campaign against

the Division's admission. An American Jewish Committee list of Ukrainian Nazi collaborators was culled for
more names. It wasn't much, but the names were sent
to Ottawa.[35]

The Minister of Immigration agreed to forward the
names to Canadian officials abroad "for their information," but he underscored the fact that with two possible exceptions, those listed were not linked to the
Division.[36] In a personal letter to Samuel Bronfman, a
long-time Liberal Party supporter, the minister again
politely dismissed the Congress argument for the wholesale rejection of Division members. Simple membership
in the SS, the minister explained, was no longer sufficient reason in and of itself to exclude any individuals
from Canada, nor would Canada abide any blanket
condemnation of all SS members as criminals. In defence of the Galicia Division the minister pointed out
that non-Germans were not permitted into the regular
army. They were shuffled into special SS Divisions.
"You will understand," he reassured Bronfman, "that
these troops were not necessarily of the training or
mentality we usually associate with Hitler's personal S.S.
formation."[37]

Bronfman and Congress officials were not reassured.
Failing to persuade immigration authorities that SS
membership was cause for rejection, they tried an end
run around the Immigration Minister. A hurried meeting was arranged with the Minister of Justice in hopes
of persuading him "of the dangers of ordinary routine
screening if applied to . . . Germans and Ukrainians."
The Minister of Justice listened but gave little. He
would not "for jurisdictional reasons" interfere in immigration affairs. The decision to admit the Division
members was not his to reverse. He would, however,
"insist that the security net be made very tight to prevent politically undesirable elements from passing
through." Congress Executive Director Saul Hayes
came away from the meeting almost empty-handed, but
he put the best possible light on the meeting. "It
showed the Minister, that we were prepared to fight

through an unpopular cause because of the principles involved."[38]

But, Hayes wondered, was there still a small opening left by the Minister of Justice — screening to prevent the admission of "political undesirables"?[39] In the past, Congress had not been pleased with political screening. This type of action was, as often as not, used to reject the immigration of individual Jews on the political left. But could it now apply to the Division? In its efforts to gather information on the Division and its members, Congress officials had become marginally acquainted with the political infighting both between various factions of the Ukrainian nationalist camp in Europe and between these nationalists and the Ukrainian left in Canada. There was finger pointing by one Ukrainian nationalist faction against the other that efforts to transplant members in Canada were merely a ploy to use Canada as a staging ground for further political activities. There were also warnings from the Ukrainian left of further political turmoil if the right-wing nationalists tried to regroup in Canada. Could Congress build a case that the Division was a political threat to Canadian stability? In the end Congress did not know enough about the matter and, again, the Ukrainian infighting did not deal specifically with members of the Galicia Division. The idea was dropped.[40]

The Jewish campaign against the Division had failed. In early January 1951, Hayes sent a confidential memorandum to his national executive.

There is a good deal of derivative material and oblique references all of which have been submitted to Government and several dossiers have been sent to the Ministry involved. In the main, however, it has to be conceded that most of the allegations against the Halychyna [Galicia] Division membership is of the hearsay variety and all our attempts to obtain statements from the Nuremberg Crime Commission or other officials thereof have proved abortive . . . . To reiterate, unless and until more evidence is forthcoming from sources which we don't know of since we have exhausted all known sources, the matter will have to be considered as closed.[41]

Congress's surrender bespoke not only the Jewish community's inability to dent the government's determination to admit Division members but also signalled the emergence of Ukrainian-Canadian lobbying strength, in this case on behalf of the Division. Of course, not all Ukrainian Canadians were united in support of the Division's entry. As we have seen, the left-wing Association of United Ukrainian Canadians mounted its own anti-Division campaign. The AUUC offered "to work with Congress on this matter and supply [Congress] with all the information we have on this problem."[42] Congress rejected the offer. It had only just gone through a process of expelling the Jewish equivalent of the AUUC, the United Jewish People's Order, from the Canadian Jewish Congress. Given the anti-Communist temper of the time, any working relationship with the AUUC would have been problematic at best.

Indeed, Congress officials were concerned lest the AUUC's campaign undermine the legitimacy of their own. If the AUUC staked out a claim to this issue "as proof that the Canadian Government was favouring pro-Fascist and anti-Semitic elements" it was feared the Canadian Jewish Congress's arguments would be tarred by association. As a result Congress took pains to carefully and publicly dissociate itself from any AUUC initiative.[43] But as they scrambled for incriminating evidence against the Division and its members, Congress staff quietly monitored AUUC statements, reports and publications, hoping to pick up leads to reliable data.

If the Canadian Jewish Congress rejected overtures of co-operation from the AUUC, it also had almost no contact with the Ukrainian Canadian Committee (UCC), then still lobbying for the Division's entry into Canada. The UCC was stung by Congress's effort to undermine their campaign. In a letter to Congress's Winnipeg office the UCC president dismissed any and all allegations against the Division. Several investigations, he protested, had "completely exonerated the said Division from the accusations levelled against them." Even more, he continued, the "authorities found that the accusations were merely a communist propaganda that was indiscriminately circulated at the time by the communists against anyone who disagrees with them." As far as he was concerned, authorities had "given this division a clean slate."

> To be able to make an accusation of the nature you have made, you must be in possession of some documentary evidence that was not available to the above-mentioned Allied Military Authorities or to the Nuremberg Court. We, therefore, would appreciate if you would be kind enough to submit the said evidence to us for our perusal.

> May we assure you that we are no less anxious than you are to maintain harmony among the various ethnic groups in Canada and trust that you will cooperate with us in solving the difficult problem created by the action taken in this connection both by your press and the Canadian Jewish Congress.[44]

Congress was conciliatory. Hayes offered a UCC-designated representative both access to copies of Congress representations to government and full and free access to files covering Congress's Galicia Division investigation. The UCC accepted.[45]

The civility of this tentative UCC-Congress contact was not long sustained. Just as the Jewish press excoriated Ukrainians for their alleged participation in the genocidal war on the Jews, *Nasha Meta*, voice of the Ukrainian Catholic community in Toronto, editorialized:

> . . . international communism and Jewry for some reason choose to condemn only Ukrainians and

their "philo-Germans" although they offered the very smallest number to the German army and they choose to shut their eyes to the many volunteers who were offered by other nationalities. And this communist-Jewish propaganda besmirches [the] entire Ukrainian nation and blames her for crimes she never committed and was in no position to commit. At Moscow's order these Ukrainian soldiers are smeared by this propaganda because the Ukrainian soldier is the most dangerous one for communist Moscow and her tyranny.[46]

By early 1952 members of the Division began arriving in Canada, but their arrival did not end the matter. The episode left a legacy of bad feeling between the organized leadership of the Ukrainian and Jewish communities, a legacy sustained by mutual mistrust informed by a sense of historical wrong that each community laid at the doorstep of the other. While individual Jews and Ukrainians might live and work side by side as friends, community organizational life was separate, all too often punctuated by conflict.

This proved the case in the spring of 1957. The Ukrainian National Federation of Canada, a nationalist organization with roots in pre-war Europe, announced a Music Festival Jubilee to celebrate the movement's twenty-fifth anniversary. As part of the festival the federation planned to bring Andrii Melnyk, the movement's international leader, to Canada.

Melnyk's name set off an alarm for the editor of the *Jewish Post* in Winnipeg. In a *Post* editorial, he denounced Melnyk as "famous in Poland as a ruthless anti-Semite" and an active Nazi agent involved in the murder of Ukrainian Jews.[47]

The Federation was incensed. They were accustomed to attacks of this type from the Ukrainian extreme left; they almost welcomed them as a sign of their movement's vibrancy. But an attack in the Jewish press was different. After all, the Jewish community was seen by the larger Canadian community to have public respectability, economic strength and political influence. If the editor's charges were not dealt with quickly and firmly, the Nazi label could spread and besmirch the whole Ukrainian community.

Thus, it was not just the Federation that felt itself under attack — it was the entire nationalist core within the Ukrainian community. Putting aside the internal wrangling that often marked its deliberations, the UCC united in face of the *Jewish Post* challenge. The editorial was denounced and a public apology demanded.[48]

It was too late to defuse the tensions. The *Post*'s accusations had already spilled into the national and international press. Some Canadian Jews, angered that any alleged Nazi would be allowed into the country, demanded Congress act. Congress, pressed by its rank and file but uneasy lest it get caught again without a strong case, needed reliable information on Melnyk. Independently of one another, the *Post*'s editor and Congress put out a call for data on Melnyk's wartime record.[49] If damning evidence could not be found, the Congress director in Winnipeg suggested, the *Jewish Post*'s accusations must be publicly recanted. The Jewish community might harbour suspicions, "But publishing them in the *Jewish Post* before we are sure of our facts and starting a big controversy with the Ukrainian community, certainly does not look like a practical way of handling the case."[50]

A search of available historical records proved disturbing but inconclusive. "It is obvious from what has been published," wrote Saul Hayes, "that Melnyk must have had something to do with anti-Jewish activities."

> But from our point of view, the evidence is by no means enough to warrant a formal submission to Ottawa. The books, for example, contain statements like "Ribbentrop incited Melnyk to take action against the Jews," but there is no evidence any[where] that he took such action. Secondly, the excellent treatment of the major war criminals which appeared in the "Black Book" published by

the World Jewish Congress a number of years ago, does not mention Melnyk. It is obvious to the layman that he was somewhere about and unfriendly. From our point of view we need more evidence.[51]

If none of Congress's information or respondents could exonerate Melnyk or his movement from pro-Fascist sympathies or Nazi contacts, they were unanimous in agreeing no form of evidence was then available linking Melnyk to actual atrocities against Jews.[52]

As the controversy dragged on, the Ukrainian National Federation began to have second thoughts. The adverse publicity surrounding the *Jewish Post* editorial continued to embarrass those planning the twenty-fifth anniversary celebrations drawing near. A banquet in Toronto with Melnyk as honoured guest was scheduled. Among those who originally accepted invitations were the Ontario Premier, Mayor Nathan Phillips (Toronto's first Jewish mayor), federal senators, elected politicians and cabinet ministers, including the Minister of Immigration.[53] The Federation leaders feared prolonged controversy or Jewish pressure might force these prominent personalities to stay away or, even worse, lead to Melnyk's visa being revoked by the very Minister of Immigration who planned to attend the banquet. Pressed to the wall, the Federation requested a meeting with Congress officials in Toronto.[54]

A three-man Ukrainian delegation led by the secretary of the Ukrainian National Federation arrived at Congress offices in Toronto, probably unclear just how forceful they should or could be. Although convinced they were the aggrieved parties in the affair, the Ukrainians still needed to defuse a confrontation that might ruin their planned festivities. With Congress officials listening quietly, Melnyk's record was defended. "Melnyk," the delegation spokesman reportedly began, "was known as a respected national hero to all Ukrainians, a man of deep religious conviction, a leader of Catholic youth who would never stoop to any kind of pogrom action."

Ukrainians in general felt hurt when from time to time their whole nation is identified as Jew haters on the basis of the action of individuals. [The Secretary] cited the case of Germany. Many Jews and Israelis feel the time is now ready to forget the experience with Germany, this only 12 years after the gravest Jewish experience in history. But Ukrainians do not enjoy such good fortune as Germans.[55]

Could not the two communities put the *Post* editorial behind them? It would be the first step towards a larger and overdue reconciliation. In a follow-up letter to Congress, the Federation secretary appealed to "traditional Jewish justice." He requested Congress "issue a public statement disassociating itself from the article published in the 'Jewish Post.' " The statement, it was further suggested, might "condemn the use of unprovoked and unverified allegations against persons or peoples . . ."[56]

Congress refused. It denied responsibility for the original *Jewish Post* editorial and saw no need to apologize for it or repudiate its content. On the other hand, Congress leaders privately recognized the editorial had generated needless bad feelings between Jews and Ukrainians, especially in Winnipeg, all without any substantiating evidence. An apology, they realized, was in order but it had to come from the *Jewish Post*.

The *Post*'s editor was "invited" to a meeting with Congress officials in Winnipeg. A heated discussion ensued. It was made clear to him "that freedom of the press notwithstanding, an editor of a Jewish newspaper should use some self-imposed restraint when the interests of the entire Jewish community is at stake." In spite of objections to Congress censorship of his newspaper, he agreed to publish an editorial retraction as well as "lengthy letters of apology" sent to four prominent Ukrainian newspapers and similar letters mailed to major Ukrainian organizations.[57]

In the end, the Federation and the UCC were just pleased to put this round of accusations and recriminations behind them. The apology was officially accepted "recognizing the fact that [the *Jewish Post*] fell victim to unreliable information."[58]

The Melnyk banquet went ahead on schedule but not without incident. Just as the prominent guests at the fifty-dollar-a-plate dinner were finishing their strawberry shortcake, police rushed in to clear the packed hall. According to press reports, an anonymous woman caller had telephoned police and the press with a bomb threat. As the crowd of notables milled about on the street in front of the Ukrainian Federation Hall, a federal minister scheduled to deliver his government's official greetings to the gathering made light of the bomb threat. "Some people," he joked, "will go to any length to stop us [politicians] talking." A spokesman for the Federation was not nearly so amused. Melnyk, he told the assembled press, was a leading anti-Communist crusader. The Communists would not be above using bombs to silence him. No bomb was found, and at the time, no suggestion was made that Jews were behind the bomb scare.[59]

It cannot be denied, however, that throughout the post-war period there were those within the Ukrainian nationalist camp who saw Communists and Jews in league to destroy the Ukrainian nationalist movement. Jews, some Ukrainian nationalists were ready to point out, played a leading role in the 1917 Revolution and the Soviet consolidation of power which followed. Those links, they believed, remained strong still. For example, in 1960 *Life* magazine printed a feature on anti-Semitism in the Soviet Union, making special reference to the history of anti-Semitism in Ukraine. The article, quoting a representative of the World Jewish Congress, drew considerable fire from the Toronto Ukrainian-language press. *Novy Shliakh* (Toronto), the voice of the Federation, dismissed talk of Ukrainian anti-Semitism as an insulting hoax. There were anti-Semitic outbursts in Ukraine, the paper allowed, but since oppressed Ukrainians did not control their own territory, anti-Jewish acts could only be the product of Russian, Polish or most recently, Communist initiative. As for anti-Semitism under the Soviet regime, it could be little more than a "cuff on the ear" to the Jewish people who had loyally served in building Communism.

The privately owned *Vilne Slovo* (Toronto) did not deny that anti-Semitism existed in Ukraine but observed that anti-Semitism existed everywhere and that the issue was not whether Jews were disliked, but why. "If the Jews are such angels," *Vilne Slovo* asked, "why is anti-semitism so universal?" *Homin Ukrainy* (Toronto), often the voice of the Banderite League for the Liberation of Ukraine, also blamed Jews for any anti-Semitism exhibited by Ukrainians. On balance, it claimed Jews were responsible for more violence done against Ukrainians than Ukrainians ever inflicted on Jews. According to the paper, Jews had most recently allied themselves with the Communists who occupied western Ukraine in 1939; co-operating with the Soviet Militia, the NKVD, and eagerly informing on their Ukrainian neighbours. Therefore, "who if not the Jews is responsible for the thousands of prisoners murdered in Soviet prisons and for other thousands sent to Siberia?" As for Jews in Canada, the paper was quoted as saying, "We should all take this into account even in our commercial relations with Jews until we can get some kind of assurance from their leaders that their hostility toward Ukrainians will be terminated."[60]

These three themes — that the scale of Ukrainian anti-Semitism was exaggerated; that anti-Semitic acts in Ukraine were orchestrated by non-Ukrainians who controlled Ukrainian territory; that any native Ukrainian anti-Semitism was largely a response to anti-Ukrainian acts by Jews — would recur again and again.

Through much of the 1950s and 1960s, formal relations between the two communities were cool. It took only a small spark to ignite underlying suspicion and mistrust. A case in point was the televising in 1960 by the French-language network of the Canadian Broadcasting Corporation of a less than flattering documentary on Symon Petlura and the trial of his Jewish assassin. According to *Press Digest*, the federal government's analysis of the ethnic press, *Vilne Slovo* declared the film yet another incident of Soviet disinformation designed to undermine the Ukrainian national cause. The paper noted that since Congress had made no public comment on the film, this must mean the Jewish umbrella organization gave tacit approval to those intent on smearing the good name of the Ukrainian people. For others, simple Jewish condemnation of the program would not have been enough. Jews could have prevented it. *Moloda Ukraina* (Toronto) felt Jewish statesmen should have used their influence to halt this and other attacks, but didn't.

The Ukrainian press uproar was reported in the *Canadian Jewish News*, which explained to its readers, many of whom had likely never heard of Petlura, why the Ukrainian leader was seen as a patriot and idealist by Ukrainian nationalists. The article outlined the role Jews played in Petlura's short-lived government, the historical controversy surrounding his role during the pogroms and his assassination. The *CJN* conceded that much about Petlura and his death was still shrouded in mystery, but one fact was crystal clear — the death of 100,000 Jews at the hands of Petlura's men. "Either Petlura's [anti-pogrom] orders were found easy to ignore," the *CJN* declared, "or Petlura himself, much as he found such bloodshed distasteful, found it useful for political reasons and did not pursue his prohibition of pogroms too strenuously."[61]

The *CJN* article was a red flag to the Ukrainian press. In retaliation, *Homin Ukrainy* decried the *CJN* story. Ukrainians, it pointed out, had suffered at the hands of "Jewish commissars," like Trotsky and Kaganovich. *Vilne Slovo* dismissed the *CJN* piece as baseless, and *Postup* (Edmonton), voice of western Ukrainian Catholics, feared there was a deliberate effort afoot to undermine relations between the two Canadian ethnic communities and stir up animosity towards Ukrainians.

"There is a hidden Communist hand behind this action," *Postup* warned, "and for this reason the Ukrainian Community in Canada will not allow itself to be provoked."[62]

The *CJN* took up the challenge. While the Jewish paper declared itself in favour of Jewish-Ukrainian "rapprochement on this continent," this could not be "based on the falsification of history." In a broadside sure to set off yet another Ukrainian salvo, the *CJN* observed that Jewish-German reconciliation could never have moved forward if the "present leaders of West Germany insisted on keeping Hitler on a hero's pedestal."

As expected, the Ukrainian press roundly condemned the comparison of Petlura and Hitler as "Ukrainian baiting." The *Ukrainian Echo* (Toronto), weekly English-language supplement of the *Homin Ukrainy*, went further. Ukrainians, it declared, were the victims of Jews, not vice versa. The Bolshevik revolution in Ukraine was spearheaded by Jews and led by a Jew, Rakovsky. As for Jewish suffering during World War II, the *Ukrainian Echo* placed that at the door of Jewish police who worked hand in hand with the Germans.

The Ukrainian Voice (Winnipeg) protested that Jews made honest discussion and intergroup dialogue impossible. Any critical comment about Jews, however intended, "and they [Jews] will immediately raise a hue and cry that you are anti-Semitic, an enemy of Jewry and thus alert public opinion against you." As to the *CJN* demand that Ukrainians renounce Petlura, the *Voice* felt this was as absurd as Ukrainians demanding Jews renounce then Israeli Prime Minister David Ben-Gurion because, as the *Voice* explained, several years earlier Israeli border guards had killed Arab men, women and children working their fields near the border. In, perhaps, the final word in this particular inter-press skirmish, the *Voice* declared no good purpose served by the attacks. "We do not consider it in Canada's interest."[63] The *CJN* did not respond.[64]

This type of press jousting was rare not because the attitudes reflected were not widely held in the two communities but because communication of any kind, even so negative, was rare. Through the 1960s, the leadership and institutional relations between the two groups were distant, formal contacts few. In 1963 the UCC invited Congress representation at a conference to commemorate the thirtieth anniversary of the Ukrainian famine, "the cruelest disaster in the history of mankind." Active participation by representatives of the Jewish community at any Ukrainian community function would have raised the ire of Holocaust survivors. Congress was saved the problem of how to respond to the invitation. The conference, as it turned out, was in the midst of the Jewish High Holidays. The invitation was graciously declined.[65]

In the 1970s some movement, albeit one-sided, developed for *rapprochement*. Tentative efforts to bridge the gulf of historical suspicion and mistrust separating Jewish and Ukrainian communities in Canada began, largely at Ukrainian initiative. In part this initiative proved a reflection of demographic shifts in the two communities. A new generation of Canadian-born, urban, educated Ukrainian and Jewish professionals were gradually making their weight felt within their respective community councils. This is not to argue the younger leaders were immune to Old World antipathies. They were not. Nor is it to argue that the older generation of leaders readily stepped aside in favour of the new. This was also not the case. But in both communities, especially the Ukrainian community, there were voices raised in favour of better relations.

Perhaps Ukrainian moves towards bettering relations also grew out of a fear that their shared heritage was now casting Ukrainians as historical villains. Ukrainian historical self-definition painted their people as an oppressed, dispossessed and victimized people. But it was also running headlong into the western world's understanding of the Holocaust and the history of European anti-Semitism which preceded it. Increasingly, Ukrainian historical truth was trampled under the weight of the larger accepted historical view that seemed transfixed on the Jewish historical drama. Not only did many Ukrainian Canadians see the Ukrainian national struggle ignored, their litany of suffering overlooked, but they also feared Ukrainians were being made the villains of Jewish and western historical narrative. The more the Holocaust captured the public and scholarly historical imagination, the more these Ukrainians felt their every spark of hard-won and short-lived national self-assertion was being dismissed as a pogromist's licence to murder Jewish men, women and children. Ukrainian heroes were vilified as collaborators and murderers in someone else's historical epic. To a Ukrainian community struggling to keep group identity alive, to retain community pride and commitment, to encourage continuity from generation to generation, this challenge to its historical sense of self was a heavy weight to bear. Perhaps if common cause could be made with the Jewish community in areas of mutual interest — the future of multicultural policy in Canada, the Soviet question, positive intergroup relations — the heat would be turned down.

For Ukrainian Canadians increasingly active in community institutional affairs there was much to learn from the Jews. Jews had blazed a path through North American urban business and professional life for others to follow. By the 1970s, as more Ukrainians were travelling this path, one-to-one contacts with Jews increased, as did appreciation of the model of Jewish mobility in America.

What was more, Jews seemed to have succeeded in carving a place for themselves in urban North America without sacrificing commitment to Jewish community. On the contrary, as individual Jews built a socially, economically and politically secure place for themselves in North American society, Jewish communal life thrived. The Jewish polity was active and took pride in both community fulfilment in North America and the growth of a Jewish national homeland in Israel. Israel's electrifying victory in the 1967 Six Day War served to further energize Jewish communal life in the diaspora. All this was not lost on the Ukrainian community. The very idea that after two thousand years of statelessness diaspora Jewry celebrated the rebirth of its homeland stood as a beacon of hope to a Ukrainian diaspora dispossessed of an independent homeland. Thus, on the individual and communal level there was much to learn from the Jews.

The time seemed appropriate. There was a precedent. If Israelis and Jews could make post-war accommodation with Germany and Germans, why not with Ukrainians? What is more, some Ukrainians believed they could offer Jews reciprocity in forgiveness. Ukrainians, after all, believed they had much to forgive the Jews.

Nothing could have been further from the Canadian Jewish consciousness than the notion that Ukrainians had historical grievances against Jews. The very idea would have been greeted with disbelief in Jewish circles. And Jews knew little or nothing of the agony of the Ukrainian diaspora experience, of the famine or the loss of Ukrainian lives during the war. If anything, Jewish leaders believed the Ukrainian community was now among the more politically powerful ethnic community voices in Canada — if not through its organizational strength, then by sheer weight of numbers.

Jewish leaders felt repeatedly frustrated in their dealings with government. They could not make headway on such basic Jewish issues as anti-boycott legislation to prohibit foreign firms or governments from demanding discrimination against Canadian Jews or other Canadian citizens as a precondition of a business contract.[66] At the same time Ukrainian political will seemed to be growing in strength. Was it not Ukrainian pressure that led to the federal government's 1971 policy of multiculturalism promising financial and political support to ethnic continuity in Canada? That was an achievement the Jewish polity, for all its supposed influence, could not match.

If Jewish communal leaders needed any more proof of the surging strength of the Ukrainian polity, it came on October 9, 1971. The very day after the government's formal announcement of its multiculturalism policy in the House of Commons, Prime Minister Pierre Trudeau flew off to Winnipeg to address the Tenth Tri-Annual Congress of the Ukrainian Canadian Committee. In his banquet address, he personally congratulated the Ukrainian-Canadian community for its key contribution in reshaping Canadian social policy. Multiculturalism was a Ukrainian victory. But the content of Trudeau's keynote address, full of the platitudes such an occasion demands, was obviously less important than the fact of his presence. By seemingly "reporting in" to the UCC, he lent credence to the notion that a new era of ethnic political influence, most importantly Ukrainian influence, was dawning.[67]

But the flexing of Ukrainian political muscle in Canada did not mean an easing of Jewish-Ukrainian relations. In Israel a small group, composed largely of recent Jewish immigrants from Ukraine, attempted to forge links to the Ukrainian diaspora while hoping to educate world Jewry to the need for inter-ethnic co-operation if Jews in the Soviet Union were to be helped. A spokesman for the fledgling group visited Canada in 1971 at the invitation of the Ukrainian community. While in Canada he met with Jewish leaders, who greeted him more as a curiosity than a prophet of co-operation.[68] Indeed, when it came to efforts on behalf of Soviet Jewry, Canadian Jewish leaders proved exceedingly shy of working with Ukrainians or others — Estonians, Latvians, Lithuanians — now dispossessed of a national state.

But in the summer of 1971, when the state visit of Soviet Premier Alexei Kosygin was in the offing, just such co-operative efforts were considered by Jewish leaders. A major joint protest was suggested as a possibility,[69] but in the end, the idea was rejected. In this instance the burden of historical grievances proved secondary to political strategy. It was argued that the

Ukrainians and their allies had very different goals from those of the Jewish community. Many among the Ukrainians and their supporters were fundamentally hostile to the Soviet system *per se*. They looked forward to the destruction of the Soviet political structure and a rupture of the federated Soviet state. The main goal of Jews, on the other hand, was to enable Soviet Jews to leave the USSR or, at least, publicly identify as Jews without fear. Thus it was concluded that to combine the Jewish protest for human rights with that of Ukrainians or other eastern Europeans for political change would blur the critical distinction between the Jewish agenda and that of other protesters.

Across Canada, Jewish leaders organized their anti-Kosygin demonstrations separately from those of others. In Toronto this proved fortuitous. The Jewish protest incorporated a twenty-four-hour candlelight vigil followed by a mass evening demonstration, all in a park across from the Soviet premier's hotel, about half a mile from the Ontario Science Centre where an official state dinner was in progress.

Ukrainian and other eastern European protesters, joined by a swelling throng of sympathizers, filled the streets in front of the Science Centre. As the night wore on, the crowd grew and tension increased. Demonstration marshals never had full control of the crowd, and a spark ignited violence. The police, mounted on horseback, waded into the crowd swinging billy clubs. A near riot erupted. Ambulances and paddy wagons took away the injured and arrested.[70]

Even though hopes of a joint protest did not materialize, Jewish and Ukrainian participation in federal advisory councils such as that on multiculturalism enlarged the circle of Ukrainian-Jewish leadership contacts and opened the door to further discussions — if only a crack. Building on these contacts, prominent Ukrainian community leaders made several overtures in the hope of engaging in further dialogue with Jewish leaders.

In Winnipeg, with its long history of inter-ethnic mixing, this was easier than in Toronto where distance was a fact, if not the rule. But even in Toronto several efforts at bridge-building were begun. In the autumn of 1974, for example, Robert (Bohdan) Onyschuk, a young lawyer and head of the UCC in Ontario, approached fellow lawyer Sidney Harris of the Congress executive in Toronto and Ben Kayfetz of the Congress staff. In what would soon become a ritualized pattern of knife and fork contacts, the three went out to dinner. "Our discussion," Kayfetz observed about the evening, "ranged across the whole spectrum of Jewish-Ukrainian concerns. We touched, of course, on the animosity and suspicion that persists in certain quarters on both sides. It was felt this might be to some extent a form of generation gap which may diminish in the course of time." In the meantime, it was agreed, informal contacts like their dinner should continue in spite of the negative feelings such contacts might generate among militant factions in both communities.[71]

And such hostility was not hard to generate. The Jewish community's official position on the Soviet Union called for Soviet adherence to the freedom of religion and freedom to migrate, as set down in the Soviet Constitution. In 1974, Congress officials felt it quite in keeping with this position to publicly support those demanding the release of imprisoned Ukrainian activist Valentyn Moroz. But even this symbolic gesture of solidarity with one whose imprisonment touched the conscience of humanity raised the ire of some in the Jewish community, predominantly Holocaust survivors, for whom negative memories of the Jewish experience in Ukraine remained fresh.[72] Whatever one might say about Moroz, his personal or political views, or his incarceration was irrelevant. It was enough that a Jewish statement of support for Moroz's human rights bonded them with Ukrainian-Canadian nationalist organizations which some Jews regarded as little more than a collection of unreconstructed Nazi sympathizers.[73]

Ironically, the Moroz statement was credited with stilling some of the more strident anti-Jewish voices in the Ukrainian community. Alex Epstein, a Toronto

Jewish lawyer with professional contacts in the Ukrainian community, repeatedly tried to find common ground for the two ethnic polities. Forever pressing Congress officials to open avenues of dialogue with Ukrainians, he welcomed the Moroz statement as a good first step by a Jewish community leadership which had previously avoided anything but cautious distance from the Ukrainian community. Ukrainians, Epstein wrote Congress, "were deeply moved by this expression of sympathy and support from the Jewish community." It was a gesture which could not but help "young and liberal" leadership then coming to the fore "in stifling anti-Semitic remarks and statements made by other Ukrainians."[74]

As a follow-up to Congress's Moroz initiative, Epstein arranged a dinner hosted by several Toronto Congress leaders with Walter Tarnopolsky, a law professor and Moroz activist. Although Tarnopolsky held no formal position in the Ukrainian community structure, he was "well regarded by them. They seek his advice on political and communal questions, as one of their leading intellectuals."[75] Tarnopolsky was not unknown to Toronto Jewish leaders. His long prominence in the Canadian Civil Liberties Association cemented his friendship with several like-minded Jewish civil liberties activists also important in Canadian Jewish Congress affairs.

The dinner meeting was held at an upscale Russian restaurant in downtown Toronto. Discussion was light, cordial yet frank. There was no agenda and except for agreeing on a second meeting to be hosted by Ukrainian leaders nothing concrete was accomplished.[76]

The follow-up dinner, three months later, in an equally elegant restaurant, this time Chinese, brought out a large Ukrainian contingent. Again nobody had any fixed agenda for the eggroll diplomacy. As heaping dishes of Chinese food were passed around the table, informal but guarded conversation ranged over topics as varied as immigration, the International Women's Year Congress in Mexico City, CBC overseas broadcasts, third-language broadcasting in Canada, reunification with family from the Soviet Union and racial tensions in Canada.[77] Dinner ended with no suggestions made as to joint actions or programs, but all agreed such meetings were useful in breaking the ice. Unspoken was a disquieting awareness that there were vocal constituents in both camps who would attack any co-operative effort, no matter how tentative, as tantamount to consorting with the devil.

Nevertheless, new lines of contact had been opened. If the mood was not one of mutual trust, at least Ukrainian participants believed a useful foundation now existed on which to build. In the summer of 1975, for example, a Congress representative was invited and attended a public demonstration on behalf of Valentyn Moroz. Congress official Ben Kayfetz was seated prominently between two local Ukrainian-Canadian politicians on a raised platform in Toronto's City Hall Square. The following year the rally fell on the Jewish New Year, Rosh Hashana.[78] No official representative of the Jewish community was able to attend, but a letter of support was sent. When, two years later, Moroz was released from Soviet prison, Congress immediately sent Moroz a telegram of congratulations through the World Congress of Free Ukrainians head office in Toronto. The telegram, honouring "a fearless champion of human rights, cultural and national freedom," was, in turn, greeted as a gesture on behalf of all those "suffering religious and political persecution in the Soviet Union."[79]

These preliminary contacts were reinforced when Rabbi Gunther Plaut, President of Congress and newly appointed to the Ontario Human Rights Commission, accepted an invitation to address the influential Ukrainian Professional and Business Club of Toronto. This association, an important and temperate voice within the UCC, was judged by Kayfetz as "an excellent forum at which to present a representative Jewish speaker . . . at this juncture in Ukrainian-Jewish relations." Rather than a bastion of the Ukrainian right wing, he saw the association as representing "an intellectual, younger group" of Canadian-born professionals. Plaut was asked to address "The Challenge of Human Rights in the USSR and the Western World"; but at his request the topic was revised simply to "Human Rights," although he promised to comment on the Soviet situation.[80]

Plaut appreciated the sense of occasion attending the event. It was, he noted, "the first occasion on which a representative of the Jewish community addresses a Ukrainian-Canadian association." Nor, he resolved, would he avoid the past which "divided us."

Plaut's audience of two hundred was identified as "the elite of the Ukrainian community of our city." As they listened somewhat uneasily, Plaut spoke of psychic associations some Jews held of Ukrainians. He explained how many Jews identified the infamous Babi Yar massacre with Ukrainian collaborators and linked Khmelnytsky and Petlura, Ukrainian national heroes, with "memories of persecution, and of widespread participation of the population in these crimes." Ukrainian Canadians must understand, he demanded, "why Jews will continue to insist that those who offended against human rights must be brought to justice — here or wherever they live at present."[81]

During the question period that followed, Plaut was struck by what he sensed was pain caused by what Ukrainians felt was the "stereotype of Ukrainian anti-semite [sic]" portrayed in the "Holocaust" mini-series shown on television that very week. Few, however, confronted the issue head on. Although one questioner called upon all Ukrainians to come to grips with the anti-Semitism in both their history and community, others queried what they saw as Jewish exclusivity in its Soviet Jewry campaign, refusing to unite with others in similar straits. Surely, they urged, anti-Soviet cooperation could help overcome any legacy of mutual mistrust. By and large pleased by the evening, Plaut reported a "desire for rapprochement was sincere; though it was apparent (and perhaps natural) that [he] met a good deal of defensiveness about Ukrainian history even that of 300 years ago."[82]

Plaut was right. History could not easily be set aside. Only a month after Plaut's Toronto speech, at the invitation of Ukrainian community leaders, a number of prominent Winnipeg Jews attended a luncheon honouring Petro Mirchuk, a Ukrainian Auschwitz survivor living in Winnipeg, whose wartime memoirs had just been published. Following a Kosher meal, Mirchuk addressed the small gathering. One representative of the Winnipeg Jewish Community Council reported that Jewish participants were taken aback when Mirchuk saw "nothing wrong in comparing Chmelnitsky [Khmelnytsky] *vs* the Jews to Bar Kochba *vs* the Romans." The very suggestion enraged the Jewish guests, who considered any attempt to parallel the Jewish position in seventeenth-century Ukraine with the might of occupying Imperial Roman legions in first-century Palestine to be nothing short of obscene. An attempt by the hosts to generate a Ukrainian-Jewish dialogue fell flat. Ukrainian speakers urged that the past be set aside. Both communities had suffered; now was the time for reconciliation, co-operation and efforts to find grounds for joint action. Most Jews sat in silence. Not even a Ukrainian survivor of Auschwitz could bridge the historical antipathies still alive in the room.[83]

Bridge-building would be difficult. Most Jewish leaders felt no urgency to make common cause with Ukrainians. They could not comprehend the Ukrainian desire to transcend the past, the need to move beyond historical grievances. But any suggestion that Jews could set aside their shared historical understanding, especially that of the Holocaust, which increasingly bonded them one to the other, was not only wrong minded, it was impossible.

If Jewish leaders remained hesitant, one must note that the desire to reach out to Jews was far from universal among Ukrainians. Some, especially among the extreme nationalists and immigrant groups, still harboured anti-Jewish feelings and had deep misgivings about any dealings with the Jewish community. Those who made overtures to the Jewish community leaders did so with some trepidation at how their initiatives would be received within community circles. When they were not responded to in kind by the Jewish community, there was some bitterness. Ukrainians had taken the first step; it went unreciprocated. In a letter to Alex Epstein, Yuri Shymko, then President of the nationalist World Congress of Free Ukrainians, lamented the lack of a positive Jewish response. Recent Jewish and Ukrainian history was marked by so much pain that these two groups, perhaps more than others, should be able to find common ground for co-operation and understanding.[84]

Epstein, still pressing Canadian Jewish Congress leaders on the value of better relations with Ukrainian organizations, again challenged Jewish leaders to respond. With "our common interest for human rights for our people in the USSR, our acute concern and fear of Soviet global policy, our desire and need for Canadian unity," co-operation was essential. As a first step, Epstein urged, it was necessary to build "links of communication with all groups, on an open and friendly basis whenever it is opportune . . . If we are to be a light to the nations, we must first get out of the darkness ourselves."[85]

Epstein's plea did not strike a responsive chord. Few Jewish leaders could object to better relations with any other group, including Ukrainian Canadians. But to the degree that Jews gave any thought to the problems of Ukrainian Canadians, which was neither much nor often, they were seen as separate and distinct from those of the Jewish community. Khmelnytsky cast a long shadow. So did war criminals.

Tentative and guarded contact between leaders of the Jewish and Ukrainian communities continued. Discussion of historical grievances remained part of almost every dialogue. Rarely, however, did discussion turn to war criminals in Canada. Perhaps it was unnecessary. Most Canadians, including Jews, might instinctively identify Nazi war criminals with Germans, but some Jewish leaders had not forgotten the Division episode of 1950 and some still doubted the innocence of the Division's wartime record. For their part, Ukrainian leaders were growing increasingly restive at a rash of investigations of Ukrainian and other eastern Europeans then under investigation in the United States for Nazi-related activities. The United States was not Canada, but could the Nazi hunt spread northward?

In the spring of 1977, several Congress officials in Toronto lunched with leaders of the Toronto-based Banderite World Congress of Free Ukrainians, again at the instigation of Alex Epstein. The mood was positive. Informal discussion again ranged over a broad series of topics but eventually and for the first time focused on the Jewish community's efforts to force the government's hand on Nazi war criminals. Yuri Shymko assured his Jewish luncheon partners "that his organization would not knowingly harbour war criminals and he was interested in seeing a positive policy on this question enacted."[86] The pledge seemed unequivocal.

It took very little, however, to test the pledge. Several months after the pleasant luncheon, an anonymous flyer was mailed to Ukrainian organizations across Canada. It requested information on one Ivan Solhan (Sovhan) said to have been a ranking Ukrainian police official accused in the death of several hundred Jews. Solhan was thought to be living in Canada. "It is hoped," the flyer stated, "people in Ukrainian circles will be able to find Solhan." The flyer requested that any information be sent to Wiesenthal's documentation centre in Vienna. It was signed "a concerned Canadian."[87]

Perhaps smarting at the suggestion that Ukrainian organizations could snap their fingers and deliver up Nazi war criminals, Shymko wrote to Ben Kayfetz who had attended the recent lunch meeting. Shymko affirmed the "bond of friendship between the two communities" and the co-operation of his organization "in bringing to justice any individual who has been responsible for premeditated murder whatever his racial or national origin, whatever his political or ideological motives." But the assurance was not without an accompanying caution. There had been, Shymko noted, "a number of mistaken accusations against innocent individuals which were legally challenged and withdrawn." The flyer, he suggested, smacked of the same slander; but this time the victim of the accusation could not defend himself. The accuser remained nameless. Shymko urged that henceforth Jewish officials communicate directly and openly with "the numerous central organizations of our communities in the world, rather than by anonymous channels."[88]

Kayfetz was concerned at any suggestion that Congress was linked with the anonymous flyer, and he was equally amazed anyone could believe the Jewish community was so tightly organized that a word from Congress could rein in those circulating the flyer. This monolithic vision was as far from true of the Jewish community as it was of the Ukrainian community. In a memo to Congress leaders, Kayfetz noted that the offending flyer was clumsily produced but it was not an accusation of guilt. It was a request for information — information necessary to avoid the very kind of false accusations Shymko protested. As to Shymko's declaration of support for bringing war criminals to justice — Kayfetz was now somewhat sceptical. "On close reading of the letter, I see it is something less than that."[89]

For jurists the terms "war criminal," "war crimes," "collaborator" and "crimes against humanity" have very specific legal meaning. But legal and semantic niceties aside, the sense of Jewish community pain that persons who knowingly aided and abetted in the Holocaust might be alive and well, living peacefully in Canada, remained real. If the term "war criminals" as used by many in the Jewish community and larger civic culture lacked legal precision, it was still a term fraught with meaning.[90] And for decades Jews had tried to get the Canadian government to act.

Official Jewish concern in this matter, of course, stretched back to the Galicia Division episode. In the years immediately following, few doubted that the mass immigration of Displaced Persons and others had included war criminals. But it was one thing for Canadian Jews to feel incensed that war criminals had secreted themselves in Canada, perhaps with the connivance of the Canadian government, church officials or ethnic political leaders; it was another thing that year after year the government and larger civic culture had refused to do anything about it. Pressed on the subject, Canadian authorities had always had one answer — they lacked an evidential or legislative basis for action.[91] Most Jews suspected that they did not care. Throughout the fifties, the Holocaust had remained a Jewish memory and war criminals a Jewish concern.

In May 1960, however, Israeli Prime Minister David Ben-Gurion announced the apprehension of Holocaust mastermind Adolf Eichmann. Ben-Gurion proclaimed that Eichmann would stand trial in Israel for war crimes, crimes against humanity and, under Israeli law, crimes against the Jewish people. Eichmann's kidnapping and lengthy trial, front-page news around the world, captured the public imagination. It sensitized Jews and non-Jews alike to the reality of the Holocaust as no previous event had done. The trial helped turn the Holocaust from a private Jewish agony into part of the western historical legacy — an event of monumental proportions destined to plague historians, moral philosophers and the conscience of the world. After the Eichmann trial, thoughtful people could no longer dismiss the Holocaust as the momentary excess of a few Nazi extremists run amok; it was now revealed as the centrepiece of a political and racial ideology with deep historical roots, an ideology that commanded the loyalty of millions.[92]

Nor did the Eichmann trial close the book on Jewish efforts to apprehend and bring war criminals to face justice. It intensified it. In 1964, world Jewry was galvanized by the realization that the German twenty-year statute of limitations on war crimes would soon take effect. If this was allowed, many Nazi war criminals would escape accountability. Some feared they could emerge from the shadows in which they were hiding to again proclaim dedication to Nazi ideals, perhaps to rebuild for the future. The Canadian Jewish Congress joined Jewish organizations around the world to protest the German statute of limitations. They pressured the Canadian government to endorse the protest.[93]

The statute of limitations issue was put high on the agenda when a Congress delegation gathered in the office of Prime Minister Lester Pearson in October 1964. Pearson was asked to intercede personally with the West German government. Canada, he was reminded, had "no statute of limitations whatever for crimes involving murder or, for that matter, other homicidal crimes."[94] Surely Canada should not sit by and let those who murdered millions go free. Pearson agreed. In part because of the world Jewish protest and the diplomatic representations by friendly governments like Canada, West Germany proclaimed a ten-year delay in the implementation of its statute of limitations in the case of war crimes.

But even as the Eichmann trial and the statute of limitations controversy were still fresh, events in Canada brought the threat of a Nazi revival home to Canadian Jewry. In 1965 a small band of self-styled Canadian Nazis, trying to ape the American Nazi party of George Lincoln Rockwell, organized a series of public meetings. Nazi regalia and swastika-emblazoned flags were unfurled in a Toronto park. The popular press splashed stories of these home-grown Nazis across the front page, and television brought their provocations into every home. The reaction of the Jewish community was instant. Congress and its constituent organizations immediately demanded appropriate police action and received the support of responsible civic, media and church leaders. But for some Jews this was not enough. Younger more militant Jewish groups, reinforced by Holocaust survivors, organized counter-demonstrations which occasionally spilled over into violence. As exaggerated rumours of a growing national neo-Nazi movement percolated through the Jewish community, Jewish self-defence groups sprang up and Holocaust survivors set up their organizational infrastructure, dedicating themselves to combating any manifestation of Nazism, commemorating the Holocaust and promoting a public program of Holocaust education.[95]

One other event which reinforced Jewish sensitivity to the Holocaust was the Israel-Arab War of 1967. The weeks preceding the outbreak of fighting in June were traumatic ones for diaspora Jewry. What they saw were Arab armies massing on all sides, threats being issued, United Nations troops pulled out of dangerous zones, and the straits of Tiran blocked to Israeli shipping. Many feared an imminent replay of the Holocaust; and again the non-Jewish world seemed ready with eulogies but no help.

Israel's lightning victory was seen as miraculous. It also served as a symbolic corrective to those who pointed fingers at the alleged passivity of Jews during the Holocaust. Understandably, the spectre of a second Holocaust also served to reinforce commitments to sanctify the memory of the first and seek justice against Nazi war criminals. The problem now was not community commitment to the issue. It was tactics.

Given the Canadian government's dismal record of inaction in following up any information on alleged Nazi war criminals passed along by Congress, simply appealing to the government's sense of justice seemed pointless. But no other strategy seemed effective. One approach again brought to the fore was "naming" alleged war criminals and exposing them to the court of public opinion. Perhaps public reaction to revelations about specifically named war criminals living freely in Canada might just force politicians, police and immigration authorities to act.

But this plan had its pitfalls. Hasty allegations made without incontrovertible evidence could leave the accuser and the Jewish community open to charges of ha-

rassment if not libel or slander. The embarrassment of
the Melnyk episode was not forgotten. Moreover, naming could undermine the moral authority of the Canadian Jewish community and make any campaign to
bring Nazi war criminals to justice seem more like an
indiscriminate witch-hunt.[96]

As we have seen, naming and trial by press or in the
court of public opinion were dangerous. They could,
and did, backfire on both the press and the Jewish community when evidence proved less than solid. But trial
by press was troubling on another count. Why must it
be left to victims or the press to indict a murderer in
the name of justice? In a society based on the rule of
law, prosecution is the duty of the state through its legal system. What can be done, however, when the state
refuses to act or claims it does not have the legal authority to act? And even as knowledge of the Holocaust
grew, the problem of war criminals in Canada remained
too distant a problem for most Canadians — including
old allies of Jews in the post-war human-rights crusade.
As a result war criminals remained, for the most part, a
parochial Jewish concern easily dismissed by government.

The Liberal Party of Pierre Trudeau, with the lion's
share of Jewish voter support and prominent Jews, both
active in Jewish communal organizations as well as Liberal organization and fundraising, yielded few divi-
dends. Why then was the Liberal government so
unbending? Several factors suggest themselves.

Trudeau, a firm believer in meritocracy, surrounded
himself with the most able men and women he could
find, including Jews. But if Trudeau harboured no ethnic intolerance or would not tolerate it in others, he felt
little or no sympathy for the politics of ethnic particularities. The Trudeau who in 1971 approved multiculturalism as an instrument of domestic cultural policy still
believed Old World antipathies should be discarded
when immigrants entered Canada. Accordingly he had
little sympathy with Japanese-Canadian demands for
reparations associated with their World War II intern-

ment, with Chinese calls for repayment of their head tax and the Ukrainian call for an apology for internment of community members during World War I. It was his view that recycling the past might serve the needs of ethnic communities but not the needs of Canada. The road to ethnic harmony, he held, lay more in ensuring future equality than in resurrecting the injustices of the past. It is likely he placed Jewish community pressure on war criminals in the same class. Certainly his ministers knew the Prime Minister was less than enthusiastic about any initiative in this area, and they took their cue from him.[97]

Long in power, old Liberal political hands must also have sensed that the Nazi war-criminals problem posed a potential minefield of inter-ethnic tension. Most Canadians might equate Nazis with Germany, but key Liberal strategists likely understood the sensitivity eastern Europeans felt on this issue. Almost forty years of experience in government had taught them something. The Liberal Party may have had limited voter support in eastern European communities where the party was often identified as too soft on Communism, but party strategists, aware of domestic reaction to American initiatives against war criminals, felt such action could exacerbate inter-ethnic tensions in Canada. With the Jewish vote already in the Liberal bag and nothing political to gain, it was better to avoid the issue.

The failure to engage government interest in war criminals as a matter of human rights is clear in the case of Harold Puntulis. A post-war Latvian immigrant and naturalized Canadian citizen, Puntulis was accused and tried in absentia for war crimes by the Soviet Union. Although Canadian Jewry had ample reason to mistrust the workings of the Soviet legal system, the evidence of Puntulis's participation in mass murder of Jews seemed irrefutable to them. A Soviet request to Canada for Puntulis's extradition was rejected. Congress acquired, translated and forwarded a copy of the Soviet trial transcript to the federal government in hope of changing the government's position. It claimed that

Canadian respect for justice, human rights and dignity demanded it. Congress failed.[98]

For more than ten years Congress badgered the federal government on Puntulis and other cases which periodically came to the attention of Jewish authorities. Nothing was accomplished. To every appeal the government's answer was the same. Desirable though it might be, action against Puntulis or others was legally impossible. In the Puntulis case, for example, the government claimed extradition was out of the question; Canada had no extradition treaty with the Soviet Union. But with or without a treaty it was not Canadian policy to submit individuals to foreign courts where different rules of evidence apply (and especially to a Communist court). Puntulis was also a naturalized Canadian citizen. He had spent five years of peaceful domicile in Canada, as required by Canadian law, before being granted Canadian citizenship. He had committed no crimes in Canada. While government officials agreed it was unfortunate such a person should have the protection of Canadian citizenship, they warned denaturalization procedures were, at best, a dubious legal procedure.

Puntulis was not alone. In 1974, for instance, David Geldiaschvilli was tried in the Soviet Union and sentenced to death for the murder of 4,000 innocent people, 3,000 of them Jews. Geldiaschvilli was a naturalized Canadian citizen arrested on a visit to his native Soviet Georgia. It was claimed at his trial that in 1968 the Soviet Union had requested Geldiaschvilli's extradition from Canada to stand trial for his crimes. Canada had refused, even though the government had information that Geldiaschvilli was a suspected mass murderer. Three years later "Geldiaschvilli applied for and received Canadian citizenship."[99] Eminent Canadian jurist and McGill law professor Maxwell Cohen dismissed the government's legal gymnastics. Yes, there were legal problems, Cohen argued, but they could all be overcome if the government had the political will to do so.[100]

Old hands in the campaign shrugged their shoulders. The government already knew there were war criminals in Canada and didn't seem to care. The public didn't seem to care. Nobody cared except Jews, who could and would not let the matter pass. Increasingly outraged by seeming public indifference, they repeatedly broached the issue with politicians and public servants alike, even though they already knew the government's answer. Time after time the government offered sympathy but claimed their hands were tied by the lack of a remedy in Canadian law.

As Canadians vacillated, Americans confronted Nazi war criminals in their backyard. Unlike Canada, the United States acted. The Americans prepared to strip Hermine Braunsteiner Ryan of her naturalized American citizenship in 1971. Braunsteiner Ryan, a former concentration camp guard, was known as the mare of Majdanek for allegedly stomping an innocent victim to death with her boots. American authorities claimed that as a Nazi, Braunsteiner Ryan had never been eligible for entry into the United States or for American citizenship. The government was ready to argue in court she could only have achieved both by fraud. In the end, Ryan surrendered her citizenship and was extradited to Germany to stand trial. It is worth noting that Braunsteiner Ryan entered the United States from Canada, where she immigrated after the war.[101]

In the winter of 1975, a Jewish delegation that included several Holocaust survivors visited Ottawa. They asked the minister responsible for Canadian citizenship if Canada could not do the same. Once again the answer was not one of right or wrong, but of legal barriers. Canadian and American law and legal systems, it was explained, were not parallel in the area of immigration and citizenship. What was legally possible in the United States was not necessarily possible here. Indeed, even if stripping away immigration and citizenship status were possible, there seemed some doubt whether fraud in applying for immigration could be proved in Canadian cases. Unlike the United States, it was unclear whether prospective post-war immigrants to Canada were asked about "past Nazi associations . . . although questions were put on Communist association." Could an immigrant be held guilty of withholding information about a Nazi past if he or she was never asked about it?

The Immigration Minister, as always, was sympathetic but promised little. "His departmental aides," he allowed, "would carry out a detailed investigation to determine if any loopholes could be found in the records" to see if the American model might work in Canada. But his words had a hollow ring. The Jewish delegation left as they had come — empty-handed.[102]

As Canadian authorities waffled, the Americans took another step. In 1977 the US Congress passed the Holtzman Amendment enabling immigration officials to investigate alleged Nazi war criminals who might have entered the United States by falsifying their past. Two years later the Office of Special Investigations, the OSI, was organized within the Justice Department to take over these investigations. More denaturalizations and deportations seemed likely.[103] These American moves inflated expectations in Canada, especially among survivor groups and their children, the second generation.

On the heels of the American initiatives came the impact of television's "Holocaust" mini-series. The Canadian public, some argued, might now be ready to support rooting Nazis out of their Canadian sanctuary. Some survivors advocated a dramatic protest to dramatize their anguish at the Canadian government's inaction on war criminals. One group was dissuaded only with difficulty from undertaking a mass demonstration or a hunger strike to bring this to the attention of the public. Survivors were told that the problem was not that the public did not know, it was that the government steadfastly refused to act.

In Toronto, frustrated Congress leaders met yet again to assess their campaign against war criminals. While they agreed that the program of public information — reaching out to other groups and keeping the war-

criminals issue present in every official government contact — must continue, they were only too aware of the
weakness of their approach. The Jewish community had
for years discussed human rights. The government responded with the law. It was time, it was suggested, to
respond in kind, to see what legal arguments could be
mustered to counter those of the government. The war-
criminals problem was referred to the Legal Committee, a committee of Congress in Toronto made up of
lawyers.[104]

The lawyers quickly settled on several possible avenues of legal argument to be explored and committee
members were assigned to do the legal spade work on
each. They were aided by Kenneth Narvey, a former
law student from Winnipeg, who offered himself as legal consultant to Congress. Narvey proved self-
motivated and single-minded, with a crusader's zeal for
rooting out war criminals. After ten months as a volunteer he was given a small stipend. Nobody thought that
more than thirty years of government inaction could be
ended without a struggle, but at least among Congress
insiders, there was now a new sense of momentum.[105]

Chapter 4

The Stage Is Set: The Emergence of the War-Criminals Issue

He was not the first federal cabinet minister to visit the imposing Bronfman House, Canadian Jewish Congress national headquarters, across the street from Montreal General Hospital. But the visit by John Roberts in the late autumn of 1977 was different. Roberts, minister responsible for citizenship and the Liberal member of parliament for a heavily Jewish riding in central Toronto came to talk about war criminals. It was less a public meeting than a quiet discussion between friends. Following the minimum of fanfare required of such an occasion, Congress leaders again relayed the Jewish community's continuing indignation that Nazi war criminals should find a haven in Canada. In August the Americans had set up a "special litigation unit" aimed at denaturalizing and deporting Nazi war criminals. Congress leaders then made their pitch. They wanted the minister to champion a similar program against war criminals in Canada. Roberts listened quietly, politely, even sympathetically; but, knowing his prime minister's attitude towards the war-criminals issue, Roberts promised nothing.[1]

Congress leaders were not really surprised. On the problem of Nazi war criminals the federal government proved unmoved by moral argument. But would it bend under the weight of legal argument? As political spade work continued in Montreal, the Congress Legal Committee got down to serious work in Toronto.

111

Congress Executive Director Saul Hayes privately doubted the value of this effort. As a lawyer, he was all for forcing the government's legal hand to uncover a remedy in Canadian law. But he argued that this should not be the responsibility of the Canadian Jewish community; it was government's responsibility. Congress should apply itself to forcing government to find a remedy; this was a function of political will. If Nazi war criminals were ever to be dealt with, Hayes was convinced, the best way was to confront the government not with legal theories but with an actual and documented war criminal living in Canada and identified by witnesses. It would then be up to government to find the appropriate legal remedy. Congress could bring relevant legislation to government attention, but it was for the public authorities, not Canadian Jewish leaders, to find or create legal remedies.[2]

Hayes may have been a little shortsighted. If it was not the role of the Jewish community to find a legal remedy to deal with Nazi war criminals in Canada, then why should it be the role of the Jewish community to unearth Nazi war criminals? Surely finding criminals, not just drafting legislation, was the duty of government under its policing powers. What is more, Congress had previously passed along information on alleged Nazi war criminals in Canada much as Hayes suggested, and nothing had come of it. What then were the options left to the Jewish community except to press in every way possible? The alternative was to do nothing, and that was unthinkable.

Kenneth Narvey's contract with Congress was renewed at six-month intervals, first to finish his legal research project, then to assist in gathering evidence and legal support documentation necessary to again approach government for action on specific cases along the lines advocated by Hayes. But Narvey's passion could not be contained by the financial or administrative constraints imposed by Congress. Narvey remained self-directed, and gave his duties a maximalist definition. To the chagrin of Congress's fiscal controllers, he marshalled Congress photocopying machines and long-distance phone facilities like a general preparing for battle. But whatever headaches he caused his superiors, one cannot deny that his energy and commitment helped to heighten the issue of war criminals on the Canadian Jewish Congress agenda.[3]

For all the tumult he generated, Narvey functioned under the Congress umbrella. Not so with other community members equally incensed by the notion that Nazi war criminals and collaborators lived peacefully in Canada. In Toronto, for example, Holocaust survivor Sabina Citron spearheaded the Canadian Holocaust Remembrance Association. Citron's wartime memories allowed her no peace so long as any vestige of Nazism remained to be confronted. She also had little patience with Congress. Until the summer of 1978 Citron was a force within Congress in Toronto, although her relationship with some Congress leaders was fractious. She charged that on critical issues Congress leaders, like Jewish leaders in pre-war Europe and America, waited too long, reluctant to take decisive action. Usually they opted for quiet, diplomatic and, in her view, ineffectual means of response. As in the pre-war case, she warned, such methods were doomed to fail. It was time to directly confront issues such as war criminals, using every legal means at hand, including public protest. The suffering of six million martyrs required it; the dignity of those who survived demanded it.

In the summer of 1978, for example, members of the tiny American Nazi Party announced they would march in full Nazi regalia through the heavily Jewish Chicago suburb of Skokie. Skokie's Jewish community was incensed. Citron, feeling their pain and sharing their rage, insisted that Congress in Toronto endorse Canadian Jews going to Skokie to stand side by side with Skokie Jews in the expected counter-demonstration. The CJC, she recalled, refused. It opted instead to organize a massive Toronto meeting of solidarity with the Jews of Skokie.

Citron interpreted this as yet another sign of Congress weakness, an unwillingness to confront the enemy head on. Before long she withdrew from Congress, and with a small band of like-minded supporters organized the Canadian Holocaust Remembrance Association. She promised her followers that the new and independent association would conduct an unrelenting campaign against Nazis and neo-Nazi supporters, unencumbered by what she dismissed as the bureaucratic inertia and ingenuous posturing of the Canadian Jewish Congress. The issue of war criminals in Canada was high on the new association's list of priorities. Indeed, during her last days in Congress Citron promoted a petition calling for a government initiative against Nazi war criminals in Canada, a petition she believes did not have the whole-hearted support of fellow Congress leaders. When she withdrew from Congress she took her petition and passion with her.[4]

Among the newly organized association's first efforts was to lobby Citron's local member of parliament, Robert Kaplan, then a government backbencher. Kaplan, representing one of the most heavily Jewish ridings in Canada, York Centre, recalled seldom if ever being approached by Congress leaders on the war-criminals issue. Perhaps Congress officials felt the Jewish MP was already on side or that the relative powerlessness of the Liberal caucus of the day meant it was far better to focus their lobbying efforts on Cabinet members, Jewish and non-Jewish. In any event, according to Kaplan, it was Citron's band of followers, not Congress, who approached him first on the issue.[5]

Kaplan was not unresponsive. On October 30, 1978 he introduced a private member's bill in the House of Commons, *Bill C-215 — An Act Respecting War Criminals in Canada*. The bill proposed an amendment to the Canadian *Citizenship Act* calling for the automatic revoking of citizenship from any person previously convicted of a "grave breach" of the 1949 Geneva Convention, the articles of war to which Canada subscribed. By "grave breach" was meant "among other things, wilful killing, torture or inhuman treatment, including biological experiments, and wilfully causing great suffering or serious injury to body or health."[6]

Cynics might shrug off Kaplan's effort as little more than a ploy to curry favour with his heavily Jewish constituency. Others might applaud him for finally challenging Parliament to address the war-crimes issue. Whatever his motive, in the end it hardly mattered. As a private member's bill, unsupported by the rest of the Liberal caucus, Kaplan's effort went nowhere.

For Congress the focus was still fixed on lobbying Cabinet.[7] In January 1979, for example, another Congress delegation pressed Secretary of State John Roberts to deal with suspected Nazi war criminals in Canada. Again the minister was polite, even encouraging of action, if evidence were forthcoming of specific cases. Congress again passed along what materials it had collected on several alleged Nazi war criminals living in Canada. But hopes were not high. Despite subsequent gentle prodding, nothing happened.[8]

But what became of the information the government received from Congress and others? A small flurry erupted when the Montreal *Gazette* reported that on "Roberts' desk there are dossiers accusing eight Canadians of murder and atrocious crimes." The article included an interview with Nazi-hunter Simon Wiesenthal in which he again accused the Canadian government of deliberately stalling on action against known accused Nazi war criminals in Canada. The government, he said, is "presented with evidence and it does nothing. Since the war ended, not one criminal has been tried or deported."[9]

Wiesenthal, who reportedly announced he would never again set foot on Canadian soil until decisive action was taken against Nazi war criminals, did not hold the government alone responsible for the lack of action. Like Citron, he was said to feel it was lack of organized Jewish community pressure not government recalcitrance which was at fault. Wiesenthal dismissed

Congress's efforts against war criminals as half-hearted at best.

Learning of the accusation, Ben Kayfetz responded that Congress did not control government. Government inaction did not result from any lack of Congress lobbying, but in spite of it. What is more, Kayfetz lamented, if Wiesenthal had information on Nazi war criminals in Canada he refused to share it with Congress. Wiesenthal had been something less than co-operative in answering Congress requests for material.[10]

But Wiesenthal was not convinced. According to him, while Congress did little, war criminals in Canada breathed free. How many alleged criminals were there in Canada? *The Gazette* (Montreal) quoted Wiesenthal as claiming there were "no known West German war criminals in Canada. The majority of the 1,000 . . . at large are Ukrainians and other Eastern Europeans who emigrated directly after the war."[11]

Whatever the actual number of alleged war criminals in Canada or their origin, the federal government seemed to want no part of the issue. Ironically, and after some prodding, Canada was again prepared to encourage Germany to continue with its war-crimes prosecution. In the autumn of 1978 Canadian Jewry joined the world Jewish community in yet another campaign designed to pressure Germany into again postponing application of its statute of limitations in the case of war criminals or, even better, disallowing the statute in war-crimes cases once and for all. Across Canada Jewish groups organized high-profile public meetings, letter-writing campaigns and formal representations to German diplomatic authorities.[12]

After some hesitation Canada's voice was finally added to the international chorus of states calling on West Germany to rethink its planned application of the statute of limitations.[13] In early July 1978 the Bundestag responded to the world-wide outcry. It abolished application of the statute of limitations in the case of Nazi war crimes.[14] But even as the Bundestag was wrestling with its statute-of-limitations problems, Canadian voters were preparing to elect a new government. A Liberal government, tumbling in popularity, faced a challenge from new Conservative leader Joe Clark and the NDP's Ed Broadbent. During the 1979 election campaign an activist Jewish student group, The North American Jewish Students' Network–Canada (Network), polled all major candidates and the three party leaders on questions of special interest to the Jewish community. Among the issues raised was that of alleged Nazi war criminals in Canada. In his reply Trudeau referred to the legal difficulties attending any course of action against Nazi war criminals. Unlike the Prime Minister, neither leader of the two opposition parties saw any legal encumbrance standing in the way of immediate and decisive action should either of them form the next government. The results of the survey were published in *The Globe and Mail* and discussed in the *Canadian Jewish News*.[15]

It would be incorrect, however, to conclude that the issue of Nazi war criminals was in any way a national election issue. It was not. Nor is it likely that many Jews picked one party over another on the basis of its stand on this one issue. Far from it. But for Jewish leaders the election was an opportunity to make their agenda better known to those who would form the next government.

The May 22, 1979 election left Canada with a minority Conservative government under Joe Clark. Congress leaders were quite prepared to remind the new government of its election promise on Nazi war criminals,[16] but Congress might not have the same entrée to the federal Progressive Conservatives as had been painstakingly cultivated with the federal Liberals. Even though the Liberals had been generally unresponsive to Jewish community concerns during the Trudeau years, a majority of Canadian Jews, especially in Quebec, still voted Liberal. Links to the Liberal Party machine were well established. Lines into the Conservative Party, especially for the Quebec-based Congress national staff, were softer. But Jewish fears of being frozen out proved wrong. The new minority Conservative government, scrambling to hold onto power, made every effort to reach out to voters, including the Jewish community, some of whom just might be wooed into supporting Conservative candidates the next time out.

Several months after the new government took power Congress leaders met with Clark's staff and that of key cabinet members on the question of Nazi war criminals. Private conversations were also held with Conservative Party strategists. Congress officials felt that progress was made; the mood was upbeat. An optimistic Alan Rose, successor to Saul Hayes, even reported to Congress National Officers in early September 1979 that federal "consideration is being given to establishing a special office to investigate and possibly prosecute suspected war criminals resident in Canada." The recently organized American OSI offered an obvious model.[17]

Celebration was premature. The new government was not nearly ready to follow the American lead. Nevertheless, the direction seemed clear and signals seemed positive. A meeting on war criminals was scheduled with Conservative Justice Minister Jacques Flynn. In anticipation of the meeting he ordered a departmental review of the legal and administrative complexities of the issue.[18] Perhaps, just perhaps, thirty-five years of inaction was coming to an end.

But, optimistic Congress officials would suddenly find the Clark government door slammed on any public policy initiative which might be interpreted as pro-Jewish. In a politically disastrous move initially designed as an act of goodwill to the Jewish community, the Prime Minister announced he was going to move the Canadian embassy in Israel from Tel-Aviv to Jerusalem. The move, never a high-priority item on the Canadian Jewish community agenda and certainly not one on which Congress officials had actively lobbied, set off a storm in Ottawa. Protests from Arab governments threatening diplomatic retaliation, pressure from Canadian business interests fearing they would be frozen out of Arab markets and warnings from Canadian External Affairs and trade officials of the need for damage control shook Clark. The press was merciless in attacking the government and the opposition Liberals had a field day. Even the Rhinoceros Party jumped into the fray. They promised that if elected they would even outdo the Clark government by putting all Canadian embassies on wheels and keep them forever on the move.[19]

Poorly advised on Jewish matters, the Clark government was suddenly gun-shy of Jewish lobbying. Wilting under opposition to the Jerusalem move, the government was not about to be accused again of pandering to Jewish interests. Action against Nazi war criminals, seen by government insiders and Tory policy planners as a parochial Jewish concern and not as an issue of wide national attention, would just have to wait. It was not even put on the government's back burner — it was taken off the stove.

Nor was the Jewish community left unscathed by the Jerusalem episode. Caught off guard by Clark's Jerusalem embassy discussion, Jewish officials worried about widespread mutterings of an all-powerful Jewish lobby winning its way with government. In the face of such talk, any concerted community push on Nazi war criminals could well prove counter-productive. As a result, a beleaguered Congress lay low. They had little choice. They were not about to get positive government action on Nazi war criminals or much else for that matter until the Jerusalem fiasco receded into the shadows of memory.

In contrast to Congress's retreat, some Jewish community activists demanded the pressure be kept up. In November 1979 a self-styled "Conference of Jewish Activists," rumoured to have ties to the militant Jewish Defence League, identified an alleged war criminal living in Toronto. Picketers marched in front of his home in a quiet residential neighbourhood as police kept a watchful eye. The picketers, basking in the light of local media attention, appeared as much to challenge the less than successful efforts of the Canadian Jewish establishment on the issue of Nazi war criminals in Canada as they did government inaction.

When Kayfetz enquired about the picketers' organizational affiliations and further plans, he received a stinging rebuke from Sabina Citron. "Rather than go after the group," Citron blasted Congress officials, "Kayfetz should go after the war criminals."[20] Within Congress, it was suspected by some that Citron had her own line to Simon Wiesenthal in Vienna and reinforced Wiesenthal's apparent impression that it was cap-in-hand Congress leadership, not government resistance, that was the biggest stumbling block to any Canadian housecleaning of war criminals. A visitor to his Vienna headquarters wrote that Wiesenthal dismissed the Canadian "Jewish establishment," particularly in Toronto, as " 'Uncle Toms' [who] don't want to offend the goyim [non-Jews] and don't want to 'rock the boat.' "[21] Such a charge was particularly galling to Gunther Plaut, the CJC President. A rabbi, scholar and himself a German-Jewish refugee, Plaut rejected any allegation of softness and defended Congress actions to Wiesenthal.[22]

Even as Congress suffered from the aftershocks of the Jerusalem affair, the minority Conservative government of Joe Clark fell on December 13, 1979. An election was called. Only ten days before the February 18, 1980 election, the Conservative Minister of Justice sent Congress officials a letter outlining the results of the public-service review he had initiated on the war-crimes issue. It was not good news. It was the opinion of the government's legal advisers "that no body of Canadian law exists for the prosecution of war criminals in Canada."[23]

This was not the first time Congress officials had heard this argument. It was, however, the first time this public-service excuse for inaction was laid out in such detail. Even as Congress officials attempted to digest the implications of the letter, Robert Kaplan was courting voters in his heavily Jewish North Toronto riding. Kaplan reminded voters of his lonely backbencher's effort to promote a bill to prosecute Nazi war criminals in

Canada. He promised that if elected he would carry the ball on the issue and that a Liberal government would be unyielding in its vigorous pursuit of these criminals.

After February 8, 1980 Kaplan, it seemed, might have his chance. Pierre Trudeau and his Liberal team regained office, and to the surprise of many, Trudeau brought Kaplan into Cabinet as Solicitor General, responsible, among other things, for the RCMP. But the Solicitor General's position is not among the more powerful Cabinet posts. What is more, some of Kaplan's Cabinet colleagues dismissed the new Solicitor General's pre-election promises on the Nazi war-criminals problem as either posturing for his Jewish constituents or giving vent to a personal passion. It was not something to be taken seriously. With Trudeau at best cool to any movement against Nazi war criminals, no Cabinet colleagues would support a Kaplan initiative. When he pushed on the issue, Kaplan felt stung by Cabinet and public-service whispers that he was using his position to advance a parochial and self-serving Jewish cause.[24]

Dismissed in Cabinet, Kaplan had another card and played it. As minister, he still had latitude for personal initiative. Indeed, on his first day on the job as solicitor general, Kaplan lined up briefings from his deputy and the Commissioner of the RCMP on the question of Nazi war criminals. Kaplan was supplied with the Justice Department brief on war criminals drawn together at the behest of the previous Minister of Justice. According to that brief no Canadian initiative under the *War Crimes Act, Citizenship Act, Immigration Act* or *Extradition Act* was possible. It allowed only one avenue for action — that any country with which Canada had an extradition treaty might demand a particular individual, even a naturalized Canadian, be extradited for specific criminal acts which fall into the war-crimes or crimes-against-humanity categories. This, of course, required another country to initiate proceedings.

Further, the new minister was advised by his deputy that without specific instructions from cabinet, the RCMP had no mandate to involve itself in ongoing investigations for which there was no framework in Canadian law. With no such framework or without an official request for the extradition of a specific individual, the RCMP had no independent jurisdiction to look into the matter of war criminals in Canada.[25]

Kaplan reserved judgment on the legal opinions offered up by Justice officials. He served notice, however, that he "wished to pursue the matter further." He requested a meeting of his own officials with those in the Justice Department and, equally important, instructed his officials to arrange a meeting between himself and Simon Wiesenthal who was scheduled to visit the United States in April 1980.[26]

In an interview with a Jewish student newspaper only days before meeting Wiesenthal, Kaplan stated he was prepared to leave the questions of the law and enabling legislation "on the back burner for the time being." Perhaps if enough evidence could be amassed against the "worst offenders living in Canada," it might be possible to overcome cabinet reticence and to find a legal method to deal with real criminals rather than hypothetical cases. A meeting with Wiesenthal might produce the necessary evidence.

In the meantime, at Kaplan's initiative, an interdepartmental committee was assembled with representatives from the RCMP and government departments with an interest in the Nazi war-criminals issue. It was chaired by Martin Low, an official in the Justice Department. The interdepartmental committee initiated yet another comprehensive examination of the war-criminals issue, at times moving beyond the question of legal remedies and into policy questions and likely political fallout.[27]

Those on the committee had no doubt as to Kaplan's commitment. Their mandate was not to forestall action. On the contrary, the minister wanted a plan for positive action, and as one official recalled, "the marching order was to find a way." But if the interdepartmental committee knew Kaplan's mind, they also knew he was not high in the Cabinet pecking order. Other ministers, echoing the Prime Minister, showed less enthusiasm for a concerted effort to deal with the issue. It was not just Kaplan's position but that of other ministers and the entrenched opposition of ranking public servants that had to be taken into account.[28]

While the interdepartmental committee was proceeding with its work, the Canadian Jewish Congress 1980 triennial assembly in Toronto elected a new national president, youthful McGill professor of international law Irwin Cotler. Cotler's strength did not lie in day-to-day supervision of Congress administration; far from it. His individual organizational style was soon part of the folklore of Congress, but there was no denying Cotler's power as an orator, his commitment to the Jewish agenda or his sense of the political moment. Two Canadian issues soon commanded his attention: the Trudeau initiative in repatriating the Canadian Constitution and the festering problem of war criminals in Canada. The two would soon be interlocked.

Convinced that Jewish views on any new national constitution should be forcefully made to government, Cotler organized a Select Congress Committee on the Constitution under the leadership of eminent Canadian legal scholar Maxwell Cohen. The committee studied Ottawa's draft constitution and drew up a report supportive of a constitutionally entrenched bill of rights in Canada. The committee, with input from Kenneth Narvey, now at Network, voiced some concern that restrictions on retroactive legislation in the proposed Charter of Rights and Freedoms might inadvertently make Nazi war criminals immune to subsequent criminal action. To avoid the likelihood of Nazi war criminals suddenly and inadvertently escaping prosecution and the Constitution making Canada "a safe haven for Nazi War Criminals," the Congress committee recommended to government that the protection against retroactivity of criminal offences not apply to any act which, "when it was committed, was criminal according to the general principle of law recognized by the community of nations." Con-

gress's recommendation was accepted and eventually incorporated in the new supreme law of the land — Section 11(g) of the Canadian Charter of Rights and
Freedoms.

But just because Congress and Network had the fore-
sight to recommend that the legislative road for government action be kept clear did not mean the government
would ever travel that route. Unless the legal advice the
Justice Minister received from his officials changed, that
seemed most unlikely. Even Kaplan seemed stymied.
His initiatives seemed to be going nowhere. His much-
vaunted meeting with Wiesenthal produced more press
coverage than it did hard evidence against individuals in
Canada. Wiesenthal did not deliver. What is more, the
feedback Kaplan was getting from his interdepartmental
committee was discouraging. They held fast to the view
that there was no legal remedy to the problem.[29]

Kaplan's efforts to generate Cabinet interest in the
problem of Nazi war criminals scored him few points
among his colleagues, and his failure to deliver government action left him vulnerable to attack from his Jewish constituents. He was out on a limb, unable to
muster Cabinet support but, in the name of solidarity,
publicly forced to defend the government's record.

To make matters worse, in early March 1981 the interdepartmental committee, which Kaplan helped to organize, delivered its review of the war-criminals
problem. The secret report, drafted by Martin Low, re-
affirmed the earlier contention that no legal remedy or
possibility of a remedy in Canadian law existed to deal
with alleged war criminals in Canada. The thirty-seven-
page double-spaced Low Report, labelled a "Discussion
Paper," also dismissed the probability of ever gathering
sufficient evidence acceptable in Canadian courts to act
against war criminals even if a legal route to prosecution could be found. Evidential material on hand from
foreign governments, the Jewish community and individuals was dismissed as "lacking in detail and impre-
cise or containing factual inconsistencies." Low also
intimated that Canadian courts trying to give legal

meaning to the term "war criminal" as commonly used could open a Pandora's box of name-calling charges and counter-charges which would be difficult to unscramble.

If there was one point to be drawn from Low's "Discussion Paper," it was that Low saw no need for further discussion. Although Low conceded that "a small number of persons now in Canada could be shown to have committed offences of greater or lesser magnitude in Europe during the Second World War," the report left little doubt that government could or perhaps should do nothing. The whole matter was best avoided and would eventually self-destruct as accused and accusers died off.[30]

Cut short by the Low Report, Kaplan seemed left with few options — encourage requests for extradition by foreign governments and, perhaps, find a legal argument the Low Committee had overlooked. But even these alternatives were fraught with difficulties. Extradition required that a foreign state sure of the Canadian domicile of a wanted criminal initiate proceedings against that individual. What is more, not all foreign states were equally welcome to apply for an individual's extradition — only those states with which Canada had an extradition treaty and, in effect, only those states with a legal system compatible with that of Canada. In the past Canada had proven reluctant in the extreme to deport persons back behind the Iron Curtain for trial, whatever their offence, and certainly not where capital offences were involved. Neither did Canada have an extradition treaty with the Soviet Union, nor did it officially recognize the Soviet annexation of Latvia, Lithuania or Estonia, where many of the Nazi crimes took place. Unless the West German government was willing to press for the extradition of a specific individual who had acted in eastern Europe under German jurisdiction during World War II, the extradition option, especially for any eastern European war criminals, was remote.

Kaplan did what he could. On a European visit he talked with West German and Dutch authorities, hoping they would search their files for any accused war criminals who might be in Canada. He returned with a Dutch "list of collaborators and war criminals who might be in Canada" and against whom "Dutch authorities are willing to commence extradition proceedings, if found in another country."[31] He instructed the RCMP to seek out the possible Canadian whereabouts of anyone on the list.

He also spoke quietly with Czech authorities. Even though Czechoslovakia was behind the Iron Curtain, Kaplan reminded Czech authorities of their still valid pre-war extradition treaty with Canada. He hinted to the Czechs that an alleged Nazi war criminal from Czechoslovakia on whom the Canadian government had a substantial file might be available for extradition at their request. But Czech authorities might have feared the international attention on the inner workings of their judicial and political system that a war-crimes trial might bring. Perhaps they were also concerned lest any trial exacerbate still-raw antipathies between Czechs and Slovaks awkwardly sharing a single bi-national state. Whatever their reasons, the Czech government was cool to Kaplan's offer.[32]

Encouraging foreign countries to press for extradition was a long shot. It would be much better to have convincing legal arguments at hand to counter those in the Low Report. Kaplan turned to the CJC and its new president, Irwin Cotler. He could not give Congress the secret Low Report, but he could brief Congress officials on the legal stumbling blocks in the way of action. Cotler assured Kaplan that Congress would quickly produce a legal brief to counter the notion that there was no remedy available in Canadian law to mete out justice to Nazi war criminals.[33]

But Kaplan still had problems in the larger Jewish community. While Kaplan again pressed his Cabinet colleagues quietly and discreetly, his public posture remained steadfastly in defence of the government's record on Nazi war criminals. This was hardly a defensible position in the eyes of the Jewish community.

Kaplan defended the government before a largely unsympathetic Toronto Jewish audience in April 1981, and as the *Canadian Jewish News* reported, his remarks were greeted with "disappointment and shock."[34] Even Cotler thought Kaplan could do more, much more. In June 1981 Cotler wrote to Kaplan to complain of the government's inaction. In the widely circulated letter Cotler protested, "If the political will was there, the appropriate remedy would be found." No Holocaust survivor "could understand how a government that can organize itself for the collection of taxes or the enforcement of traffic laws cannot bring to justice the greatest mass murderers in history." He went on to argue that the existence of Nazi war criminals in Canada was not just a Jewish issue. It was a moral outrage to all Canadians. "I can assure you the intensity of concern 'loses in translation,' and a letter filters out the depths of feeling behind it. But let there be no mistake about it. We see this — we feel it — as a matter of the utmost concern, and for Canada, as a matter of conscience."[35]

Privately Cotler doubted Kaplan's ability to defeat opposition from inside Cabinet, and saw him as stymied by advice from public officials that action against war criminals was not legally possible. And when Kaplan turned to Congress for assistance in developing counter legal arguments, Congress agreed to do it. In fact, they were eager to do it.[36]

Whatever their reservations about Kaplan, unspoken among Jewish leaders was a far greater concern that except for the Jewish community, few in Canada really cared about Nazi war criminals. Even a well-publicized resolution passed by the Constitutional and International Law section of the Canadian Bar Association calling for legal action against Nazi war criminals in Canada was less a grassroots plea for justice than the product of lobbying by a few Jewish lawyers at the Association's annual meetings.[37]

But Congress itself was not immune from attack. The Canadian Holocaust Remembrance Association leaders submitted a brief on Nazi war criminals to federal authorities in May 1982. When they learned that Congress was also preparing a legal brief, the Association wrote directly to Trudeau denouncing Congress, not government, as a major stumbling block to action. The Association claimed that but for Congress's unwillingness to raise the issue of war criminals with government, "due to their fear of anti-Semitic backlash," the federal government would have initiated a Nazi cleanup years earlier. "It should not be necessary," the Association's president wrote, without seeing the Congress brief, "to waste precious time studying a 100 page [Congress] document which is largely irrelevant."[38]

All talk of a one-hundred-page Congress brief was premature. Preparation of a first-rate legal brief would take time. Much as he had done on the Constitution, Cotler organized a national committee. He appointed as chairman David Matas, a dedicated Winnipeg civil liberties lawyer active with Amnesty International. Kenneth Narvey joined as a member of the committee. The National Legal Committee took over the legal work begun by Congress's regional legal committee in Toronto.[39]

In Matas, Cotler found a kindred spirit. Matas too saw the issue of war criminals as an issue of human rights and dignity. He concluded that the most promising legal route, more promising even than denaturalization and deportation, was for Parliament to enact new retroactively binding legislation allowing trials of war criminals in Canada. Such legislation was possible under the very revision to the Constitution Congress had helped to frame.

Cotler, while not disagreeing with the value of such new legislation, was uneasy with a brief that only stressed one option. At Cotler's initiative Matas reworked the brief to show the proposed new legislation as one of several alternatives available to the government if it truly wished to deal head on with the war-crimes problem.[40]

Suddenly, before the revised brief could be submitted, the question of Nazi war criminals in Canada ceased to be an abstract question of law. It had a human face. In the spring of 1982 Albert Helmut Rauca, a seventy-three-year-old immigrant to Canada, was taken into custody by the RCMP on a German extradition warrant. Picked up at his suburban Toronto home, Rauca stood accused of direct involvement in the murder of thousands of Lithuanian Jews during World War II.

Congress leaders were delighted by the Rauca extradition proceedings. Not only did it promise the removal from Canada of an accused Nazi mass murderer, but it also riveted national attention to the problem of Nazi war criminals in Canada as nothing had done before. Ironically, however, the Rauca hearings forced Cotler and Matas to keep the now-completed Congress brief under wraps. Congress's key position was that there were legal remedies for dealing with Nazi criminals in Canada; Canada did not need to wait for extradition. Rauca's lawyer was arguing much the same thing and until all Canadian legal remedies were exhausted, he opposed his client's extradition to West Germany. Rather than have Congress face the embarrassment of seeming to support Rauca's legal arguments, the Congress brief was withheld pending a final determination of Rauca's legal fate.[41]

Public sensitization on Nazi war criminals received another jolt in September 1982. As the Rauca hearing continued, *None Is Too Many* was published. The book, a scholarly study of the Canadian response to the plight of European Jewry before, during and after the Holocaust, did not directly address the question of Nazi war criminals entering Canada. It did, however, detail the rigid Canadian rejection of Jewish refugees during the years of Nazi terror. In this, *None Is Too Many* inadvertently set up a contrast between the conscious Canadian refusal to offer sanctuary to the victims of Nazi brutality and a growing realization that Canada may have given haven, perhaps unknowingly, to their murderers. The book and the wide publicity it received left many outraged at the shame of past Canadian immigration practices. It further stiffened the resolve of Canadian Jewry to demand action.[42]

But what action? The ongoing Rauca proceedings seemingly confirmed that extradition was still an option, just as the Low Report had allowed. But all knew that extradition was a very limited one. In December 1982 a delegation of Congress leaders made yet another pilgrimage to Ottawa to lobby political leaders, including the Minister of Justice and the Prime Minister, on the war-criminals issue. The reception was as always warm and concerned. But as always the government was hesitant to commit its hand to anything beyond Rauca-like extraditions. Trudeau, flanked by Kaplan and fellow Toronto Liberal Cabinet Minister John Roberts, also representing a heavily Jewish riding, met the delegation but promised nothing. For Trudeau, Cotler concluded, the war-criminals issue was not a basic issue of human rights. It was, in fact, a parochially Jewish issue that, if acted upon by government, might prove divisive of the larger civic culture.[43]

Was Trudeau right? After the Rauca affair ended would interest in war criminals just fade away? Was there no vocal constituency for the issue outside the Jewish community? Compared to Israel-related matters, problems of Soviet Jewry and the fight against contemporary anti-Semitism, how high was the problem of war criminals on the communal Jewish agenda? In spite of Trudeau's assessment, the issue just refused to go away.

On October 12, 1982 Rauca was ordered deported. But he could still appeal, first to the Ontario Court of Appeal and, if necessary, the Supreme Court of Canada. In the meantime Cotler and Matas continued to hold back the Congress legal brief. But how long could Congress hold back? There was some concern that if Rauca took his appeal all the way to the Supreme Court, there would be further lengthy delays. In addition, what if the Supreme Court ruled against Rauca on the grounds there were no domestic legal remedies besides extradition? Then Congress's key arguments that there were domestic remedies would also be undermined.[44] Thus, it seemed essential, if the Rauca appeal went to a higher court, that the CJC obtain leave to argue the case that extradition, appropriate for Rauca, did not preclude Canadian trial in other instances.[45] It was probably with a sigh of relief that CJC received the news that Rauca would forgo his final avenue of appeal to the Canadian Supreme Court.

Almost coinciding with the deportation of Rauca in May 1983 came the election of Milton Harris, a wealthy Toronto businessman, to replace Irwin Cotler as president of the Canadian Jewish Congress. Before Congress could release its long-awaited legal brief, Harris decided to put his own stamp on the Congress's campaign against Nazi war criminals and on the brief. As a well-known Liberal partisan, Harris hoped to have the access to Cabinet members necessary to make the Congress case and make it stick.[46]

Harris, like Cotler, had closely followed the Rauca extradition proceedings and also like Cotler, agreed the government must be pushed beyond extradition as the only available remedy. Extradition may have been "an appropriate remedy in the Rauca case" but, Cotler wrote to Harris, extradition is of "limited value" against most Nazi war criminals of eastern European origin suspected of being in Canada. The Congress brief, once released, must prove other legal remedies existed and "fidelity to law and justice" required such remedies be used.[47] But Harris, a self-confessed "frustrated lawyer" still demanded the brief be revised yet again, this time to stress the denaturalization and deportation option he preferred. Once more, the Congress brief would be delayed.[48]

But the clock did not stand still. Even as he waited for the Congress brief Kaplan pressed ahead. Citing reports of covert post-war American intelligence assistance to known war criminals entering the United States, Kaplan ordered RCMP Commissioner Simmonds to investigate the possibility that Canadian officials were somehow implicated. Further, in response to a CBC news item suggesting Canadian complicity in the arrival of Nazis in Canada after the war, Kaplan demanded the allegations "should be pursued" in interviews with those who might have been involved or through examination of such records as might be available.[49]

Among Jews, however, his government was savaged for lack of action. In April 1983, 15,000 Holocaust survivors from across North America had gathered in Washington. In the glare of international media coverage Irwin Cotler publicly attacked Ottawa for years of inaction. In the highly charged atmosphere of the gathering he congratulated the government on its Rauca action but lamented, "It took 36 years for the first Nazi war criminal in this country to be brought before a Canadian Court." He pledged Rauca would not and could not be the last.[50]

For Kaplan the Jewish campaign was a mixed blessing. While it lent weight to his own efforts, it also kept him in an awkward position. He was the Cabinet spokesman in the Jewish community. After making the war criminals his "issue" in Cabinet, he was repeatedly forced to defend Liberal inaction or, as he explained to less than sympathetic delegates at the 1983 CJC Plenary Assembly in Montreal, the lack of a legal vehicle other than extradition to pursue war criminals.[51] All the political advice Kaplan received from his officials served to affirm this course of action — or lack of it. The Low Report and, according to Kaplan, a secret 1983 RCMP report on Nazi war criminals, also prepared at Kaplan's request, only reinforced one another.

But in the spring of 1983 the government was presented with an alternative legal opinion, not from Congress but from Christopher A. Amerasinghe, crown prosecutor in the Rauca extradition hearing. During the course of the lengthy proceedings, Amerasinghe became an expert on the issue of war criminals in Canada. He was asked by the RCMP to assess their report and, more particularly, to comment specifically on the possibility of revoking Canadian "citizenship conferred on Nazi war criminals in Canada."

Amerasinghe disagreed with the RCMP conclusions and, by extension, those of the Low Report. He argued that revocation of citizenship leading to deportation from Canada was not only possible, it was likely the most effective way to deal with Nazi war criminals in Canada. Amerasinghe claimed that the pre-conditions under which Canadian citizenship was offered included legal immigration into Canada. If someone's immigration was in itself illegal, their subsequent citizenship was invalid and could legally be revoked. The acts committed by war criminals would have ruled out legal entry into Canada and the fact that they were not specifically asked about wartime activities did not lessen the illegality of their entry. It was, he argued, the responsibility of each and every immigrant to volunteer critical facts about themselves relevant to the admission process. Such information, even if brought to light later, could retroactively be used to deny an individual's legal right to be in Canada.

Amerasinghe was certain enough of his reasoning to recommend validating his analysis in one or more test cases. If the courts found fault in his line of reasoning, a legislative remedy would be called for. If however, the case were "successful, it would serve as a precedent and cases where extradition is not possible could be dealt with in this way."[52]

Kaplan carefully read the Amerasinghe analysis and saw an opening. In the absence of the Congress brief, in early July 1983 Kaplan pointed out to his Cabinet colleague, the Minister of Justice, Mark MacGuigan, that this might just be the legal opening needed to go to court against Nazi war criminals. If so, Kaplan pressed, "I would like to develop a program to identify some cases for action."[53]

A CJC delegation headed by Milton Harris, new president of Congress, also met with Justice Minister MacGuigan. Harris, too, pressed for a program of denaturalization and deportation. MacGuigan promised a reappraisal. For his part Harris promised to make Congress's legal brief, now revised to emphasize the denaturalization and deportation procedure, available for Justice Department review.[54]

In its final incarnation the Congress brief, heavily weighted in favour of the denaturalization and deportation option, was forwarded to Justice officials in September 1983. Matas, who saw his report twice revised to incorporate the views of two different CJC presidents, was both disappointed and frustrated. He drifted away from Congress and took what was left of his original brief to the B'nai Brith League for Human Rights, where he soon found a new home as legal counsel.[55]

The ball was now squarely in the Justice Department's court. They had Kaplan's test case proposal together with the Amerasinghe report and the Congress brief. But would they do anything with them?

Within Congress, expectations of an imminent break in forty years of inaction were again on the rise. Surely the government would have to respond to the Congress brief, to Amerasinghe's report and Kaplan's prodding. In December 1983 Harris led yet another CJC delegation to Ottawa, hoping to come away with a firm commitment. Before meeting with the Minister of Justice, Harris visited with both Ed Broadbent, leader of the New Democratic Party, and, more important, Brian Mulroney, new leader of the opposition Conservative Party. Both politicians pledged their support to any initiative to rid Canada of war criminals, although Mulroney seemed somewhat ill briefed on the issue. The meeting with the Minister of Justice seemed even more encouraging. Harris, a life-long Liberal supporter, left the meeting elated. MacGuigan, Harris recalled, declared the government was now prepared to move on several test cases. The minister explained to Harris and the other CJC delegates that a letter had gone to Kaplan requesting that several of the best cases on which the RCMP had dossiers be made ready for action. He pleaded for a little more patience but promised patience would be rewarded.

Unfortunately, Harris was eventually forced to conclude that his Congress delegation had been misled.

Unbeknownst to Congress, MacGuigan's letter to Kaplan fell far short of a ringing endorsement of testing the law. Rather, MacGuigan again reviewed the problem of prosecution set out in the Low Report and challenged by Amerasinghe and the Congress brief. He fell in behind Low. The question of whether a person's knowing concealment of an incriminating past for purposes of gaining Canadian entry could later be brought to bear as a factor in a subsequent denaturalization remained far from clear. In Canada, unlike the United States, immigration and naturalization legislation are separate. Fraud in obtaining admission to Canada does not necessarily mean fraud was used in obtaining citizenship. Thus revoking citizenship may not be as straightforward as might be hoped.

The courts, MacGuigan allowed, had yet to rule on the question. But would they get a chance? Maybe not. In as lukewarm an endorsement of action as one could imagine MacGuigan wrote to Kaplan, ". . . it may be appropriate to consider at a later date the possibility of proceedings against a suspected Nazi war criminal on the facts of a particular case as a 'test case.'" But not now. As to when, MacGuigan offered no timetable.[56]

With Harris still convinced prosecutions were in the offing, Kaplan grasped at straws. He instructed his RCMP officials to "proceed to work up a few cases as we are invited to do by the Minister [MacGuigan] at the end of his letter. The sooner the better."[57] It would not be soon enough. MacGuigan's commitment to act against Nazi war criminals, whatever its depth, was soon cast aside in the political free-for-all that erupted in Ottawa. The Liberal government, scraping bottom in national popularity polls, awaited the resignation of its leader, Prime Minister Trudeau. Trudeau was in no hurry. For months he kept the nation, the media, his caucus and aspiring prime ministerial hopefuls cooling their heels while he pondered his future. Finally, on February 29, 1984, Trudeau announced he was stepping down. Political pandemonium broke out in Liberal Party circles. Leadership hopefuls, including

MacGuigan, were soon criss-crossing the country testing their respective political strengths. MacGuigan, never an advocate of legal innovations regarding war criminals, now had other irons in the political fire. As he turned his attention elsewhere, the test-case option went nowhere.

Three months after the less than halfhearted MacGuigan letter to Kaplan and after MacGuigan's seeming promise of action in return for Congress's patience, nothing was happening. Patience was running out. One Congress leader concluded that politicians and public servants alike were using the political uncertainty in Ottawa to stall. "I am very much concerned," he wrote Harris, "that the issue will be placed in abeyance with the excuse being given that all are concerned with the leadership race within the Liberal party." He suggested that perhaps a public outcry on war criminals could force action or a promise of action out of the Liberal leadership hopefuls precisely because of the political vagaries of the leadership race.[58] Others disagreed. Congress had already learned that public outcries, especially those engineered by the Jewish community, were seldom heard in Ottawa.

In mid-March, as the Liberal leadership campaign continued, it appeared as if Congress's concern was premature. An overly optimistic Solicitor General Kaplan and RCMP Commissioner Simmonds appeared before the Commons Justice Committee. Kaplan indicated that the crown was preparing to move for the denaturalization and deportation of several war criminals against whom sufficient evidence had been gathered. Harris and other Congress leaders were elated. In a rare moment of celebration Harris wrote other key Congress leaders "it appears that we are reaching the successful culmination of an arduous and determined effort by the Canadian Jewish Congress, and its War Criminals Committee and legal Sub-Committee."[59]

However, self-congratulation again proved premature. Kaplan may have been certain he could gather the evidence necessary to go to court, but it was Justice officials who needed to initiate proceedings. What is more, Kaplan's police officials were less certain that the cases were airtight. They felt the dossiers being prepared for the proposed test cases might not hold up in court and requested more time.[60] Harris, who had assured Congress leadership prosecutions were imminent, again wondered what was holding up court proceedings. "With the greatest of respect," one Congress leader wrote Harris, "I think you and I are being diddled, and . . . if there was any loss of credibility, I do not think it should be directed to you or to me."[61] Kaplan felt the heat. Squeezed on one side by Congress and on the other by his less than sympathetic Cabinet colleagues and public servants, Kaplan tried to head off any Jewish community protest. He asked for time. "I know you're impatient. I appreciate forbearance, but criticism would be undesirable."[62]

Harris, however, could only wait so long. He had put his credibility in Congress on the line by accepting MacGuigan's promise at face value. He felt he'd been had, and he was angry. In June he met with Kaplan who again rehashed the advice he had from his legal experts that there was insufficient evidence to move ahead on any one denaturalization and deportation test case. Harris would not be pacified. If cases were weak, government should not throw in the towel. It should go and get the evidence. He requested a joint meeting with the Solicitor General, the Minister of Justice and their respective officials. But in the heat of a leadership race, especially one in which the Minister of Justice was a candidate, no meeting could be arranged immediately.[63]

In late spring of 1984 the Liberals convened their leadership convention. Front-runner John Turner, riding on the crest of national popularity polls, was chosen as new Liberal leader and sworn in as Prime Minister on June 30, 1984. He quickly installed a new cabinet, including a new Minister of Justice.

Liberal supporter Harris hoped to push the issue of war criminals high on the new minister's agenda. He privately and confidentially informed the new minister of the groundwork already done by Congress and the Solicitor General's office, and most importantly, he reminded the minister of his predecessor's "commitment that a test case would be launched against an alleged war criminal who entered this country by lying about his activities during the war." Harris requested a meeting "as soon as possible."[64]

A meeting was arranged, but just days before Harris was scheduled to be in Ottawa, the new Liberal prime minister called a snap federal election. The issue of Nazi war criminals was set aside and barely raised in the popular press during an election in which personality took precedence over issues. In the end, voters delivered a crushing blow to Liberal Party fortunes. It was a Conservative landslide. On September 17, 1984, Prime Minister Brian Mulroney was sworn into office, backed by the largest majority ever awarded a Canadian government.

And what of the war-crimes issue? Congress leaders feared that after years of lobbying the Liberals, of coming preciously close to squeezing possibly precedent-setting court test cases out of them, it might now be necessary to start again from zero. Although Congress leaders had failed to move the previous Liberal government on Jewish issues, at least they had had access to important government ministers and often the Prime Minister. Even during the short-lived Clark government, Jewish community leaders had found a generally open door in Ottawa — at least until Clark stumbled into the Jerusalem embassy fiasco.

The Mulroney government was another matter. There were important Congress leaders who supported the Conservative Party, and Mulroney was also rumoured to have several Jewish friends in Montreal and Toronto with whom he consulted from time to time. But they were not the same people. When Mulroney took office, Congress and leaders of the mainstream Jewish organizations felt themselves without access to the Prime Minister or his key ministers. However, not all Jewish communal leaders were dismayed at the change in government. Like much of the country, a good portion of the Jewish community may have become tired of over two decades of nearly unbroken Liberal rule and begun to creep out of the Liberal corner. Data from a survey of young Jewish leaders in Toronto and Montreal are illustrative. In both cities, a greater number supported the Conservatives than the Liberals in the 1984 elections.[65]

A long-time Congress leader and Conservative supporter wrote to Ottawa requesting appointments with Solicitor General Elmer MacKay and Minister of Justice John Crosbie to discuss the still-pending Nazi war-criminals issue. His request was denied and he was dismissed with a reassurance that the new government was aware of the problem and would look into it in due course. "Over the next few months," responded the Solicitor General, "I will be discussing war criminal matters with my colleague, the Minister of Justice. I will certainly bring your letter and your prior brief on denaturalization and deportation to his attention." For his part, Justice Minister Crosbie noted that "inquiries" were being "undertaken" that might lead to "possible proceedings." Neither minister offered to meet with Congress leaders or showed any awareness of the new priority the Jewish community placed on dealing with the long-festering Nazi war-crimes problem.[66]

But if most Congress leaders felt frozen out of Ottawa, Harris was upset to learn that persons he considered marginal to Canadian Jewish organizational life did meet with government representatives. Congress, Harris wrote to one Jewish Conservative party supporter, "will sooner or later force me to tell our Community in public that this Government has no interest in dealing with representatives of the Canadian Jewish Community on an issue of critical importance to us."

You can imagine our astonishment when we read in the newspaper that Sol Littman, who was representing the American Wiesenthal Institute, met with Mr. MacKay and in the subsequent press conference stated there were at least 3,000 War Criminals living in Canada. I need not tell you the expectations that the number would raise in our Community could not possibly be fulfilled by any Government.

I cannot understand the political wisdom of refusing to meet the representatives of the Canadian Jewish Community, who have the ear of the total Community . . . but would meet with an American organization that has no political standing in Canada.[67]

Sol Littman was not unknown in either the Toronto Jewish community or the larger community. Born and raised in Toronto, he had earned a B.A. in sociology at the University of Toronto and an M.A. in sociology and anthropology at the University of Wisconsin, returning to Toronto to complete a social-work degree in 1952 while working for the B'nai Brith Youth Organization. For the next twenty years Littman was an employee of the B'nai Brith. He moved from the Youth Organization to be regional Anti-Defamation League Director, first in Omaha, Nebraska, then Detroit and New York City. He moved back to Toronto as B'nai Brith Canadian director for several years before his career took another turn. In 1971 he became managing editor of the *Canadian Jewish News*, just reorganized as the Jewish community newspaper.

Littman, charming and soft spoken, could also be unpredictable and headstrong. Some saw him as something less than a team player, one who attracted controversy and kept his own counsel. As a servant of the Jewish community he sometimes bristled at the timid positions taken by the community's lay leadership. Always independent of mind, Littman left Jewish community employ. Now an experienced journalist, he used his considerable writing skills and investigative talents in the service of the CBC, *The Toronto Star* or in freelance writing for other Canadian publications. In December 1982, while he was covering the Rauca trial, he parted company with the CBC but stuck with the trial and in 1983, shortly after Rauca's extradition and death in German custody, Littman wrote *War Criminal on Trial: The Rauca Case*.[68]

Research on the book immersed Littman in the issue of Nazi war criminals in Canada. As a journalist, he had covered the war-criminals story before, but the research he did for the volume convinced him that Rauca was just the tip of the iceberg.[69] His research also brought him into contact with others of a like mind associated with the Simon Wiesenthal Center in Los Angeles. The Center was respectfully named for the famed Nazi-hunter, but according to a Wiesenthal Center spokesman, Wiesenthal had neither administrative responsibility nor policy veto over the organization. The Center was not without Canadian interests. The Los Angeles group was organized and directed by Rabbi Marvin Hier, previously of Vancouver. Hier received much of his seed money and continuing financial support for the Center from wealthy Jewish supporters in western Canada.

According to Littman, the Wiesenthal Center had a paid membership of approximately 3,000 in Canada and was anxious to heighten its Canadian profile. Littman, already deeply concerned with the issue of war criminals in Canada and knowledgeable about both the Jewish community and the workings of the media, became the Center's official Canadian representative in early 1984, just after his book on Rauca was published.[70]

Prior to publication of the book, Littman prepared an article for *Saturday Night*. Drawing largely on his manuscript, he focused on Canadian government complicity in the post-war admission of alleged war criminals into Canada. To illustrate his point, Littman raised the example of the Galicia Division members. They might have been understandably shy about being discussed in an article on Nazi war criminals but they were more concerned at Littman's assertion that Division members had been assigned guard duty at concentration camps and members had participated in putting down the 1943 Warsaw Ghetto uprising, at the cost of thousands of Jewish lives. The Warsaw Ghetto uprising, the veterans pointed out, was over before the Division was even organized. While historians are aware that questions could be asked about the activities of individual Galicia Division members before they volunteered for the SS, Division members protested that their unit was never involved in anti-Jewish actions. The Division veterans filed a libel suit against *Saturday Night*. The offending sentences were not in the final published manuscript of Littman's book which contains the publisher's note, "Material in this book appeared in somewhat different form in *Saturday Night* magazine."[71]

Littman pressed on. Even before he became Canadian representative of the California-based Simon Wiesenthal Center, Littman also began researching a more comprehensive volume on Canada and the Nazi warcriminals problem. Solicitor General Kaplan, perhaps hoping anything Littman might eventually publish would further sensitize public opinion, put Littman under a short-term contract to gather research data on Nazi war criminals in Canada. But while Littman was under contract to Kaplan's department, his research possibilities were limited. He was not permitted to see the dossiers on those alleged war criminals against whom Kaplan hoped test prosecutions could be brought, nor was he allowed access to RCMP files or other materials restricted to researchers from outside government.[72]

Littman and the Simon Wiesenthal Center he represented were clearly outside the national umbrella of the Canadian Jewish Congress. The election of a Conservative government in December 1984, which left Congress out in the cold, provided an opening for Littman. Even as Congress representatives requested and were denied a meeting with Prime Minister Mulroney's new solicitor general, Elmer MacKay, Sol Littman, cloaked in the mantle of Wiesenthal's name, requested and was granted a meeting with the minister. As Congress looked on in amazement Littman, accompanied by several spokesmen for the California-based organization, arrived in Ottawa.

The meeting, Littman recalled, was cordial and frank. He was, however, uninformed at the time about Congress's long record of lobbying a reluctant government on the issue of Nazi war criminals in Canada and unaware that several test cases needed only ministerial approval to be taken to court. The Center pressed its own agenda. Littman later confirmed that the test cases on which Congress had pinned so much hope did not come up in the discussion. The minister reassured the Wiesenthal Center delegation that he was sympathetic to their concern.[73]

Littman had alerted the media that members of the Wiesenthal Center would be meeting with MacKay. The press were waiting when Littman and company emerged from the minister's office. The press wanted a good news story, and Littman had one for them. Littman asserted that at least 1,000 Nazi war criminals were alive and well in Canada and repeated his demand that something be done. With seeming access to the new government, Littman was suddenly the darling of the press when it came to war criminals. The media dubbed Littman, like Wiesenthal, a Nazi-hunter.

Littman was again in Ottawa several weeks after his initial meeting with the Solicitor General when he received an urgent telephone call from the Simon Wiesenthal Center's California headquarters. The Center had obtained documents under American freedom of information legislation indicating, among other things, that in 1962 a Dr Joseph Menke had applied to the Canadian embassy in Buenos Aires for admission to Canada. His request, Littman was informed, was referred to the Canadian visa control office in Cologne which, in turn, requested information on Menke from American intelligence authorities in Europe. According to the documentation, Canadian authorities were advised that

Joseph Menke was a known alias used by the notorious Dr Josef Mengele, the wanted Nazi war criminal who conducted barbaric medical experiments on inmates at the Auschwitz concentration camp.

Littman tried to follow up the information. He checked with both the Canadian Immigration Service and the RCMP. Neither divulged any record of the Menke application or whether or not the application had been rejected. Athough he had little to go on, Littman concluded that Menke and Mengele were one and the same and could not ignore the possibility that the mass murderer had actually come to Canada. He wrote to the Prime Minister on December 20, 1984, using Wiesenthal Center stationery, and also sent a copy of the letter to the Minister of Justice.

In his letter Littman offered little doubt that Mengele had indeed tried to enter Canada. "This," he cautioned the Prime Minister, "leaves us with the frightening possibility that Mengele may actually be living in Canada today." On behalf of the Simon Wiesenthal Center, Littman demanded a release of all documentation and "an immediate investigation, ordered at the highest level" into the Mengele affair.

> The dimension of Mengele's crimes, and the legacy of his 400,000 victims, demand that no stone remain unturned in the quest to bring this man, who is the personification of evil, before the bar of justice. Only a thorough investigation ordered by your government can ascertain what role Canada played in the bizarre case of Joseph Mengele.[74]

While Littman awaited a reply, a second meeting with MacKay was hastily arranged at which Littman raised the Mengele story. MacKay was not particularly moved by the Mengele revelations, but, Littman recalled, the minister again hinted that something was in the offing. He refused to be more specific.

Almost four weeks after sending Mulroney his letter, Littman was informed by the Wiesenthal Center that

The New York Times now had the file from which Mengele's alleged Canadian connection had been pulled. Rather than have the Canadian angle get lost in a larger *New York Times* story, Littman called a press conference in Toronto for January 20. He told reporters he would reveal the contents of his letter to Mulroney.[75] He also filled in *The New York Times* on his Mengele accusations.[76]

The media smelled a good story. As Littman later learned, *Maclean's* magazine, jumping the gun, phoned the Prime Minister's Office, which was taken by surprise. Not only did the PMO not reveal what was in the letter, they also seemed never to have heard of it. A mad scramble to find the letter ensued. It had apparently been misplaced in the wave of Christmas greetings that flooded the PMO during holiday week. Just before his scheduled press conference began, Littman was summoned to the phone. According to Littman, a Mulroney aide apologized for the delay in answering the now-located letter. It was hinted that Littman should postpone his press conference until after the Prime Minister could consider the letter's content, but Littman refused. He released his letter and the accompanying documentation to the press. The story made headlines across Canada the following Monday and was also carried in *The New York Times*.[77]

The flurry of media controversy generated by the Mengele story caught the PMO off guard. Stumbling around for an appropriate response — a response that would keep the Mulroney government on the side of the angels, distance it from accusations of indifference to the Nazi war-criminals question being levelled against the Trudeau Liberals, and perhaps grant the new government time for cooling off while appearing to take decisive action — Mulroney latched upon the idea of a judicial inquiry. On February 7, 1985, the government announced that Quebec Superior Court Justice Jules Deschênes had agreed to conduct an inquiry into the presence of Nazi war criminals in Canada, including

Mengele, and to determine if any remedy existed in Canadian law to deal with them.

Why did the Prime Minister do it? There is an obvious one-to-one link between Littman's Mengele accusations and the formation of the Deschênes Commission. But in retrospect one can rightly argue that concern over the Mengele story was less the cause of the Deschênes Commission than it was the excuse for it. Mulroney was already predisposed to act on the issue of war criminals in Canada. The Mengele episode determined the timing and, to some degree, the format of Mulroney's initiative.

Mulroney's readiness to respond to the subject of Nazi war criminals in Canada after forty years of Liberal inaction was partly out of personal conviction. Mulroney may have been responding on a Jewish issue out of fondness for his Jewish friends. Following his 1976 defeat for the Conservative leadership at the hands of Joe Clark, Mulroney was said to be at a low point. According to one insider, it was at that time that the "WASP establishment turned their back on" the Irish Catholic of modest social origins, while Jewish friends and supporters remained steadfast. His friends may never have mentioned the war-crimes issue to him, but Mulroney may well have been pleased to offer them a gift for their loyalty.[78] Mulroney, the plucky boy from Baie Comeau, saw himself as an underdog; in that respect he identified with Jews. By striking a blow against Nazi war criminals, he was perhaps asserting a commitment to fair play, taking a swipe at bullies everywhere.[79]

It is, perhaps, this background which also helped shape Mulroney's reaction to the Rauca extradition hearings. Several of those close to him indicate Mulroney was personally upset by the extradition proceedings. He was reportedly offended both by the magnitude of Rauca's crimes and the very idea that Rauca and perhaps other Nazi murderers should have been allowed to live peaceful and undisturbed lives in Canada, seemingly beyond the reach of justice.[80]

Yet if Mulroney was privately sensitive to the issue of Nazi war criminals in Canada, this did not mean that he was fully aware of Canadian Jewry's campaign to win government action on this issue or that he had his own plan to deal with war criminals. As a fledgling leader of the opposition he had met with a Congress delegation, but his conversations with it were not specific and ended with his pledging vague support for action against Nazi war criminals should he ever come to power. But no promises were demanded or made. Mulroney did not strike Milton Harris, the head of the delegation, as being particularly well briefed on the legal or political niceties of the issue.[81] Thus, if the Conservative leader was sympathetic to action on the issue of Nazi war criminals, he was most certainly not subject to any ongoing Jewish community lobbying effort. His Jewish friends were not, it seems, plugged into the leadership of Congress or other major Jewish organizations. Congress and especially its Montreal headquarters may well have been seen as controlled by pro-Liberal party supporters. Nor was Mulroney's sympathy informed by a detailed understanding of the legal controversy or information on the promised test cases which were still pending when the 1984 federal election was called. It was not an election issue. No Conservative election promises were made regarding Nazi war criminals and the party emerged victorious "with no fixed private or public position."[82]

When the Mengele story broke, Mulroney was obviously taken by surprise. But he instinctively grasped at this opportunity to right what he had already concluded was a shameful wrong.[83] A political warhorse, Mulroney was certainly not unmindful that there were also political points to be scored. The Jewish vote in Montreal and Toronto had proven more fluid in the 1984 election than was previously the case. If taking the morally high ground on the issue of war criminals won the Conservative Party added support in Jewish circles, why not? And who could argue against flushing out Nazi war criminals? Taking decisive action on the war-crimes issue would certainly show the Conservative government as more responsive to a public outcry against Nazi war criminals than the previous Liberal government had proven during several decades of almost unbroken rule.[84]

Content his course was morally right and politically astute, Mulroney allegedly acted without consultation — not even with Jewish leaders, not with his caucus, not with close colleagues and certainly not with the public service. There were those in the caucus, especially from western Canada or from ridings with a heavy eastern European flavour, who might have welcomed an opportunity to discuss the political implications of the Prime Minister's thrust. They were not asked.

What is more, there is no evidence Mulroney consulted his Cabinet, not even those with portfolios touched by the Prime Minister's initiative. One key Mulroney aide was "not aware of any significant consultation" by the Prime Minister with Cabinet on this question. The issue of war criminals in Canada, the aide allowed, was "one of those cases where the Prime Minister, as he often does, short-circuited the system and said there will be an inquiry and an inquiry now."[85]

Mulroney may have been tempted to keep his own counsel, in part, because he wanted the initiative to be seen as his own — not that of the key ministers who would be directly involved. Two of these were old political adversaries. The Ottawa rumour mill spoke of cool distance between the Prime Minister and both the then Minister of Justice, John Crosbie, and Minister of External Affairs, Joe Clark. Both Crosbie and Clark had earlier challenged Mulroney's drive for party leadership. It is doubtful either was among the Prime Minister's confidantes and at least not when it came to action against Nazi war criminals, although it is conceivable that some political advisers in the Justice Department may have played a role.

If Mulroney cut himself off from his ministers, he seemed equally distant and perhaps untrusting of key public servants with experience on the war-crimes issue. In the politically messy atmosphere of post-election Ottawa, tension between the new prime minister and a sea of public servants with years of service to the preceding Liberal government was unavoidable. Talk of public-service shakeups, purges of Liberal loyalists and efforts by the PMO to ride roughshod over the public service were common. Whether out of lack of trust or because Mulroney had already concluded that public servants had little to offer except excuses for years of Liberal inaction, those who had previously advised the government on war criminals, including some in the Justice Department, seemingly had no input. Had caucus, ministers or public servants been systematically consulted they might have raised legal, political or evidential questions. The Low Report might have been discussed. Justice officials might have notified the Prime Minister about existing dossiers on suspected war criminals which were all but ready to go to trial. None of this seems to have happened. Unencumbered by tempering advice, offended by forty years of government inaction, convinced of the rightness of his course and apparently working only with his immediate office staff, the Prime Minister initiated the Deschênes Commission.

On February 7, 1985 the Commission was announced. The caucus and Cabinet were surprised. Some huddled together discussing the political fallout which might result. Congress leaders reacted with disbelief. They had never pressed for a Deschênes-like inquiry. They had not gotten close enough to Mulroney or his cabinet to press them on anything. While the Mulroney initiative was welcomed publicly, Jewish leaders privately were very uneasy. They did not know what Mulroney was up to. What about the long-awaited and some felt promised test cases? Were they a dead issue? It seemed as if years of Congress lobbying had been to no effect. They had been so close to prosecutions and now all they had was a commission which might take everything back to ground zero. Whatever was said publicly, Congress insiders saw the announcement of the Deschênes Commission as a major setback for their campaign. They thought it had been a failure.[86]

Milton Harris, President of the Canadian Jewish Congress, certainly felt frustrated. Had he not made a deal with the previous Liberal government to proceed into court against several suspected Nazi war criminals? Now the new Conservative government ignored both the agreement and the leadership of the Canadian Jewish Congress. Instead they flirted with Sol Littman and the California-based Simon Wiesenthal Center. The result was not court proceedings against actual Nazi war criminals but a commission of inquiry "to conduct . . . investigations regarding alleged war criminals in Canada."[87] Surely, Jewish leaders lamented, the government was ignoring the obvious if it failed to prosecute Nazis it knew about and, instead, set out to rediscover what it already knew — that there were Nazis in Canada.

In a hurried press release the day of the Deschênes Commission announcement, Harris seemed testy. The government, he said, "must do more than merely have an inquiry into Nazi war criminals in Canada." It must act, and act soon. Was the Deschênes Commission an alternative to prosecution or a precursor to it? "If this inquiry represents the total action the government wants to take, we don't accept that, and we assume that the Canadian people do not accept that either."[88]

Whatever Harris was promised or thought he had been promised by the Liberals was now history. The Deschênes Commission was the government's policy and its only policy. There would be no test cases during the Deschênes process. All that remained to be determined was how the Quebec Superior Court Justice would carry out his mandate, his proposed *modus operandi* and what input would be expected or allowed from interested parties. Congress had no option. It fell into line.

Canadian Jewish Congress officials began culling their archives and files in preparation for the brief they expected to present to Deschênes. Nor were they alone.

For some time the mass membership B'nai Brith and the Canadian Jewish Congress, umbrella organization of Canadian Jewry, had not always seen eye to eye. There had long been turf battles between the two. B'nai Brith portrayed itself as a populist organization in contrast to a timid "establishment" Congress. Congress, in turn, stressed its professionalism and legitimate role as the Parliament of Canadian Jewry.

Some Jewish leaders harboured fears the Deschênes Commission would choke off any hope of real government initiative against Nazi war criminals. Ukrainian leaders may have had different concerns. Many Ukrainian Canadians, especially post-World War II immigrants and their children, were alarmed lest the Deschênes Commission degenerate into a wholesale assault on the good name and integrity of the Ukrainian community in Canada. A belief that Sol Littman, already suspect for his charges against the Galicia Division, was the prime mover behind Mulroney's decision to appoint the Commission only strengthened that view. In the splash of media attention accompanying Littman's Mengele revelations and the announcement of the Deschênes Commission, the Canadian "Nazi-hunter" had held the spotlight. The media and some in government too often failed to distinguish the California-based Simon Wiesenthal Center, which Littman represented in Canada, from the separate and distinct Vienna-based operations of Simon Wiesenthal. Similarly, some in the Ukrainian community could no longer distinguish Sol Littman the determined crusader from Sol Littman the personification of all that threatened their community.

Only two days after the government's announcement of the Commission, Simon Wiesenthal was interviewed on Israeli radio. In a report carried by Canadian Press, he was said to have charged that "218 former Ukrainian officers of Hitler's s.s. (elite guard), which ran death camps in Eastern Europe, are living in Canada." Before long, copies of Wiesenthal's Vienna Documentation Center *Annual Report* for 1984 circulated through press and Ukrainian-Canadian community circles. In it

Wiesenthal stated he had submitted "a list of 218 s.s. officers who had been volunteers of the Ukrainian s.s. division and of general s.s. formations" to Canadian authorities. *The Globe and Mail* reached Littman for comment, and in a front-page article, he reportedly supported Wiesenthal's charges that members of Ukrainian ss units had entered Canada after the war. Indeed, as Littman explained, his organization, armed with a copy of Wiesenthal's list and using only the local telephone directory, easily located twenty-eight of those named, of whom fourteen were "validated." The juxtaposition of Littman's seeming influence in arranging the Commission and his role as Wiesenthal's agent shook some in the Ukrainian community. Was he only hunting Nazi war criminals, or was he hunting Ukrainians?

Estimates of the number of war criminals or "war criminals and collaborators" in Canada, most said to be from eastern Europe, continued to pop up in the press. Littman was most often associated with the number 3,000. The press did not challenge his head count.[89]

Among some Ukrainian Canadians, Littman was now a bogeyman. What, they wondered, was his real agenda? Was his charge that there were thousands of eastern European war criminals in Canada also implying that the larger Ukrainian-Canadian community harboured these criminals? Certainly they suspected his motives. And whom did he really represent? After all, were these not exactly the kind of charges, if they stuck, that would benefit the Soviet campaign to delegitimize the Ukrainian nationalist struggle for a free, independent and non-Communist Ukrainian homeland? Could the Jews be in league with the Soviets? For dyed-in-the wool post-war Ukrainian nationalists this made sense. Canada was not the centre of their psychic universe. They remained dedicated to the liberation of the homeland. The war-criminal accusations seemed obviously designed to hurt their cause.

The post-war nationalist camp was most entrenched in Toronto — less so in western Canada. In western Canada the critical mass of pre-war Ukrainian Canadians was large enough to partly deflect the onslaught of the post-war nationalist political agenda. In southern Ontario and Quebec nationalists dominated. One astute observer of the Ukrainian-Canadian scene noted that in western Canada, those of the DP generation who wished to be part of the Ukrainian mainstream "assimilated" into the dominant Ukrainian-Canadian world. In eastern Canada the post-war nationalists were the mainstream. So much so, he explained, that in Toronto even transplanted Canadian-born Ukrainians from the west had to adopt the mind set of the post-war arrivals if they wished to participate in community affairs.[90]

But even in the east, unity was absent. The political infighting between various factions of the nationalist camp and disputes over control of the Ukrainian Canadian Committee prevented the flowering of a truly representative national umbrella organization. Each faction jealously guarded its own autonomy, relegating the central body, the UCC, to plod along with neither authority nor resources.

Anti-Soviet fears may have been more pronounced in eastern Canada, but an anti-Soviet world view was an accepted tenet of faith among many in the Ukrainian community across Canada. Nor was this simple paranoia. Ukrainian nationalists, religious leaders and political dissidents faced harassment and incarceration in Gulag prisons or psychiatric institutions for their views. Ukrainian prisoners often languished side by side with Jewish prisoners of conscience. In the Ukrainian diaspora, many were convinced Soviet agents were intent on discrediting those who had called attention to Soviet abuse. But for some the single-mindedness of this anti-Sovietism drew them into a world view filled with dark shadows, conspiracies and ulterior motives. It is, however, with this frame of mind that some in the Ukrainian community approached the Deschênes Commission.

Some were already on edge regarding alleged Nazi war-criminal accusations. The mainstream Ukrainian-Canadian press repeatedly attacked the American OSI as, at best, an unwitting dupe of the Soviet Union. Others went further. They were convinced the Soviet Union was secretly behind the war-crimes charges against members of the Ukrainian-American community. What better way to discredit the Ukrainian nationalist cause in the United States than to tar its supporters as unreconstructed Nazi collaborators? And if the Soviets were behind the spate of accusations of Ukrainian Nazi atrocities, how could evidence supplied by the Soviet Union be anything but tainted? Indeed, why all the sudden American interest in Nazi war criminals so many years after the fact if the real agenda, a Soviet agenda, was not to delegitimize the cause of Ukrainian and other anti-Soviet nationalist groups?

Thankfully, Canada seemed different. For forty years Canadian authorities had given little or no sign that they would fall into the Soviet trap — this from successive Liberal governments which were otherwise none too friendly to the Ukrainian nationalist cause. When the Mulroney Conservatives came to power there seemed even less to worry about. Ukrainian Canadians were, in the main, longtime Tory supporters and the Tories knew it. What is more, the Conservatives had generally pledged support for the anti-Soviet stance of Ukrainian and other dispossessed minority groups. Several people of eastern European descent were key players in the Mulroney cabinet and prominent in caucus. If there was little to worry about with the Liberals, surely there was nothing to worry about with the Conservatives.

The Deschênes Commission surprised many Ukrainian Canadians. Added to their sudden anxiety the supposed role of Sol Littman and Vienna's Simon Wiesenthal, both regarded as less than friendly to Ukrainian Canadians, and community anxiety grew more intense. But even as Ukrainian leaders weighed their options, one thing remained clear — the Soviet Union stood to gain most from a Ukrainian witch-hunt. Rumours of secret plots grew in credibility with each repetition. Talk of conspiracy was heard. For example, Soviet agents in the PMO had paved the way for the

Deschênes Commission. Littman and Wiesenthal were either Soviet agents or their mindless dupes. And most bizarre of all, some felt Jewish pressure on western governments to prosecute Nazi war criminals was part of a secret deal hammered out between Edgar Bronfman, President of the World Jewish Congress, and the Soviets. Accordingly, in exchange for the Soviet release of Anatoly Scharansky and easing restrictions on Jewish emigration, Jewish organizations would do all in their power to discredit Ukrainian nationalists as nothing less than a pack of Nazi war criminals.[91]

On the other hand, the appointment of the Deschênes Commission was generally greeted with favour by the popular press. An editorial in the *Winnipeg Free Press* was typical. The Commission, the *Free Press* insisted, was long overdue, and it was hoped that it would finally lay to rest painful doubts one Canadian citizen might harbour about the wartime activities of another. "The accusation that hurts most is that criminals are going unpunished because Canada has not tried. By creating the Commission, Canada is at least making an effort."[92]

The media may have applauded the creation of the Deschênes Commission but it aggravated Ukrainian anxieties by raising the profile of Littman as an authority on the war-criminals issue in Canada. As the then president of the UCC recalled, telephones in UCC offices across Canada did not stop ringing. Individuals complained of alleged slurs, press distortion and anti-Ukrainian incidents. They demanded the UCC do something and do it fast. The Deschênes Commission, some warned, would become a showcase for anti-Ukrainian slander. The community must defend itself now before it was too late.[93]

First off the mark in public defence of the community was the UCC office in Edmonton. On February 13, 1985 it issued a press release decrying "vaguely formulated charges that give rise to innuendos against entire communities of people." Any accusations against the Division came in for special comment.

In view of the Ukrainian experience during the
Second World War it is understandable that recent
allegations concerning the presence of Ukrainian
war criminals in Canada have aroused a great deal
of concern in the Ukrainian community. We
strongly oppose vaguely formulated accusations.
We insist that those making allegations be fully in
command of the historical facts and make their
charges as specific as possible in order to avoid
damaging entire communities.[94]

The next day, Valentine's Day, the UCC National Executive in Winnipeg issued a separate press release prepared in Toronto several days earlier. Over bread and
cold cuts, several Toronto lawyers and community leaders had gathered in the office of Yaroslaw Botiuk, legal
adviser to the Galicia Division veterans' organization.
They carefully prepared a draft statement affirming support for the Deschênes initiative and endorsed the prosecution of war criminals "in Canadian courts to the full
extent of Canadian Law." However, the statement demanded an immediate end to "erroneous and
inflammatory reports that have appeared in the Canadian media." The release protested that Ukrainian Canadians had been "slandered," the memory of
Ukrainians who had suffered in the war "besmirched,"
while press reports only served to promote "social and
ethnic intolerance against the Ukrainians."[95]

In an effort to show that Littman had a history of unwarranted attacks on the Division, even predating his
Saturday Night article, the UCC press release appended
an August 1980 Toronto *Sunday Star* clipping. The clipping was a "correction" to a story by Sol Littman run
two months earlier which raised the name of the Division in connection with the search for Nazi war criminals in Canada. In its published apology *The Sunday
Star* described the reference as an "unwarranted connection" and regretted "any embarrassment to veterans
of the division now resident in Canada."[96]

On the day of the Winnipeg press release, Toronto Ukrainian spokesmen held a press conference at the Royal York Hotel, chaired by Orest Rudzik, lawyer and past president of the Toronto UCC. Several speakers demanded that the alleged organized campaign against their community must stop. According to *The Globe and Mail*, Rudzik spoke out against the media "for repeating Mr. Littman's assertion that the war criminals are Ukrainian." The press kit included a brief synopsis of the Galicia Division's history exonerating the Division of any crime.[97]

Alex Epstein, who had earlier tried to promote Jewish-Ukrainian dialogue, echoed Ukrainian concern. Epstein, in a letter to the Canadian Jewish Congress, explained that many Ukrainians then saw Sol Littman as leading a concerted attack on their community and its organizations. Although Epstein himself knew full well that Littman did not speak for Congress, he pointed out that many Ukrainians and other eastern Europeans believed that he did. He suggested, therefore, that Congress publicize the fact that Littman was not their spokesman.[98] Congress's reply was short and to the point.

As you indicated, Mr. Sol Littman is the official representative, in Canada, of the Simon Wiesenthal Center of Los Angeles, and is not a spokesman for Canadian Jewish Congress.[99]

The fact remained, however, that a larger-than-life Sol Littman was widely identified among Ukrainians as a spokesman for the Canadian Jewish community. Even if he was not an "official" spokesman for the Canadian Jewish Congress leadership, he was thought by some to be their stalking horse, saying what they believed but were too timid to say publicly. Imagining that Jewish organizational life was both hierarchical and well disciplined, it was difficult for some Ukrainian leaders to believe Congress could not call off Littman if it so wished. Since Littman continued to attract media attention, some Ukrainians assumed he was encouraged to do so by Canadian Jewish leadership.[100] What is more, with the continuing confusion in name between the California-based Simon Wiesenthal Center and Simon Wiesenthal's own Vienna-based Documentation Center, it was also incorrectly assumed that Littman was operating hand in glove with the Vienna Nazi-hunter.

Among those who challenged Wiesenthal were some intemperate voices. During a Ukrainian-language broadcast over radio station CHIN in Toronto, Father Myron Stasiw, a veteran of the Division, read a lengthy commentary originally published in a local Ukrainian-language newspaper. The commentary, with which Father Stasiw said he agreed, charged that Wiesenthal — and all those who supported him — were motivated by a hatred of Ukrainians. Rather than attack Ukrainians, the commentary demanded, they should clean their own houses of Jews who collaborated with the Nazis against their own brothers. The commentary read by the priest then proceeded to list wrongs Jews had allegedly committed against their Ukrainian neighbours. If the broadcast received no rebuke from the organized Ukrainian community, it did not go unnoticed by some in the Jewish community.[101]

In an interview granted to a Ukrainian newspaper several weeks after his broadcast, Father Stasiw explained why he and thousands like him had enlisted in the Division. They were, he recounted, patriots who had enlisted to battle for a free and non-Communist Ukraine. They were not Nazis. "His voice husky and firm," the priest disclaimed anything to do with "anti-Semitic activities."

Referring to the radio commentary, Father Stasiw denied it was an attack on Jews and considered it mild in tone, compared to Wiesenthal who was repeatedly caught "attacking Ukrainians and the division." Nevertheless, as a result of Father Stasiw's broadcast, the newspaper reported, "threats of legal action" were made against CHIN's owner.

Father Myron Stasiw is a bewildered man, a man who wonders why this matter [of Nazi war criminals] was resurrected after all these years. "Who is gaining by it?" he asks impatiently. Ukrainians are, says Stasiw, "scapegoats." He feels that those responsible for crimes committed during WWII should be tried and brought to justice.

As we [the interviewer and photographer] leave his crowded office, Stasiw smiles and firmly shakes our hands.

"You have to defend your rights."[102]

Provocation, however, is in the eye of the beholder. Some Ukrainian students at the University of Toronto were infuriated by a lengthy article entitled "A Blind Eye to Murder: National Socialist War Criminals in Canada," published in a University of Toronto student newspaper. The February 1985 article painted a picture of a post-war Canada, immigration barriers lowered, welcoming tens of thousands of Displaced Persons including many Ukrainians. "A sizable minority of the refugee population," the article asserted, " . . . was composed of Nazi collaborators, former ss men and concentration camp personnel, and members of the mobile killing units (*Einsatzgruppen*) that roamed German held territories in the East exterminating the Jewish population."

While it would be a gross injustice to tarnish the reputations of entire ethnic groups now in Canada by over-emphasizing the crimes committed by a minority of their countrymen, evidence presented during the Nuremberg War Crimes Trials clearly demonstrated that the Nazis found many willing accomplices in the Baltic, Ukrainian and Byelorussian populations.[103]

In spite of the author's explicit denials of any intent
to defame specific groups, Ukrainian-Canadian students
on campus felt the article once again tied the Nazi can
to the Ukrainian community tail. Why would the author
lump Ukrainians and the Nuremberg Trial together unless he wanted to give the impression that the Ukrainian diaspora was implicated in the crimes against Jews?
If this was the intent of the article, a response was in
order. But what? The University Ukrainian Student Association invited Yury Boshyk, a moderate community
member and sessional assistant professor in the Slavic
Studies Department, to discuss the issue. All agreed
that a response in kind could only lead to further
"provocations." Better to battle slander with scholarship. The students agreed to help Boshyk organize a
day-long symposium on Ukraine during World War II
and its aftermath, including the Nazi war-crimes controversy. The time line was tight. The conference was
scheduled for Saturday, March 2, 1985, less than a
month away.[104]

Funds were raised, publicity organized and presenters
contacted. A Jewish viewpoint was thought essential,
especially as discussion focused on current events. A
spokesman from the American Jewish Committee accepted an invitation to speak but, at the last moment,
could not come. Matas, who had also been invited, did
participate. Invitations announcing the symposium were
also sent to leading Jewish organizations, but as the
event fell on Saturday, the Sabbath, Jewish organizations could have no official representation. Given the
distance between the two communities, it is unlikely
that the symposium would have gathered much official
Jewish participation even if it had been scheduled on a
different day of the week.[105]

Aside from Matas, most of the presenters were either
prominent American and Canadian spokesmen against
the OSI and OSI-type operations in Canada or academics, mostly Canadians of Ukrainian descent. They addressed various historical or current subjects dealing

with wartime Ukraine. This included the situation of the Jews.

Symposium attendance was well beyond the planners' expectations. The audience was heavy with senior members of the Ukrainian community but not without a strong contingent of younger community members. Ben Kayfetz, recently retired from the Canadian Jewish Congress staff, attended out of personal interest. When he arrived at St Vladimir Institute on the western edge of the University of Toronto campus punctually at 9:00 in the morning, the scheduled start of the symposium, the Institute auditorium was already packed. He was "diverted to the overflow room which was equipped with three closed-circuit TV screens. The attendance was nearly 700 or 800."

Kayfetz stayed riveted to his chair for nine hours. He kept detailed notes as speaker after speaker addressed the wartime Ukraine experience. None denied Jewish suffering or the complicity of individual Ukrainians. But a distinction was made between complicity of individuals and wholesale participation in or support from the Nazi murder of Jews by the larger Ukrainian population or their organizations. As speakers acknowledged the incomparability of the terror inflicted on Jews, they reminded their audience that Ukrainians were also victims, victims of both Nazis and Soviets. Speakers were equally at pains to distance the Ukrainian people as a whole from those individual Ukrainians who found a place in the Nazi-organized "auxiliary police who worked with the S.S. in the ghettos and death camps." These individuals, one speaker explained, "were drawn from the lowest and criminal elements among Ukrainians. Such elements being present in every society." Indeed, if speakers downplayed the issue of collaboration, they repeatedly stressed efforts by Ukrainians to save Jews, most notably the work of Metropolitan Sheptytsky whom Kayfetz acknowledged as "truly one of the *chassidei umot ha'alam*" or righteous gentiles.

Kayfetz left the symposium before the more politically charged evening session on the OSI and other more current war-criminals matters began. Even so, he had heard enough to submit a ten-page memorandum of observations and comments to CJC leaders. Kayfetz was impressed by the size, organization and drama of the event. He was far less taken with the content of the speeches. Well read in the history of Ukraine during World War II, including Yiddish-language materials, Kayfetz wondered if Ukrainian involvement with the Nazi machine had received full review and if "there were certain matters that were not dealt with or dealt with inadequately." For example, he could find no assessment of Ukrainian public attitudes towards Jews, attitudes which might have influenced some Ukrainians to participate in the Nazis' murderous campaign against the Jews.[106]

The emotional electricity which charged the symposium gripped the audience. The chairman at the sessions tried to keep a lid on public outbursts, not always to the pleasure of the assembly. True, there were very few echoes of Father Stasiw's more extreme views. Nevertheless, one woman expressed disappointment that spontaneous applause during one speaker's controversial presentation of a paper entitled "Ukrainian-Jewish Relations During the Soviet and Nazi Occupations" was cut short by the chairman. The paper which, among other things, touched on Jewish co-operation with the Soviet occupation and Ukrainian efforts to save Jews during the Nazi years was, she noted, worth cheering, and heartfelt outbursts from the audience should be recognized, not stilled.[107]

By and large, however, the symposium was judged a great success. Most of the papers were edited and published by the Canadian Institute of Ukrainian Studies, and a scholarly examination of Ukraine during World War II was issued. The community found comfort in the knowledge that they had a case to make.

But the symposium offered more than reassurance. It was a catalyst to action. During the breaks between sessions the corridors were filled with talk about Deschênes and the need for organization — the momentum of the day must not be lost; now was the time to organize a defence committee not just to deal with what were seen as anti-Ukrainian attacks in the press and elsewhere but to protect Ukrainian interests before the Deschênes Commission.

Riding a wave of enthusiasm, the local UCC announced a meeting of interested parties for the following Friday evening at the office of the Ukrainian Credit Union. What would the meeting discuss? One option was already on the community table. Lubomyr Luciuk, who had recently completed a Ph.D. on Ukrainian DP immigration to Canada, had presented the UCC with his draft proposal for a Research and Documentation Group which would document the Ukrainian historical experience and make findings available to the public. His budget called for just under $80,000 per year.[108]

The group convened around a large table was symbolically split between the younger and Canadian-born at one end and the older immigrant generation at the other. One participant recalled that there was no fixed agenda and discussion rambled. The meeting did not spend much time on specifics like Luciuk's proposal. All agreed research was desirable but it would cost money which they did not have. Gathering money would take organization and organization was also a commodity in short supply. But it was agreed that in the atmosphere of community crisis the meeting should constitute itself a working committee. It was also agreed that whatever final form the new committee took, it must have a Canadian face and reflect Canadian issues. The key issue was defence of the Ukrainian-Canadian community and its good name. The postwar immigrant generation — those most immediately touched by the cloud of accusations hanging over the community — must keep a low profile.[109]

Two days later a small Toronto deputation was in Winnipeg to put the new committee's plans before the UCC National Executive. The Executive, already battered by grass-roots demands for decisive action in defence of the community, welcomed the Toronto initiative, and legitimized the group as a formal committee of the UCC. At a regular Executive meeting a week later the endorsement was made official.[110]

The new committee needed a name. Back in Toronto insiders rejected several suggestions including Canadian Friends of Due Process, a simple Canadianization of the key American anti-OSI lobbying group. They finally agreed on the Civil Liberties Commission of the Ukrainian Canadian Committee (CLC).[111] The UCC Director in Toronto approached several prominent community members to chair the new CLC, but each declined in turn. Finally John Gregorovich became the reluctant groom. The Alberta-born Gregorovich, a lawyer with Ford of Canada and a stalwart of Toronto's organized Ukrainian community, was part of the inner circle which pulled the CLC together. Then President of the Ukrainian Professional and Business Club of Toronto, Gregorovich had originally set his sights no higher than overseeing the Committee's legal activities. However, with no other candidates willing to take on the responsibility, Gregorovich accepted the position and decided to make the best of it.[112]

The early days of the CLC's existence smacked of amateurishness and a trial-and-error approach to problems. That was unavoidable. Unlike the Canadian Jewish Congress, the Ukrainian Canadian Committee in Toronto had little viable administrative infrastructure and certainly none it could offer the CLC. Nor was there a community tradition of fundraising necessary to support the full-fledged effort. On the local level, especially in western Canada, a Ukrainian corporate infrastructure was slowly emerging. But, in the main, when confronted by a national challenge, the Ukrainian community had no experienced mechanism in place and ready to respond. This seems as true for the national office of the UCC in Winnipeg as for the new headquarters of the scrappy and single-issue CLC.[113]

Thus, the CLC began from scratch. With more enthusiasm than experience Gregorovich assembled space, equipment and volunteers to set up an office. A telephone line was installed; letterhead paper was ordered. Gregorovich pulled together a grand organizational chart, replete with subcommittees responsible for fundraising, public relations, research, legal issues and coordination of community political action. As laid out on paper, each subcommittee would report back to an executive committee headquartered in Toronto but with representation from Ukrainian communities across Canada. But what looked good on paper was not easily converted into a working structure.[114]

Fundraising and outreach, assuring community members "the recent unsubstantiated accusations in the media regarding the harbouring of war criminals in the Ukrainian Canadian community" were being attacked head on, were priorities. A statement of goals was widely circulated to Ukrainian communities across Canada.

1. To take a public stand against slanderous allegations which have resulted in the defamation of all Canadians of Ukrainian descent.

2. To represent the Ukrainian community at the [Deschênes] Commission of Inquiry on War Criminals.

3. To show that membership in the Ukrainian Insurgent Army, the First Division, Ukrainian National Army and the Ukrainian Nationalists is not proof of participation in war crimes as these organizations [sic] purpose and operations were to advance the cause of Ukrainian freedom.

4. To prevent the use of Soviet evidence in Canadian Courts against Canadians.

5. To require that any Canadian accused of war crimes be tried not in a civil court but in a criminal court of law where stricter proof of guilt is required.

6. To extend the terms of reference of the Deschênes Commission to include all criminals against humanity, past and present.[115]

The CLC Community Action Committee kicked off the campaign. It planned to bombard federal members of parliament, the Prime Minister and relevant cabinet ministers with citizens' letters of concern about the Deschênes Commission. To "help defend the good name of Canadians of Ukrainian origin" against media allegations which "have begun to blacken the name of our Community," pre-printed postcards were made available and sample protest letters were circulated. Local Ukrainian groups were also encouraged to lobby their MPs "face to face."[116]

But who would pay the bills? Lubomyr Luciuk, now chairman of the CLC subcommittee on research, had not lost his grand vision. He presented a "minimum annual budget" of almost $100,000 per year for as many years as was necessary to initiate a program of information retrieval and publication. The executive reserved judgment on the scale of research it could fund, but the need for funds was obviously critical. However, no ready pool of money was available. Priority was given to a one-million-dollar fundraising campaign. Local branches of the UCC, Ukrainian credit unions and Ukrainian churches across Canada were encouraged to solicit and collect financial contributions, no matter how small. But the going was rough from the start. With little tradition of communal giving and no fundraising apparatus in place, fundraisers continually fell short of their goal.[117]

Still, Gregorovich was pleased. "To date," he noted, "defense by Ukrainians has been on a sporadic reactive basis by individuals and organizations when attacks have occurred. The current Ukrainian organizational network has not dealt with the problem on an ongoing basis." The CLC, he believed, represented change.[118]

Not everyone climbed onto the CLC bandwagon. As the CLC delineated its role, the organized veterans of the Galicia Division decided to strike out in defence of their own interests. While appreciative of the community-wide effort, they pleaded special and immediate needs which would be best served by organizing their own response to specific accusations directed at them.[119] The Brotherhood of Veterans of the First Division of the Ukrainian National Army (UNA), engaged legal counsel to defend their interests.

Whether Division veterans or CLC, all sensed the lurking presence of the Soviet Union behind their current troubles. It was the Soviet Union which would celebrate any discredit which fell on the Ukrainian diaspora.

But what of the Jews? What was their role? An internal CLC discussion paper entitled "Coping With Anti-Ukrainianism" identified Jewish community pressure to bring Nazi war criminals in Canada to justice as but a thinly veiled assault on Ukrainians. The suggestion was that in engineering an attack on Ukrainians, Jews had again climbed into bed with the Soviets.

Anti-Ukrainianism is defamation designed to create hatred, ridicule and contempt of the Ukrainian ethno-cultural group and Ukraine. During the last century and a half there has been active anti-Ukrainianism by Russians, Poles, Czechs, Slovaks, Hungarians, Romanians and Jews as a matter of state, community and individual policy. The general aim has been desire for Ukrainian territory and the necessity of bolstering that case by asserting that Ukrainians, the Ukrainian language and Ukraine do not exist, but are an intellectual, German, romantic or other invention. Jewish defamation of Ukrainians has been partly motivated by Jewish participation in support of the ruling ethnic group and partly by direct Jewish community interests. Although there is a residue of this activity by all of the afore-mentioned groups, at the present time the significant activity is by the Russian state apparatus, Russian organizations, Russians, and the Jewish community and individual Jews.

At the present time the bulk of the damage to Ukrainian aspirations and to Ukrainians in the diaspora, and particularly to North American Ukrainians, comes from activity by the Soviet Russian state and the Jewish community. The most significant damage arises from the actions of the Jewish community, assisted by the Russian Empire through the KGB. Accordingly the focus is on dealing with the Jewish problem although the solutions apply to the significant Russian activity as well as to the residue of activity by other groups.

With the CLC then building up a head of steam, the paper saw no benefit which might accrue out of seeking accommodation or even dialogue with the Jewish community. Here was a sharp break with efforts of recent years to initiate *rapprochement* with the Canadian Jewish community. For the CLC the Deschênes Commission had heightened a sense of community crisis; dialogue was no longer a priority. "While nominal efforts should be made to deal with the problem of contacts with the Jewish community," the discussion paper concluded, "it is a pointless waste of time and energy to try to deal with the situation primarily by dialogue with the Jewish community or with individual Jews. The effort has to be directed elsewhere." The "elsewhere" was the popular media and the government.[120]

Most certainly those guiding the CLC had no clear notion of the Canadian Jewish community or its institutional infrastructure. In the haze of their own isolation, the CLC leadership continually blurred Littman and Wiesenthal as one into a seemingly well-orchestrated Jewish campaign to tar the Ukrainian diaspora as unrepentant Nazi war criminals. Jews might be doing the bidding of the Soviets, but they believed it was the Soviets who were the prime movers and would be the beneficiary of any discredit which fell on the Ukrainian-Canadian community.

It is doubtful that many mainstream Jewish leaders were especially knowledgeable of or concerned about Ukrainian anxieties. Irwin Cotler and David Matas, two who focused on legal questions regarding the Nazi war-criminals issue and who would remain high profile during the entire Deschênes Commission proceedings, gave no thought to any Ukrainian or other ethnic dimension to the war-criminals issue until the Ukrainian protest erupted.[121] Neither, apparently, had the Mulroney government. Several who more closely monitored the unfolding politics of the war-criminals question were less surprised by the eastern European response.[122] But heated Ukrainian reaction or inflamed sensibilities would not deter the Jewish community. It had committed itself to seek legal redress against any and all Nazi war criminals living in Canada. That took precedence.

In any event, the mounting Ukrainian community uproar was initially less disturbing to Jewish leaders than their private doubts about the Deschênes inquiry itself. But whatever reservations Congress leaders harboured, they would co-operate fully with Deschênes. They had no choice. They planned no organized or costly lobbying campaigns. To what end? Deschênes would do what Deschênes had to do. If some worried what course the proceedings might take, none felt the Jewish community was under attack.

But unlike Ukrainian communal organizations, the Canadian Jewish Congress, if called upon, was organizationally prepared to meet the challenge of Deschênes. The CJC's community relations staff had extensive experience in monitoring issues of inter-group tension. The hunt for Nazi war criminals was but one among many. Always answerable to lay leadership and mindful of grass-roots Jewish sentiment, Jewish professional staff carried the community ball in dealing with anti-Semitic incidents, hate literature, human-rights issues and other public concerns which touched the Jewish community as a whole. If they were hard pressed to juggle all items on their plates, at least there was an assured budget, support staff and a core of volunteers already in place. When the Deschênes Commission was announced, there was no need to go, cap in hand, to the community to raise money for whatever would be felt necessary. No need to borrow filing cabinets, office space or secretaries. Nor was there need to learn, trial and error, how and whom to contact in the press, when to issue a press release or which labour leaders or church spokesmen might be counted on to voice solidarity with the Jewish community.

This is not to say that all in the Jewish community were content with mainstream Jewish political leadership whether Congress or B'nai Brith. To some like Sabina Citron, who pressed charges against Ernst Zundel, or newly dubbed Nazi-hunter Sol Littman or the militant Jewish Defence League, the organized Jewish leadership was too often soft, fearful of offending or satisfied by half victories. These dissident voices were often adept at winning the popular media's ear. They remained an irritant to the mainstream Jewish leadership.

Nevertheless, unlike the Ukrainian CLC, especially in Toronto, the mainline organized Jewish community's response to the Deschênes process remained in the hands of moderates and seasoned professionals. Many of the more militant voices found themselves outside the family of Congress organizations or the B'nai Brith.

The difference from the Ukrainian community could not be more striking. In the absence of a community infrastructure, the most impassioned rushed in to organize their own. Emotion initially substituted for experience. To them the Deschênes Commission was of singular importance in Ukrainian-Canadian history. They and the single-issue CLC they had created would learn on the job. They were dedicated but they were flying by the seat of their pants.

Would the CLC survive Deschênes? Would it develop seasoned professionals to deal with other matters after the Deschênes process was long past? This remained to be seen as April 10, 1985, the day of the Commission's first hearings, approached.

Chapter 5

One Is Too Many: The Deschênes Hearings

Marika Bandera stood quietly before Judge Jules Deschênes in Ottawa's Supreme Court Building as her counsel, Alex Epstein, explained her reason for being there. Externally she controlled her emotions. Yet her prepared brief mirrored the anguish and anger of many Ukrainian Canadians faced with what they felt was defamatory media coverage of the Commission's hearings. Accompanied by her fifteen-year-old son, Stepan, she had come "with a mother's interest in defending her children." Her message bespoke the turmoil which had racked her life and that of many in her community.

> My name is Marika Bandera, and I am appearing on behalf of my family: my son Stepan, who is here with me today, and my two young daughters. My husband Andriy, who was the son of Stepan Bandera, the Ukrainian nationalist leader in Ukraine's struggle against both Nazi Germany and Soviet Russia, died July 19th of last year.
>
> It is my duty, as the surviving widow and mother of three children born in Canada, to defend the honour and integrity of the Bandera name, a name that was unscrupulously maligned by Mr. Sol Littman during your Commission hearing in Toronto, Wednesday, April 24th, 1985.[1]

What had moved Marika Bandera to seek leave to testify before the Commission? In testimony before the

Commission a few days earlier, Sol Littman, offering an analysis of World War II events, stated that "The Ukrainians, by reason of their larger numbers and historic hatred of Poles and Jews, proved themselves particularly pernicious collaborationists . . . leaders of the Ukrainian nationalist movement, Bandera and Melnyk, readily joined in the expectation that Hitler would create a totalitarian Ukraine under their leadership, free of Poles and Jews."[2]

Many Canadian Jews with any roots in or knowledge of the history of their brethren in Eastern Europe would have found nothing surprising about Littman's view. In a tragic replay of the cases of Bohdan Khmelnytsky in the seventeenth century and Symon Petlura in the 1920s, these wartime Ukrainian national heroes were thought to be major historical villains by many Jews, identified as perpetrators or abetters of anti-Semitic savagery. As Littman wrote to Judge Deschênes in response to Marika Bandera's defence of her family name, "Bandera may have been a saint in the eyes of his family and his followers, but to others he was a murderous villain . . . The massacre of the Jews of Lvov is also too well known to be explained away."[3]

Andrii Melnyk was already a known commodity to Canadian Jewish leaders, dating back to the controversy over his visit to Canada in the 1950s. So was Bandera. But the case of Bandera also yielded painful ironies. The same "anti-Semitic, pro-Nazi" Bandera had been imprisoned in the Nazi concentration camp of Sachsenhausen, near Berlin. In addition, his two brothers were brutally murdered in Auschwitz. According to eyewitness testimony cited by Maria Bandera, they were executed by having cement poured over their water-soaked bodies.[4] Stepan Bandera himself survived the war but was murdered by KGB assassins in 1959.

True, Littman's comment on Bandera, an important actor in the historical events of his day, represented but one line in a submission of forty pages of text. Similarly, it had taken but two sentences in his *Saturday Night* article of July 1983 on the Rauca case to enrage the Division leadership and to bring on a libel suit against the magazine. The issue was no longer simply how much Littman said nor, to some, what he said. It was that the words were said by Littman, already in the eyes of many Ukrainians, an exaggerated bugbear for the evils that threatened their community.

In his presentation to the Commission, Littman had gone — he thought — to great lengths to avoid group defamation. He was careful to indicate that only a small minority of eastern Europeans had actively collaborated with the Nazi occupiers, that many had risked their lives to save Jews or through involvement in underground operations against the German forces, and that some Jews had themselves collaborated with the Nazi death machine as ghetto policemen or *Kapos* in concentration camps. He allowed that, by extension, they also could possibly be guilty of war crimes and liable for prosecution.[5]

For Marika Bandera, all these disclaimers and qualifications painstakingly crafted by Littman were not sufficient. For her, Bandera was not a historical figure. He was her father-in-law. And in step with mainstream Ukrainian-Canadian organizations, she vehemently rejected any charge of anti-Semitism directed against him or his followers. They had fought the Nazis, suffered at their hands. How could they also be partners in the Holocaust?

To Littman the Nazis' imprisonment of Bandera and other Ukrainian nationalists had nothing to do with their attitude towards Jews and everything to do with their nationalism. The disagreement between Bandera and the Nazis was not over Jews, it was over the Nazis' rejection of a truly independent Ukraine. Whatever their differences, Banderites and Nazis shared anti-Semitism. Littman's views on Banderite anti-Semitism could not be shaken.[6]

Nor could Marika Bandera's faith in her father-in-law. She concluded her brief with an emotional appeal: " . . . in the memory of my late husband and his father, and for the future of my children, I beseech the commission not to allow hate-mongers and bigots to abuse your just intentions, and to protect innocent individuals and communities who are entitled to respect and protection of their rights."[7]

It was into this maelstrom of Old World passion and prejudice that the Deschênes Commission was plunged, almost from its inception. The Commission staff, like the Mulroney government, were unprepared for the ethnic tensions which quickly assumed centre stage. People had been thinking of a few black-shirted Nazis, à la Mengele, but not Ukrainians. Yet instead of black, they were confronted with shades of grey.

The original mandate of the Commission, as defined in its terms of reference under the Inquiries Act, made no mention of ethnic groups or communities in Canada. Why should it? Ethnicity was not an issue. The Commission was mandated to determine whether individual war criminals were present in Canada, how they might have arrived and what remedies were available to bring them to justice. The preamble to the text, moreover, was quite specific in limiting the mandate to Nazi war criminality, as opposed to a more inclusive focus which would cover all war crimes or crimes against humanity.[8]

On April 10, 1985, several weeks before Marika Bandera would take the stand, the Commission convened its first public hearing in the Supreme Court Building on Wellington Street in Ottawa — symbolically situated about equal distance between the Parliament Buildings and the Public Archives of Canada. If those in attendance expected an instant flurry of revelations, they were disappointed. Housekeeping was the first order of business. The Commission's Rules of Practice and Procedure, drafted by Judge Deschênes, were laid out. They offered a general framework within which witnesses would be examined and evidence considered. Rule 9 stood out. It allowed that the Commission might permit "outside parties or their counsels" standing. The granting of standing would permit them to do more than monitor hearings or submit briefs. They could cross-examine witnesses on matters relevant to their interest. They would, in effect, become part of the Commission's structure.

Even before the first day of hearings, Kenneth Narvey twigged to the possibility of obtaining standing. Still possessed by a single-minded determination to pursue war criminals, Narvey was no longer with Congress. He had rejoined Network, the activist Jewish interest group, some two years earlier as its researcher and representative on war crimes matters.

Narvey, excited by the possibilities of what standing could offer, decided to apply for it on the first day of hearings, and suggested to other Jewish organizations that they do the same. David Matas, now counsel to the League for Human Rights of B'nai Brith Canada, jumped at the opportunity. In a sudden flurry of activity, Matas telephoned B'nai Brith officials in Toronto. They in turn reached Howard Spunt, a B'nai Brith member and public servant in Ottawa. In Spunt's oral application for standing, which followed Narvey's, he argued that B'nai Brith had within its membership not only students but many actual victims of Nazi war crimes. Justice Jules Deschênes agreed. B'nai Brith had a special and direct interest, he ruled, and would be granted standing. Network would be permitted to file written briefs, and to make an in-person presentation, but would not be granted standing. After a brief second day of hearings, in which only three questions were asked of witnesses, the commission adjourned for two weeks.[9]

But standing for B'nai Brith was a bombshell. It triggered a chain reaction rocking both Jewish and Ukrainian organizations. In the organizational tug of war between B'nai Brith and the Canadian Jewish Congress, one Congress official recalled, Congress had been bested. Congress officials smarted at the very idea that the B'nai Brith should represent Canadian Jewish interests at the Deschênes hearings. It was Congress not B'nai Brith, they held, which spoke for Canadian Jewry. But would Deschênes allow for more than one representative from the Jewish community?[10]

As the hearings reconvened in Toronto, prominent lawyer Morris Manning rose to request standing for the Canadian Jewish Congress as the voice of Canadian Jewry, which had a vital stake in the proceedings. Deschênes had obviously done his homework. He knew the organizational pecking order of community groups. Congress was granted standing. A hint from Deschênes that perhaps Congress and the B'nai Brith might agree on joint representation was ignored.[11]

Other Jewish groups came forward. A survivors' group in Montreal, the Toronto-based Canadian Holocaust Remembrance Association, the Jewish Defence League and the Simon Wiesenthal Center all requested standing. All were turned down. Between Congress representing the interests of Canadian Jewry and the B'nai Brith looking out for Holocaust survivors, it seemed that all Jewish bases were covered.

But Jewish groups were not the only ones to come forward. Concerned by the B'nai Brith coup, John Gregorovich of the newly organized Ukrainian Civil Liberties Commission applied for standing in the name of its parent Ukrainian Canadian Committee. He did so, he later recalled, with some trepidation. He was not sure what standing would mean but if Jewish interests had standing, the UCC had to get it too. If not, he observed, it "would look like we weren't doing our job." Deschênes granted his request on the grounds that the UCC represented Ukrainian Canadians who "have been linked rightly or wrongly with war crimes, and the Ukrainian community itself have felt aggrieved as a result of various attacks or insinuations in recent months." Three other Ukrainian organizations, including the Ukrainian Youth Association, were rejected but all agreed to work with the UCC.[12]

One additional Ukrainian group, the Brotherhood of Veterans of the 1st Division of the First Ukrainian Army in Canada, the Galicia Division, requested and received standing. They argued that their interests, like those of the Holocaust survivors, were separate and distinct and, as such, deserved separate standing. After all, they had been attacked as war criminals.[13] The Division veterans also had a second and equally compelling reason to want independent status. From its inception the CLC was determined to present itself in all public forums as a Canadian group defending Canadian interests. This was in part to avoid any implications that spokesmen for the CLC were in any way personally implicated in war crimes. But as a result, one Ukrainian observer recalled, the foreign-born were required to keep a lower profile and consequently may have felt "tainted." In the "sparring between Canadian perspective and the old world perspective," veterans of the Division may have felt slighted. They were determined to speak for themselves.[14] Deschênes granted the Division's request.

Perhaps none of the groups with standing had any clear idea what they wanted standing for or what exactly they were going to do with it. But there is no doubt that granting intervenor standing to spokesmen for ethnic interests helped sharpen an inter-ethnic stake in the proceedings. This is what the counsel for the Commission feared. They warned Deschênes to proceed with caution lest the proceedings get cumbersome and divisive. He may have taken this advice to heart.[15] Deschênes rejected all additional requests for standing, not just from other Jewish and Ukrainian groups but from those of other ethnic communities as well.

Any Commission or its report is in large part the product of the men and women who serve as commissioners and members of the staff. The major players on the Commission staff were Judge Deschênes himself and the two Commission lawyers, Yves Fortier and Michael Meighen.

Few jurists in Canada command the respect that Jules Deschênes does. He is a legal scholar and jurist of impeccable integrity. Mulroney no doubt assumed that selecting a man of his stature would add weight to any recommendations which might be forthcoming. Born in Montreal in 1923, Deschênes received his law degree from the Université de Montréal, was called to the bar in 1946 and named a Queen's Counsel in 1961. From 1966 to 1972, he was senior partner in the law firm of Deschênes, de Grandpré, Colas, Godin and Lapointe. He then served as Chief Justice of the Quebec Superior Court, and throughout his career has been active on provincial, national and international legal bodies.[16]

There is a fearful tradition in Jewish folklore which suggests that the non-Jewish world is filled with real or potential danger. In the world of modern politics, this tradition has been reformulated into the oft-heard Jewish question, equally the product of insecurity, posed about any event or person of authority: "Is it (he or she) good for the Jews?" Was Deschênes good for the Jews? Notwithstanding the Judge's eminence, revelations during the course of the Commission hearings raised questions about possible bias on his part which could be extended to the issue of prosecution of alleged war criminals.

The first incident, which did not surface in public, related to a paper prepared by Judge Deschênes in May 1985 for the Sub-commission on Prevention of Discrimination and Protection of Minorities of the UN Commission on Human Rights. The paper was an attempt by Deschênes to develop an acceptable definition of the term minority. In a section entitled "The will of the minority to survive" the Judge touched a raw Jewish nerve. "Lastly," he concluded, "the Jewish minority provides a mixed example in many countries since its members wish to be integrated into the local economic system, but isolate themselves in their own family and religious system. How is it possible to achieve the former while at the same time preserving the latter?"[17]

By itself, this one paragraph out of 182 which composed the Judge's report would appear rather innocuous. Indeed, the first sentence of the quote is reasonably accurate. The second is an insightful question which should be posed in every good college course in ethnic relations. Yet the World Jewish Congress delegates present at the UN Commission on Human Rights meeting felt obliged to press for further clarification of the meaning behind the paragraph. It was felt that one possible interpretation was that Jews might only be able to participate fully in any society if they were also prepared to assimilate culturally and religiously. For Jews, that view was unacceptable.

A private discussion between the WJC representative and the Judge on August 15, 1985 and a subsequent exchange on August 20, 1985, while cordial, seem to have been substantively inconclusive.[18] By early September 1985, well after the Commission of Inquiry had been established, private reports of this episode reached Congress. Jewish leaders were uneasy. Was the Judge insensitive to Jewish concerns? Or worse, did he harbour an anti-Jewish bias? While at least one Congress official felt uneasy, it was decided to let the matter ride, at least until after the Commission had concluded its work. Neither the Jewish nor general media reported the incident.[19]

A second issue which did emerge publicly, in mid-November 1985, concerned the Judge's views of the fairness of the Nuremberg war-crimes trials of 1945–46. In a paper entitled "Politics and the Rule of Law" the Judge questioned the legitimacy of trials of the vanquished by the victors:

> There is no doubt that these proceedings have marked a considerable progress towards assuring a better respect of the rule of law among nations, even in times of war. Yet they still fall short of the true measure of justice that should be meted out to victors and vanquished alike after an armed conflict.
>
> Field Marshal Goering complained rightly that Nuremberg represented the justice of the victors and that the tribunal should have also comprised judges from the neutral and the vanquished countries.
>
> But it is difficult to conceive of an imperial tribunal to apply such an imperfect body of laws as the "jus

gentium" [international law], when no superna-
tional body can maintain peace or, at least, prevent
a recourse to military force. A trial in the wake of
a military victory cannot easily be seen as truly impartial. Indeed the statutes adopted at the London
Conference prohibited the defence of "tu quoque"
[charging an adversary with being or doing the
same as oneself] albeit the German armed forces
could not have monopolized all the wrongdoings in
Europe and Africa as well as in the Mediterranean
and the Atlantic.[20]

These revelations stirred up a hornet's nest. Would
the Judge's views on Nuremberg make him reluctant
about launching an aggressive search for alleged Nazi
war criminals in Canada four decades after the war?
Littman, for one, suggested that Deschênes's analysis
raised "troubling questions" and argued that there is "a
tremendous difference between a planned campaign
with murder squads, concentration camps, gas chambers
and crematoria — and the occasional excesses of a soldier in the heat of battle."[21] That distinction was echoed by Bernard Finestone, former Congress Quebec
region president and Progressive Conservative activist.
He resented anyone equating his own wartime experiences in the Canadian armed forces to the allegations
against Nazi war criminals.[22] Maxwell Cohen, respected
professor of international law at the University of Ottawa, also challenged the Judge's thesis. According to
The Globe and Mail he pointed out that the consensus
of legal scholarship was that the trial of the Nazis was
not an exercise of the trial of the victors over the vanquished. "The systematic effort at genocide and the systematic plans for aggression," Cohen asserted, "make
all the difference in the world. A lawyer who doesn't
understand that doesn't understand the law."[23]

The Judge, for his part, was stung by the criticism of
his Nuremberg evaluation, and was sorely tempted to
respond. Yet to do so would have kept the debate sim-
mering, deflecting attention from the main task at hand.

The media's attention span was not long. The Judge kept his silence, and the issue faded from the headlines in a few days.[24]

The press may have forgotten; the Jews didn't. The UN and Nuremberg episodes heightened Jewish anxieties about the attitude of Judge Deschênes to Jews and the Jewish community. But these doubts did not lead to any public questioning of the impartiality and fairness of the Judge by mainstream Jewish organizations. Reservations — if any — by Congress or B'nai Brith officials were kept private.

Unlike Deschênes, the two Commission lawyers had no public track record on the issue of war criminality, but they were comparably high profile, with substantial clout in Canadian legal and political circles. Yves Fortier, born in Quebec City in 1935, received his law degree from McGill University and was awarded a Rhodes scholarship at Oxford University. A senior partner in the prestigious Montreal firm of Ogilvy and Renault, and past president of the Canadian Bar Association, he had also held directorships in a number of Canadian corporations. During the 1984 federal election, he resisted Liberal Party urging to run as a candidate in a Quebec City riding but remained identified with the party. His Liberal ties proved no barrier in his maintaining a close personal friendship with Prime Minister Mulroney. He was, and remains, a touted candidate for a position on the Supreme Court.

Michael Meighen, the other Commission counsel, was born in Montreal in 1939. A long-time personal friend of Mulroney, Meighen completed his law degree at Université Laval in 1963. With his blue-blood credentials as grandson of former Prime Minister Arthur Meighen, and as a senior partner in the Toronto firm of McMaster Meighen and holder of several corporate directorships, he also brought political balance to the team. Meighen had long been active in the Conservative Party, and had held important administrative posts.

Both lawyers brought to their tasks the personal trust of the Prime Minister, valuable political connections, as well as reputations for intelligence and efficiency. Their Liberal and Conservative affiliations would serve to avoid appearances of political partisanship in the outcome of the deliberations. The political risks were real. The Liberals might be damaged should the Commission Report emphasize a perceived — and perhaps actual — record of inaction on the issue stretching back close to forty years. And the Conservatives were now alert lest the Report's recommendations satisfy neither Jewish nor Ukrainian groups, with harmful results at the polls.

Neither Fortier nor Meighen had extensive legal experience in areas of law closely linked with the Commission's work: immigration law, human rights law or criminal law. Fortier's practice did involve a great deal of international law; Meighen's work was primarily in the corporate law sector. Both lawyers freely admitted to very limited familiarity with the history of eastern Europe before and during World War II, and neither was familiar with the passions which the historic Jewish-Ukrainian relationship could arouse in seemingly well integrated Canadian citizens. The two were taken by surprise when they realized that they had stumbled into an ethnic minefield.[25]

How could it be otherwise? They were raised in the cocoon of Canada's two founding communities, with multi-generational roots in Canada far removed from the passions of Old World conflicts. In this, of course, they were no different from the Prime Minister and those other government officials who were taken by surprise as the Ukrainian-Jewish confrontation heated up.[26]

It appears the commission lawyers were selected to reflect the English-French, Liberal-Conservative duality of Canada. The key historical researchers, however, were chosen to reflect another ethnic duality — Jewish and Ukrainian. Alti Rodal had studied Jewish history at Oxford, and had a background in Holocaust studies and familiarity with Yiddish and Hebrew. Roman Waschuk was a bright young graduate student in history from the University of Toronto, familiar with Ukrainian history and literate in Ukrainian. While relations between the two were amicable, the intrusion from outside of conflicting interests and episodes of ethnic tension was not unknown.

A case in point was the issue of the correspondence and related documents of Gordon Bohdan Panchuk, a well-known Ukrainian-Canadian leader. While still in the Canadian military he had personally visited the veterans of the Galicia Division in Italy and England and had played a key role in the effort to have them resettle in Canada.[27] The Commission felt that his personal papers, now housed in the Archives of Ontario, might contain pertinent information. But Panchuk had offered his papers to the Archives on condition that he retain the right to control access to them for a specified period. In fact, Panchuk had encouraged historians working on Canadian wartime history to examine them. Lubomyr Luciuk had used the papers for his doctoral dissertation on Ukrainian DPs. Luciuk, called upon by Panchuk to evaluate requests to see his papers, served as his adviser and "trustee."

Panchuk decided that the Commission could have access, but only under certain conditions. Luciuk, like Panchuk, was concerned lest the Ukrainian-Canadian community should be ill-served. Thus, it was stipulated that the Commission would have to identify the background and professional training of any prospective researchers before access would be granted.[28]

These restrictions were concretized in practice. The Commission sent two of its researchers, Alti Rodal and another historian, Paula Draper, both Jewish, to study the papers. After an initial survey of the collection, the Commission's Jewish researchers were refused further access. Roman Waschuk, the Commission's Ukrainian-Canadian researcher, was subsequently given access. The Commission had acceded to the restrictions, "bowing upon a matter of principle," albeit reluctantly. In practice, the restrictions meant that Jewish employees of the Commission were barred.[29]

Other key players at the hearings included the counsels chosen by the groups with standing to represent their interests before the Commission. For the B'nai Brith and the Division, this was no problem. David Matas was already counsel to the B'nai Brith: Matas, active in both Canadian Amnesty International and the Canadian Bar Association, welcomed the opportunity to represent the organization at the hearings. The Division finally appointed the avuncular and affable Yaroslaw Botiuk. Botiuk, well known in the Toronto Ukrainian community, was singleminded in his concern that the Division's name be defended from any and all accusations of wrongdoing.[30] But he was pre-empted in that effort. Early in the proceedings the Judge ruled explicitly that simple membership in the Galicia Division of the ss would *ipso facto* not constitute grounds for investigating any individual. Deschênes ruled that the Commission's hearings were not the appropriate venue to address accusations concerning the activities or character of the Division.[31] Botiuk, while plainly delighted, now had a relatively minor role in the proceedings, but he attended diligently.

For Congress and the UCC the problems of finding counsel were somewhat more complex. Morris Manning who had appeared before Deschênes to request standing for Congress had other commitments. There was no shortage of lawyers like Manning ready to help. But help was not what was needed; it was an experienced and knowledgeable legal advocate. McGill law professor and past president of Congress, Irwin Cotler, seemed an obvious choice. He had the knowledge and interest, was obviously dedicated and could devote the necessary time. He had tried unsuccessfully to get Commission standing for a Montreal survivors' group.

But would Cotler work well with Congress president Milton Harris, who prided himself on his layman's knowledge of the law? Both men, obviously dedicated to the campaign against Nazi war criminals in Canada, had very different administrative and leadership styles. In the past they had not always seen eye to eye on the

best political or legal strategy to use in prodding a reluctant government into action against war criminals.
Each maintained an independence of mind and spirit
which might have left some, including Cotler and Harris, wondering how any joint team effort would work.

The choice would be made when Congress's National
Officers met in Ottawa at the end of April 1985, just
three days after Deschênes granted Congress standing.
Officers' meetings usually alternated between Montreal
and Toronto, but this one was different. The last few
days of April 1985 were special days on the Jewish calendar. A gathering of Holocaust survivors and their
children assembled in Ottawa to mark the fortieth anniversary of the Allied victory in Europe. The event
proved more than a remembrance of the past. It exploded into a celebration of human resilience, a re-
dedication to life by those who had witnessed so much
death. Nor was the solemnity of the event lost. As discussion focused on the role of the survivor, talk of the
Deschênes process was never far from mind.

Against this backdrop Congress officers assembled.
Whatever doubts Cotler or Harris had were soon set
aside. Cotler was appointed counsel for Congress, *pro
bono*.[32]

The Ukrainian Canadian Committee also needed
counsel. Here too there were sympathetic lawyers ready
to help. Several among the more prominent CLC leaders
were lawyers, including Gregorovich. But as they sur-
veyed their options, they decided to reach into the private sector. One person seemed an obvious choice —
Toronto lawyer John Sopinka, with the prestigious law
firm of Stikeman, Elliott. His name, Gregorovich recalled, "just kept coming up."[33]

No doubt Sopinka was a name to be reckoned with in
the Canadian legal fraternity. Sopinka included among
his recent clients nurse Susan Nelles, accused and exonerated in the case of the mysterious deaths at the Toronto Hospital for Sick Children, and Sinclair Stevens,
the former Conservative cabinet minister whom he defended on conflict of interest charges before the Parker

Commission Inquiry. Though of Ukrainian origin, he was without deep roots in the organized community. His father had immigrated to western Canada after World War I, but economic difficulties pushed the Sopinka family off the land and eastward to Hamilton, Ontario, where the father found a blue-collar job. The family had some contact with Hamilton's small Ukrainian community — but on the political left. Sopinka attended Ukrainian language classes at the local Ukrainian Labour Temple, where his regional Ukrainian accent sounded foreign to many ears. He recalls other children laughing at him, "You're not Ukrainian, you're Polish."

Although Sopinka was not active in the Ukrainian community, the CLC was convinced he would "dignify the cause by who he was." He could, they also hoped, be "educated" to their cause. To their great delight and even greater surprise, Sopinka agreed to take on the job.[34] In Sopinka the CLC felt they would be getting the best and they expected to pay for it. When he approached Sopinka, Gregorovich made it clear the CLC did not expect bargain-basement legal advice. There was no question but that they would pay Sopinka's "normal rate."[35]

For the most part, the four partisan lawyers seemed to get along with one another, as they did with Fortier, Meighen and the Judge. Their paths had all crossed before. Fortier knew Sopinka well as "an opponent on the court — both the law court and the squash court." He knew Matas from joint involvement in the Canadian Bar Association and Cotler from early professional associations in Ottawa and Montreal. Meighen, likewise, had come to know both Cotler and Sopinka over the years.[36] Yet despite their familiarity and mutual respect, there were interesting differences within the legal fraternity involved with the Commission.

Like Sopinka, Fortier and Meighen were being well paid for their efforts. Yet by the standards of high-profile law firms, these amounts could well represent a cut in income. Their culture was that of the high-priced corporate lawyer, and by sitting on the Commission they were doing well by doing good. In contrast, Cotler's milieu was the academy and the Jewish community. His seeming disregard for his own personal finances was legendary in Jewish leadership circles. Not only was he not getting paid for his Deschênes work, but he neglected to answer memos from the Congress comptroller who literally begged him to submit claims for his expenses. In desperation, the comptroller finally estimated his likely expenses and sent out cheques accordingly. Matas of B'nai Brith was likewise not a lawyer in the Bay Street mould. Splitting his time between his private practice in Winnipeg and Deschênes, Matas's commitment of time and effort was not made without economic sacrifice.

These four attorneys, of course, were not the only outside counsel for the two ethnic groups present at public hearings. A total of twelve appeared for Jewish organizations, and six for Ukrainian.[37]

Few people knew what to expect as the hearings began on April 10, 1985. Those hoping for tearful confessions or identification of Nazi monsters hiding in Canada were to be disappointed. No names of suspects were permitted in public sessions. When the Judge convened the first session in Ottawa, he made it clear that public testimony and submissions would deal in the main with two broad themes. First was the attempt to set straight the post-war Canadian historical record. The immigration experience was to be scrutinized to see whether, or how, Nazi war criminals evaded screening procedures and settled in Canada. The Commission would also review the actions — and inactions — of the government and the RCMP, regarding their zeal, or lack thereof, in trying to identify or apprehend alleged war criminals. As often happens when history is rehashed, new truths emerged. The testimony offered during the inquiry yielded more than a few startling revelations dealing with events of the immediate post-war period right through to the early 1980s.

The second theme of the Commission's activity was purely legalistic. The Commission was charged with recommending what steps the government could take if it established that there were indeed alleged Nazi war criminals living in Canada. These steps might involve legal remedies like denaturalization, deportation, extradition or trial in Canada. The legal arguments brought before the Commission would eventually shape the specific recommendations of the Judge's final report.

Because the Commission was specifically mandated to examine the Mengele immigration issue, early in the hearings, testimony of key witnesses focused on Littman's charges. Corporal Fred Yetter of the RCMP, chief investigator of war crimes for the force, testified that his investigations included pursuit of Mengele's aliases as provided by Interpol. He found no incriminating landing records or passports under those names. As Meighen summarized the matter: "We have not a shred of evidence to suggest that Josef Mengele, under his own name or under any known alias ever came to Canada or applied to come to Canada."[38] Littman's Mengele allegation, which served in large measure as the spark that ignited the Commission and was mentioned in the Commission's terms of reference, would come back to haunt the inquiry and Sol Littman himself. Interestingly enough, in Littman's forty-page brief to the Commission of April 24th, 1985, there was no mention of Mengele.

But then Littman had already admitted his charge had been wrong. In a letter of March 25, 1985 to the Prime Minister, he took pains to concede he was in error on the original Mengele story.[39] He noted, however, there was a wanted criminal with a similar-sounding name; perhaps it was this other war criminal who was involved. But since Littman's Mengele accusation was still seen as largely responsible for prompting the setting up of the Commission, some might accuse him of unwittingly misleading the Prime Minister and the country.

Littman's testimony before Deschênes re-opened an ongoing parade of numbers. The numbers game — guesses as to the actual numbers of alleged war criminals in Canada — was kicked off with his assertion that "as many as 3000 Nazi war criminals and wartime collaborators may have made their way to Canada after the war and as many as 2000 of them are still alive and continue to live in Canada." However, some time later Littman privately explained that the 3,000 number was based on "his own studies." But whence the 3,000 figure? In his "original" figure he included 2,000 former Ukrainian and other ss personnel who he said came to Canada. He allowed he did not know what each and every individual had done, but they all had been members of the ss, which had been declared a criminal organization by the Nuremberg Tribunal. He estimated 1,000 others from other countries, yielding a 3,000 total.[40]

Yet even before Littman's testimony, *Maclean's* had quoted Justice Minister John Crosbie as believing "no more than 30 or 40 Nazi war criminals may be at large in Canada." The same article re-cycled Simon Wiesenthal's well-publicized charge that "218 former Ukrainian officers of the ss who had operated death camps in Eastern Europe were now in Canada."[41] Indeed, the Commission's final report would list thirty-one such estimates in the public record, made from 1971 to 1986, and ranging from "a handful," according to Justice officials, to a high of "6000" attributed to Wiesenthal by the *New York Daily News* in May 1986.[42]

Part, but only part, of this numerical confusion could be traced to different definitions of who was being counted. No doubt, popular understandings of what constituted a war crime varied greatly. And further complications would yield additional variation. How many Nazi war criminals had come to Canada in the first place? How many were still alive? How many might be successfully identified? How many of these might be prosecuted based on acceptable evidence? Coming as it did from Littman, the estimate of 3,000 was particularly jarring. Some likely understood it as implying that all the Ukrainian members of the Galicia Division who immigrated to Canada in 1950 stood accused.

For Jewish Canadians, and certainly for establishment Jewish communal leaders, numbers were never the issue. Few would doubt that the apprehension and conviction of even one war criminal was a worthwhile undertaking, and that evaluation of the need for the Commission ought not to rest on a dubious cost-benefit calculation. It did not matter if the number was much less than 3,000. As the title of a B'nai Brith pamphlet on war criminals asserted, "One Is Too Many." Even convictions of "a handful of obscure old men," a term used by the UCC to deflate the urgency of the whole exercise, would be important as substance and symbol.[43] And while Littman's brief may have opened the bidding in the high range, his next page presented a more realistic view about the possibilities of large-scale trials.

If we manage to extradite, denaturalize, deport, and try even fifty in the next five years, we will have done extremely well. The important thing is that numbers should not be used to trivialize the search for war criminals, to suggest the number is too small to merit the government's attention. There is an intolerable biological clock ticking away that suggests we must get on with the job before death and infirmity combine to defeat justice.[44]

Littman saw justice in a race against time. He also knew that for all the heated debate it generated south of the border, the OSI had been unable to bring more than a handful of alleged Nazi war-criminal cases forward for legal hearing. Mass murderers might die peacefully in Canadian beds.

The early hearings of the Commission were also marked by the presentation of confidential "lists" of alleged war criminals. It was time to put up or shut up.

Littman offered to give the Commission a list of names. Meir Halevi, national director of the militant Jewish Defence League, showed up with a large cardboard box stuffed with names, including eight to ten members of the proto-Fascist Rumanian Iron Guard. Sabina Citron, the fiery representative of the Canadian Holocaust Remembrance Association, who had initiated charges against publisher Ernst Zundel, brought a list but did not divulge the number of names on it. Even the Croatian Committee for Human Rights added to the drama of the hearings. Concerned by accusations that some Croatian nationalists had collaborated with the Nazis, they claimed to have a list of Italians and Serbs who had committed atrocities against Croatians. However, according to Canadian Press, their leader indicated that in the interests of minimizing inter-group conflict he would only release the list with a guarantee that no one would be "prosecuted criminally."[45] The Commission took those lists unconditionally supplied and names culled from other sources and began a case-by-case review.

Gathering information was not always easy. A batch of names, including some who had served in the Galicia Division, had originally been served up to Kaplan by Simon Wiesenthal. Commission lawyers Fortier and Meighen flew to New York in November 1985 to meet personally with Wiesenthal. He refused to come to Canada. They met the elderly Nazi-hunter and his attorney mid-morning at Manhattan's Doral Hotel, and talked through lunch. The lawyers laid out the evidence they had on the names Wiesenthal had originally given Kaplan, and requested any additional information he might have in his files. Wiesenthal, "cordial and pleasant," promised to supply more detail. He sent nothing. Follow-up letters requested the material. Nothing came. If the Commission was going to find more evidence on those Wiesenthal fingered, it would not come from him.[46]

While Commission investigators began to sift through names collected, the hearings also focused early on the

Canadian government's own role in the immigration of possible Nazi war criminals. True, the Commission heard the ringing assurance from the RCMP's Yetter that investigations in 1962 and 1985 had turned up no evidence of the Mengele connection. Many of the early Mengele leads may have arisen due to similar-sounding names, such as Joseph Menke or George Menk. The Commission also heard the story of Nazi officer Wilhelm Mohnke, who had ordered the shooting of fifty-nine Canadian prisoners of war in 1944, and who was found living in Lubeck, West Germany, in 1976. German officials informed External Affairs that the case had been closed.[47]

Additional testimony by George O'Leary of the Immigration Department and Randalf Schramm of the RCMP fleshed out a picture of deliberate government laxity in immigration processing. O'Leary recounted the gradual loosening up of entry restrictions for Nazi party members in 1950 and for SS members by 1955. (Approval of the Galicia Division admitted in 1950 had been a special case in exception to the rules.) He described the pre-1950 screening as inconsistent. Both war criminals and Communists were designated as undesirables. But it was acknowledged that Cold War hysteria focused attention more on the left than on the right. If anything, Nazis or Nazi sympathizers were proven anti-Communists. Indeed, according to O'Leary, it should not have been surprising if low-ranking Nazis and war criminals had emigrated to the west. After all, senior Nazi intelligence officers like Klaus Barbie and scientists like Wernher von Braun were eagerly recruited by the Allies.[48]

Schramm further testified that there was no policy of pursuing suspected war criminals until 1962, and no policy of following up tips from private citizens until twenty years later. In fact, a 1962 policy paper advised that legal action would not be taken in most cases, on the grounds that Canadian courts could not try citizens for offences committed in other countries. According to Canadian Press, an angry Littman minced no words:

"Our security arrangements in terms of checking out immigrants were so loose you could drive ten tanks through them."[49]

William Kelly, former deputy commissioner of the RCMP, in charge of security investigation for European immigrants from 1950–54, and Albert Greening, who worked with the RCMP visa control group in Germany from 1954–62, added further details. Kelly reported that at least one unnamed Allied nation falsified documents to facilitate emigration of Europeans to Canada after the war. At any rate, Canadian Press reported the thirty RCMP officers stationed in Europe after the war did not have access to the master list of 40,000 suspected war criminals compiled by the UN War Crimes Commission.[50] The RCMP officers involved in the screening were young and inexperienced in this type of work. Highway patrol duty on the prairies did not equip them with the political savvy needed to ferret out security risks among the European immigrants. They did little investigative work themselves, relying on British, French, American and German intelligence to verify information.[51]

This was a picture of administrative incompetence and bureaucratic lethargy. But more damaging revelations, dealing with political and governmental decision-making, were yet to come, not just in testimony but from the press. Using the new *Access to Information Act*, David Vienneau of *The Toronto Star* unearthed a series of early 1960s memoranda among consular officials, External Affairs and other ministries. Both the newspaper accounts and the ongoing testimony pointed in the same direction: away from action against any alleged Nazi war criminals.

Most of the memos unearthed by Vienneau centred on the need to avoid antagonizing Canada's ally and European trading partner, West Germany. But one confidential memo of May 25, 1962, from the External Affairs European Division was more blunt, and for Jews, far uglier. Investigations of war criminality against two suspects identified by Jewish groups, it warned, would smack "very strongly of a witch-hunt. Both cases have been brought to light in what looks like a spirit of revenge instigated by Jews, and in my view anti-German baiting by the Jews is just as reprehensible as Jew baiting by the Nazis." In a more restrained but similar vein, a member of External Affairs' legal division also cautioned that two opposing political considerations ought to be weighed by government before deciding whether to pursue Nazi war criminals in Canada. One was the possible damage that could be done to relations with West Germany, the other was criticism from the Jewish community for failing to act. His implication seemed clear: he would rank German relations above Jewish concerns.

These discussions among lower-ranking government officials seeped up the chain of command. A June 30, 1962 memo by External Affairs under-secretary of state Norman Robertson to then External Affairs Minister Howard Green urged action against war criminals in Canada only if it would credit Canada and not embarrass West Germany. Speaking of the West German authorities, Robertson reportedly wrote: "If they were given a choice, they would probably prefer that we let sleeping dogs lie." So, apparently, did the Diefenbaker cabinet. No action on the two suspects was taken.[52]

Throughout the Deschênes Inquiry, press reports continued to expose the government's inertia. The legal division of External Affairs continued its cautious approach to the investigation of Nazi war criminals into the 1980s. An exceptional 1983 suggestion by Brian Corbett of the Justice Department recommended that Canada sign an extradition treaty with the Soviet Union limited to war criminals. In a foreshadowing of the arguments placed before the Commission, that recommendation was vetoed on July 28, 1983 by External Affairs. They argued that war crimes were not an extraditable offence. Furthermore, if the door to Soviet extraditions was opened, some extradition requests might be forthcoming for political acts which would not be offences in Canada.[53]

Other evidence produced during the public hearings showed that Canada was not alone in its neglect of the war-criminals matter. Indeed, the tone of response may well have been set by a 1948 secret cable from the British Foreign Office to all Commonwealth countries. The British urged that all cases of Nazi war criminals be disposed of before August 31, 1948 and that no new ones should be opened thereafter. The cable minced no words — for a bureaucratic memo — in explaining this *de facto* statute of limitations. "In our view, punishment of war criminals is more a matter of discouraging future generations than of meting out retribution to every guilty individual. Moreover, in view of future political developments in Germany envisioned by recent tripartite talks, we are convinced that it is now necessary to dispose of the past as soon as possible."[54]

The stream of press and Commission revelations culminating in the 1948 cable had a profound and disquieting effect on the Commission hearings. Clearly, the do-nothing message must have been taken to heart by later generations of government officials. Fortier allowed that the British directive helped explain the chill which greeted all calls for investigations in Canada and elsewhere after 1948. For Jewish representatives, the cable, like the earlier evidence about lax Canadian screening procedures, was further proof that Canada had a self-imposed lack of any clear commitment to apprehend Nazi war criminals. Said Irwin Cotler, "In 1948, shortly after the Holocaust . . . when many of the victims were still in displaced persons' camps, you have here a clear unequivocal policy statement saying we should suspend the bringing of Nazi war criminals to justice."[55]

Hardly had the uproar over the 1948 memo died down when another bombshell burst. No revelation which surfaced during the Commission's hearings matched the possible intrigue of the story of the untimely destruction of the immigration files. Former Liberal Solicitor General Robert Kaplan, during his Commission testimony of October 9, 1985, revealed a tale with possible cloak-and-dagger overtones, smacking of a mini-Watergatelike cover-up. Kaplan reported that earlier in the 1980s, hundreds of thousands of immigration files recording data on applicants for entry had been mysteriously destroyed while in the hands of the Public Archives of Canada. The destruction occurred shortly after he had requested that the RCMP make use of any information contained in the files on Nazi war criminals. According to the testimony at the hearings, RCMP Commissioner Robert Simmonds secretly advised Kaplan on April 30, 1984 that the files had been destroyed between February 1982 and September 1983. Kaplan was outraged. He ordered an immediate investigation. Deputy Solicitor General Fred Gibson reported back to Kaplan that the action was either a "culpable act" or a "monumental blunder," but at any rate, seriously ". . . impaired the ability of Canadian authorities . . . to take effective action against war criminals in Canada."[56]

Jewish representatives at the Deschênes hearings were angry and suspicious. How was it that the destruction had begun, coincidentally, just after Helmut Rauca's arrest for extradition to West Germany? Cotler demanded a full-scale independent investigation. Ivan Whitehall, a senior Justice Department lawyer, jumped to the defence of the Archives. Himself a member of a family of Holocaust survivors, he protested there was no evidence of any conspiracy to destroy the files. Furthermore, he doubted if the files contained any information pertinent to the Commission's work. Perhaps he was right. But the incident did little to instil confidence in the integrity of the government's commitment to the pursuit of Nazi war criminals. Speculation remained rife. Rumours of nefarious motives and sinister plots relating to the incident abounded.[57]

Two weeks later, Minister of State for Immigration Walter Maclean responded for the government. He claimed that file destruction was a routine housecleaning operation and that, at any rate, all immigrant landing records were kept on microfilm. Indeed, the key documents of interest, the applications for admission to

Canada, were not even in the destroyed files. They were kept — and destroyed — in the countries in which they were made, again according to normally established procedures. This explanation apparently did not satisfy Sol Littman. He is quoted in *The Toronto Sun* as accusing the federal government of a "cover-up" on the matter.[58]

Given the controversy over the missing files, Judge Deschênes decided that the Commission would have to conduct its own inquiry into the matter.[59] Less than a month later, Fortier reported on his results. He found that the destruction of the files was, indeed, in keeping with government policy. There was no evidence that the files held any information which would be of interest to the inquiry.[60]

But that was not the only "missing-file" story to emerge. In late December, *The Toronto Star*'s David Vienneau reported that several files relating to four Nazi collaborators from France were missing from the Public Archives of Canada. In 1948 the four had been given special cabinet permission to remain in Canada. They included Count Jacques de Bernonville, a close associate of Klaus Barbie. He fled Canada in 1951 after being tipped off by Prime Minister Louis St Laurent about a deportation order. Vienneau found that several "secret" Privy Council files, including one containing correspondence between de Bernonville and the federal government, were empty. An August 28, 1948 External Affairs memo to St Laurent on de Bernonville was also missing. The implication was that the missing documents might have contained material damaging to the reputations of former Liberal party leaders.[61]

Talk of possible deliberate destruction of files, tampering with government records and sanitizing of documents was soon overshadowed by another flare-up. In a heated session in early December as the Commission hearings were winding to a close, Littman explained that even before the Deschênes Commission began he had been satisfied that Josef Mengele had never tried to enter Canada. He thus allowed that his initial allegation, which had received international publicity and which, most believed, had precipitated the creation of the inquiry, was false. "The conclusions were mine and mine alone. If there were any mistakes, they were mine."[62]

Littman's admission infuriated Whitehall, counsel for the Justice Department. The standard Justice Department line, even pre-dating the Low memorandum, had been that Canadian law offered no remedy to the war-criminals problem. Many Justice Department officials may have seen the appointment of a commission on war criminals as a slap in the face, a rejection of their advice and perhaps further evidence of the Conservative distrust of the "Liberal" public service. To them discrediting Littman may have seemed sweet revenge. Whitehall argued that, considering the scanty information Littman had at his disposal, no reasonable man could have concluded that Mengele had come to Canada. Littman responded that his original letter to the Prime Minister had not declared an established fact. It was simply a request that the government investigate the matter. A bitter exchange ensued. "I think," explained Littman, "that is an entirely appropriate letter to address to a government body, unless you want to turn me into a vigilante going out running around looking for Mr Mengele." "You may already be one, sir," retorted Whitehall.[63]

At that, Jewish representatives exploded in rage. In the tumult Judge Deschênes, visibly upset, threatened to end the hearing unless order was restored. He ordered Whitehall to withdraw his remark, and Whitehall, satisfied he had made his point, complied. But tempers remained hot. Irwin Cotler feared that Whitehall's attack on Littman could leave the "suggestion that maybe we shouldn't have had the Commission to begin with." At the conclusion of the public hearings the following day, after the Judge had left the chamber, the press reported a confrontation between Cotler and Whitehall. Cotler reportedly accused Whitehall of possibly undermining the Commission's work. In the noisy debate that followed, Cotler was joined by Kenneth Narvey. White-hall responded by stalking out of the chamber. Cotler was seized with anger. As he told the press, "after forty years of government inaction," a spokesman for the Justice Department might jeopardize the Commission's integrity.[64]

The Whitehall uproar did not deter the Judge. The hearings were over for the time being, but the work was far from complete. No decision had been taken on the thorny question of whether to travel to the Soviet Union to take evidence against individuals in Canada accused of war crimes. Such a trip, if approved, would take time, and the Commission's deadline for submission of a report was fast approaching. At Judge Deschênes's request, Justice Minister Crosbie granted the first of several extensions. The life of the Commission was extended to the end of June 1986.

Other contentious issues continued to surface, again pitting Jewish organizations against the government or the Commission itself. The Judge had commissioned outside legal consultants to prepare secret reports on various issues. These reports made Jewish groups, especially the B'nai Brith, uneasy. They reminded Matas of the role played by the secret report of Martin Low in persuading the Liberal Cabinet that little could be done on the war-criminals issue. They feared that these current reports might again fall victim to either faulty reasoning or specific interpretations of statutes and precedent, thus harming the Jewish cause but remaining unchallenged because of their secrecy.[65]

In January 1986, David Matas, counsel for B'nai Brith, petitioned before the Federal Court of Canada that Judge Deschênes should be required to release the consultants' work prior to writing of his final report. Deschênes had indicated that he might include these studies as appendices to his final report. He did not yet wish to make their content public.[66]

In early February, the Federal Court denied the B'nai Brith motion, arguing that release of these reports would only delay the final report of the Commission. That had been the fear of Judge Deschênes himself, who seemed worried that release of the reports would lead to lengthy rejoinders, which would in turn require still further rebuttals, resulting in endless rounds of legal disputations.[67] But Matas was not satisfied: "If the commission should come to an erroneous conclusion based on those reports," he told the press, "the government isn't going to appoint another commission to conduct another study."[68] B'nai Brith decided to appeal the ruling. Congress, while in agreement about making public the reports, was less certain of the value of continuing court proceedings. They thus supported, but were not party to, the B'nai Brith initiative.[69]

On May 13 1986, B'nai Brith won its case in a unanimous ruling of the Appeal Court. The three appeal judges decided that the reports should be made public. In addition, they declared that interested groups should be given a reasonable opportunity to respond prior to the termination of the Commission's work. Since the deadline for termination of the inquiry was approaching, the Appeal Court was explicit. "The need to meet that time limit," it declared, "cannot be permitted to deprive the parties entitled thereto of their meaningful opportunity to comment."[70]

As it happened, the controversy proved to be a tempest in a teapot. The fears of the Jewish organizations were misplaced. Both Congress and the B'nai Brith found that, with one exception, the large part of the legal opinion in the reports paralleled their own reasoning or did not contradict it. They were clearly not, on balance, facing a replay of the Low memorandum.[71] Nevertheless, an important point had been made. For years Jewish leaders pressing the war-criminals issue had repeatedly encountered a wall of negative responses constructed from the chiselled stone of government secrecy. Now, perhaps the wall had been breached once and for all. Future decisions on the Nazi war-criminals issue would be made in the open arena of public scrutiny.

If Jews were obsessed with the openness of legal argument, Ukrainians were equally obsessed with "Soviet evidence." The term "Soviet evidence" proved problematic. This might more properly be called "evidence located in the Soviet Union." Many Nazi war crimes had taken place on the soil of eastern Europe in countries now part of the Soviet bloc. Much documentary evidence of these crimes was captured by the Red Army as it advanced westward against the Nazis in the latter stages of the war and was deposited in Soviet bloc government archives. In addition the Soviet bloc was home to many eyewitnesses to war crimes whose testimonial evidence could be important. Thus, while the press and the Commission latched onto the shorthand term "Soviet evidence," it was only Soviet by geography, not origin. But whatever term one used to describe the evidence, could the documents now be guaranteed to be free of Soviet tampering? Could testimony of Soviet bloc citizens be guaranteed to be accurate and trustworthy?

Jewish groups argued that the Commission should seek out evidence wherever it could be found, as long as Canadian courts and officials, using Canadian standards, could rule on its admissibility or quality. Eastern European ethnic organizations, particularly the CLC, as well as its like-minded supporters, publicly argued with equal passion that all Soviet evidence would be tainted, often deceptively so. No efforts should be made to obtain it.

Deschênes had first approached the Soviet Union in November 1985, asking whether the Commission could visit the Soviet Union to collect oral testimony and documentary evidence. It was rumoured that Deschênes was seeking information on only fifteen of more than eight hundred individuals who had been identified to the Commission as possible war criminals living in Canada. While the Soviets acknowledged receipt of the request, no reply was forthcoming for months. Coincidentally, while Soviet officials were pondering, some thought stalling, their reply to Deschênes, reports emanating from the Soviet Union told of village meetings, notably in Ukraine, in which residents recalled their wartime experiences and denounced specific individuals now residing in Canada. Alexey Makarov, spokesman for the Soviet Embassy in Ottawa, told the press these meetings were "an expression of the people's indignation."[72]

Meanwhile, Deschênes's June 30, 1986 deadline was fast approaching. In early May, the Commission heard the final arguments by the counsel for the various groups. All took the opportunity to reiterate their positions on the issue of Soviet evidence. The Judge and his advisers were, of course, aware of the dangers of using evidence provided by a totalitarian regime. As a result, they had stipulated a number of conditions for any Soviet visit. These included the presence of independent Canadian translators, access to original documents, access to any previous statements by any witnesses, freedom to conduct examinations in accordance with Canadian rules of evidence and confidentiality of identities. Soviet Counsellor Makarov had already violated one of the Deschênes preconditions. He identified by name two Toronto residents who were in fact under investigation by the Commission.[73]

In early May, the Commission received its first official response from the Soviets. They were told they could come to the Soviet Union, but not before June 10, just three weeks before the expiration of the Commission's mandate. That left no time for gathering and analysis of the evidence before the report was due. In addition, while the Commission had reportedly requested information about fifteen suspects, the Soviet Union only admitted having evidence about two, both Ukrainian, and both the targets of previous Soviet vilification. "As to the others", said Makarov, "upon the arrival of the Canadian delegation in the Soviet Union, it will be discussed." The Soviet response made no mention of the conditions outlined by the Commission. Needless to say, Commission officials were not pleased with what was at best a preliminary response. Meighen

felt that the reply left a "myriad" questions
unanswered.[74]

The timing also wouldn't allow the Commission to
co-ordinate visits to Poland, West Germany and Great
Britain. The Commission requested confirmation of the
original conditions for the visit and also added another
— the right to videotape all proceedings.[75]

Things now moved quickly. On May 28 the Canadian
Embassy in Moscow received a reply from the Soviet
Union that ostensibly agreed to the Commission's conditions. Yet when the Commission staffers examined
the Soviet reponse more closely, they discovered there
was less to the reply than met the eye. True, the Soviets had agreed to permit independent interviewers (not
translators) and videotaping by Canadians of witnesses'
testimony. But, they had remained vague about other
conditions.[76]

They had not indicated whether they would provide
the inquiry with the original Nazi documents confiscated
after the war. Photocopies were unacceptable to the
Judge, who was concerned with possibly fabricated documents. The Soviets also ignored the question of access
to previous statements made by witnesses. The Soviets
had already violated the confidentiality of the names of
suspects in leaks to the press from their Ottawa embassy. In addition, Meighen contended that the Soviets
had failed to guarantee that witnesses would be interviewed under Canadian rules of evidence. He claimed
that the Soviet contention that "Canadian lawyers will
be given the opportunity to clarify from witnesses all
questions of relevant interest" was an insufficient guarantee of fidelity to Canadian rules of evidence. As a result, the Commission declared it would not go to the
Soviet Union.[77]

Eastern European groups hailed the Commission's
decision. "What they wanted to present was well re-
hearsed ahead of time. The witnesses, and I use that
term in quotations, perform like actors in a play," argued Yaroslaw Botiuk, Division counsel. Jewish groups
who had hoped for a different outcome were disap-

pointed. But the negative decision was not wholly unexpected. Congress leaders felt "a bit disappointed," but
thought that it was not a fateful decision. They made
representations to have the issue reopened but there
was no sustained pressure following the decision to
have it reversed.[78]

Only days after the decision, Justice Minister Crosbie
granted the Commission yet another three-month extension to complete its already twice delayed report. Cotler hoped that the extra time would allow the
Commission to visit the Soviet Union. He argued that
attempting to organize the visit through correspondence
had been and would remain less productive than face-
to-face negotiations with Soviet authorities. This was
not to be. The extension had been granted, in part, because Deschênes was suddenly taken ill and needed
time to recuperate. The issue of going to the Soviet
Union was now settled.[79]

Once the fireworks, dramatics and oratory were done,
what were the key legal and political arguments in the
eighteen legal briefs presented to the Commission
which Deschênes would have to wade through? The
Jewish position focused on developing as many remedies as possible to the problem of alleged war criminals
in Canada. In separate briefs Congress and B'nai Brith
first developed an historical and moral framework,
rooted in the story of Canadian governmental apathy
to, if not collusion in, the immigration of suspected war
criminals in the post-war period, and subsequent inaction about their apprehension. Against this shortfall in
state moral authority and imputations of guilt against
state authorities, they postulated a variety of legal alternatives for action.

The Ukrainian briefs, submitted to Deschênes after
the Jewish briefs were made public, also combined
communal passion with legal argument. The moral position comprised two elements. First, that the proceedings might smear the good name of a community of
Ukrainian Canadians, 90 percent Canadian born,

through the possible guilt of a very few. Indeed some felt that this, not the apprehension of a few Nazi criminals, was the hidden intent of what they thought of as Ukrainian-baiters. Second, that Ukrainian immigrants who had entered Canada after the war after having served in the Galicia Division were not by definition war criminals. The legal arguments focused on the discrediting of the use of any Soviet evidence, and on outlining objections to possible remedies proposed by Jewish organizations.[80]

Sol Littman submitted an early brief on behalf of the Simon Wiesenthal Center. In his submission, which had elicited the emotional response from Marika Bandera, Littman tried to defuse the ethnic issue by suggesting that ethnic labels were merely descriptive, "like trying to write about the FLQ without any reference to French Canada." Littman also argued that any war criminal, including Jewish collaborators with the Nazis, ought to receive equivalent treatment.[81]

The B'nai Brith submission avoided discussing ethnic issues but did not hold back on emotionalism. Spokesman Frank Dimant set the tone: "I will not dwell on the policy of Canada during World War Two when refuge was denied to my parents and to my relatives." He cited a series of rationales for the legal pursuit of war criminals: love of justice, respect for law, compassion for victims of the Holocaust; a desire to prevent a recurring Holocaust; obligations to Jewish ancestors who perished in the Holocaust; obligations to our society to prevent historical truth from being obliterated (a reference to high-profile Holocaust deniers). Yet Dimant, like Cotler who spoke later, attempted to avoid the appearance of Jewish partisanship on the issue of war criminals. He appealed to Canada's conscience as a democratic society, a Christian society and a member of "spaceship earth."[82]

The Jewish demand for urgent action was driven by the spectre of governmental inaction against Nazis throughout the post-war period. As Cotler argued before the Commission, that record raised a "reasonable apprehension of obstruction of justice," particularly with regard to the deliberate role of the government in admitting alleged war criminals. Bad enough that the government terminated prosecution of war criminals in 1948; bad enough that the government enabled Barbie associate Count Jacques de Bernonville and other Vichy collaborators to enter Canada; bad enough that the Diefenbaker government in 1962 believed that prosecutions of Nazi war criminals could be construed as pandering to "Jewish revenge"; bad enough that immigration files were revealed to have been destroyed in 1982. The policy of the RCMP, until 1983, was that Nazi war criminals were not to be investigated unless "otherwise instructed."[83] All this was bad enough — at least let the government act now before the biological clock made it too late for any of those who had committed crimes to face justice.

In their briefs to the Commission, the Jewish representatives also took issue with the ghost of the Low memorandum, even as they laid out options for future policy.[84] Indeed, Kenneth Narvey submitted to Deschênes a detailed ninety-two page legal critique of the Low report. Cotler, in another twenty-eight page critique, called the report less a discussion paper than a "series of conclusions" which foreclosed from Cabinet a full range of choices and a "sophisticated rationale for continued inaction" showing little ingenuity or creativity.[85] B'nai Brith counsel David Matas was even more scathing. During a speech in Montreal, he had complained that the Low report did not even meet the minimum standards demanded of a law review article in that Low failed to present and analyse contrary precedents, law or arguments.[86]

Oddly, there is little disagreement in the Low report, the Jewish submissions and the Ukrainian briefs on the list of conceivable legal remedies. The disagreement arises with regard to which, if any, of these are acceptable, feasible or desirable. Even the Low report allowed that extradition was a viable option. But Jewish briefs urged the Canadian government to adopt an interventionist stance, and not wait for other countries to initiate proceedings.[87]

The Canadian government could, the Jewish groups suggested, request the West Germans to initiate extradition proceedings against alleged war criminals of either German or non-German origin, for commission of war crimes on German-controlled territory during World War II. To date, Germany had sought the extradition of only Helmut Rauca, a German national. In 1982, however, West Germany announced that in appropriate cases it might also request the extradition of alleged war criminals of non-German origin. It has yet to do so.

Moreover, Canada could honour, if not openly encourage, requests for extradition from countries with which it already had extradition treaties, including Czechoslovakia, Hungary, Yugoslavia and Rumania. Indeed, in 1981 a Yugoslav was extradited from Canada to face a charge of rape. In the United States, the more telling example was the extradition of eighty-six-year-old Nazi collaborator Andrija Artukovic to Yugoslavia to face charges of mass murder.

More controversially, the Congress briefs also put forward the idea of extradition to Israel as an option to be considered. That would require Israeli co-operation in an amendment to the existing extradition treaty between Canada and Israel, to enable the treaty to apply to offences committed before the treaty came into force in 1969. In addition, the Canadian government and courts would have to recognize the jurisdiction of Israel over war crimes. That posed no problem in the view of Congress, since war crimes and crimes against humanity were considered "universal." Jurisdiction was not limited to specific states. Congress cited an American precedent for extradition to Israel. An alleged camp guard at Treblinka was recently ordered to be surrendered to Israel under the US–Israel extradition treaty. His name was John Demjanjuk.[88]

To move beyond extradition was to challenge the Low recommendations again. In advocating denaturalization and deportation, along an American model, the Jewish briefs again attacked the Justice Department's conventional wisdom. War criminals in Canada could be deprived of their citizenship, the briefs urged, if fraud on entry or during the citizenship process could be established. It was argued that applicants for landing or citizenship have a "duty to disclose" histories of criminality. The government could also amend the *Citizenship Act* to allow specifically for denaturalization of war criminals.

Following denaturalization, Canada, like the United States, could press for deportation. The United States had deported Feodor Feodorenko, a death-camp guard, to the Soviet Union following his denaturalization. Canada had yet to deport anyone to the Soviet Union. Deportation could apply to any Nazi war criminal who was a landed immigrant or a naturalized citizen, who had made false statements at entry. The attraction of deportation was that it could occur without having to prove fraudulent intent, and thus could be the more far-reaching remedy if applied rigorously.

While denaturalization and deportation were the preferred route, they were cumbersome to implement under Canadian law. Denaturalization is done by a Canadian federal court, while deportation is handled by immigration adjudicators. Some streamlining of procedures might be in order.

The Jewish briefs also sought options in existing legislation. It was suggested that prosecution in Canada could be undertaken under the Canadian *War Crimes Act of 1945*. That act was an instrument designed originally to facilitate military trials during wartime, and had been used by Canada as the legal basis for four trials which Canada held in occupied Germany just after the war. Matas had argued that these trials could be revived as remedies in Canada, and that a military tribunal could be considered as an "expert tribunal."

If the government preferred, finally, it could introduce new legislation to facilitate trial in Canada. War crimes and crimes against humanity could be designated as offences under the Canadian *Criminal Code*. Indeed, Canada's *Criminal Code* had already incorporated amendments which listed international offences such as hostage taking, airplane hijacking and diversion of nuclear materials as criminal offences.[89]

Any such new legislation would have to confront the problem of retroactivity. The Canadian Charter of Rights and Freedoms, reflecting prevailing views of the western legal tradition, prohibits retroactive criminal legislation. But Canada had already allowed an exception, in cases where Canadian law retroactively makes criminal acts which were criminal at the time according to the international law of nations. This was done through Section 11(g) of the Charter, which had originally been proposed by Congress to facilitate prosecution of war criminals.[90]

These were the range of options, and the Jewish briefs urged the government to consider all of them, but showed a slight bias towards extradition as the ideal remedy. They did, however, recognize that other remedies, such as denaturalization and deportation from Canada or trial in Canada might, in the end, be the more practical route to justice.[91]

Apart from these precise remedies, the Jewish briefs raised two other legal issues. They recommended that a Canadian equivalent to the American Office of Special Investigations of the US Justice Department (OSI) be established. As Matas argued, the Deschênes Commission, while it was sitting, was acting as a *de facto* OSI.[92] It was in fact investigating over 800 allegations of war criminality. Matas's recommendation reflected the sense that the track record of the RCMP and the Justice Department, over the past forty years, had demonstrated neither zeal nor competence in the pursuit of war criminals. Perhaps new players, in a new organizational unit, could do the job.

The second issue was that of evidence. In any investigation, it was urged, evidence ought to be accepted regardless of its source, including the Soviet Union or Soviet bloc countries. Both Cotler and Matas were only too aware of the limitations of the Soviet legal system. Cotler's long-distance defence of Soviet dissident Anatoly Scharansky had brought him into direct contact with fabricated evidence. But the Jewish position was that evidence obtained from sources under Soviet control would be studied by Canadian courts, under Canadian rules of evidence. It ought not to be rejected out of hand.

Indeed, part of the evidence used in the Rauca extradition hearing was a report by Rauca's Nazi superiors which outlined the murders for which he was responsible. It had come from Soviet archives.[93] Moreover, the experience of both West Germany and the OSI with evidence which had come from Soviet sources had, on the whole, been quite favourable.[94]

The major Ukrainian briefs, notably that prepared by John Sopinka, were as much a refutation of Congress and B'nai Brith conclusions as an independent statement of legal philosophy. In general the Ukrainian briefs began by setting the historical context of events in Ukraine before and during World War II.[95] The central thrust of these historical overviews was to demonstrate, for the record, that Ukrainians were victims of Nazi and Soviet oppression alike. The submissions were also at pains to demonstrate that wartime Ukrainian nationalist groups were not organizational accomplices of the Nazis, and that the Galicia Division of the SS was a unit engaged in fighting the Soviet Army. None had any role, the briefs claimed, in organized war criminality.[96]

This need to "set the record straight" reflects the preoccupation with a possible tarring of Ukrainian Canadians as being either war criminals — an absurdity in a community over 90 percent Canadian born — or as knowingly harbouring war criminals in their midst. Thus UCC counsel John Sopinka urged "the Commission should make it abundantly clear that members of the OUN and UPA are not under investigation."

Any other result would lend credence to the Soviet effort at historical falsification, and deal a grave blow at the efforts of the Ukrainian Canadians to represent their cultural heritage. If there is any evidence that any Ukrainians are suspected of involvement in the commission of atrocities by the Nazis (which is denied), it is of fundamental importance to the Ukrainian Canadian community that the isolated nature of such actions outside the purview of the organizations which enjoyed broad popular support through the Ukrainian population should be underlined.[97]

Closely linked to the defence of the community's name was the argument against Soviet evidence. Sopinka warned that Soviet authorities could intimidate witnesses and coerce testimony. The Soviet Union could not be trusted to abide by Canadian rules of evidence. There was, he continued, ample reason to question the Soviet justice system. He cleverly cited Cotler's own massive brief prepared for Jewish dissident Anatoly Scharansky, as supporting the unreliability of Soviet evidence. Original documents, Sopinka allowed, might be "slightly more reliable" since they could be subjected to expert examination. But such evidence should only be "used in accordance with the ordinary Canadian rules of admissibility. No relaxation in the rules can be justified in favour of Soviet evidence when the liberty of a Canadian resident or citizen is concerned."[98]

What is ironic about the Ukrainian arguments, with their emphasis on competing versions of the historical record, is that Congress and B'nai Brith representations make essentially no mention of European history. They carefully avoid mention of the role of any Ukrainian or other groups in war criminality or anti-Semitic persecutions.

In a sense, Congress and the B'nai Brith didn't have to. The Jewish record of victimization during the Holocaust had become the universally accepted narrative.

The decision to set up the Commission itself, and the Commission's acknowledgment that non-Germans played a role in the commission of war crimes, demonstrated as much. As for the issue of Soviet evidence, it was simply one of many issues in the Jewish briefs. For some Ukrainians, on the other hand, the fight over Soviet evidence was part and parcel of a broader agenda, that of opposing any *de facto* recognition of the legitimacy of the Soviet regime. Militants accepted as fact that the impetus for the search for Nazi war criminals was largely a KGB-inspired scheme aimed at discrediting Ukrainian communities abroad.

Against this background, it is not surprising that Ukrainian arguments sought to broaden the Commission's legal mandate, which would then enable Ukrainians, like Jews, to claim their rightful place as historical victims. Why, they demanded, focus only on Nazi war crimes? The concern with Nazi war criminals, they felt, should be expanded to include any and all war crimes, including those which may have taken place at the behest of a Soviet bloc regime. This should include people responsible for orchestrating the Ukrainian famine of 1932, or those who collaborated with invading Soviet troops in Ukraine 1939–41, during which time so many Ukrainian national leaders were systematically murdered.

On procedural matters, extradition to West Germany was considered acceptable, but any extradition to eastern bloc countries, with or without treaty, was opposed. Sopinka argued, moreover, that the Canadian Charter of Rights and Freedoms does not permit extradition to a country whose standards of justice are possibly inadequate. Thus the extradition of the alleged Yugoslavian rapist, which took place in 1981 prior to the Charter coming into effect, should not now be permitted. The Ukrainian position also opposed extradition to Israel. The Ukrainian brief argued that Israel has no material or legal claim for crimes not committed against its citizens, nor on its territory, before the Israeli state was formed.

The Ukrainian position also rejected denaturalization and deportation as possible remedies. These decisions would be made in a non-criminal court proceeding where the actual proving of war criminality need not occur. In these proceedings the issue would be illegal entry not war crimes. Thus, the suspect would be punished for a lesser crime because, it was argued, he had committed a worse one. In other words, Sopinka claimed, before this could be seen as a remedy to rid Canada of war criminals, it must first be established that these suspects were indeed war criminals. Thus denaturalization and deportation put the cart before the horse. Moreover, the deportation remedy could also strike terror into the hearts of many immigrants who might have — deliberately or inadvertently — misrepresented some fact upon entry, and who might suddenly feel threatened under strict enforcement of the law.

Furthermore, prosecutions under existing law in Canada were seen as impossible. Among other points, it was argued that international law, which includes the category of war crimes, has the status of common law, the corpus of legal precedents with status in Canadian law. Thus it could not form the basis for a criminal prosecution, under Section 8 of the Canadian *Criminal Code*. That provision states that no one can be convicted of a common-law offence under the *Criminal Code*.[99]

The only possible option might be to change the *Criminal Code* or to amend the *Citizenship Act*. If there had to be a solution, trial in Canada was preferred to any other. However, the Ukrainian briefs raised the question of whether the benefits of such actions would be worth the costs. The number of war criminals waiting to be found was small, Sopinka noted, and the potential for social disharmony great.

If your investigations have revealed only a relatively small number of suspects, and if the actions attributed to them do not constitute major war crimes but may well be actions on the borderline between legitimate warfare and illegitimate warfare, and especially if any subsequent proceedings would need to place significant reliance upon Soviet supplied evidence, it is my submission that it would be more advisable for the Commission to recommend that no new legislation be introduced.[100]

Finally, and not surprisingly, the Jewish and Ukrainian briefs differed on the need for a separate investigative unit. The Ukrainian submissions strongly opposed the setting up of an OSI-like organization. It was not only unnecessary, they claimed, but could also lead to witch-hunts and to ethnic discord, as in the United States.

In short, the Ukrainian position would appear to have been pro forma support for the attempt to discover and prosecute war criminals, combined with assertions that the numbers might not warrant a major effort. It did not exhibit enthusiasm for any possible remedy to facilitate investigation or prosecution. If the government was committed to action, trial in Canada was the most acceptable of a poor lot of options.

As the formal hearings concluded, the Ukrainian and Jewish communities were left to wait for the report. And wait they did. The actual drafting took longer than anticipated, and required several extensions. When a final draft was presented to the government, in December 1986, the end was still not in sight. The cabinet feared that even in that section of the report which would be released to the public, there was possibly too much descriptive detail about individual cases brought before the Commission and this might lead to identification of possible suspects and violation of confidentiality. The report was sent back to the Commission, to expunge the offending portions.[101]

But behind the scenes, the Ukrainian and Jewish communal organizations were doing more than waiting. From day one of the announcing of the Commission, both sets of communal organizations had swung into action. Even before Deschênes heard his first witness, each had mobilized for a public-relations blitz directed at the government and the Canadian public. As always, there were a few token efforts at outreach or damage control between the two communities, notably at the top echelons of the UCC, Congress and the B'nai Brith. But most communal energies were directed inward, to arouse members of the group.

For Jewish leaders, already highly organized, the war-criminals issue, along with relations with the Ukrainian community, was only one item among many on a crowded communal agenda. The appointment of the Commission simply changed the order, putting war criminals ahead of other Jewish community concerns.

For Ukrainian leaders, and indeed for many in the organized Ukrainian-Canadian community, the war-criminals issue swamped all other issues. It mobilized the community as had nothing else in the post-war Canadian experience. The Jewish community had been the main actor on the war-criminals issue prior to Deschênes, but the Ukrainian community, feeling threatened, emerged to share the spotlight during the period of the Commission's mandate. The passions which occasionally surfaced during the Commission hearings continued to percolate, in even more extreme form, within the communities at large.

Chapter 6

The Perils of Ethnic Politics: What Happened Behind the Scenes

To the casual observer the Deschênes process must have seemed a peculiar but self-contained universe — a strange mixture of one part dry judicial hearing, one part detailed history lesson and one part wild street brawl. The press kept close tabs on the Commission. The war-crimes issue was not only an important story, it was also sexy journalism. Revelations about the seedy underbelly of Canada's immigration past, the intrusion of cold-war politics into the hearings and, not to be overlooked, finding two of Canada's senior ethnic communities represented by high-profile lawyers locking horns in public was the stuff that sold newspapers.

Nor did the hearings exist in a vacuum. Jewish and Ukrainian community support groups were involved in research, public relations, lobbying and, especially in the case of the Ukrainian Civil Liberties Commission, fundraising.

The CLC launched a public campaign to raise $1,000,000 to cover costs and carry out special programs such as research. But unlike the Canadian Jewish community, the Ukrainian community, as one CLC official acknowledged, was "not used to digging into its pocket deeply."[1] With no community-wide fundraising apparatus in place, competing local needs and little history of such campaigns, the million-dollar goal seemed enormous. However, Lubomyr Luciuk, the CLC's research director, warned that the war-criminals crisis was "probably the single greatest threat to the Ukrainian Diaspora that we have faced since the Second World War."[2] Money had to be found.

Still the flow of money was not what was hoped. But instead of engaging professional fundraisers, a network of voluntary fundraisers was pressed into service. Their expectations were often low and, without a core of big "givers," so were contributions. Thus, however deeply concerned Ukrainian Canadians and their supporters might be, their concern was not readily translated into dollars.

The CLC's budget and fundraising campaign, such as it was, generated other problems. Some western Canadian Ukrainian leaders worried that the CLC in Toronto couldn't raise money because the CLC was running the community's fundraising campaign as it did the rest of its activities — poorly and amateurishly. "Fundraising," they charged, "was totally unco-ordinated, with different groups appealing to the community for funds." With so much at stake, some of the discontented western leadership pressed the UCC leadership in Winnipeg to wrestle control of the Deschênes issue back from Toronto.

This was not done. But western anxiety that a faltering and unprofessional fundraising campaign was but the most visible sign of a larger ineffectual CLC performance in representing the entire community's interests had to be dealt with. John Gregorovich of the CLC was saddled with the task of reassuring the western group — a community seen by some in Toronto as too Canadianized, too lacking in commitment to the national cause as compared to Toronto and Montreal communities.[3] Nevertheless, in part to allay growing dissension in the western ranks, the CLC announced a national conference to be held in Toronto in late summer 1985 "to inform its members about the latest proceedings of the Deschênes Commission of Inquiry on

War Criminals and to discuss its strategies for the future.[4]

If the $1,000,000 campaign helped stir up internal Ukrainian-Canadian discord, it also left Sol Littman unsettled as to the $1,000,000 agenda of the Ukrainian lobby. On July 25 he held a press conference in the fashionable Harbour Castle Hilton in Toronto. Picking up on Ukrainian press stories about the fundraising effort, Littman issued a press release declaring it "a $1,000,000 'information campaign' designed to thwart the Commission of Inquiry on War Criminals in Canada and weaken Parliament's will to bring Nazi war criminals to justice." The collected funds, Littman warned, would be a "war chest" to set the stage for claiming that the number of war criminals in Canada did not warrant an inquiry.[5]

According to the *Toronto Star*, Littman was challenged by Lubomyr Luciuk, CLC research director, who "arrived uninvited" at Littman's press conference. Luciuk denied that Ukrainians or their allies wanted to "undermine" the Inquiry. Nevertheless, the press indicated that Luciuk, perhaps trying to deflect attention from the $1,000,000 campaign, attempted to redirect the discussion to the issue of Soviet evidence and questioned why Deschênes's mandate did not extend to all war criminals, not just Nazis. When the dust settled, Littman could be satisfied that he had focused media attention on the "war chest" revelation, and Luciuk that he had passionately confronted Littman on his own turf. The media got what it wanted — drama.[6] The popular media coverage, augmented by that of the Canadian Jewish press, did, however, raise within the Jewish community the spectre of a Ukrainian community intent on spending as much as was necessary to undermine the Deschênes process. The result was that some Jews may have wondered why the Ukrainian community would go to such lengths to protest, raise so much money, if it did not have something to hide.[7]

The denunciations back and forth between the CLC and the Wiesenthal Center's Sol Littman did not go unnoticed by the mainline Jewish leaders. They feared it would only serve to ethnicize the Deschênes debate. Casting the Nazi war-criminals issue as a parochial confrontation between Jews and eastern Europeans could not help but trivialize the issue in the public mind and make it a political hot potato for government. That was to be avoided. Privately Jewish leaders were not blind to the inter-ethnic nature of the current tension; but publicly they had to avoid any slugging match with eastern Europeans. The effort to rid Canada of Nazi war criminals must be seen by all as a matter of principle, upholding the honour of Canada and delivering to all Canadians justice long overdue.

These ongoing inter-ethnic tensions offered the press the confrontational copy it enjoyed, and kept the ethnic pot boiling, much to the chagrin of Congress leaders. Congress could not still the Ukrainian community, nor could it dismiss Littman. He had credibility, associated as he was with the prestigious Simon Wiesenthal Center. Littman was not dependent on Congress for his funds nor bound by Congress's resolutions.[8] But Congress could keep Littman at arm's length. His early offer to share his files and to work co-operatively on Deschênes-related matters with Congress was turned down.[9] In part, Congress may not have wanted to enhance Littman's credibility. It may also have feared dragging mainline Jewish organizations even deeper into inter-ethnic conflict associated with Littman and, some may have felt, diverting public focus away from war criminals in Canada.[10]

Several Congress leaders, already angered with Littman's seemingly aggressive style, became incensed when, in mid-October 1985, he sent a package of "well chosen articles and editorials" to all members of parliament. Nobody denied his right to lobby MPs, nor did anyone complain about the press clippings he enclosed. But some were displeased that he described his package as a corrective to the lobbying effort "by a coalition of Baltic and Ukrainian emigre organizations to discredit the Deschênes Commission." The term "emigre" seemed loaded, implying that the issue of Nazi war criminals, including the Jewish community's efforts, were somehow outside the context of Canadian society — the property of "emigre organizations" without the best interests of Canada at heart. In a letter to all MPs Milton Harris, president of Congress, rejected the "emigre" label as "unacceptable." While he expressed "regret" at the "activities of any group which attempts to inhibit and impede the activities of the Commission . . ." Harris affirmed that the "CJC rejects allegations that any ethnic groups be identified as culpable of genocide."[11]

Littman, seeing this as an unwarranted attack on his integrity, fired a broadside at Congress. He wrote to Alan Rose, executive head of Congress staff in Montreal, describing Congress's letter to MPs as touched by a spirit reminiscent of the *Judenrate*, Jewish councils in the ghettos of wartime Europe, accused by some of co-operation with the Nazis. Nor would he retract the term "emigre." The term was deliberately picked, Littman noted, and had been employed both by the World Jewish Congress to describe similar organizations in the US and in Ukrainian and Baltic publications to denote refugees escaping political tyranny.

Any implication that he or the Wiesenthal Center were prepared to hold specific ethnic groups responsible for the Holocaust was also rejected. Littman challenged Congress to locate anything, published or spoken, by which he or the Wiesenthal Center labelled any ethnic group as being guilty of genocide. Furthermore, he suggested that Congress staff was in the dark as to the true nature and strength of the Ukrainian lobbying effort. Littman wrote that Congress's staff was so misinformed on unfolding events that they could not properly brief Congress leadership.[12] Littman also wrote to all MPs defending himself and the Wiesenthal Center. Again he rejected any implication that the Center held any group "culpable of genocide" or that the term "emigre" was intended to put a slur on immigrants.[13]

Harris responded to Littman. He claimed Littman's original letter to MPs "did severe injury" to the cause of flushing out Nazi war criminals in Canada and bringing them to justice. Littman had succeeded only in "exacerbating the feeling in the Ukrainian Canadian Community and their political supporters against the Deschênes Commission. Our [Congress Executive] Officers were determined that the Members of Parliament know that you have no mandate from the Canadian Jewish Community to represent them and I do."

But the real problem, according to Harris, was not Littman's attempt to speak for Canadian Jewry. It was the possible damage his actions inflicted on the government's political will to act positively once Deschênes presented his recommendations to cabinet.

> The terrible danger of public attacks on other ethnic communities, or their 'emigre organizations,' will heighten the perception amongst the Canadian public, followed inexorably by the politicians, that the whole question of bringing Nazi War Criminals in Canada to justice is simply a dispute between Ukrainian and Jewish Canadians. If that perception were to take hold then any action that might be recommended by the Deschene [sic] Commission will be blocked at the political level.[14]

Did the exchange take its toll of Littman? Would he be isolated, left out in the cold by the establishment Canadian Jewish community? He seemed as much a thorn in the side of some mainline Jewish leaders as he was a bogeyman to Ukrainians. He had been publicly criticized by Congress in front of national political leaders. His press credibility was at stake. Bad enough to be seen as a pariah by many in the Ukrainian community; still worse to be regarded in that way by Jewish leaders.

Littman approached several key Toronto Congress personalities, reconfirming his willingness to work with them. Over lunch in the coffee shop of a downtown Toronto hotel, Littman explained to them his desire for openness and co-operation. Those listening knew Harris was determined to keep Littman at arm's length.[15] But Littman felt that he had at least made the effort and lines of communication to other leaders had been re-opened.

Outside Congress Littman did have a sympathetic following who saw him as the personification of the forceful effort to uncover war criminals, as much as some in the Ukrainian community saw him as the personification of evil. For some in Congress there remained the uneasy fear that as a lightning rod for Ukrainian hostility, Littman might inadvertently help make the Nazi war-criminal issue even more ethnically divisive. But if Congress was too publicly disapproving of Littman, this could further arm those marginal dissident Jewish groups long protesting that Congress was more worried about rocking the boat than delivering Nazi war criminals to justice. Thus public disassociation from Littman's letter to the MPs was about as far as Congress dared go in separating itself from Littman. However, if Congress's response was too much for Littman, it was too little for the CLC. It would appear that nothing less than a public denunciation of Littman would please them.

To the uninformed, this uproar might have seemed to be an unfortunate side show compared to the drama then unfolding at the hearings. Nothing could have been further from the truth. The sputtering controversy that surrounded Ukrainian-Jewish relations served as a catalyst for the CLC campaign. Not only did invoking Littman's name help to rally Ukrainian community foot soldiers to the cause, it also heightened the perception of some that the Nazi war-criminals issue was ethnically divisive and a political minefield. This was precisely the point the CLC and its eastern European allies wanted to impress on government. As the Jewish community demanded that Deschênes be left to do what Deschênes had to do, unimpeded by outside political influence, the Ukrainian lobby hoped to impress on government that political fallout not just from Deschênes's possible recommendations but from the Deschênes process itself would be serious. Thus, while Congress was transfixed on the Deschênes hearings, the CLC left the hearings to John Sopinka and focused on the political arena.

In blurring the line between public debate and interest lobbying, the CLC could count on the support of a small band of Tory backbenchers that included several of eastern European background or representing ridings with heavily European constituencies. None had been informed or consulted by the Prime Minister before establishment of the Commission. A key player was Andrew Witer, proud of his Ukrainian ancestry and representing the heavily eastern European Toronto riding of Parkdale–High Park. His Ottawa office became a clearing house for press clippings and other documentary material mailed to a list of those key individuals sympathetic to the cause. Witer, who personally felt a "conscious" and perhaps even "organized and orchestrated" attack on the Ukrainian-Canadian community was under way, did not shrink from battle.[16]

The Conservative caucus was warned that Deschênes could be the cause of fundamental realignment in eastern European voting patterns. In June 1985 a discussion paper advised members of caucus that the war-crimes issue would generate mass defections from the Conservatives at the next election. The paper, stamped "Confidential," described the Commission as "a quick and easy solution made in haste."

Eastern Europeans' groups in Canada feel that they specifically have been targeted. They feel they have been unjustly smeared and maligned in the press and that the press has been selective, and at times, even unfair to their side of the story. There have been accusations by individuals that had been interviewed, that reports had been distorted.

The Deschênes process, especially the "Soviet evidence" controversy, was being laid at the door of "the Mulroney government." As a result, "good will" towards that government "has been seriously damaged among Eastern European electorates. This loss of faith and trust in the Tory party will inevitably manifest itself in the next election."

Ethnic groups tend to vote in blocks, and where there is as little as 5% of any ethnic group concentrated in a riding, that percentage can have a dramatic impact on the outcome of the election. Collective block swings across the country could significantly alter the results of a general election.

The paper speculated on likely Deschênes recommendations, pointing out the downside of each, especially if Deschênes sanctioned the introduction of "Soviet-supplied evidence" which "most certainly will be fabricated." But it reserved its parting shot for the problems Deschênes would represent in swing ridings where even a small eastern European vote could be the key to victory or defeat.

The consequences for the Progressive Conservative Party, under whose tenure in office the events are occurring, would manifest themselves at the ballot box in 1988, with potentially irreparable damage being felt in the Prairie provinces, large Metropolitan centres such as Toronto, Montreal, as well as the Niagara Peninsula.[17]

Reinforcing this warning about a restive and increasingly anti-Tory eastern European backlash, a mass demonstration broke the quiet of a usually sleepy Ottawa summer. As reported in the Ukrainian press, several thousand Ukrainian Canadians and their supporters gathered in the capital, many bused in from Toronto and Montreal. They gathered on Parliament Hill, some carrying placards reading "Hitler and Stalin were Blood Brothers" and "Prosecute Soviet War Criminals" but none was more telling than that of a pained Ukrainian concentration camp survivor holding aloft a sign reading, "I was in Auschwitz."

The main speaker was Yuri Shymko, a longtime outspoken Ukrainian stalwart and Tory member of the Ontario legislature for a heavily eastern European riding in Toronto's west end. He demanded the Commission's mandate be expanded to include all war criminals, not just Nazis. ". . . Just as we do not discriminate between victims," he urged, "we cannot discriminate between murderers and war criminals, be they survivors of the long bankrupt regime of Adolf Hitler or the reigning survivors of the presently ruling heirs of Josef Stalin."

Following the official ceremony on the Hill, demonstrators paraded towards the Soviet embassy. The procession stopped at the Cenotaph, the National War Memorial. Here two children laid wreaths to commemorate the millions of Ukrainians who died in World War II. The parade, stretching more than a mile, then swung past the American Embassy to protest OSI use of evidence from the Soviet Union and finally arrived at the gate of the Soviet Embassy. A red flag bearing two symbols — the hammer and sickle and the swastika — was burned.[18]

Witer and several sympathetic Conservative MPs combined to raise the Deschênes issue in caucus on several occasions. Many members privately agreed the Deschênes inquiry was a political blunder but publicly there was no turning back. The judicial process must move ahead. The government would just have to ride out whatever political storms brewed.[19]

At least the Jewish community was now supportive. Some might originally have doubted the sincerity of the Mulroney government, but most in the community now saluted it for taking action. At an Israel Bond Dinner in Montreal, Mulroney received an enthusiastic welcome. In a prepared speech, full of the effusiveness demanded of such an occasion, the Prime Minister promised that any Deschênes recommendations "will be dealt with as a matter of great urgency by the government." Repeatedly interrupted by applause, Mulroney continued: "The Holocaust is an indelible stain on the conscience of history. We shall never forget. And Canada shall never become a safe haven for those guilty of or associated with such monstrous acts."[20]

But what of any eroding eastern European and Ukrainian Tory support? Here damage control was necessary. Publicly, the government never wavered from support of the Deschênes process. Privately, eastern Europeans needed to be reassured of the government's awakened sensitivity to their concerns. Prominent and high-profile cabinet ministers reached out to eastern European leaders. Ray Hnatyshyn and Don Mazankowski, identified as ranking eastern European voices in cabinet, were joined by others like John Crosbie and Michael Wilson, who had personally and actively courted eastern European support for the Conservatives in the years before the Mulroney landslide.[21]

Ukrainian leaders across Canada picked up a simple message from meetings with politicians. The Deschênes inquiry may have been a blunder, a political error, but there was no turning back now. Deschênes would be allowed to fulfil his mandate. The government, however, was now mindful of eastern European interests, and community leaders were reminded that it was Cabinet, not Deschênes, which would make the final determination on any action which lay ahead. Consultation was promised. The Deschênes cloud also had a silver lining. It would once and for all lay to rest the divisive issue of Nazi war criminals that had too long festered in the Canadian body politic.[22]

Eastern European spokesmen reportedly listened politely, but some, especially Ukrainians, remained cautious. They were not ready to let up their pressure. In private fence-mending talks with Crosbie, for example, several Ukrainian spokesmen made it clear they shared their community's anger with a government so insensitive to Ukrainian interests. How could they have been so blindly ill-informed? One spokesman later recalled that he demanded to know if the outspoken minister from Newfoundland had been in Ottawa so long he could no longer recognize an iceberg when he saw it. Surely Crosbie must "know as he saw the war crimes iceberg float by" that there was far more to it than broke the surface.[23] In response to a routine Conservative fund-raising appeal, longtime Conservative supporter John Gregorovich, head of the CLC, again made his sharp displeasure with the government known. Instead of his regular contribution, he discontinued his support until the war criminal issue subsided.[24]

Tory insiders may have worried about withering grass-roots party support among eastern Europeans, but neither the Prime Minister nor Judge Deschênes would tolerate political intrusions into the Commission's affairs. Ministers set out quietly to soothe ruffled eastern European feathers, but public utterances by MPs and Cabinet ministers alike were discouraged lest they be seen as interfering in the judicial process.

Otto Jelinek was a case in point. As minister responsible for multiculturalism, he was also responsible for promoting inter-ethnic harmony, but he was also personally caught up in the issue. Originally a refugee from Czechoslovakia, he could not help but sympathize with the anti-Communist thrust of those railing against gathering evidence in the Soviet Union. His every instinct told him to enter the fray. If he could not speak out publicly, he was ready to appear before Deschênes, an act that would generate even more publicity.[25]

Jelinek's staff proved far less enthusiastic. He was advised to avoid speaking out lest his intervention be seen as political interference. To help restrain their minister, senior staff sought and received an advisory from their legal services office. Jelinek was informed he had best desist from addressing any statement to the Deschênes inquiry.

What is more, it was strongly suggested that any statement, whether before Deschênes or in any public forum, would only exacerbate Ukrainian-Jewish tension which he, as Minister of State for Multiculturalism, should be seeking to ease.[26]

But individual members of parliament were not gagged. They could and did speak out in the Deschênes process. A band of hard line Tory backbenchers, typified by Andrew Witer, were incensed at the very idea that potentially "tainted" evidence from the Soviet Union might find its way into Canadian courts. Witer requested leave to appear before the Deschênes Commission. He was turned down on the grounds that "the hearing of representations on the legality and advisability of collecting evidence abroad is restricted to those counsel for groups who have standing before the Commission." A written submission, however, would be appropriate.[27]

Several like-minded Tory backbenchers or those with substantial eastern European constituencies, including Pat Boyer, Alex Kindy and William Lesick, were also denied permission to address the Commission. They could, if they wished, submit written statements. In what seemed to the press as an incipient backbenchers' revolt, they wrote Deschênes to protest. Several MPs also unsuccessfully pressed the Justice Minister to intercede with Deschênes against allowing the gathering or use of evidence from the Soviet Union. They got nowhere.[28]

The brewing revolt in the backbench gave signs of spreading. Several more Tory backbenchers came forward to lend support to the anti-Soviet evidence group. They were joined by Toronto Liberal John Nunziata, his party's critic of the Solicitor General.[29] Even Edmonton Conservative MP David Kilgour, usually very warm towards Jewish concerns and head of the parliamentary Committee for Soviet Jewry, joined the protest, though he tried to minimize any rupture with the Jewish community. He protested to Deschênes against use of Soviet evidence and any expedition to the Soviet Union in search of such evidence, but he also sent a copy of his carefully worded Deschênes letter to Alan Rose, Executive Vice-President of the Canadian Jewish Congress. He wanted Rose to receive his complete letter rather than excerpts from the press, perhaps taken out of context.[30]

The explosion of press attention attending what seemed to many in the Jewish community as undue political meddling in the Deschênes proceedings coincided with a full-page Saturday *Globe and Mail* advertisement in September 1985 sponsored by key Ukrainian, Lithuanian, Latvian, Estonian and Slovenian organizations in Canada. The ad entitled "Why Discriminate" was prepared by an ad agency and published at a reported cost of $37,000. The CLC, which paid the lion's share of the cost, had a twin agenda. In part it hoped to convince the larger Canadian public that an injustice was in progress, that eastern Europeans were selectively and unjustly singled out for abuse. But the main target of the ad was the influential members of the Canadian media for whom *The Globe and Mail* was required reading.[31] But were the text and its message clear?

Does Moscow have a vested interest in discrediting refugees who were forced to flee Eastern Europe?

Why is the Commission of Inquiry on War Criminals focussing on political enemies of the Soviet Bloc?

Why are not all war criminals — in Nazi Germany, in the Soviet Union, Vietnam, Cambodia, Angola, and the Middle East equally horrible?

Who are being excused from investigation by the Commission?

It's a tragedy for all Canadians of Eastern European descent that the memory and the history of our homelands are being defiled by Soviet allegations of war crimes in Eastern Europe more than a generation ago.

If there are differences tell us what they are, so we can explain them to our children, our friends, our neighbours, and our colleagues at work. We're sure they must be wondering.

Below a drawing of an innocent little girl in folk dress and with flowers entwined in her hair was the plaintive plea. "How do we explain to our children?"[32]

The *Canadian Jewish News* had an answer. In an editorial entitled "Tell Them the Truth," it agreed the signatory group "owes their children — and themselves — an honest and historically verifiable explanation." It was time, the *CJN* asserted, for those who paid for the ad to squarely face the issue of "involvement" of local populations in the Holocaust rather than "pretend that nothing of the sort ever happened."

Justice will be served if our fellow Canadians do not try to interfere with a legitimate investigation and do not confuse the issues by splattering the pavement with red herrings. The issues are complex and emotional enough without such self-serving distractions.[33]

But the ad and the backbench protest seemed ominous to Jewish leaders. If the CLC was successful in muddying the political waters by churning up fears of a Soviet-inspired witch-hunt or complicate the process with talk of non-Nazi war criminals, there was no telling how the Cabinet or general public would respond to even the most reasoned recommendations from Deschênes. And if the Cabinet became convinced the continued hunt for Nazi war criminals was too ethnically divisive, too costly of national harmony, let alone Tory support, might it not shy away from decisive action? If this, as many suspected, was the underlying agenda of the Ukrainians and their allies, they seemed to be succeeding.

Perhaps Jewish leaders had been too transfixed on the Deschênes hearings while Ukrainians focused their energy on Parliament Hill. The CLC may not have been a model of lobbying efficiency but it might just be effective, in spite of itself. Jewish leaders realized they would have to respond. But how? The object was to keep the Nazi war-criminals issue from being seen as a problem of ethnicity rather than justice. But how could Congress counter the Ukrainian thrust without further ethnicizing the issue?[34]

In Toronto an ad hoc committee of the local Congress Joint Community Relations Committee gathered over a light lunch to consider "issues arising out of the campaign by certain East European groups pertaining to the Deschênes Commission." The committee was carefully briefed on deep-seated Ukrainian fears that the Deschênes inquiry was little more than a Soviet-inspired "witch hunt" designed to discredit the entire Ukrainian national cause. Talk soon focused on the role of MPs and the likely impact of the CLC-organized publicity campaign on them. The issues of "Soviet evidence" and enlarging the mandate of the Commission to include all war criminals were dismissed as "red herrings." These issues, most felt, were designed to ambush the inquiry before its recommendations ever got to Cabinet. If public doubts as to the Commission's gullibility could be raised, any recommendation it might make would be regarded as suspect.

But what to do? It was obviously important to avoid a "mud-slinging campaign." That would only exacerbate problems by playing into the hands of those who wanted the issue of Nazi war criminals seen as a discordant ethnic problem — a political hot potato. Nevertheless, something had to be done. It was decided they would first approach federal MPs from Ontario, "first and foremost those who expressed themselves on the issues of evidence" to "provide them with insight to what we see as the real issue: specifically bringing Nazi mass murderers to justice." Congress representatives in other parts of Canada were requested to do the same with their local MPs.

It was also suggested that "sympathetic" Ukrainian moderates be identified and lobbied in the hopes that they could use their influence, if any, to blunt some of the more intemperate aspects of the CLC campaign. There was some fear that the moderate voices had been pushed to the margins of the Ukrainian community and would not be listened to in the present climate. But all agreed the effort had to be made.

Finally, the ad hoc committee also suggested the old human rights coalition of labour, churches, other ethnic groups, academics, jurists and other progressive community spokesmen be reactivated. After all, wasn't ridding Canada of Nazi war criminals an issue of Canadian justice and human rights? This grouping might be supported by veterans' groups and others on record as calling for forthright action against Nazi war criminals in Canada. With "support and understanding" of a public coalition, it could be argued that catching Nazi war criminals commanded wide support in the larger civic culture.[35]

A series of meetings was arranged with MPs in and around Toronto, but they proved less than satisfactory from the Jewish point of view. MPs with direct and personal links into eastern European communities were also openly partisans of the Ukrainian campaign. Some had political problems speaking their mind. One with a large and vociferous eastern European voting bloc in his riding begged the political sensitivity of the question. Though he privately held counterviews, he dared not say so publicly. Still another proved so rude, ill informed and, in the eyes of his Jewish visitors, uncaring of the problem, that any further discussion was thought to be a waste of time and energy.[36]

Even as federal MPs were being contacted, the issue of Nazi war criminals and especially that of evidence from the Soviet Union spilled over onto the Ontario provincial stage, specifically the Ontario Conservative Party leadership campaign. In October 1985 MPP Yuri Shymko wrote to each of the then three provincial Tory leadership hopefuls soliciting their views on the Soviet-

evidence issue. Normally an issue like Nazi war criminals would have little place in a provincial leadership
campaign, but there was a feeling that if new legislation
were ever to be enacted, it might fall to provincial authorities to enforce that legislation. In any event, this
was not a normal leadership race. The front runner was
Larry Grossman. He was dogged by a whisper campaign — was the party ready to have a Jew carry its
banner into the next Ontario election? According to
The Globe and Mail, one of Grossman's opponents was
forced to purge his ranks of several workers after some
were reported to be publicly raising the question of
"whether the religion of candidates made a difference
to delegates."[37]

Replying to Shymko, all three leadership hopefuls endorsed the Deschênes process, but each also had reservations about the collection and use of evidence from
the Soviet Union — including Grossman. In a letter to
Shymko, Grossman stated, "I fully share your concerns
and those of your constituents with respect to the quality and admissibility of any evidence collected in the Soviet Union or its satellite countries."[38] The Shymko-
initiated exchange was publicized in the Ukrainian and
mass press.[39]

Grossman's reply to Shymko caused some consterna-
tion among Jewish leaders. Grossman had never been
particularly active in Jewish organizations, but in his
personal life he identified firmly with the community
and its traditions. Moreover, he did represent a largely
Jewish riding and never shrank from informing his provincial colleagues of Jewish concerns. For instance, he
was both forceful and effective in moving the provincial
Conservative government to pass legislation making it
illegal for Ontario firms to participate in the Arab boycott of Jews and Jewish-owned businesses, a step the
federal government had yet to take. But on the issue of
evidence from the Soviet Union, it appeared to some
that Grossman now ignored the Jewish community in a
mad scramble to snare the party leadership.

Congress hastily arranged meetings with all three Conservative leadership candidates. Grossman's opponents committed themselves to bring Nazis to justice but acknowledged reservations about the possibility of tainted Soviet-supplied evidence finding its way into Canadian courts. They also expressed concern about the politically volatile nature of interethnic tensions surrounding the issue. Politics was politics, and condemning the Soviet Union was good politics. There would be no retractions.

The meeting with Grossman proved equally discouraging. All knew he was in a tight race for party leadership. A few votes one way or the other could spell the difference between victory and defeat. The very idea that a Toronto Jew could be a serious contender for leadership of the Ontario Conservatives was an epoch-making event. He was obviously torn but the best he could do was pledge that should he win the leadership, he would be in touch with the Prime Minister to pass along the Jewish community's views.[40]

Meetings with MPs and others in hopes of de-emphasizing the ethnicity of the Nazi war-crimes issue accomplished little. Public statements distancing the Jewish community from any inference of group slander seemed to fall on deaf ears.[41] And the ethnic issue, especially as regards the Ukrainians, refused to go away in discussions within the Jewish community. Indeed, on the local level in Winnipeg, Edmonton, Calgary and Toronto, Jewish analysis of the Deschênes Commission became less a debate on the merits of this or that approach at the official hearings and more a discussion on how to deal with the problem of deteriorating Ukrainian-Jewish relations and its spin-off in the national political arena. All the while Jewish spokesmen at the hearings or in other public forums continued to insist the war-criminals issue was not an ethnic issue; privately they knew it had become one.[42]

One might still find a *modus vivendi* with the Ukrainian leadership. In an almost complete reversal of precedent, especially for Toronto and Montreal Jewry, Congress leaders, led by Milton Harris, wrote and otherwise put out word that they wished to make contact with their Ukrainian counterparts. But Harris did so knowing he did not have unanimous Jewish community support. There were some still convinced that the organized Ukrainian community harboured an "ideology of antisemitism [sic]."[43]

Others also attempted to initiate conciliatory dialogue between Ukrainians and Jews. Within weeks of the announcement of the Deschênes Commission, the Canadian Council of Christians and Jews, acting as honest broker, identified the deterioration in Ukrainian-Jewish relations as an area for Council intervention. In Montreal the Council had previously organized informal discussions between prominent Jews and Ukrainians. Now, with dark storm clouds hanging over Ukrainian-Jewish relations, the Council President again offered the Council as neutral ground for a friendly exchange of views. It did not work.

Victor Goldbloom, the Council President, was well acquainted with Montreal's Jewish leadership. He was cut from the same cloth. Softspoken and widely seen as a conciliator, Goldbloom had long been active in both Quebec politics and Jewish community and Congress affairs in Montreal. But he also had contact with the Montreal Ukrainian community. In Toronto he knew few in the Ukrainian organized structure and certainly few in leadership capacities. Nor did those within the UCC or CLC have any history of ongoing contact with Council. But using those connections he had, Goldbloom pressed on in organizing a preliminary meeting.

As chance would have it, just as a tiny group assembled in the Council's office in downtown Toronto, news broke of the B'nai Brith's official standing at the hearing. Caught off guard and with no sense of what the B'nai Brith move boded for the future, all agreed more dialogue was necessary, but not until the dust settled. Except for suggesting the names of others who might come to a subsequent gathering, this first meeting accomplished little.[44]

A meeting in Montreal in May 1985 under Council auspices was no more fruitful. The gathering at Temple Emanuel was, according to one Ukrainian participant, supposed to turn out two dozen delegates from each community. Congress, on the other hand, thought a large delegation would only make the gathering unwieldy and preclude a frank exchange. They wanted "no more than six participants on each side." When the group assembled, it was instantly clear that both sides had failed to communicate. The Ukrainians brought their full complement of twenty-four. Only twelve Jews attended, twice what Congress thought best, but that may have been interpreted by Ukrainians as a sign of the unwillingness of Jews to take interethnic dialogue seriously.

In advance of the meeting, each group was also asked to prepare a paper dealing with points of friction — "what irks us about the other." The Ukrainians prepared a paper. The Jews did not — yet another sign it seemed to Ukrainians of Jewish indifference to the discussion process. On the other hand, the Ukrainian paper seemed to Jews little more than an effort to instigate argument. To the Ukrainians' disappointment, Jews proved uninterested in scheduling follow-up meetings. Unlike Ukrainian leaders, Jewish leaders always thought of the Temple Emanuel meeting as a one-time event. The Ukrainians may have wanted a larger Jewish audience before whom their community's case could be made, but Jewish leaders left unconvinced that any further meetings were worth the effort. They preferred discussion between high-ranking Congress leaders and those of the UCC.[45]

In late June 1985 Goldbloom was able to assemble a small group including Sydney, Nova Scotia-born Father John Tataryn, priest at the large Ukrainian Catholic St Demetrius Church in suburban Toronto. St Demitrius was at the cutting edge of Toronto's more "Canadianized" Ukrainians, dominated by a second- and third-generation of Canadian congregation. But, he recalled, they were no less concerned than their parents and grandparents about attacks on their community.

At the time of the meeting, the issue of evidence from the Soviet Union was heating up. The discussion reportedly got off to a poor start. Goldbloom, Tataryn felt, threw a "wet blanket" on dialogue by opening with a list of historical grievances Jews had against Ukrainians. Tataryn replied in kind. When the group finally got back to discussing how to assure "the war criminal issue not poison relationships between the two communities," the atmosphere in the gathering was already so poisoned that most were grateful when it broke up. Additional unproductive meetings under the wing of the Council were held for a time in Winnipeg and Montreal but not in Toronto, centre-stage for militants in both Ukrainian and Jewish communities.[46]

Under whatever auspices contacts between mainline Jewish and Ukrainian leadership took place, Littman was not invited. Nevertheless, his shadow fell across any Ukrainian-Jewish discussion. Congress leadership tried to publicly distance themselves from Littman's operations. Yet distance was not denunciation and public denunciation of Littman was what some Ukrainian leaders wanted. When instead of being denounced, Littman was offered an audience at the April 1985 Canadian Gathering of Jewish Holocaust Survivors in Ottawa, sponsored by Congress and B'nai Brith, some Ukrainians were incensed. In letters of protest to Congress and the B'nai Brith, the Secretary-General of the Canadian League for the Liberation of Ukraine protested what he saw as offering Littman a community platform from which to further inflame anti-Ukrainian sentiment. "While Littman may not formally be associated with the Canadian Jewish Congress," a claim which had a hollow ring for some in the Ukrainian community, he was still given a forum at a Congress-sponsored event. What is more, continued the Secretary-General, "we note that there is no record to suggest that anyone present at the Ottawa rally protested his prejudicial comments, nor that the CJC divorced itself from them."[47]

Alan Rose responded for Congress. He reiterated the Congress position that no ethnic community could be held culpable for the Holocaust. But on the Ukrainian demand that Littman be publicly rejected, the Congress official was far less forthcoming. Once again, Rose drew a line between Congress and Littman but made no denunciation. "I am sure," he wrote, "that you will understand that Canadian Jewish Congress cannot be responsible for statements made by individuals at public gatherings."

But the Secretary-General apparently did not understand. If Littman spoke at a Congress-sponsored event, then he spoke under Congress auspices. Congress, the Secretary-General protested, must take responsibility for his remarks. If Congress refused to publicly condemn Littman's comments, Congress would be understood to have condoned them.[48]

Thus as public debate heated up, efforts to bring Jews and Ukrainians together went nowhere and official communication, such as it was, proved a dialogue of the deaf. Each tried to make a case which the other would not or could not hear. But each also thought there were those, if they could be found, who would listen. The Canadian Jewish Congress resolved to seek out moderate Ukrainian leaders, while some Ukrainian leaders, in a reversal of the CLC's earlier caution on opening the door to dialogue with Jews, also determined to find a similar core of Jewish moderates. At a July 1985 meeting, discussion focused on the Jewish community and concluded that "large sections of community [are] opposed to what's happening." It was now time to find these Jews and under the UCC umbrella "meet with them informally."[49]

Thus, like giants tiptoeing through a minefield, both Congress and CLC leaders began to feel their way towards contact. Each hoped to find a sympathetic if not supportive ear in the other camp and each also hoped to find it before the whole exercise exploded in their face.

Working through the Director of Community Relations of the Winnipeg Jewish Community Council in June, Alan Rose, Executive Vice-President of Congress, requested a meeting with John Nowosad, National President of the Ukrainian Canadian Committee. Nowosad, in the wholesale fruit business in Winnipeg, was acquainted with many in the local Jewish community. Indeed, pre-Deschênes relations between Jewish and Ukrainian communities in Winnipeg were generally good. For example, after the Winnipeg Board of Education approved a Holocaust curriculum for the schools, at the request of the Ukrainian community a Jewish community staff member worked with interested members of the Ukrainian community to create a similar educational package on the Ukrainian famine. Ironically, it was a left-wing Ukrainian local school-board member who scuttled the Ukrainian famine curriculum proposal. The eruption of the Nazi war-crimes issue further split the Winnipeg Ukrainian community right and left. It also chilled relations with the much smaller Winnipeg Jewish community.[50]

UCC President Nowosad at first welcomed a meeting "involving leaders of our respective communities." Without consulting with his executive Nowosad allowed "that a meeting would be very much in order." He asked that Rose get in touch with him directly to set a date and "discuss who should be invited." Nowosad wanted the meeting in Winnipeg, perhaps to reinforce Winnipeg's role as headquarters of the UCC and also to show symbolically that Ukrainian leadership were not going cap in hand to meet with Jews.[51]

Rose responded quickly. He phoned Nowosad and arranged to fly to Winnipeg with Milton Harris, National President of Congress, for a dinner meeting.[52] But in his rush to better relations, Nowosad had miscalculated the potential resistance at home. He immediately faced a house revolt. More militant members of his executive, mostly of post-war immigrant vintage, protested any contact with Jews or, at least, any discussion that led to reconciliation while, as they saw it, Jewish interests were still out to destroy their community. Nowosad, joined by more moderate voices, pleaded against a total rejection of Congress's overture. But the best he could get was a compromise calling for a meeting only after an agreeable and itemized agenda had been set. "On receipt of the agenda," Rose was informed, "we will propose a date for the meeting. The Committee felt that meeting just for the sake of meeting will not serve a useful purpose for improving relations." Rose phoned Winnipeg to sound out UCC officials on just what they meant by an agenda. Wasn't bettering relations agenda enough? Obviously not. But what other items the UCC had in mind remained unclear. He wrote again suggesting that the only item on the agenda should be relations between the two communities. This was again met with the Ukrainian reply that Congress submit "an agenda for a proposed meeting between our respective Presidents."[53]

For almost four months Congress leaders unsuccessfully sought a way to bring Ukrainian leaders to the table. Did the Ukrainians want to discuss problems face to face or not? Why all the mixed signals? Congress could not know that a meeting with Jewish leaders had become an extremely divisive issue within the UCC. It threatened to split moderates from hardliners, the immigrant generation from Canadian born and, in part, exacerbate Ukrainian-Canadian east-west tensions. In an organization that ran on the basis of unanimity, unanimous support for a meeting with Congress officials was not to be had. But the UCC could not simply say no to dialogue. That could prove a public relations black eye — so they stalled.

Unaware, Congress tried an end run. If a simple request for a meeting could not flush Ukrainian spokesmen out into the open, perhaps Senator Paul Yuzyk could. Senator Yuzyk, appointed to the Senate by John Diefenbaker, had long been a spokesman for Ukrainian Canadians on Parliament Hill. A University of Mani-

toba historian by training, Yuzyk was a pioneer of the
multicultural ideal. He was well known to Canadian
Jewish leaders but thought by many in the Ukrainian
community to be past his political prime and out of
touch with the newer generation of predominantly eastern Ukrainian-Canadian activists.[54]

But Yuzyk still commanded respect. He was, after
all, a member of the Canadian Senate. Alan Rose, who
had known Yuzyk for years as a conciliatory voice of
moderation, requested Yuzyk intercede to set up a
meeting. Rose also sent the UCC a tentative three-point
agenda. Discussion of the Deschênes impact on relations, consideration of an ongoing intercommunity dialogue and informal exchanges on multiculturalism policy
and race relations were just variations on a single
theme: bettering current Ukrainian-Jewish relations.[55]

With a proposed agenda in hand and Yuzyk on their
backs, the UCC was finally drawn into discussions, although not without conditions. Hoping to forestall internal criticism from its own militants dead set against
high level Ukrainian-Jewish contacts, the UCC demanded the meeting be downgraded from one between
presidents to "a preliminary meeting of the executive
directors of our representative organizations . . . prior
to the meeting of our Presidents. The purpose of such a
meeting would be to finalize the agenda and other specific arrangements for the Presidents' meeting." The
scale of the meeting was also kept small and informal
on neutral ground or in Ottawa. At Yuzyk's instigation
the meeting was expanded to include the B'nai Brith
since, according to Yuzyk, they represented an independent influential voice both in the Deschênes process
and the Jewish community at large. Now, fully six
months after the idea of a meeting of presidents was
first broached and seemingly accepted, a preliminary
meeting of senior professional staff was set. Yuzyk
agreed to act as chairman.[56]

The small group, two representatives from Congress,
two from B'nai Brith, Yuri Weretelnyk, the young,
bright but inexperienced executive director of the UCC

in Winnipeg, and Senator Yuzyk, assembled at high noon a week before Christmas 1985 at the fashionable Courtyard Cafe in Ottawa's Market district. Ukrainians and Jews might have had trouble agreeing on some issues of mutual concern, but eating was never one of them. Wine and lunch were ordered — fish seemed a general favourite of the day. Over the hubbub of the noonday crowd, Weretelnyk reported he had brought with him from Winnipeg a proposed agenda drawn up and approved by his executive.

To get things going, Weretelnyk was invited to read his agenda without interruption. As the Jews listened in silence Weretelnyk began his presentation with a preamble attacking alleged Jewish slanders of the Ukrainian community. He then ran through the proposed agenda. It is a wonder the meeting did not break up then and there. The agenda items seemed to have nothing to do with building bridges between the two communities in the New World and everything to do with tallying Ukrainian grievances towards Jews, current and historical. Among other things on the UCC discussion list were items on Jewish involvement in orchestrating the famine, Jews in the Soviet Communist Party and NKVD (Soviet secret police), Jewish "war criminals" and collaboration with the Nazis. Jewish war criminals? Jews at the meeting looked at one another in bewilderment. After six months of effort to get a meeting, after delays and compromise, this seemed, to the Jews around the table, an insensitive effort to derail discussion, a thinly veiled effort to destroy any chance for intercommunity co-operation in Canada. If this was to be the basis of dialogue, there would be no dialogue.[57]

Senator Yuzyk, sensing the imminent collapse of the meeting, jumped in to save the day. He dismissed the proposed Ukrainian agenda as just that — a proposal. Since the agenda was obviously neither appropriate nor acceptable, there was no point in belabouring it with further discussion. Indeed, he urged, perhaps there need be no agenda in the usual sense of the word. After all, what was the ultimate object of bringing the presidents of the respective organizations together if not to come up with a joint statement of principle — a motherhood statement — on better relations between groups, rejecting group slanders and affirming principles of justice? Why not then make life easier for everyone by making approval of such a statement of principle the only formal item on the agenda? In the meantime draft statements could be circulated for comment. Indeed, in the process of hammering out a draft statement, all could have ample opportunity to air their concerns. It might not be easy, but Yuzyk was convinced a joint statement was an exercise worthy of group effort.[58]

Congress and B'nai Brith officials accepted the Yuzyk proposal. Weretelynk guaranteed nothing. He was on a short leash. He had no mandate from his executive to do anything else except present the proposed agenda. That done, Weretelnyk had no fall-back position. Nevertheless, he was likely uneasy about bucking so respected and senior a member of the Ukrainian community as Senator Yuzyk. When Senator Yuzyk promised to personally sell the joint-statement idea to the UCC, Weretelnyk fell in line. The meeting was pulled back from the brink. Coffee and dessert were ordered.

While much of his power in the community had long since been eclipsed by others, Yuzyk still had some clout and he used it. He presented the idea of the statement of principle to the UCC as less a proposal than a *fait accompli*. To say no to it could be a public-relations headache. In any event, the UCC would have its input and, of course, would reject what was not acceptable, just as the Jewish leaders would. A final draft would be a matter of negotiation and compromise, not, Yuzyk promised, sleight of hand. The UCC had no choice but to agree. Yuzyk set about writing a first draft — so did the other participants.

There was another reason why UCC's agreement was easier to muster than it might otherwise have been only a few weeks earlier — Littman suddenly did not seem the bogeyman he was earlier. On December 6, 1985, as plans for the Ottawa meeting were set, Littman testified before the Deschênes hearings, acknowledging that his original Mengele accusations had been misguided. In a bitter exchange with Ivan Whitehall, lawyer for the Justice Department, Littman's unfortunate choice of words left some convinced he had been condemned as a "vigilante."

Editorial writers tried to separate Littman from the Deschênes process his efforts helped spark. Whatever credibility he might lose from the "vigilante" exchange with Whitehall, noted *The Ottawa Citizen*, Littman should still be applauded for initiating the Commission.[59] By responding with the Deschênes Commission the government had taken a long overdue step in the direction of justice.[60]

Jewish leaders assessed whether the damage done to Littman by his "vigilante" remark might spill over to damage the credibility of the entire Deschênes process. But the Ukrainian press was jubilant. *The Ukrainian News* of Edmonton declared in a headline "Littman Called 'Vigilante', Commission Ends Hearings Under Cloud." *The Ukrainian Echo* crowed "Littman Allegations Prove False."[61] Littman no longer seemed the looming threat he had so recently appeared to be.

However, if Ukrainian leaders were reassured that Littman's star was in eclipse, that did not eliminate the flash points of tension, especially those that erupted whenever the question of evidence from the Soviet Union — "Soviet evidence" — was raised. With Deschênes now on record as prepared under certain conditions to both accept evidence from and gather evidence in the Soviet Union, anti-Communist lobby groups fell in line behind the CLC. A case in point was Vancouver lawyer Douglas Christie, best known to the Jewish community as the lawyer for both Ernst Zundel and James Keegstra. Christie wrote to Gregorovich offering, if not pleading, to be allowed to assist. Although he was not of Ukrainian descent, Christie assured the CLC that he feared for the erosion of freedom and expanding impact of the Soviet Union. In that, he claimed, he was at one with the Ukrainian cause.

Gregorovich's reply was polite but non-committal. He sent Christie a package of material that might be of interest and very briefly outlined the Deschênes threat — not for the Ukrainian community but for "Canada."

As far as the Deschênes Commission is concerned there are three recommendations that could harm Canada:

1. retroactive legislation

2. the creation of a Canadian O.S.I.

3. the acceptance of materials and witnesses from the Soviet bloc as evidence in Canadian courts.

The recommendation of the Commission need not, of course, be accepted by the government. Accordingly we will be persuading the cabinet, Conservative M.P.s and Senators, and members of the other two parties that such recommendations should not be implemented.[62]

Whether this was the case remained to be seen. As 1985 drew to a close, the door to Ukrainian-Jewish dialogue seemed to be open, if only a crack. Yuzyk was carrying the ball. But barely had the new year dawned than a trial half-way around the world threatened to choke off whatever little momentum had been building.

In February 1986, after years of legal manoeuvring, John Demjanjuk, accused of operating the gas chambers at Treblinka, was deported from the United States to Israel to stand trial for war crimes. The Demjanjuk trial concretized for Ukrainians all the fears which the Deschênes hearings had raised in the abstract. It involved reliance on Soviet evidence, in this case a controversial identification card retrieved from Soviet archives; trial in a strange, perhaps hostile jurisdiction; perceived defamation of the Ukrainian nation in the eyes of the world. For many Ukrainians, Demjanjuk was already a symbol, a Ukrainian Dreyfus. It had happened in the United States. It could happen in Canada too. And always there was a fear that the Soviet Union was the impresario standing just off stage, reaping the benefits of the entire production.

The deportation of Demjanjuk from the US for trial in Israel cast a dark shadow over diaspora Ukrainian life and added greater urgency to the work of the CLC in Canada. Worried that Deschênes might lead to a string of Demjanjuk-like cases, some in the CLC were drawn to his plight. A CLC delegation met with Mark O'Connor, Demjanjuk's lawyer, for a briefing. His presentation left the CLC in a quandary.

In the nine years that his case had percolated through the American courts, Demjanjuk had been unable to prevent his own extradition to Israel. Thus there was a strong possibility that he might be convicted by the Israeli courts, with the rest of the world feeling that, like Eichmann, he was truly guilty and justly convicted. In that event, it could well be tactically counter-productive for the Ukrainian-Canadian community to climb into the glass booth with Demjanjuk. "This is dangerous for us" reported John Gregorovich to the CLC executive, "when we are in the process of campaigns to disengage ourselves from precisely that kind of association." Montreal historian Roman Serbyn also counselled caution. Too close a tie to Demjanjuk might, if he were found guilty, hamper community efforts on other fronts.[63]

And yet many Ukrainian Canadians felt a visceral desire to believe in Demjanjuk's innocence. Toronto activists jumped to his defence. But should the CLC itself undertake fundraising on his behalf? The case was complex. Gregorovich argued that the actual guilt or innocence of Demjanjuk, which meant so much to Ukrainians, was incidental to the Israelis. Rather, the trial served a much broader Israeli agenda. It would again allow Israel to indict the West again for having failed to save Jews during the war. Portraying the Jew as victim might produce benefits to internal and foreign policy for Israel, increasingly portrayed as an aggressor *vis-à-vis* the Arabs. Gregorovich reportedly argued that the publicity surrounding the trial would "assist the Israelis in their internal and external politics," and would help the process of maintaining identity by "frightening the younger Jewish generations around the world." Gregorovich accurately anticipated the hopes of Israeli leaders — who would bus in schoolchildren to view the trial once it began — that it would serve to educate a new generation of Jews to the horrors of the Holocaust.[64]

The CLC monitored events relating to Demjanjuk, and like Ukrainians everywhere, debated the issue intensely. The Ukrainian press in Canada did not let up in its coverage, but, in the end, the CLC did not become officially involved. Eventually, a separate Demjanjuk Committee was formed under UCC auspices. The CLC took that as a cue to withdraw from any overt activity on Demjanjuk's behalf.[65] Nevertheless, the CLC realized that anxiety about Demjanjuk kept community attention focused on the war-criminals issue. Some worried, however, that the CLC fundraising campaign might suffer. Ukrainian pockets were only so deep.

The CLC's ambitious and multi-dimensional lobbying efforts continued to be hamstrung by shortages of cash. While fundraising efforts persisted through 1986, they met with less success than had been hoped. The CLC's original fundraising drive, with its target of $1,000,000, fell short of the mark. As of late September 1986, contributions totalled only $695,000. Indeed the breakdown of donations reflected the regional differences among Ukrainian Canadians, and Ukrainian organizations in particular. Toronto remained the centre of the post-war generation, the west earlier and more Canadianized generations. While only one quarter of Ukrainian Canadians lived in Ontario, they provided almost two-thirds of the donors and cash. Thus measured in dollars,

Ukrainian Canadians in the west were seemingly less interested, or less committed to the cause.[66]

It is possible that the fundraising problems encountered by Ukrainians reflected a self-fulfilling prophecy. The normative expectations for the average donation may have been set too low. As an example, the Saskatchewan Branch of the CLC based its provincial campaign on an average gift of $25. A 1983 national study of the Ukrainian experience in Canada also illustrates the acceptable range of giving. The list of donors to the project identifies only five individuals who donated more than $100. The modal or most frequent donation is in fact $25. All contributions, down to $2, are listed.[67]

Budgetary constraints forced the CLC to develop a trim operation, low on overhead, with concern for getting the biggest bang for the buck. All in all, the CLC was remarkably successful. Moreover, the budgetary belt-tightening did not prevent coming up with the money for key projects, where the return was considered worthwhile. This was true of *The Globe and Mail* ad of 1985, replicated in another ad in 1987. It was also the case with the decision to publish and distribute the pamphlet *Trial and Error* written by Nikolai Tolstoy.

Count Nikolai Tolstoy, a British historian and a descendant of the great Russian family, was invited by the chair of Ukrainian Studies Foundation of the University of Toronto, at the suggestion of Lubomyr Luciuk, to deliver one of its annual William Kurelek memorial lectures. Before a large and sympathetic audience in December 1985, he argued the equivalence of Soviet war criminality to that of the Nazis. While in Canada, Tolstoy also familiarized himself with the Deschênes Commission of Inquiry and with Ukrainian concerns. He expanded the written text of his lecture to include harsh criticisms of the Commission and Sol Littman. "It appears," he wrote, "that in 1985, Mr. Sol Littman . . . woke up one day under the impression that the notorious war criminal Josef Mengele (now dead) might once have tried (unsuccessfully) to apply for a visa to emigrate to Canada. Having washed and breakfasted, Litt-man suddenly realised that his discovery further implied that 'about 500' other war criminals were actually within the country . . . Then, as he laid down his coffee cup, a fresh thought struck him. Why just 500? . . ."[68]

Some CLC spokesmen felt that the Tolstoy text made a highly effective pamphlet, suitable for wide distribu-tion. Didn't it dovetail with the CLC case? It argued strongly against the use of Soviet evidence, and for the prosecution of all war criminals, notably Soviet ones. It also reminded readers of the anti-Semitic and anti-Zion-ist track record of the Soviet state. Its style was both polemical and scholarly, and of course the Tolstoy name had its own magic.

Funds were set aside for the pamphlet project, which would be combined with a June lecture tour by Tolstoy himself. Plans called for 20,000 copies to be printed in English, and 10,000 in French. Free copies were distrib-uted to libraries, the media, government officials and academics across Canada.

The Tolstoy pamphlet, like others which followed, was a key ingredient in the CLC's public-education and research campaign designed to blunt potentially harmful fallout from the Commission. Ukrainians felt they had a message to get across, one that had not yet been heard. The Canadian-made documentary, *Harvest of Despair*, served a similar role. The film, made years earlier by the Famine Research Committee, an ad hoc Toronto-based group of academics and others affiliated with the UCC, had won major international awards in 1985. In September of that year it was broadcast coast to coast by CBC-TV.

The film had two themes. One was the recounting of the horrors of the famine. It made its point with graphic photographs and film footage, including those of stacks of corpses reminiscent of Nazi death camps. The second theme was the duplicity — or *naïveté* — of the western media, which failed to report the story to the outside world. Why, the film asked, was the world so easily taken in by Soviet lies? Walter Duranty, *New*

York Times Moscow correspondent and Pulitzer Prize winner, for example, insisted there was no famine in Russia, even as thousands were dying.

Perhaps surprisingly, the film ran into major barriers in its American distribution. The educational network PBS, its natural constituency, refused to air it, claiming that it was "inadequately documented," and that it had a "perceived bias."[69] When the film was eventually shown on PBS, it was broadcast on the William Buckley show. As a result, the film may have been regarded by many viewers as but a reflection of the host's well-known conservative views rather than as a neutral historical account of the famine. The showing of the film was followed by a panel discussion focusing on the degree of accuracy of the film and its ideological and political context.

But there is no doubt that the film packed a powerful punch. MP Andrew Witer urged the CLC to guarantee its distribution to all MPs.[70] Efforts were also under way to authorize the film for school showing, so that the famine, like the Holocaust, might be understood by youth as a major tragedy of the twentieth century.

Ironically, this effort hit a brick wall at the Toronto school board. The film was screened for a meeting of interested educators, but before the famine could be discussed, the authenticity of the film itself was called into question. In a verbal battle reminiscent of the old left-right battles in the Ukrainian community, it was alleged, and conceded, that some of the still photographs used in the film were actually taken from film of an earlier famine in the 1920s, not that of the famine of 1932–33. Far fewer photos were available of the latter tragedy. "You have to have visual impact," York University historian Orest Subtelny reportedly argued. "You want to show what people dying from a famine look like. Starving children are starving children." But, to the delight of those who opposed the anti-Soviet thrust of the film, some educators joined in questioning whether a film that misrepresented evidence would be suitable for use in school board programs.

Those who advocated education about the famine felt aggrieved at the setback. The man who pulled the plug and aroused suspicion was Douglas Tottle, a self-described jack of all trades, from Winnipeg, identified with the left. From whence his expertise on the famine? What brought this Winnipegger to a meeting of the Toronto Board of Education? He was already well known to Winnipeg Ukrainians for his aggressive letters to the editor casting doubts on the famine, and attacking the Ukrainian nationalists' role during World War II.

At any rate, his attack was on target. The effort to add the famine to the Toronto Board of Education's curriculum was put on hold. The film's producers offered to add an introductory note to the film, pointing out the use of the earlier footage. It was hoped that the revised film, along with the famine educational unit, would pass muster.[71]

At first glance, the famine would appear to have little to do with the hunt for Nazi war criminals. But raising wide public consciousness of the famine was of great importance to the Ukrainian community. Just as the Holocaust had assumed such symbolic importance for modern Jewish identity, so had the famine among Ukrainians. As part of Ukrainian proximate history, it would surely reinforce the bonds of ethnic solidarity.[72] And if the story of the famine were better known beyond the Ukrainian community, it would also reinforce the image of Ukrainians as victims. That image, were it to seep into the larger public consciousness, might well blunt the force of efforts to picture Ukrainians as ruthless oppressors of Jews during the war. Finally, awareness of the horrors of the famine would help discredit the Soviet Union. Breaching the deliberate Soviet policy of disinformation concerning the famine might well spill over into the current debate on the acceptability of Soviet-supplied evidence on war crimes. The key was to drive home the magnitude of the famine's devastation. As Robert Conquest, author of *The Harvest of Sorrow*, testified before the US Senate, the Soviet Union would have to shoot down a 747 airliner every day for seventy years to match the death toll of the famine.[73]

A Research Committee was established early by the CLC, and if hobbled by lack of funds, it did not lack for ideas. Under Lubomyr Luciuk's vigorous leadership, some successes were enjoyed in putting the CLC case before the public and academic community. For example, Luciuk and anthropologist Ron Vastokas published articles in *The Globe and Mail*. Scientific papers were presented. An oral history project was initiated.

But, some Ukrainian leaders still chafed at what they felt was the abysmal lack of knowledge and concern among Canadians about the suffering of the Ukrainian people. More research, widely disseminated, was needed to expose the Ukrainian version of history which had been distorted or usurped by others. But more research would require more money. Dreams cost nothing. And Luciuk and the CLC dreamed of a massive research effort to set the historical record straight. The short-term benefits might lie in shaping the response to the Deschênes recommendations, but the long-term payoff was equally important: creation of symbols with which to anchor Ukrainian historical memory. The task would be difficult. Over the next twenty years, the CLC envisioned the need for perhaps fifty committed Ukrainian Canadians to attain social-science positions in Canadian universities.[74]

Luciuk's vision was long-term and, perhaps, infused with a sense that Ukrainian research institutes at the University of Alberta and Harvard could do more in defence of the Ukrainian polity and its historical legacy but did not. In late 1986 the CLC had identified six substantive areas or topics, relating to Ukrainian-Jewish relations, which required further explanation. Each represented a challenge to supposed anti-Ukrainian biases in the accepted scholarly literature — a literature too dominated, it was felt, by a Jewish world view. The new topics — "bases of Jewish anti-Ukrainianism; creation of the myth of Ukrainian anti-Semitism; Khmelnytsky, Nathan Hannover, and Jewish deaths during the

Ukrainian struggle for independence in the 1600s; Russian anti-Semitism; creation of the myth of Petlura's anti-Semitism; Jews and Ukrainians in World War II" — described an agenda of debunking conventional, and Jewish, wisdoms. Additional topics were identified for research specific to World War II. Most of these focused on Ukrainian suffering at the hands of Nazis or Soviets. Naturally enough one dealt with Babi Yar. Another referred explicitly to Ukrainian-Jewish relations: "Creation of the myth of Ukrainian massacres of Jews in World War II."[75] This was more than a disinterested search for knowledge. It was a proposal for purposeful scholarship in the interests of communal priorities. But without funding, it was only a pipe-dream.

As the Deschênes proceedings ground on, the CLC, like Witer's Ottawa office, continued to serve as the clearing house for information and advice to all segments in the community. This sometimes entailed cooling out hotheads whose public expression of passion might discredit the cause. Like its counterparts in the Jewish community, the CLC now recognized the need to head off wild pronouncements or inflammatory letters to the media or politicians. In particular, the CLC was concerned lest its campaign be tarred by and dismissed for anti-Semitic outbursts. A typical case concerned an unsolicited letter to the CLC offering a seven-page tract for transmission to the Deschênes Commission. The statement in question, written not by the sender but by a third party, described a "sinister force" plotting to set up a permanent Office of Special Investigations in Canada. It also speculated about possible war criminality among the thousands of recently arrived Soviet Jews, including elderly immigrants likely implicated in murders of Ukrainians during 1939–41.

The CLC knew that presenting such a statement to Judge Deschênes would just not do and pleaded that it not be sent.

. . . the most damaging part of it is the continual reference to individual Jews, and to the Jewish community. The situation in the English speaking world, indeed in the Western world, is such that the slightest indication of criticism of Jews is automatically classified as anti-semitism. Once a statement is classified as anti-semitism or a spokesman is classified as anti-semitic, credibility is completely lost. No mainstream media person, academician, government official or politician will have anything to do with the person making the statement. We may consider it unfortunate, because it means that legitimate references to actions of Jews cannot be raised without being smeared as anti-semitism. While we may regret this double standard, we have to recognize that it exists, and recognize that we can be effective only if we live within the rules that are laid down by the outside society. Our objective is to be effective, not to vent our frustrations.[76]

The cautious considerations that applied to public pronouncements did not always apply to private contacts. Gregorovich continued his communications with Doug Christie, lawyer for Zundel and Keegstra, through 1986. He turned to Christie on behalf of Paul Zumbakis, the American lawyer whose massive brief against the use of Soviet evidence was incorporated into the CLC's submission to the Commission. Zumbakis had taken a strong public position against the OSI and other features of the hunt for Nazi war criminals. He had apparently also been following the trial of Ernst Zundel in Toronto. Gregorovich wrote to Christie asking for "copies of the transcripts in which . . . [Christie's] devastating cross-examination of Hilsberg [sic], the professional holocaust history witness, is contained."[77]

Christie was pleased to oblige, and he informed Gregorovich that Zundel would deliver the transcript. Christie also repeated his support for the UCC campaign and indicated he was urging the Canadian Free Speech League, of which he was general counsel, to write to the Minister of Justice along those lines. Christie again congratulated the CLC on their efforts. They were appreciated not only by Ukrainians but by those like himself who, he claimed, cherished truth and freedom.[78]

In June 1986, the CLC sent Christie a copy of the Tolstoy pamphlet. Christie, who had already attended Tolstoy's public lecture in Vancouver and had been much impressed, passed on copies of the pamphlet to his friends. His only regret, he wrote the CLC, was that Count Tolstoy made negative references to Germans. Whatever Tolstoy may have said did not deter Christie or Zundel from supporting the CLC campaign. Back in February the CLC had been told that "a person associated with Zundel" was thinking of laying criminal charges against Sol Littman. At the complainant's request, the CLC had provided what information it could but raised the question of whether such a charge might not best be laid by a Ukrainian Canadian.[79]

Nothing further developed on the matter until February 1987, when none other than Zundel himself filed documents with an Ontario justice of the peace, hoping to prosecute Littman under the very provisions of the *Criminal Code*, Section 177, by which Zundel himself had been convicted. Zundel argued that Littman's exaggerated claims about the numbers of war criminals in Canada constituted "false news" likely to cause social or racial unrest. "They are running out of Germans to hound," said Zundel, "and now they are going after Ukrainians." Zundel's charge was eventually rejected.[80]

CLC leaders, like their Jewish counterparts, also remained in constant touch with comparable communities in the United States and elsewhere in the diaspora. For many in the CLC the war-criminals issue was an international problem, with Soviets secretly pulling the strings behind the scenes. Trouble could erupt in any western country to disturb the peace of resident Ukrainian communities.

But contact was not always productive. At times, Ukrainian Canadians would find that the commentary from their brethren south of the border was more critical than fraternal. It was difficult enough for the CLC and the UCC to keep the lid on internal, ideological, regional and organizational differences. Criticism by the American big brother did not help. In one instance the CLC was criticized for apparently publicizing details about its campaign on Deschênes, and for the lack of co-operation with other groups. "We suggest," wrote the major American-Ukrainian newspaper, "that the community adopt a more sophisticated approach in its lobbying effort."[81]

Lectures such as these were not appreciated by some Ukrainian-Canadian leaders. Certainly their community, in terms of numerical weight, political clout and cultural vibrancy, had little to learn from their American cousins. Ukrainian-Canadian leaders knew it was in the United States that the OSI had been active for close to a decade, and where people like Demjanjuk had been extradited. So what had this vaunted sophistication achieved for Ukrainian Americans? Perhaps it was the Americans who had much to learn. Indeed, Canada was a centre of the Ukrainian diaspora. Toronto ranked with Munich as a major focal point for militant Ukrainian nationalism, and smaller Ukrainian communities, such as the Australian, were more than pleased to consult with Canada and to accept Canadian advice.[82]

The CLC also continued to monitor the media. This involved the usual techniques, also common in Jewish lobbying efforts — keeping up routine letters to the editor, as well as longer, more thoughtful letters to and meetings with media officials to press the Ukrainian position. But Gregorovich also decided to hit the media where they were most vulnerable — in their pocketbooks. He set about trying to convince the government not to advertise in newspapers that had published material the CLC considered defamatory to specific groups. By and large, Canadian newspapers, and notably editorialists, supported the Deschênes Commission in 1986, as they had in 1985. *The Globe and Mail, The Toronto Star, The Ottawa Citizen* and *The Gazette* (Montreal), the flagships of the Canadian press, continued to sup-

port the Commission against charges that it was con-
ducting a witch-hunt. They editorialized in favour of extending Deschênes's deadline to facilitate the full
investigation which was the Commission's mandate.
They also supported efforts to gather evidence in the
Soviet Union, with appropriate safeguards.[83] This did
not please the CLC. Worse still was what Ukrainians
identified as a provocative coupling of the term "war
criminal" with "Ukrainian." For those who had over-
stepped the reasonable bounds of journalistic licence,
stronger measures were needed.

Southam News was a case in point. Southam newspapers published, among other articles, a controversial
column by Keith Spicer in which he emphasized
Ukrainian oppression of Jews. Gregorovich wrote to a
battery of Cabinet ministers, urging that their departments desist from funnelling tax dollars, via advertisements, into Southam papers, but he got nowhere. Otto
Jelinek, Minister of State for Multiculturalism, suggested that Gregorovich complain to the Ontario Press
Council. The Minister of Supply and Services suggested
that if Gregorovich felt the articles were in fact defamatory or constituted hate literature, he could use the appropriate legal remedies. Others brushed him off. The
Southam advertising boycott would not work.[84] Yet if
Gregorovich lost this battle, the war was ongoing. The
subtle benefits of sensitizing politicians and the media
to Ukrainian concerns might come later.

Dr Stephen Hladkyj, an Ontario dentist and a stalwart of the Ukrainian community, had better luck with
the media. He was personally, passionately committed
to the cause; his father had suffered at the hands of
both Nazis and Soviets. For some time Hladkyj battled
what he saw as press bias if not anti-Ukrainian coverage. His success did not come at once. First he encouraged the federal Attorney General to prosecute
journalist Michael Solomon under the hate literature
laws of Canada. In a December 1985 story carried by
the Jewish Telegraphic Agency, Solomon had referred
to cases of "eight Canadians of Ukrainian origin sus-

pected of war crimes." This, Hladkyj claimed, was group defamation.[85] But he had no luck.

Finally Hladkyj hit paydirt with *The Toronto Star*. He lodged an official complaint with the Ontario Press Council, relating to a September 28, 1985 article by *Toronto Star* Ottawa correspondent David Vienneau. Vienneau had written that "Not once had there been disclosed a single case of a forged document or a perjured witness" regarding the use of Soviet-supplied evidence. But Hladkyj argued that four such cases had in fact been documented in testimony given to the Deschênes Commission itself in the summer of 1985. He received no satisfaction from *The Toronto Star*, but the Press Council supported him.

In its defence, the *Star* cited a November 14 Commission document. But that document, the Press Council noted, had focused on the admissibility of Soviet evidence, not its authenticity. "Not once had the admissibility of Soviet evidence been questioned." Furthermore, the document did not exonerate the Soviets from perjury or falsification of documents, which were the issues raised in the Vienneau article. Evidence might well be admissible, and later discovered to be forged or otherwise deficient.[86] The dentist won his point, at least with the Press Council.

B'nai Brith's David Matas was taken aback by the ruling. Perhaps it might influence the Commission's thinking about the entire issue of Soviet evidence. In a letter to the Press Council, Matas argued that *The Toronto Star* had been correct all along. The four American cases cited by Hladkyj were cases where "the courts decided not to consider the Soviet evidence. None of these courts found any of the documents to be forged or the witnesses to have perjured themselves." But the Press Council ruling stood.[87]

But in the age of McLuhan, media monitoring involves far more than print. Most Canadians get their news from television and radio. Moreover, harmful images or stereotypes are more likely to be transmitted through electronic media than through newspaper arti-

cles. Ethnic groups have always been alert to such pur-
veying of stereotypes. Italian organizations have long
protested the use of the word Mafia as a codeword for
organized crime. Visible minorities have protested media stereotyping which commonly portrays blacks involved in crime. Chinese spokesmen have protested
ballet performances of *The Nutcracker* where dancers
wore pigtails. And Jews have always feared the spread
of anti-Semitic stereotypes, from Shakespeare's Shylock
to Dickens's Fagin to contemporary characters like
Mordecai Richler's Duddy Kravitz.

Eastern European groups prove no exception. In
March 1986, the Baltic Federation of Canada, a steadfast supporter of the CLC, protested to the CTV network
about a case of group defamation on an episode of the
American television show, "Highway to Heaven." The
March 12 episode featured the story of a fictitious Jan
Baltic, a neo-Nazi terrorist who harassed a concentra-
tion-camp survivor. The president of the Federation, representing 100,000 Canadians of Lithuanian, Estonian,
and Latvian origin, had been trying for weeks to persuade CTV to make changes in the program, perhaps
dubbing in another name.

CTV was not impressed. As reported in *The Globe
and Mail* Murray Chercover, CTV President, replied that
given "the program's dedication to human rights . . ."
he could not believe ". . . how anyone could take offence even through the inadvertent use of a fictional
name." CTV Vice-President Marge Anthony was even
less sympathetic. "I don't know what to say to them.
It's like saying that if there were a bad guy named John
Ireland, you had to take his name out and next week if
it's someone called John White you can't have him because it's against all whites, or if it were Joe Black, it
would be against all blacks. There couldn't be any bad
guys named anything. We've just reached a point in our
civilization in this country where we are really getting
so paranoid about everything."[88]

Surprisingly, when the Baltic Federation of Canada, a
supporter of the CLC campaign and co-signatory of the

CCL's *Globe and Mail* advertisement discovered its appeals were to no avail, it turned to the Canadian Jewish Congress for support. Congress was quick to respond, just as the World Jewish Congress had done on the same issue in the United States. While not agreeing that the program warranted prosecution under Canada's hate literature laws, Congress recommended some form of action through the federal regulatory agency, the CRTC. Congress made inquiries with legal counsel for the CRTC and researched TV broadcasting regulations. David Satok of Congress's Joint Community Relations Committee expressed the Canadian Jewish concern. "To give the name Baltic to the villain unfairly and gratuitously cast aspersions on a whole group of Canadians whose ancestry is one of the Baltic republics. We therefore very much share the concern of members of Canada's Baltic community on this matter."[89] In any case, neither the protests of Congress nor a similar protest by Victor Goldbloom of the Canadian Council of Christians and Jews was able to prevent the airing of the program.

Though the Jewish intervention was unsuccessful, the case showed there was still room for a common stand on a matter of principle. Of course, it was even better when the principle coincided with communal self-interest. To be sure, JCRC support for the Baltic position reflected longstanding Jewish concerns about ethnic stereotyping. But secondary political considerations were not lost on Jewish leaders. As JCRC leaders well knew, the action could be seen as building a bridge to the Baltic community, which indeed might help soften opposition on the war-criminals issue in the future.[90]

A year later, a similar controversy developed in the United States, and was widely reported in the Ukrainian-Canadian press. A CBS TV movie entitled *Escape from Sobibor* was based on a true story of the escape of Jewish inmates from the Sobibor concentration camp. Ukrainian-American organizations took offence at the film's portrayal of Ukrainian camp guards assisting the Nazis; they argued it contributed to the spread of a negative stereotype of Ukrainians as anti-Semites. Ukrainian-Canadian organizations were alerted and lent their support in letters of protest to CBS, urging changes in the film.[91]

Unlike the Baltic episode, however, efforts at Jewish-Ukrainian mutual support on this issue blew up. Representatives of the Ukrainian community asked Eli Rosenbaum of the World Jewish Congress to join in their protest against CBS. Rosenbaum complied, although in his letter of support he pointed out that the majority of camp guards at Sobibor were Ukrainians. But he did identify residual problems: "The impression possibly created thereby that all Ukrainians are somehow responsible for the killings at Sobibor arguably will be strengthened by the film's failure to depict even one other European nationality group among the camp personnel . . . and by the practical reality that the story of Sobibor provides no opportunity to recount the extraordinary heroism of those Ukrainians in the Ukraine itself who risked, and sometimes gave, their lives shielding Jews from Nazis and their acolytes."[92]

Rosenbaum's letter was published in *The Ukrainian Weekly*, the leading Ukrainian-American journal, thus provoking an exchange between columnist Myron Kuropas and Rosenbaum. Kuropas found the letter half-hearted at best, and claimed it reasserted harmful stereotypes about Ukrainians while ostensibly defending them. His column, entitled "Thanks a lot Mr. Rosenbaum. For Nothing," labelled the letter a "sanctimoniously self serving diatribe." Rosenbaum responded in kind. He claimed that it was Kuropas's "ill informed and venomous posturing" that could help explain "why there are only a very few of us left in the Jewish community who are still prepared to meet with Ukrainian leaders."[93]

If the media was one focus of attention, politicians were another. The CLC stepped up its lobbying campaign through the course of the year and won sympathetic support from Conservative backbenchers in Ontario and Alberta, and they aggressively lobbied cab-

inet ministers and the Prime Minister. The Ukrainian
lobbying effort operated at many levels. A massive pre-
printed postcard campaign flooded the Prime Minister's
office in a demonstration of populist, grass-roots
Ukrainian sentiment. The 1984 Mulroney victory had
been greeted by eastern European anti-Communists
with enthusiasm. Now, they let the government know
they felt betrayed, their expectations dashed.[94]

In support of the populist postcard campaign, organizations sent letters to the Prime Minister and to Cabinet ministers. A Ukrainian seniors' discussion group in
Toronto wrote to complain about attacks from uniden-
tified Jewish groups creating conflict with eastern Europeans in Canada. The Conservative Association of
Andrew Witer's Parkdale–High Park riding added their
voice. They urged Justice Minister Ray Hnatyshyn not
to take action against people identified by the Commission and not to release any names. The Conservative
caucus had already been warned that votes could be
lost as a result of Deschênes. The Toronto branch of
the Ukrainian Canadian Women's Committee minced
no words. "We have watched you commit blunder after
blunder," they wrote to the Prime Minister, "not the
least of which was the creation of the Deschênes Commission . . . Don't flatter yourself about the last Federal
election. We did not vote you in, we were voting the
Liberals out . . ." MPs with large eastern European
constituencies got the message. Patrick Boyer, a leading
figure in the group of Tory backbenchers monitoring
the Commission, wrote to both the Prime Minister and
the Justice Minister. He urged that *Criminal Code*
amendments apply to all war criminals, that any trials
take place in Canada, and that no OSI be established.[95]

None of this surprised the Prime Minister, who had
already received a personal taste of Ukrainian antipathy
on January 12, 1986, as the Ukrainian community celebrated the Ukrainian New Year. About 3,000 community members, many in their late twenties and thirties,
gathered for the annual *Malanka*, an evening of festivities, at Toronto's Harbour Castle Hilton. As TV camera

crews arrived, word swept the dance floor that the Prime Minister was about to make a surprise visit. Following some delay, Mulroney and his wife, Mila, were led in by MP Andrew Witer.

The reception was cool at best. Lukewarm applause was punctuated by scattered booing. After a noble effort by Mila to say a few words in Ukrainian and brief remarks by Witer, the party beat a hasty retreat. The next day the cold shoulder given to the Prime Minister was the talk of the local Ukrainian community. Most agreed that the tone of the evening reflected the celebrants' bitter mood in the wake of Deschênes.[96]

Backbench Conservative MPs remained nervous; especially those from ridings with sizeable eastern European populations. But what could they do? Deschênes would not hear them and their prime minister wanted a lid kept on Cabinet and cooled caucus debate. In an absence of options Conservative MP Patrick Boyer, with the help of Liberal Senator Stanley Haidasz, organized a Parliamentary Study Group on the Canadian Nazi War Criminal Inquiry. Some of the group's founding members were grateful for a forum in which they could be seen to defend and promote interests of eastern European constituents fearful of Deschênes.

After its initial meeting, news of the study group spread. Other MPs, including Liberal Sheila Finestone, representing the heavily Jewish riding of Mount Royal, turned up at meetings. As membership broadened, the group quickly refocused onto Ukrainian-Jewish tensions. In the words of Conservative MP Don Blenkarn, "We're trying to cool Deschênes out." Co-chairman Boyer's stock was high among Jewish leaders, because of his active role on behalf of Soviet Jewry. He also represented a heavily eastern European Toronto riding. Boyer looked to the committee to "find common ground." Easier said than done.[97]

In their meetings, the study group heard presentations from representatives of both eastern European and Jewish constituencies. First invited was American lawyer Paul Zumbakis who spoke, and showed a film about the dangers of accepting Soviet evidence. At sub-sequent meetings the group heard from Irwin Cotler and David Matas. The two Jewish lawyers presented arguments in favour of gathering Soviet evidence with appropriate safeguards, and spoke on the entire range of Jewish communal concerns and legal positions. At times, the meetings were tense. As David Matas looked on at the January 16 meeting, Conservative MP Alex Kindy reportedly raised the allegations of Austrian leader Bruno Kreisky that Simon Wiesenthal had co-operated with the Gestapo during the war. In addition, Conservative MP William Lesick and Andrew Witer attacked the use of Soviet evidence. Witer, according to the Ukrainian press, compared Littman's allegations against Ukrainians to those of Zundel or Keegstra against Jews.[98]

Federal politicians were not the only ones to keep abreast of the Deschênes developments. Indeed, Ukrainian and Jewish leaders knew it was possible that provincial attorneys general might well be implicated in any future recommendations of the report. Some provincial politicians were already in the fray. One champion of the Ukrainian cause was Ontario Conservative MPP Yuri Shymko, who had earlier lobbied Ontario Tory leadership candidates on the subject of war criminals. At one point Shymko wrote to Deschênes, attempting to discredit Sol Littman. He asserted that Littman in his research relied on articles written by a known Soviet propagandist and journalist, Valery Styrkul. Shymko based his claim on an information packet distributed by Witer's office. In an odd twist of fate, Shymko's charge was quickly revealed to have been the result of clerical error and his own honest confusion. The packet contained articles by Styrkul, along with a copy of a Littman letter to MPs and copies of other articles. Shymko had erroneously assumed that Littman was also promoting the Soviet articles. He duly apologized to the Judge, and to Littman.

But the incident did not end there. Littman regarded Shymko's letter of apology as half-hearted. In his letter

Shymko indicated, parenthetically, that Littman had previously corresponded with Styrkul and was familiar with his work. Littman countered that his contacts with Styrkul had been limited to challenging his claims and asking for proof. But what also pained Littman was the loss of another Ukrainian friend over the fallout from Deschênes. "Yuri Yuri Yuri!" he wrote to Shymko,

> After all the years we worked together on various multicultural committees, after all the TV pieces and newspaper articles I did on behalf of Ukrainian art, dance and drama, and after all the support I gave to Ukrainian language classes in the public schools, I was shocked by the viciousness of your attack on me in your original letter to Justice Deschênes. . . . Doesn't it say something about the unfortunate atmosphere that you and others have created in the Ukrainian community, the hysteria which prevents people from distinguishing friend from foe?[99]

But the days when platitudes about ethnic food or folkdancing could sustain ethnic coalitions were over. For Ukrainians, reputations — and lives — were now on the line.

No such tragi-comedy of errors followed the interventions of the federal MPs. But the concern of the Conservative backbenchers was understandable. Although they had not been consulted or even informed about the intention to appoint a Commission, it was they who now felt the pressure from constituents and from contacts in eastern European community organizations. Some of the expressions of hostility were coming not only from old-timers, where it might be expected, but from younger members of the communities. "They're coming out with lines that I hoped had disappeared from this country," Don Blenkarn is noted as saying in the *Canadian Jewish News*. "What is developing is racial hatred . . . Ukrainians are blaming Jewish people in general because Jewish people blamed them. . . . I hope [Deschênes] can find some evidence that's incontrovertible against some individuals. If he can't, the government is going to pay for it heavily, politically. And the Jewish community is going to suffer."[100]

Whether or not the Conservatives would have to "pay" for the Deschênes blunder, of course, depended on many things. The Commission had yet to make any recommendations, and the government had yet to act. Elections were still a long way down the road. But there was no mistaking the rumblings that were beginning to be heard in Metro Toronto and in the west. For a second year, John Gregorovich led Ukrainians in letting Conservatives know exactly where he stood. "Unfortunately, as a consequence of the government's creation of the Deschênes Commission," he wrote to Conservative fundraisers, "my donations have had to be shifted to the defence of the Ukrainian and other East European communities from the media and organizational defamation of Ukrainians and East Europeans."[101]

The Liberals, for their part, were maintaining a relatively low profile on Deschênes. Even if party strategists knew or felt that the Tories might suffer at the polls, Liberals realized that they had little to gain on the issue. After forty years of inaction, the Liberal party was now on record as supporting both the apprehension of war criminals in principle and the appointment of the Deschênes Commission. There was no evidence of any major effort to play the "Deschênes card" in a bid to woo disaffected eastern European voters. At any rate, Liberals did not have great strength among eastern European voters. On the other hand, the last election had seen erosion in the usually solid Jewish support for the party. The last thing Liberals needed was to be seen to be pandering to eastern Europeans on the war-criminals issue — that might undermine Jewish support even further. Of course, that logic applied more in the Liberal strongholds of Toronto and Montreal, with their large and influential Jewish communities.

In the west, however, Liberal fortunes had nowhere to go but up. Laurence Decore, mayor of Edmonton, was a rare Liberal fish in a sea of Conservative strength. Of Ukrainian origin (his father, an Alberta MP, had lobbied for admission of the Division), Decore was outspoken in his criticism and opposition to the use of Soviet evidence. If his fellow Liberals might pretend not to hear him, the Ukrainian press did take notice. "We realize that our Tory members of government are privately working to do what they can, but that's not enough," editorialized the *Ukrainian Echo*. "No member of the government is going to speak out the way a Liberal like Decore will, because otherwise they won't be members of government for much longer."[102]

Meanwhile, government policy advisers were also making their own calculations. In the view of Conservative insiders, the Deschênes Commission could well turn into an embarrassing fiasco, and an ultimate ethnic zero-sum game — for every perceived Ukrainian victory, there would be a Jewish defeat, and vice versa. It would be hard for policy makers, regardless of what Deschênes recommended, to chart a middle course which would please both Ukrainians and Jews. Some compromise would have to be worked out so that both Jewish and eastern European community leaders could save face, even if militants in both camps cried foul. Poll data would prove useful in the months ahead to help the government avoid setting off too many land mines.

But what if the Deschênes recommendations were unequivocal, and the government was forced to choose between the two constituencies? If one group would have to be alienated, then in the confidential view of one Tory strategist, it would have to be the Jews. There were just too many factors in favour of Ukrainians and other eastern European allies. The consensus among some Tory advisers was that the Jewish community was gradually becoming less important politically. Conservative officials were aware of the demographic trends. There were now many more Ukrainian and Baltic voters than Jewish. What is more, the Jewish proportion of the population would continue to fall in the future. And more importantly, eastern Europeans would soon begin to rival Jews in their occupational and income profiles, as well as in their involvement in the political process. Given the belief that Jews were predominantly loyal to the Liberal Party, there would be too little payoff for Conservatives to be overly concerned about Jewish sensibilities.[103]

Some Jewish leaders, who viewed the Ukrainian campaign with concern, did not sit by idly. Increasingly, through 1986 and 1987, Jewish organizations remained active, emphasizing private, ongoing lobbying efforts rather than public pressure. Congress and B'nai Brith acted, as always, independently of each other. B'nai Brith members were warned that "there still exists a danger that a number of interest groups and MPs are critical of the Commission's investigations of Nazi war criminals in Canada." B'nai Brith executive members and Lodge presidents were urged to continue to write letters — personal ones wherever possible — to MPs and senators, making the Jewish case.[104]

Congress activists were likewise exhorted to press their positions to MPs and senators, in person where possible, but with little or no publicity. Congress remained concerned about aggravating ethnic tensions and urged supporters to be scrupulously careful to avoid maligning any ethnic group. "Failing to do so would give the appearance that action against war criminals is an inter-ethnic issue rather than what it really is, namely an issue of Canadian law and morality, and this could undermine the whole process." wrote Executive Director Jack Silverstone. "Rather you must take the 'high road' as it were — the appeal must be to morality and law. In order to make this most effective you need to be well informed."[105]

But one community's information was another community's defamation. Among the packet of "well written and thoughtful editorials" included in the Congress

information packet was none other than Keith Spicer's
column which had triggered John Gregorovich's campaign against federal advertising in Southam newspapers. Its references to "Ukrainians' lively anti-Semitic
tradition," the Ukrainian community's "misguided and
self-defeating $2 million anti-Deschênes campaign," its
assertion that Ukrainian-Canadian leaders "lacked common sense" and its claim that "History has seen
Ukrainians hurting Jews. Never the opposite," inflamed
many Ukrainians.[106]

What is more, in the Jewish community were those
who still believed that the Ukrainians had blood on
their hands. Here and there an accusation was made
against a neighbour or fellow citizen. Any accusations
against individuals, no matter how flimsy, which were
sent to Congress or B'nai Brith were dutifully forwarded to the Deschênes Commission, just as earlier allegations had been passed along to the RCMP. Neither
Congress nor B'nai Brith investigated the accuracy of
allegations. That, they claimed, was not their responsibility. If it was their duty to pass along all names that
came their way, it was for government, not voluntary
organizations, to ferret out any criminals and apply the
law. Of course Jewish officials logically knew that most
of these allegations did not rest on any solid foundation
of evidence. If but one lead, however, helped uncover a
Nazi war criminal, the exercise would be worthwhile.
But an inevitable result of the process would be a
finding by the Commission that the number of alleged
war criminals in Canada had been greatly exaggerated.
That was unavoidable.[107]

Meanwhile Littman, seemingly undaunted by the uproar over the Mengele charge and by the pending lawsuit in connection with his *Saturday Night* article,
maintained his relentless and very public crusade. Indeed, he carried his cause beyond Canada's borders. In
an article for Israel's leading newspaper, *Maariv*, Littman detailed his analysis of the war-criminals story for
the Israeli public. In an article headlined "End of the
Cease-fire," Littman described the rapid escalation of

tensions between the Jewish and Ukrainian communities. With the pending trial of Demjanjuk in Israel, Littman argued, Jews would be subjected to even harsher attacks from militant post-war Ukrainians in Canada.[108]

Mainstream Jewish lobbying efforts continued in the mode of quiet diplomacy. Excessive populism was out. There were no marches or mass postcard campaigns, lest they ignite the public fear of inter-ethnic tension. Periodic meetings with Cabinet ministers and other politicians were the rule. The ministers seemed surprisingly well informed about the internal squabbles of both the Ukrainian and Jewish communities. Thus in one meeting, while Solicitor General Perrin Beatty expressed concern about rising ethnic tensions, he also reportedly commended Milton Harris as "forthright and gutsy" for his effort to still extremists in the Jewish camp.[109]

In addition to quiet lobbying a good deal of Congress energy was devoted to outlining possible scenarios and responses to whatever Deschênes was likely to recommend. Target groups from which to build a post-Deschênes coalition for positive action against war criminals were identified. These included interest groups such as the Canadian Legion; ethnic groups such as the Germans and the Poles could perhaps be brought on board. But building ethnic coalitions could well turn into a tricky business. ". . . we should understand that the ethnic groups have their own fish to fry," noted Congress's Alan Rose. "It is more important when meeting with these communities that we reiterate the CJC position that this is not an ethnic issue."[110]

In short order, Congress fleshed out a detailed political plan of action in anticipation of Deschênes's report. The effort was entirely predicated on the assumption that there would be a prolonged period during which to influence the government's response to the report after its release. The Congress plan, a combination of public advocacy and private lobbying, was to be unfolded in four phases. These ranged from a three-week pre-release program to the fourth phase, a year-long period of sustained advocacy. Whatever Deschênes recommended, Congress would be ready.[111]

Yet for Jewish and Ukrainian leaders, mobilizing their own constituents, monitoring the media and pressuring the government were not the only priorities. Throughout 1986 ethnic leaders knew there would be a world after Deschênes, and that Jewish and Ukrainian politics in Canada would need to find a way to deal with one another. Even as each polity protected its interests, Senator Yuzyk was pressing for a joint statement of principle — a sign of reconciliation.

It would not be easy. Reports from the field told of incidents of name-calling and insults. At a public discussion of Deschênes at the University of Toronto, including both David Matas and John Sopinka, one woman told of her eleven-year-old daughter being called a Nazi. At the same meeting, a Jewish student angrily chided those who refused to distinguish between non-Jewish collaborators and members of the *Judenrate*. Ukrainian speakers had argued that if there was any Ukrainian collaboration in war crimes, it had occurred under duress, no different from that of the members of the *Judenrate* or the *Kapos*. According to the *Canadian Jewish News*, the student's counter-argument that eastern European camp guards were volunteers, whose alternative was privation, while Jews faced certain death, was not persuasive. His effort was punctuated by hoots of derision.[112]

Ukrainians also reported an upsurge in anti-Ukrainian episodes. MP Andrew Witer reported knowledge of two to three dozen incidents of prejudice in the winter of 1986 during the Deschênes hearings. Some blamed such episodes, whether a child taunted in a park or a newspaper account allegedly linking Ukrainians and war criminality, on Deschênes or the Jews. "Why," some demanded, "are the Jews doing this to us?"[113]

Relations between Ukrainian and Jewish organizations continued to be marked by a bizarre mixture of hostile encounters and fence-mending efforts. Many of the high-level contacts, including those mediated by Yuzyk, were unpublicized. In late December, even as Yuzyk hosted a meeting in Ottawa, Gregorovich and other Ukrainian leaders joined Eli Rosenbaum, then general counsel of the World Jewish Congress, in a meeting set up by Toronto's Alex Epstein. Rosenbaum had worked for three years with OSI and was in a position to answer troubling questions. For the Ukrainians, meeting with Rosenbaum was like meeting with an enemy during a battlefield ceasefire; he had crossed swords many times with their American counterparts on the war-criminals issue.

Rosenbaum's motive was different; he had a message to deliver. He tried to defuse Ukrainian hostility, using the argument that the conflict was not at root an ethnic one. He cautioned the Ukrainians against rallying around alleged war criminals. "It is a shame that Ukrainians know the name of John Demjanjuk, and not that of . . . Ukrainian freedom fighters." The Ukrainians were adamant; they were not prepared to concede the guilt of Demjanjuk or anyone else Deschênes or the OSI might identify. Moreover, since the evidence was, in the Ukrainian view, always suspect, guilt could in all probability never be established. The meeting was, however, polite and civil.[114]

Civility is one thing, *rapprochement* another. Following the stormy pre-Christmas lunch meeting in Ottawa the two sides, with the mediation of Senator Yuzyk, began drafting a statement. He hoped to isolate militants on both sides, while affirming the need for better relations. This was to prove no easy feat. Congress also worked out a draft in January 1986, and sent it to Yuzyk and B'nai Brith for comment.[115]

Yuzyk's background as a historian, plus his later experience in politics, told him that Ukrainians had no choice but to seek accommodation with moderate Jewish leaders. But he understood militant Jewish passion, as indeed he understood the passions which animated many Ukrainians. For some, it was a case of "children defending their parents." Nevertheless, he was convinced a joint statement could moderate tensions.[116]

But it was not to be. The draft written by Congress was spare in content and narrow in focus. It combined support for the pursuit of Nazi war criminals with a pledge to oppose any effort at group slander or defamation.

> We are concerned that relations between Jewish Canadians and Ukrainian Canadians be maintained and strengthened in the interest of both communities. We agree that those Nazi mass murderers who dwell among us should be brought to justice in conformity with the Canadian law and the Deschênes Commission continue its investigations in terms of its mandate. We cannot permit those who have committed mass murder to go unpunished. We reject as repugnant that any group in Canada be identified with war criminals. We are solely interested in identifying war criminals as individuals irrespective of their ethnic origin.
>
> We join as Canadians in vigorously condemning bigotry directed against any group of our fellow citizens and commit our organizations to work to this end.
>
> Canadian Jewish Congress and B'nai Brith join with the Ukrainian Canadian Committee in reaffirming our commitment that all Canadians — regardless of origin — must unite to enrich the unique multicultural mosaic of Canada. In this regard we intend to confer on matters of mutual concern, which include multiculturalism, human rights and such issues as may be of interest to our respective organizations.[117]

The UCC was not satisfied, nor was its Deschênes watchdog, the CLC. The Ukrainians wanted a broader statement which would reflect the passion which sustained their concerns. They hoped for a statement which would, somehow, touch on issues such as the famine, ongoing Soviet oppression, the activities of Jews in the Soviet Communist party, and alleged

Ukrainian baiting in the current impasse.[118] The Congress statement, dry and antiseptic, did not fill the bill. Yuzyk drafted a counter-statement.

Since the 19th century, Jews and Ukrainians immigrated to Canada in large numbers to escape the persecution and privation which were so much a part of life in the old country.

Happily, Canada has provided us with a life full of freedom and prosperity, and our communities, in turn, have been working harmoniously to build a stronger Canada. There have been no czars or commissars to foist hatred and malevolence in our midst.

Regrettably, the indescribable horrors that occurred in Nazi-occupied Europe have given rise to repugnant accusations against the Ukrainian people by some irresponsible Jewish individuals . . . These scurrilous charges by extremists and scandal mongerers have caused Ukrainian Canadians to believe that they themselves are under attack, even if they are fourth generation Canadians, or Canadian war veterans.

It is this provocation that has caused Ukrainian Canadians to be defensive in regard to the Deschênes Commission and that has led to insensitive, inflammatory statements by some irresponsible Ukrainian individuals.

Therefore, be it agreed that we the undersigned shall work together to reverse the estrangement which helps no one but our enemies; that we will do our utmost to combat derogatory statements against Jews or Ukrainians, or any other group; that we support the Deschênes Commission in its mandate to investigate war criminals who may be living in Canada; and most important, that as we attempt to resolve the issue which has divided us, we are determined to work together to strengthen multiculturalism and human rights, and to solve any other issue that is of direct interest to our communities or to Canada's well being."[119]

To some, the two statements might seem nearly identical. But Yuzyk's version was unacceptable to Jewish leaders. It pointed to anti-Ukrainian outbursts from individuals within the Jewish community as the source of ethnic tensions and found no comparable conduct in the Ukrainian community. The statement also spoke of war criminals generally, not Nazi war criminals. It emphasized the issue of provocations aimed at Ukrainians rather than the justice of the hunt for Nazi war criminals living in Canada. It too would not do.

Negotiations now began in earnest, with drafts and revisions flying. B'nai Brith proposed wording of its own. Alan Rose and Milton Harris of Congress redrafted a statement in late February. It reflected some of the concerns of Ukrainians while keeping the tone of the original draft, apportioning equal blame to irresponsible statements from both communities. This was better but not totally acceptable to the UCC.[120]

By March it had become clear that a compromise would be very hard to reach. Winter vacations as well as fundamental conflicts of interest had slowed down the process. Jewish leaders began to wonder whether in fact Senator Yuzyk could deliver as mediator, given a persistent militancy in the Ukrainian camp. Perhaps a communiqué was really not that essential, or worth the effort. The top priority for Congress had always been a tripartite meeting of presidents, to hash out the issues. The UCC now demanded as a priority the issuing of a statement in advance of any such face-to-face meeting. Even the process, not just the content, divided the two groups.

Spring came, and advisers in the two communities were still poring over drafts. The goal seemed to be slipping away. Congress leaders suspected there was no pleasing the UCC. Could it be that increasing internal disarray, with tensions escalating between CLC militants and moderates made it impossible for them to agree on anything? Senator Yuzyk, who was seriously ill and sapped of strength, seemed no longer to have the political energy to move UCC leaders.[121]

Yuzyk, it must be said, never gave up on the idea of a tripartite summit conference of Congress, B'nai Brith and the UCC. B'nai Brith, seizing the moment, invited the ailing Yuzyk to address the annual meeting of the B'nai Brith Board in April 1986. While a public address was a poor substitute for a joint statement or a frank exchange of views among the leaders of the three organizations, Yuzyk's invitation certainly had a symbolic impact. Yuzyk used the occasion to urge that a tripartite committee be established to meet regularly, twice yearly, to discuss matters of mutual concern. Many nodded in agreement; few believed it would come to pass. In a last-ditch attempt at compromise, Congress and B'nai Brith leaders invited Yuzyk and UCC President John Nowosad to a mid-summer luncheon meeting. The UCC declined. While willing to continue the dialogue, wrote Nowosad to B'nai Brith President Harry Bick, "with the great number of issues yet to be resolved, it is difficult to meet at this time." There would be no joint statement.[122]

While these behind-the-scenes efforts at *rapprochement* were floundering, there were several public displays of successful Ukrainian-Jewish cooperation. In March 1986 a previously unknown organization called the Ukrainian Defence League surfaced. The group posted flyers in downtown Toronto claiming "Let My People Go! Stop Jewish Persecution of Ukrainians in Canada and the USA."[123] Whoever was responsible for the posters had been influenced, in name and slogan, by the Jewish Defence League, which had long been active in Canada. The JDL had taken a particularly hard-line position on the war-criminals issue. So some retaliation was apparently in order.

Condemnation of the flyers was swift, not only from Jewish organizations, but from the UCC. Congress, ever ready to accept a Ukrainian olive branch, welcomed the UCC condemnation. Milton Harris went further. He dismissed the flyers as likely the work of people or groups outside the Ukrainian or Jewish communities, racially motivated, out to sow discord and hostility between the two groups.[124]

Indeed, public acts of extremism provided ready-made occasions for public displays of ethnic co-operation. For example, April 1986 saw the victimiza-tion of the Ukrainian community in Edmonton, though not with inflammatory flyers. One Sunday evening, van-dals spray painted the words "Nazi Lies" on a monu-ment honouring the victims of the Ukrainian famine. The Alberta branch of the UCC and the Jewish Federa-tion issued a joint statement just two days after the de-facing. "This is an outrageous act of political vandalism," the statement declared, "reminiscent of Nazi defacements of Jewish synagogues and cemeteries that occurred during the rise of the Nazi regime. It is an insult to the memory of the millions of victims who died in 1932–33."[125]

In fact, Jewish-Ukrainian relations in Edmonton, and western Canada generally, were more positive than in Toronto, the eye of the Deschênes storm. In western Canada both communities were largely native born. Representatives in Winnipeg and Edmonton met re-spectfully to discuss and try to improve relations. The Jewish community in Edmonton, for example, smaller and politically weaker than its Ukrainian counterpart, was certainly alert to the value of ethnic harmony. And Ukrainians could point to a series of much appreciated gestures by Jews or the Jewish community, affirming the spirit of ethnic goodwill.

Jewish representatives had participated in the services originally dedicating the Edmonton monument to the victims of Stalin's brutality, and noted the similarities between Hitler's slaughter of the Jews and Stalin's mass murders. On another occasion, the Jewish community of Edmonton had also pointedly told the militant Jew-ish Defence League that it was not welcome in Edmon-ton. The Ukrainian community in Edmonton, moreover, had been solid in support of government action against James Keegstra, the Alberta schoolteacher who taught his students that the Holocaust never happened. Symbolic co-operation extended to electoral politics as well: ". . . there was that dramatic moment during the recent Progressive Conservative leadership convention when a candidate of Jewish origin, Ron Ghitter, walked over to a candidate of Ukrainian origin, Julian Koziak, and threw his support his way even though it was evident only a miracle would prevent Don Getty from winning on the second ballot."[126]

These kinds of open-hearted gestures were far rarer in the east, where tensions simmered close to the surface. But tactical considerations would often serve to moderate potentially explosive flashpoints involving the two communities. A case in point was the anti-American protest of the Toronto Croatian community against the deportation of the alleged Nazi war criminal Andrija Artukovic, Minister of the Interior in the Ustashi pro-Nazi puppet regime in Croatia, from the United States for trial in Yugoslavia. Artukovic stood accused of the murder of thousands of Serbs and Jews. Two thousand Croatian protesters rallied outside the American Consulate in Toronto in February 1986. Passions exploded unexpectedly. One militant Croatian doused himself with gasoline and lit a match. As reported in *The Globe and Mail*, a poster found in his van read, "Dear God, Help stop Genocide on my Croatian People."[127]

Croatian nationalists maintained a round-the-clock vigil outside the American consulate. They approached the Ukrainian community for support in manning the pickets. After all, they asked, was not the fate of Artukovic possibly the future fate of a Ukrainian falsely entrapped by Nazi-hunters? But regardless of the degree of sympathy for the Croatians, the CLC felt wary of committing whole-hearted public support. They could not deny their Croatian allies assistance. Croatian organizations backed the CLC effort. But it was decided that only a handful of Ukrainian protesters ought to be seen at the pickets, lest provocateurs incite trouble. Ensuing negative publicity could harm the Ukrainian cause. The ethnic background of the vigil remained focused on Serbian-Croatian rivalries, with little spillover onto Ukrainian-Jewish relations. Nevertheless, Croatian and Ukrainian flags flew side by side on the median in front of the American Consulate.[128]

But so long as the Deschênes process continued and the stigma of war criminals and the Holocaust was attached to the Ukrainian community, better Ukrainian-Jewish relations remained a problem. And for the Canadians following the news during the course of 1986, the Holocaust seemed everywhere. Moreover, it might seem that everyone was involved except the Germans. Individual Ukrainians, Balts and Croatians were being pursued as war criminals. French collaboration was a sub-theme of the Klaus Barbie trial in France. Polish collaboration and anti-Semitism were the subject of the award-winning film *Shoah*. Austria's historical claim as Hitler's first victim was brought into question by the Waldheim revelations. Each day's news seemed to highlight the complicity of non-Germans.

Even Canada's Hungarian community was pulled into the limelight. Readers of Toronto's *Globe and Mail* were treated to an account of an almost sectarian conflict raging within Toronto's Hungarian community. Tempers flared over an exhibit in a Hungarian community centre, devoted to memorabilia of the Hungarian *Gendarmerie*. Most Canadians, and even most Jews, had doubtless never heard of the *Gendarmerie*. But not so for Hungarians, and certainly not for Hungarian Jews. The *Gendarmerie* had been instrumental in the round-up and deportation of Hungary's 600,000 Jews during the war to the fate that awaited in the death camps. The group was outlawed following the Allied victory.[129]

"The question is," asked an opponent of the exhibit, "would the German community here in Toronto open a museum commemorating the memory of the Gestapo, or the Italian community open up an exhibit glorifying Mussolini's fascist police? No way." Defenders of the exhibit countered, ". . . There are things in the exhibit that do not always show the good parts of our history, but it is a part of our history."[130]

The Hungarian *Gendarmerie* connection would surface again. A 1983 segment of the CTV public-affairs show "W5" had accused one Imre Finta, then resident of Toronto, of war crimes while he was a member of the *Gendarmerie*. A native of Hungary, Finta was allegedly implicated in the deportation and subsequent deaths of Hungarian Jews, and survivors had testified that Finta was the *Gendarmerie* commander who confiscated Jewish valuables and organized the deportation from Szeged in Hungary. Finta brought a libel suit against CTV, but CTV fought back. Its lawyers, led by none other than John Sopinka, assembled testimony from several countries, including Hungary, on Finta's wartime activities. Rather than go to court, Finta decided to discontinue his suit. The news was hailed by the Jewish community. "In our view," said Congress's Manuel Prutschi, "Finta has totally surrendered." All evidence from the Finta case was subpoenaed by the Deschênes Commission.[131] This was not the last to be heard about Imre Finta.

Events in Israel also continued to colour Jewish-Ukrainian relations. Both the Jewish and Ukrainian press in Canada, for example, covered the efforts of Yakov Suslensky and his Israeli Society of Jewish-Ukrainian Contacts. Suslensky, a recent immigrant to Israel from the Soviet Union, had been imprisoned side by side with Ukrainians before being permitted to emigrate. Once in Israel, he sought to further the *rapprochement* of Jews and Ukrainians, wherever and however possible. In September 1985, a Jerusalem monument honouring the Jewish and Ukrainian victims of the Holocaust, and the victims of the famine, had been demolished. Time passed, and the Israeli police made no headway in solving the crime. Nor, some charged, did they appear to attach much urgency to it. In December of that year Suslensky led a small protest at the site of the desecrated monument, decrying what he termed deliberate government inaction. In April 1986 the CLC publicly condemned the Israeli authorities for the lack of action on the matter.[132]

The Ukrainian press also monitored news of interest from Israel. The *Ukrainian News* of Edmonton carried a *Jerusalem Post* report alleging that some Israeli political leaders had actually justified the destruction of the monument. Yet the paper also carried an account by an Israeli of his encounter with two Ukrainian men who had suffered in the labour camps of both the Nazis and the Soviets. "I am therefore angered," he protested "by the cynicism of those who claim that Ukrainians did not suffer from the Nazis. . . . They defile the memory of those Ukrainians who died of hunger and forced labor." These stories were highlighted as examples of unusual Jewish sensitivity to Ukrainian pain.[133]

Suslensky also doggedly carried on his efforts. The fact that some Jewish communal leaders viewed his efforts with suspicion did not deter him. In autumn 1986, at Ukrainian urgings, Suslensky embarked on a cross-Canada tour, meeting with Jewish and Ukrainian groups. As he discovered, some Jews questioned the Ukrainian refusal to come to grips with the dark underside of their history. Yet by the same token, Ukrainians complained that Jews did not properly appreciate Ukrainian suffering or the heroism of those Ukrainians who did save Jewish lives. One sore point which continued to rankle was the case of Metropolitan Andrei Sheptytsky, who saved Jews and spoke out against the Nazi actions and admonished his Ukrainian flock against co-operation in anti-Jewish actions. Yad Vashem, Israel's Holocaust Institute, persisted in refusing to designate Sheptytsky as a "righteous gentile." Close to 7,000 non-Jews had earned this meritorious designation denoting people who took risks to save Jewish lives during the war. Sheptytsky is not one of them.[134]

Stories of Sheptytsky's efforts on behalf of Jews — and there is no dispute at all over the fact of his having used his offices personally to save scores of Jews — appear repeatedly in the Ukrainian press. For some observers, the steadfast refusal of Yad Vashem to acknowledge Sheptytsky's courage can only be explained as persisting prejudice against Ukrainians.

On the matter of Sheptytsky, representatives of Yad Vashem present their counter-arguments. In essence, they parallel arguments made by Jews about the role of Pope Pius XII and the Catholic Church in saving Jews during World War II. Yes, individual churches and monasteries did save Jewish lives, particularly children, and yes, the Pope did countenance quiet initiatives to save Jews. But far more was expected, far more was needed, and far more could have been done.[135] Likewise, "If Sheptytsky were a plain man, or just a simple priest, he would certainly deserve a tree," said one Yad Vashem historian, referring to the tree symbolically planted in honour of each righteous gentile. "Sheptytsky may have been personally responsible for saving 150 lives during the war. But he was a leader, and could have done more." Thus his record is seen as being somewhat ambiguous. Moreover, it is possible that the responsible committees at Yad Vashem feel that by honouring Sheptytsky, they may implicitly exonerate the Ukrainians in general and the entire Ukrainian Catholic Church in particular. This they may be reluctant to do.[136]

But the continuing controversy over Sheptytsky proved nothing compared to that surrounding Demjanjuk. Even before the trial began, many Ukrainian Canadians were incensed. Ukrainian-Jewish relations in Canada could not help but be affected. Some diaspora Ukrainians expressed fears that Demjanjuk might not receive a fair trial in Israel. They were also concerned about pre-trial comments of some Israeli government leaders, and the fact that Demjanjuk had been held for several months after his arrival in February 1986, without formal charges being laid. These concerns were relayed to Israeli officials by Americans for Human Rights in Ukraine (AHRU), a nationalist Ukrainian group, in a letter to all members of Knesset. The letter asserted that these conditions were "contrary to your laws and in violation of John Demjanjuk's human rights."[137]

No one could have expected the explosion that ensued. The response by Deputy Speaker of the Knesset Dov Ben Meir caught Ukrainians, and indeed many Israelis and diaspora Jews, off guard. The letter must certainly be judged unusual in the history of governmental correspondence. It combines intemperate language with unflattering generalities about Ukrainians and Ukraine. For example, Ben Meir reminded Ukrainians that "since the days of Bogdan Chelmnitsky [sic], the Jewish people has a long score to settle with the Ukrainian people," and recalled further the "uncounted numbers" of Ukrainians who collaborated with the Nazis. For Ben Meir, it was intolerable that Ukrainians would raise questions about the quality of Israeli justice. "To you and your friends, I suggest that you go to church not only on Sunday but on every day of the week," Ben Meir concluded, "and that you kneel there until bleeding at the knees in asking forgiveness for what your people has done to ours."[138]

Ukrainians were outraged. Bozhena Olshaniwsky, President of the AHRU, responded in an open letter, which was, like Ben Meir's, widely publicized in the Ukrainian press. The response tried to set the historical context of the murders of Ukrainian Jews during the Khmelnytsky rebellions. As the leaseholders, tax collectors and agents of the Polish nobles, Jews had become enmeshed in the system of social oppression imposed upon Ukraine by the Polish regime. Next came the problem of collective guilt. "Do you really hold the entire Ukrainian nation collectively responsible for the crimes of certain individuals?" She reminded Ben Meir that Ukrainians were also among the jury members who had acquitted Mendel Beiless, a Ukrainian Jew tried on a trumped-up blood libel charge in the early 1900s. (This trial, popularized in Bernard Malamud's book *The Fixer*, resurrected the anti-Semitic myth that Jews murdered Christian girls and used their blood in the making of Passover matzoh.) She further cited Israeli War Crimes Investigation Office estimates that Ukrainian collaborators numbered about 11,000, against a total population of 36 million in Ukraine at that time, and rejected the claim that anti-Semitism was particularly indigenous to Ukraine. Today, as in the past, she charged, outside agents were largely to blame; anti-Semitism was deliberately fomented by Moscow.[139]

News of the exchange raced throughout the Ukrainian community. What, some Ukrainians might wonder, would happen to a senior Canadian politician who wrote a similar letter about Jews? Jewish leaders tried to distance themselves from Ben Meir's attack on all Ukrainians. Ever diplomatic, Jack Silverstone of Congress called it "unhelpful." John Gregorovich reported that Ukrainian Canadians were in a state of shock. Ben Meir, reached by Canadian Press in Israel, claimed he had directed his remarks only at the hardline AHRU, and not at all Ukrainians. His backpedalling did little to assuage Ukrainian resentments. Convincing the average Ukrainian of the value of improved relations with Jews would become even more difficult.[140]

Even as all awaited the Deschênes Commission report, Ben Meir's letter underscored the worst fears of concerned Ukrainian-Canadian groups. Behind the pursuit of individual Ukrainian war-crimes suspects lurked, they suggested, a generalized prejudice against Ukrainians, and a Soviet-inspired vendetta aimed at labelling all Ukrainians as war criminals or collaborators. Beneath the polite veneer of legal argumentation flowed a subterranean river of ethnic hatred. Perhaps the repeated assertion by Jewish leaders that the issue of war criminals was not an anti-Ukrainian exercise was simply a smokescreen.

In a similar vein, Ukrainian leaders repeatedly asserted that their position on the war-criminals issue was motivated only by concern for fair treatment and the fear of group defamation. Their zeal was not fuelled by anti-Semitism or the desire to keep secret any harbouring of war criminals by the community. Their enemy was the Soviet Union, they claimed, not Jews; indeed Jews and Ukrainians shared the same enemy. It was the Soviet Union that armed the Arab states while it persecuted Jews, as it did Ukrainians, within its borders. Ukrainian leaders declared that intemperate remarks by a handful of hotheads did not mean that the community was anti-Semitic. Opposition to Jewish policy positions, or attempts to provide different interpretations of historical events, did not imply anti-Semitism. Better for Jews and Ukrainians to unite to fight the Soviet Union and the evils of Communism, not each other. No one could dispute the anti-Communist credentials of the mainstream Ukrainian organizations. And the Conservative backbenchers vocal in their opposition to the use of Soviet evidence by Deschênes included some firmly ensconced on the right wing of the party.

But many Jews were reluctant to accept that argument. Despite the urging of American neoconservatives, Jews have always questioned the bona fides of right-wing anti-Communists. Perhaps there has been too much anti-Semitic water under the right-wing bridge. True, many Jews nowadays find they have much in common with the political agenda of the right; a common commitment to the defence of Israel has been one point of co-operation, particularly in the United States. Wariness of a challenge to the meritocracy in the name of affirmative action has also bonded Jews with conservatives, but the new flirtation has not yet led to marriage. Jews still tend to hold relatively liberal opinions, and vote for the more liberal parties. It is as though even conservative Jews remain uncertain as to whether they really are on the same wave-length as other right-wing conservatives.[141]

For some Jews, it may be enough to arouse suspicion that some of the Ukrainian opposition to Deschênes is linked to right-wing anti-Semitism. Ukrainians might use the same logic to brand the OSI and Nazi-hunters like Simon Wiesenthal (who have, after all, sought out Soviet bloc evidence) as left-wing anti-Ukrainians, dupes of or in league with the Soviets. In ethnic politics, perceptions are everything.

The focus of this ethnic politics was the Deschênes process. Public hearings were over. Press reports held that Judge Deschênes had completed his report. What would he recommend? Yet 1986 came and went, with no release of the report of the Commission. Ottawa rumour mills worked overtime. Cabinet had the report — what was it doing with it? Was it being revised, sanitized to protect the privacy of individual subjects who might be identified? Perhaps the report was being delayed for other reasons? After all, David Vienneau of *The Toronto Star* had called the report a "ticking time bomb," and a later *Star* headline had predicted "Trouble looms for Mulroney."[142] Jewish leaders were becoming apprehensive. An Australian report on war criminals was released in very short order with no mysterious delays, and the Australian government seemed pledged to move ahead expeditiously to enact its recommendations. Why was Ottawa taking so long?[143]

Some Jewish spokesmen were troubled that the mysterious revisions might water down the actual content of the report, weakening it as a historical document. "I don't think the whole thing should be so antiseptic," said B'nai Brith's Matas, "that it seems the crime took place nowhere." Jews were not alone in their apprehension. A leader of Canada's Serbian community, hoping that the Commission would say something about war crimes against his people, feared that nothing would happen and that the report would be a whitewash.[144]

Of course, some Ukrainian Canadians were apprehensive too, but they received reassuring news in January 1987. Reliable sources suggested that no Ukrainians would ultimately be included on the secret list of "hot" Nazi war-criminal suspects compiled by Deschênes. While it was still possible that an osi-like agency might be recommended, or that the legitimacy of Soviet evidence would be established, it was unlikely that one of their own would be among the primary group of alleged Nazi war criminals to be identified. While several

Ukrainian Canadians had been interviewed as suspects by the Commission, none were among those notified by the Commission, as required by law, that they were to be accused of legal misconduct. By January, then, it was likely that Ukrainian names, if there were any, had been removed from the list.[145]

John Gregorovich, however, cautioned against early celebrations. Until the report was officially released, one could not be certain. Ukrainians might well be among the secondary group of suspects. He urged no let-up in the community's vigilance.[146] Nevertheless, the CLC could smell victory; relief was almost palpable. There would be no high-profile Ukrainian trials.

As Ukrainian insecurities receded and the mood became more upbeat, Alex Epstein, along with Victor Goldbloom of the Canadian Council of Christians and Jews, tried once again to find some middle ground between the two groups. They pulled together a proposal for a meeting between key members of the Ukrainian and Jewish communities. A meeting that would have been unimaginable a few months earlier was quickly scheduled for Monday, January 19, 1987, at the Toronto headquarters of the Canadian Jewish Congress. Both sides now affirmed the need to minimize possible ethnic divisions resulting from the forthcoming Deschênes recommendations, whatever they might be.

As chance would have it, January 19 brought with it the worst snowstorm of the season. Many of those invited could not even get out of their own driveways. But a core group including Dorothy Reitman, newly elected president of Congress, David Matas, Victor Goldbloom, Alex Epstein, John Gregorovich and representatives of the Latvian and Estonian communities managed to make it to the meeting.

Discussion was about discussion — ways to open dialogue, or as Goldbloom reportedly put it, "to work through what is in our hearts." All the old controversies were rehashed: Soviet evidence; control of "extremists"; playing to the media; the aborted joint communiqué; the hunt for war criminals other than

Nazis. No miracles took place. But all agreed that so long as each group recognized the sensitivities of the other, nothing should be done to provoke deliberate confrontation.[147]

Given these hopes for renewed dialogue, it came as a shock when one last spasm of ethnic politics threatened to shake the renewed enthusiasm. Only two weeks after the meeting, a full-page advertisement in *The Globe and Mail* of February 2, sponsored by the CLC, urged readers to "Protect the Innocent." It warned all Canadians that their civil liberties might be threatened, à la McCarthyism, by the setting up in Canada of an OSI-type investigative unit. "Millions of Canadians," the ad asserted, were opposed to the idea. Ethnic communities would inevitably be slandered by OSI-type activities. The individuals named or investigated would be subjected not only to unproved allegations but quite possibly to violent vigilante justice, as had happened in the United States. A general witch-hunt would ensue. All these things, the ad warned, "could happen here."[148]

Jewish leaders were upset with both the timing of the ad — prior to the release of the Deschênes Commission's report — and with its tone. The ad boasted two new departures from the earlier *Globe and Mail* ad in the fall of 1985. This invited donations to the Civil Liberties Commission to support their effort. (The CLC was not identified as linked to the Ukrainian community.) Secondly, the ad was signed by a roster of ethnic organizations which stretched far beyond Ukrainians and their eastern European ethnic allies. Signatories included the Afghan Association of Ontario (Canada), the Canadian Coalition for Vietnamese Human Rights, the German Canadian Congress and the National Congress of Italian Canadians. At least one group was left off the list by mistake. The Hungarian Canadian Federation later informed members that it had signed the ad but that a clerical error may have led to its name being excluded. The Japanese Canadians, on the other hand, had been invited to join, but declined.[149]

The advertisement in *The Globe and Mail* seemed to
some Jewish leaders to be ethnic politics with a vengeance. Was this a major, public, last-ditch effort to
influence the government prior to the official release of
the report of the Deschênes Commission? What were
the Italians doing on that list? And why the Vietnamese? Was there a new ethnic coalition emerging in
Canada from which Jews were to be excluded? Congress and B'nai Brith moved quickly to try and repair
the damage.

Congress hastily arranged for a meeting with the
president of the National Congress of Italian Canadians, to try to find out why his organization had co-
signed the ad. In a letter to Congress he claimed that
he had approved neither the layout nor the timing of
the ad and that his organization had not contributed towards its cost. While not refuting the actual substance
of the ad, he agreed that the unfortunate episode demonstrated the need for closer consultation and co-
operation between the Jewish and Italian communities
in the future. Some observers saw the incident as only
an error of judgment, and key members of the Italian
organization expressed regret and sorrow at the turn of
events and hoped the rupture would not be
permanent.[150]

B'nai Brith went further. David Matas delivered a
lengthy, detailed rebuttal to the ad at a meeting of the
Italian group's national Executive. He told the meeting
that the Italian signing of the ad was an anomaly. He
noted that except for the Italians, all of the ethnic
groups represented were groups whose territories, in
whole or in part, were controlled by Soviet-supported
Communist forces. Thus, in their struggle to help free
their brethren from the yoke of Soviet domination, anything to further weaken the Soviet state, such as an attack on the legitimacy of the use of Soviet evidence,
would be laudable. Matas wondered if the Italian community ought to be drawn into this particular cold-war
operation.

Matas also reminded his audience that "in fascist Italy proper, and in all areas occupied by fascist Italy, the Jews remained safe from deportation." He pointed out that some groups such as Ukrainians, Balts or Croatians were forced during the course of the war into the miserable choice of co-operation with the Nazis or with the Communists. That choice was not directly imposed on Italians. The unstated implication was that Italians had relatively little to feel guilty or defensive about on the matter of anti-Semitism or war criminality. "To join these groups now in such an intemperate attack on American legal institutions," continued Matas, "is a violation of the Italian historical tradition."[151]

Outreach to the other groups who had signed the ad was also the order of the day. Congress had felt particularly betrayed by the Vietnamese. "I write this letter with a sense of regret because of our sensitivity to the concerns of the Vietnamese community. You may know that Canadian Jewish Congress led the faith groups in putting pressure on the federal government to bring 'boat people' to Canada," wrote Congess's Alan Rose. "Indeed Canadian Jewish Congress guaranteed 1000 'boat people' and made additional contributions to the charitable funds set up to integrate them into our mosaic."[152]

When no reply was received, further inquiries were made. It appeared that the group that signed the ad, the Canadian Coalition for Vietnamese Human Rights, was a small, ad hoc splinter group with no formal ties to Vietnamese mainstream associations. They were not found in the telephone directory. What was unclear was how they had become linked to the Ukrainian cause.[153]

Jewish organizations were not alone in their opposition to the CLC ad. Two days after publishing the ad, *The Globe and Mail* took the unusual step of challenging its arguments. In an editorial the *Globe* charged, "In their strident, pre-emptive attack on the Deschênes report, the advertisers are themselves culpable of disinformation." They went on to say that the ad distorted the role of the OSI, and that the Deschênes process would be more likely to "forestall vigilante action than to incite it." Whereas the ad warned that it — referring to a witch-hunt — could happen here, the *Globe* responded that "it should happen here."[154]

But that was not the only controversy engendered by the ad. The Canadian Civil Liberties Association (CCLA) felt that the similarities between its name and that of the CLC might confuse *Globe and Mail* readers. The CCLA wrote a letter to the editor disassociating their organization from the ad. In addition, CCLA lawyers wrote to the CLC requesting that they "cease and desist from using the name Civil Liberties Commission or any other name likely to be confused with our client's name." The CLC would not be moved. John Sopinka, responding for the CLC, rejected the request out of hand. Sopinka denied the claim that confusion might arise. The CCLA itself had offered no such examples. Sopinka could not resist a little jibe — given the CCLA's silence on the civil libertarian concerns raised by the Ukrainian community throughout the Deschênes process, it was unlikely that they would have suddenly changed their views to help raise money to pay for the ad.[155]

The CLC's Gregorovich responded to the CCLA disclaimer by sending a letter to *The Globe and Mail* (which was not published), rejecting any charge of intent to confuse the Civil Liberties Commission with the Canadian Civil Liberties Association. After all, he claimed, the CCLA publicly defended Holocaust denier Ernst Zundel. "Those who prefer to send their dollars to an organization which champions Mr. Zundel's case are equally free to do so. The Civil Liberties Commission . . . holds no brief whatsoever on behalf of Mr. Zundel. It also shares the . . . concerns about Mr. Zundel's views on the mass murder of millions of Jews, gypsies and East Europeans by the Nazis."[156]

In late February and early March 1987, as most Canadians waited for spring, Jewish and Ukrainian leaders waited for the Deschênes Commission's report. Relations between the two communities remained in limbo.

Both groups knew there would be dialogue in their future; there had to be. But interaction on the basis of complete mutual trust might be impossible. It now rested with Deschênes and the Cabinet to set the tone for future relations.

Chapter 7

The Report and Its Aftermath

At 8:00 A.M. on March 12, 1987, with less than twenty-four hours' notice, everyone had gathered as requested in the anteroom of the House of Commons restaurant. Five representatives from each of the four groups with standing before the Commission were present, along with several government officials. The tables, arranged in a horseshoe, were set for breakfast. With no pre-arranged seating plan, the delegates divided themselves into two groups — Congress and B'nai Brith members on one side, UCC members and the Division veterans on the other. Many were familiar to each other — Gregorovich, Luciuk, Cotler, Harris, Matas, Botiuk, Silverstone.

Minister of Justice Ray Hnatyshyn welcomed everyone. He spoke not of the contents of the Deschênes Commission's report but of the hard work that had gone into its preparation and his hope that justice would now be served. Conversation at the tables was light, yet restive. Several Jewish representatives noted that the breakfast was not kosher.

Just after nine, with breakfast finished, the delegations were ushered into a private lock-up across from Parliament Hill. Each was given a copy of Part I, the public volume of the *Report of the Commission of Inquiry on War Criminals*. Cut off from any outside communication for two hours, they sat around a large conference table, again with Jews on one side and Ukrainians on the other, while a Justice Department official went through the *Report*, its recommendations and the prepared government response.

There was little intergroup discussion. Only one discordant note was sounded, and it was quickly stilled. A representative of the Galicia Division veterans at one point launched into an attack on Israel's trial of John Demjanjuk as an exercise of vengeance on the part of the victims. Before the remark could generate any Jewish reaction, Gregorovich jumped in. The official UCC position, he reminded everone, was that Demjanjuk was receiving a fair trial in Israel. Argument averted, the delegates turned their attention back to the *Report*.[1]

Even with the lock-up, which had been promised by the government, there was little time to digest the *Report*. The press was waiting for immediate reactions; so were the respective ethnic communities. Two years and four million dollars after the Prime Minister had announced the Commission, the *Report* was out. Yet those who thought the *Report* would be a political time bomb were wrong. There was no explosion. As the delegates spilled out of the lock-up, their initial response was positive. Deschênes in his *Report* and the government in its response had done the impossible: they seemed to have pleased everyone. As one Commission staffer claimed, the *Report* offered "something for everybody."[2]

Moreover, something unusual had taken place. Just as the representatives were released from the lock-up, the Minister of Justice rose in the House to respond to the *Report*. Few people expected him to both release the Deschênes report and announce the government's game plan at the same time. Commission recommendations are often ignored, or sometimes used to stimulate on-going debate; concrete government action generally follows a period of prolonged debate and consultation. But this was different. Rather than call for public discussion, the government in effect pre-empted further discussion. There would be no more consultation. The minister announced the government had laid out its course of action in choosing from among the array of

legal options Judge Deschênes had put forward. The
government intended to deal vigorously with war criminals, with a "made in Canada" solution — trials in
Canada.

To some Ukrainian and Jewish leaders, the *Report*
and the quick government response came as manna
from heaven. The Jews hoped action was imminent.
Ukrainians were convinced their community's positions
had made an impact on the government's plan of action. And both groups felt that a new era of inter-ethnic harmony might be on the way. But how had the
Commission and the government's instant reaction managed to please almost everyone? Deschênes had been
asked to address three sets of questions. Were there at
present any Nazi war criminals in Canada, and how
many? How and when did these war criminals come to
Canada? What remedies might be available to bring
them to justice?

The *Report* comprised two distinct parts. The first,
released to the public, was a mammoth volume of 966
pages divided into an overview of the Commission's investigative procedures and the various legal arguments
presented before the Commission, along with findings
and recommendations. This was followed by a longer
section consisting of a brief synopsis — without naming
names — of each of the more than 800 actual cases of
alleged Nazi war criminals investigated by the
Commission.[3]

The second — and confidential — section of the
Report reviewed the particulars of confidential testimony offered the Commission and contained the detailed allegations and summaries of evidence against
twenty-nine suspects. These were the cases in which the
Commission felt that the seriousness of the allegations
and availability of evidence "warranted special attention" and recommended that "steps be taken toward either revocation of citizenship and deportation or
criminal prosecution . . ."[4]

Anyone picking up the Commission's public volume
would be immediately drawn to page after page of brief

comments on individuals — each identified only by number — the Commission had investigated. The Commission, which never independently sought out suspected war criminals, had relied on more than 800 names gleaned from other sources. It eventually isolated the 20 serious cases, detailed in Part II of its report, from a short list of 29. (Nine cases were recommended closed without prosecution.) Of the remaining cases, 606 were recommended for immediate closure. These included 341 where the suspect never came to Canada, 21 who came to Canada but moved elsewhere, 86 who died in Canada, 4 who could not be located in Canada, and 154 where the subjects were living in Canada but no *prima facie* evidence of wrongdoing could be found. That left another 139 cases where further investigations might be warranted.[5]

Additional names continued to flow into the Commission, too late to be investigated. It received late in its mandate the list of 71 German scientists and technicians who had come to Canada after the war. Quick investigations enabled the Commission to close some of the files, but a total of 79 of the late submissions were judged to require further investigations before the cases could be resolved. That yielded a total of 218 names for further investigation, excluding the short list of 20 major suspects.

Where did these cases come from? How were these numbers derived? The figures 20, 218 or 238 were seized on by the media as representing the scope of the Nazi war-criminals problem in Canada. Jewish leaders again reiterated that "one was too many," but government officials, recalling the earlier figure of 3,000, heaved a sigh of relief. The numbers were not as high as they had feared. But were they accurate? Some said no. They pointed out that what the Commission did not, and perhaps could not do, was undertake an independent hunt for Nazi war criminals in Canada. It did not undertake a massive cross-checking of available names against lists of possible Nazi war criminals from external sources. For example, the 40,000 names listed by the United Nations War Crimes Commission (UNWCC) might have been cross-checked against lists of all post-war Canadian immigrants, or naturalized Canadians, not just those few on supplied lists.

Admittedly, such an approach was logistically formidable. Millions of people had come to Canada after 1945. Finding a match of two names would then entail a massive investigation itself, to prove whether the names weren't coincidentally similar, whether the person was alive, had left Canada or could be found. That approach might well yield more names, but required a commitment of time, staff and money which the Commission did not have.

The Commission had decided to opt for the more practical approach of building up its case-load from available lists. These included 335 files assembled over the years by the RCMP. Additional lists were received from Jewish sources in Canada, the United States, Israel and the USSR. Some names came in from the public at large, following advertisements placed in sixty-eight English, twenty-four French and eighteen ethnic newspapers.[6]

Once names were assembled, the investigations became a two-pronged affair. A major undertaking was the checking of the names listed in archives of various international agencies involved in prosecuting or studying war crimes. The Commission's names were sent to be cross-checked with data from the Berlin Document Centre; the Central Office of Land Judicial Authorities for the Investigation of National-Socialist Crimes in Ludwigsburg, West Germany; the German Military Service Office in Berlin; the Berlin Sick Book Depository; the Central Information Office of the Federal Archives at Aachen-Kornelimünster. Other sources, consulted where specifics of a case seemed to warrant it, included the *Centre de documentation juive contemporaine* in Paris, the OSI in Washington, the Wiesenthal Documentation Center in Vienna and the Yad Vashem archives in Jerusalem.[7]

As extensive as these sources were, each was limited in its scope. Some sources, like the Ludwigsburg Office in West Germany, dealt with crimes which took place on German soil, where the suspect was arrested in West Germany or where the suspect was of German origin. These criteria would obviously exclude most non-Germans guilty of war crimes. Most of the concentration and extermination camps, it must be noted, were located outside Germany and staffed largely by non-Germans. Most of the victims, Jewish and non-Jewish, were also non-German. Thus there were shortcomings in relying on German origin lists and documents. The problem was compounded by the decision of the Commission not to send any names, with one exception, to any eastern European country for checking with archives there. Many of those archives may well have had valuable data, some captured from retreating Germans or from the camps themselves.

Judge Deschênes knew full well the difficulties imposed on the Commission's work by that decision. He certainly did not rule out future investigations making use of such evidence, under appropriate conditions. But the protracted negotiations with the Soviets on the procedures for taking evidence in the Soviet Union had left the Commission with no time and no alternative.[8]

Two other massive lists existed. One was the Central Registry of War Criminals and Security Suspects, CROWCASS, which had been produced by American, British and French forces after the war. But the list had proved useless since it was just a list of names, with no corresponding archives or files.

The second list was that of the United Nations War Crimes Commission, intended to facilitate apprehension of war criminals still at large. The UNWCC holdings divided cases into three categories. An "A" classification denoted a case for *prima facie* classification as a war criminal. "S" denoted a suspected war criminal. "W" denoted a witness. However, the Soviet Union was not a member of the UNWCC, so the list held no files on people of Russian, Ukrainian or Baltic origin.[9]

Nevertheless, the Commission ran a trial sample of fifty-five names against the UNWCC list. "Only five UNWCC files could be said with any degree of certainty to be identical with the Commission's own subjects. These were files on subjects of Dutch origin, and generally speaking, they contained no new information."[10] The Commission concluded that any yield from the very time-consuming process of cross-checking with UNWCC and CROWCASS files would have been minimal.

A second line of investigation for the Commission was checking on whether subjects were actually residing in Canada. This was usually verified through police records, records of motor vehicle licences, telephone directories and the like. If the individual was located, the Commission staff would interview the accusers, witnesses or the subjects themselves.

Two subjects received special attention in the *Report*. The case of Josef Mengele, instrumental as it may have been in prompting the Prime Minister to set up the Commission, and mentioned explicitly in its terms of reference, was aired thoroughly. The Judge formally laid to rest the possibility that Mengele had ever lived in or applied to live in Canada. That finding had, of course, emerged during the course of the hearings.

More important was the Judge's decisive verdict on the Galicia Division, a source of past friction between Jewish and Ukrainian communities. The Judge ruled that membership in the Division, like membership in the Waffen SS generally, was not in itself a war crime. Drawing on a distinction elaborated at Nuremberg, the Judge pointed out that what was paramount in establishing war criminality was direct knowledge of or personal implication in a war crime. Moreover, knowledge of war crimes would have to be proven; it could not be assumed.

Evidence of such knowledge or participation among Galicia veterans was not forthcoming, not when the issue first emerged in 1950, and not during the current investigation by the Commission. Nor was it forthcoming from Simon Wiesenthal in Vienna. Of a list of 217 names supplied by Wiesenthal to then Solicitor General Kaplan, the Commission found, as of October 22, 1986, no evidence of war-crimes guilt. Indeed, 187 had never set foot in Canada, 11 came to Canada and had since died, 2 came and left, one could not be located, and 16 had no *prima facie* case against them. The estimated 600 Division veterans still in Canada were off the hook. Ukrainians were jubilant.[11]

The Judge's assessment of Wiesenthal's list was particularly damning. It was nearly "totally useless" and put the Commission to "a considerable amount of purposeless work." The Judge also lamented previously "large and grossly exaggerated figures" regarding the estimated numbers of possible war criminals.[12]

But what do we know of the names on the assembled lists? Some, particularly those whose names came from the RCMP, might already have had thick files. Some were previously subjects of media reports. A case in point was a man wanted by Dutch authorities for the alleged murder of two civilians. Convicted of treason *in absentia* by the Dutch, he had so far escaped deportation because treason was not one of the crimes covered in the Canada–Netherlands extradition treaty.

But others were obviously innocent, and their cases were dealt with quickly and quietly. There was no problem in closing the files on those subjects who had never come to Canada, or who were dead. What of the 154 cases of subjects living in Canada, against whom no *prima facie* evidence was found? Some of those cases were based on tissue-thin, indeed at times farcical, allegations. Consider the following examples:

Case no. 158
This individual was brought to the attention of the Commission by a private citizen. The only allegation initially made was that the subject was a war criminal because he was so wealthy and of German background.

Case no. 190
This family's surname was brought to the attention of the Commission by Mr. David Matas, whose source of information was an anonymous letter claiming the family came from a foreign country and deserved investigation because they were "recluses." There was no specific allegation of involvement in war crimes made against this family.

Case no. 561
This individual was brought to the attention of the Commission by the RCMP, whose source of information was the Canadian Jewish Congress. It was alleged that the subject was responsible for the deaths of "hundreds of Jews. . ."

Records of the Department of Employment and Immigration . . . indicate that the subject was born in 1941 . . .

And then there was the case of the Mengele look-alike brought to the attention of the Commission by the Canadian Jewish Congress. The Commission decided to close the file on that subject after noticing little resemblance between photos of the subject and Dr Mengele, and discovering that the subject's height was 6 feet 3 inches while Mengele's was reportedly 5 feet 8 inches.[13]
These sorts of cases, comic as they might seem, fuelled fears of witch-hunts and tarring of the innocent. Yet they ought not to obscure the significance of the very real, heinous criminality which did surface. Even in some cases where closure was recommended, it was evident that the subjects were nasty types indeed. One subject, for example, had declared to the RCMP a "love for Hitler." Another, more serious case concerned an alleged spy for Nazi Germany, sentenced to death *in absentia* for treason and war crimes by a west European country. The individual had been granted amnesty by that country in 1960. He had originally applied for Canadian entry in 1946, well before that amnesty, and entered Canada under an assumed name. The aura of

mystery surrounding the case, which was recommended for closure, is compounded by the observation that "the Government of Canada was aware of the subject's past when he applied for landing in this country. This individual was, nevertheless, admitted to Canada by Order-in-Council . . ."[14]

Several files dealing with serious criminality were recommended for closure because the subject was no longer resident in Canada. But the Commission's disposition of such cases may have been inconsistent, at least as can be gleaned from the brief reviews provided in the *Report*. Case no. 748, for example, involves allegations of participation in atrocities but evidence only of membership in the *Wehrmacht*, not the ss. The Commission here recommended that the results of its investigation be turned over to the authorities of the country in which the crime had been committed. Case no. 85, by contrast, involves an allegation of membership in the Gestapo, and evidence on file in Ludwigsburg, West Germany, confirmed that a person with a similar name to the subject was a member of the Nazi-supported police in eastern Europe, with eye-witness testimony on the subject's participation in executions. Yet in this ostensibly more serious case, there was no recommendation to notify the country in which the subject, who left Canada, now resides. There may be perfectly logical reasons here, dealing with the nature of the charges, the nature of the evidence or the specific foreign countries involved. But on the surface, the dispositions seem inconsistent.[15]

As we consider the 218 cases where Judge Deschênes recommended further information be obtained, we find cases where criminality, if established, could easily match that which we can presume for the more serious twenty. Case no. 273 refers to an individual who allegedly admitted working in gas chambers that exterminated Jews, and where evidence identified the subject as a member of the Waffen ss from late 1943 until 1945. Case no. 319 describes a subject alleged to have participated "in the liquidation of civilians in 1941–43, while acting as an investigator in the Nazi police." Case no. 399 refers to a person alleged to have "been an assistant police chief in Eastern Europe when several thousand persons were murdered by Nazis and Eastern European Nazi collaborators." Case no. 732 refers to a person alleged to have "admitted killing Jewish girls and eating and selling human flesh."[16]

The Commission's recommendations in many of these cases leaves it to the government of Canada to decide whether or not to pursue investigations through the relevant eastern bloc country and archival centres. For the second-tier cases, the ball is squarely in the government's court. To be sure, some people on the list of 218 will likely turn out to be innocent, misidentified, or people against whom *prima facie* evidence is not obtainable, even from eastern European sources. A recurring problem in many cases is the confusion of either identical or similar names. But others, where identification is established, may well turn out to be liable for prosecution for war crimes.

What do we know of the top twenty cases, where swift action was recommended? From the cursory descriptions in the public section of the *Report* we know that Deschênes made confidential recommendations offering options other than prosecution in Canada, for example, extradition, revocation of citizenship, revocation of citizenship and deportation.[17]

How did these alleged war criminals come to Canada? Commission researcher Alti Rodal was assigned the task of pulling together the details of the post-war record. Although it was not released with the public *Report*, snippets from her lengthy study, "Nazi War Criminals in Canada: the Historical and Policy Setting from the 1940s to the Present," were leaked to the press. Canadians discovered the complicity of their government in a British-American plan to settle German scientists in Canada so as to keep them out of Soviet hands. An American program, aimed at atomic scientists such as Wernher von Braun, was known as Operation Paper Clip. The Canadian program, which focused on scientists and technicians, was code-named Operation Matchbox. Those scientists and technicians entered Canada between 1947 and 1949, when official Canadian policy still barred German nationals.

The Commission discovered seventy-one Germans who may have come to Canada in that manner after the war. Several were alleged to have worked for the German corporate giant IG Farben, which used slave labour and manufactured the poison gas used in the gas chambers. But the Commission did not find any tie with these Farben operations among any of those who actually entered Canada.

The Rodal study also provided further details of the role of the Canadian government, including Prime Minister Louis St Laurent, in the case of Klaus Barbie's right-hand man, Count Jacques de Bernonville.[18] It also uncovered evidence, though inconclusive, that British and American intelligence operatives may have smuggled Nazi collaborators from eastern Europe into Canada without knowledge of the Canadian government, in order to build an anti-Soviet intelligence network. According to *The Globe and Mail*'s Richard Cleroux, none other than double agent Kim Philby may have had a hand in the British program.[19]

The Rodal study included a sensitive chapter on a number of eastern European political groups who collaborated with the Nazis, and whose members may have entered Canada despite efforts to screen them out. These groups included the Rumanian Iron Guard, the Hungarian Arrow Cross and the Latvian Thunder Cross. More potentially explosive were questions that her study addressed as to the make-up of the Galicia Division.[20]

Judge Deschênes praised Rodal's study, calling it "an outstanding contribution to the knowledge of this particular question" and claiming it deserved "wide distribution." But at the time, the government was in no hurry. Part of its hesitation came from possible embarrassment of former politicians and bureaucrats. Equally worrisome was the possibility that the report's detailed discussions of political groups within specific ethnic communities might tar all members of the ethnic groups as collaborators with Nazism. Moreover, while mere membership in these groups was not evidence of war criminality, the Rodal study might derail any ethnic healing process now under way.[21]

Government officials seemed confused about how to handle Rodal's study. One Privy Council Office official claimed that the Department of Justice "would be responsible for its ultimate release." But a Justice Department official disagreed, claiming that the PCO had withheld the report. Commission lawyer Meighen reviewed her study and felt that while it was not unusually sensitive, it was up to the government alone to release it. Days after the release of the main *Report*, Justice Minister Hnatyshyn could not commit himself to a date for the release of the Rodal study. It was, he explained, still being studied by the PCO. He would not speculate on how much would be censored on "security grounds."[22]

The clamour grew for the study's release. "I think it's essential that it be brought out," said Robert Kaplan, "so Canadians will know the whole story of war crimes." Jewish community representatives added their concern. The B'nai Brith reportedly promised to "pester the federal Justice Minister with letters and phone calls."[23] Justice Minister Hnatyshyn, feeling pressured, promised to release the study after he received it from the PCO. Like the Judge's report, it apparently also needed to be vetted. But when would it be released? Rodal claimed that her study mentioned only one suspect by name, and clues to other identities could be deleted easily, as in Deschênes's *Report* itself. A first deadline of May came and went. A second deadline for release was set for July.[24] It too came and went.

Irwin Cotler was surprised at the delay. Hadn't Judge Deschênes himself read the study and urged its dissemination? Cotler feared the government's political considerations might override a judicial assessment. As for any fears about violating privacy, Cotler was of two minds. As a civil libertarian, he had long championed legislation to safeguard citizens' rights to privacy. Yet he found it ironic that he had "never seen such concern for privacy as for Nazi war criminals" whether in Deschênes's *Report* or the Rodal study.[25]

Finally, in early August, the press squeezed a heavily censored version of her report out of Ottawa through the *Access to Information Act*. Little was new to those who had followed the Deschênes proceedings. As expected, the study documented the complicity of Canadian officials in largely CIA-orchestrated "dumping" of ex-Nazis in Canada. Most of this had already come out in press reports during the Commission itself.

What was news, however, was the revelation that Prime Minister Pierre Trudeau himself had shown no enthusiasm whatever for the prosecution of war criminals through the 1970s and the period of the Low memorandum. While the sections discussing Trudeau's opposition were deleted, Rodal herself confirmed that he was motivated by "political reasons," upon which she would not elaborate. The press hunted down the former prime minister. He, in turn, directed reporters back to Robert Kaplan.[26]

Equally upsetting to many Jews was the revelation that an RCMP officer may have been involved in lying to superiors and destroying documents to permit the entry of two war-crimes suspects to Canada as late as 1983. Even worse, the officer, described in the study as "quite right wing, German, and regarding the war criminals issue as blown out of all proportion by the Jewish lobby," was still employed in counter-espionage for the Canadian Security Intelligence Service.[27]

The study also noted that "significant numbers" of war criminals were likely found among immigrants who came from Bulgaria, Czechoslovakia, Estonia, France, West Germany, Hungary, Latvia, Lithuania, Poland, Rumania, the Soviet Union and Yugoslavia. That section was also severely edited.[28]

If the Rodal study offered few revelations to those who had closely followed the Deschênes process, it did afford the public a retrospective view on how Nazi war criminals got into Canada and, in tainting the previous Liberal government as at best indifferent to the presence of Nazi war criminals in Canada, showed how long the issue of war criminals had festered unattended. But if Rodal pricked the national conscience and the Deschênes *Report* identified twenty "hot" cases and over two hundred more to be followed up, what, finally, were the substantive policy recommendations made by Judge Deschênes? At first glance, the Judge would seem to have accepted all the legal arguments put forward in the Jewish briefs. For war criminals found in Canada, the Judge outlined three broad avenues of possible action.

First was amendment of the *Criminal Code* to permit prosecution in Canada of *all* war criminals—not only those associated with Nazi war crimes. This would apply to all war crimes, past, present and future, wherever committed.

Second was streamlining and consolidating the process of denaturalization and deportation, as well as screening out future war criminals from immigration to and naturalization in Canada. But the recommendations also implied that war criminals who could be shown to have lied about their history of war criminality to gain entry to Canada could face denaturalization and deportation. That would involve amendments to both the *Citizenship Act* and the *Immigration Act*.

A third remedy was extradition. Judge Deschênes argued in favour of honouring extradition requests from the Federal Republic of West Germany. More significantly, he recommended the amendment of the 1967 Canada-Israel extradition treaty to permit extradition for offences committed prior to its coming into force. Perhaps most surprisingly, the Judge did not reject out of hand any extradition requests from eastern bloc countries such as Poland or the Soviet Union, with which Canada has no extradition treaties. Extradition in those cases, Deschênes allowed, could be "entertained" under the provisions of international agreements

Canada has signed calling for punishment of those who commit war crimes.[29]

In addition, the Judge agreed that evidence taken from Soviet sources could well be admissible in Canadian courts. But while reiterating the legality and advisability of obtaining such evidence, he outlined again the six stringent conditions to be attached to use of such evidence, conditions more rigorous than those imposed on the American OSI. The insistence on adhering to these conditions had already proved to be a stumbling block with the Soviet government, and whether the Soviets might actually meet those conditions in the future remained to be seen.[30]

To the delight of the Ukrainian community, Judge Deschênes also recommended against the establishment in Canada of an OSI-type operation. In his view, such a move was "neither necessary nor commendable." The Judge based his decision on the need to avoid inflaming ethnic passions. "Creating an OSI in Canada would be courting dangers which must be avoided at all costs: internal peace between the various ethnic groups which form now such an important part of the population of Canada is more important, in the long run, for the good of this country than results which may be more spectacular in the short run, but are likely to inflict serious and possibly incurable wounds." The Judge chose instead to recommend that the RCMP and the Justice Department have their staffs augmented to permit them to carry out the tasks required. How or whether such an arrangement would differ in practice from the OSI also remained to be seen.[31]

When Deschênes's *Report* was released on the morning of March 12, 1987, all interested parties swung into action. With the termination of the lock-up and before they heard what Justice Minister Hnatyshyn was telling Parliament, Jewish community spokesmen met reporters at an Ottawa press conference, prepared to distribute material and respond to questions. Similar press meetings were held by Jewish officials in Montreal, Toronto and Winnipeg.

Reporters apparently had to dig a little harder to get official reactions from the Ukrainian community. One Ukrainian-American newspaper noted that the only Ukrainian Canadian its reporter could find to talk about the issue was another journalist covering the story.[32]

If there was one characteristic of the generally positive, at times euphoric reaction to the *Report*, it was that everyone — Jews, Ukrainians, and politicians of all stripes — could climb on board. And they did. The tensions of the previous two years dissipated in a warm afterglow that engulfed almost all the key players.

For its part, the government was pleased. In reading the government's response Justice Minister Hnatyshyn told the House of Commons, "it is now apparent that the problem of war criminals is not as extensive as had been feared." He continued, "the scope of this problem has been considerably exaggerated by some. There are and have been far fewer suspected war criminals in Canada than suggested." The minister's zeal in trying to minimize the problem may have been premature. Unaware perhaps of all of the details of the still suppressed Rodal study, he continued, "it is also clear from the *Report* that there was no action or policy on the part of the Government of Canada or of Canadian officials to aid or assist known or suspected war criminals in entering Canada nor to conceal or protect their presence in any way."[33]

But the Judge only made recommendations; it was for the government to act. In the months before the *Report*'s official release, while the text was being revised, Cabinet pondered the Deschênes Commission's recommendations which they already had. As the Ukrainian and Jewish players geared up for a protracted and heated tug-of-war to prod government action, the government determined its own agenda. Above all, it wanted to prevent any further divisiveness. Ukrainian-Jewish tensions during the hearings had been bad enough. If a struggle erupted over the recommendations, the government knew full well that it would be the real loser.

The government's strategy was an ingenious as it was simple. When Hnatyshyn rose in the House to congratulate Judge Deschênes on his fine job, the minister pre-emptively announced the government's response to the *Report*—no debate, no consultation, no lobbying and, he hoped, no bad blood. The minister plucked from among the Deschênes recommendations a single pre-ferred option. He announced the government would move amendments to the *Criminal Code* so as to permit the trial in Canada of war criminals, all war criminals not just Nazis — a "made in Canada" solution. The Commission's recommendations concerning use of de-naturalization and deportation, as well as extradition, including extradition to Israel, were largely ignored. The Ukrainians, opposed to deportation, were as pleased with the government's response as they were with the *Report*'s clearing of the Division. Jews were generally delighted with the promise of action against war criminals. The question now was how long it would be before the first arrest would be made.

Both opposition parties were quick to praise the work of the Commission and the promise of quick govern-ment action. They called for rapid action on the amend-ments to the *Criminal Code*. Kaplan, speaking for the Liberals, was pleased to emphasize the small number of suspects. After all, it was his party that was largely on the hook for forty years of inaction. But Kaplan was also concerned that no action had been taken on cases already in the pipeline during the two years of the Commission's work. Like others championing the war-crimes issue, he felt the pressure of time but was not prepared in his initial response to push hard for the de-naturalization or extradition options. There was no need to tell Kaplan they had been available to earlier Liberal governments but had not been used.

The NDP's Svend Robinson was more demanding. He hoped that the government would not close the door on the other remedies outlined by the Commission. Citing

the case of the man whose extradition was sought by
the Dutch government, he questioned the need for a
trial in Canada, when the man had already been sentenced to twenty years by a Dutch court. Why could he
not be extradited?[34]

Kaplan and Robinson, like officials of the Jewish
community, were eager that the government act
quickly. Said Robinson, "the biological clock is running
out on Nazi war criminals." Kaplan noted that the government had had the *Report* for close to three months
before releasing it and still had no information available
on how many new staff would be allocated to the RCMP
and to the Justice Department for implementation. The
complement of two RCMP officers assigned to look into
war-crime allegations was now clearly and woefully inadequate.

But Kaplan seemed particularly enthused about the
universal dimensions of the made-in-Canada approach.
He acknowledged that more recently war crimes have
been committed in places like Afghanistan, Angola and
Vietnam, and perhaps some perpetrators of those
crimes were now in Canada. Additional commissions, in
the Deschênes model, could address those problems.[35]

Finally, all parties included in their reactions motherhood calls for reducing ethnic tensions in the wake of
the *Report*. Kaplan saw "a great opportunity for a healing process to take place in our country, a healing process which is needed because of tensions among some
communities in Canadian society which became regrettably worse during the process of the Deschênes Commission." The NDP's Robinson was also sensitive to the
ethnic insecurities which had been aroused. "We must
make it very clear," he asserted, "that we are not sin-
gling out any ethnic community. There can be no collective indictments. There can be no collective guilt in
this area."[36]

The government, slumping in popularity polls, took
pleasure in the praise it drew from all sides for establishing the Commission of Inquiry and for its promise of
quick action. But the government had been prepared

for the best. When the government released the *Report* and its response, it already knew something of the way the Deschênes process had played to the larger Canadian community.

In the late fall of 1986, the government, through the minister of state for multiculturalism, had quietly commissioned a poll of Canadian opinion on the war-criminals issue. Several questions were written by Carleton University's Centre for Communication, Culture and Society and added to a Carleton School of Journalism poll of the four western provinces. The survey was conducted between January 3–13, 1987 and the findings presented to the government at the end of the month. Thus while the Commission's *Report* was being readied for release, government officials had a sense of what might await, at least in western Canada, with its large concentration of Ukrainian voters.

The poll results were surprising, and could not have been anticipated. Of the 2,008 respondents, 55 percent favoured investigations of Nazi war criminals, while 39 percent felt the matter could be ignored. But what also became clear is that the issue had not commanded the attention of most Canadians. This appeared true even for the 143 respondents, or 7.1 percent of the sample, who were of Ukrainian origin. Only 20 people in the entire sample—1 percent—knew of the appointment of the Deschênes Commission of Inquiry or could identify its name after being told that a war-criminals inquiry had been formed. Even if all 20 were Ukrainians, that would still comprise only 14 percent of the 143 Ukrainians in the sample. Thus, it was safe to conclude that the overwhelming majority of Ukrainian Canadians, at least in western Canada, like their fellow citizens, were not waiting with baited breath.

Another finding was equally surprising. When asked to identify an ethnic group "that has been seen to be more responsible for war crimes than any other groups living in Canada," again only 11 respondents, or 0.5 percent of the sample, mentioned Ukrainians. This suggested that despite the two years of Deschênes-related

publicity, very few Ukrainians, to say nothing of other
citizens, were influenced by any anti-Ukrainian group
defamation. Neither the Commission hearings, nor media reports, had led to a general tarring of the Ukrainian image, at least in the mind of the western
Canadian. The name-calling episodes reported in the
press and recycled by MP Andrew Witer and other
Ukrainian interlocutors may well have been isolated oc-
currences. In any event, they seemed to have made no
lasting impression.

To be sure, Ukrainians in western Canada differ from
those in the east. Ontario is the stronghold of the post-
war immigration and of the Galicia Division veterans,
and thus Ukrainian awareness of the issue might be
much higher than among the more assimilated Ukrainians in the west. But how much higher? Among the
non-Ukrainian, non-Jewish population in eastern
Canada, it is doubtful that the level of public awareness
would be much higher than in the west.[37]

How should one interpret this grass-roots disinterest
in the war-criminals issue? One might well conclude
that the Canadian public generally has a low tolerance
for public issues other than basic bread-and-butter concerns. Foreign policy matters, for example, have never
loomed large on the public's agenda, and Canadian politicians know it. Cabinet meetings rarely, if ever, are
preoccupied by issues of foreign policy, except where
Canadian economic or other interests are directly involved. The war-criminals issue might well appear to
the general public as distant, involving foreigners or immigrants, events that happened elsewhere over four
decades ago, and thus of no immediate concern.

What of the seeming low levels of Ukrainian awareness of the matter? Was it possible that the Ukrainian
national leadership was, on this issue, out of touch with
the community rank and file? Could it be that Ukrainian Canadians in the west, most of whom would be native-born Canadians, might simply feel that the war-
criminals issue had little relevance to them? Perhaps
Ukrainian leadership and ethnic media had bowed to

hardline immigrants, nationalists and Division members who had commandeered the communal agenda to reflect their own concerns. That would not be unprecedented for ethnic groups. Within the Jewish community, impassioned minorities of Holocaust survivors or other groups had often prodded mainstream leaders to adopt certain positions. And Ukrainian post-war immigrants who had fought and suffered for Ukraine assumed a moral authority that the more complacent native-born did not.

Whatever the reasons, public concern was low, and the government could feel reasonably secure. Given the tenor of the Commission findings and its recommendations, if it acted with dispatch the government expected there would be no explosions, certainly not from the general public, nor from Ukrainians and probably not from Jews. They were right.

Ukrainian spokesmen were particularly pleased. Rumour in the community had it that none of the twenty "hot" Nazi files was Ukrainian. Moreover, Deschênes had found no evidence to implicate the veterans of the Division in war crimes. No longer, many hoped, would Ukrainian claims to collective status as victims be threatened by linking of their heroes to Nazi war criminality. Newspaper headlines blared their vindication: "Ukrainian ss Veterans weren't war criminals," "Report clears Ukrainian soldiers recruited by Germans," "No charges called for in Ukrainian ss Division."[38]

The Judge and his researchers knew that his findings could not address the broader question of Ukrainian-Jewish relations before and during World War II. That was not his mandate, and this was one Pandora's box best kept closed. He also knew that some historical questions had yet to be fully answered by historians. But as far as he was concerned, the problem of culpability for war crimes, at least for the Division, had been laid to rest. If Congress or B'nai Brith officials had any reservations on the matter, they were not voiced publicly.

Not surprisingly, Sol Littman was not pleased to see the Division off the hook, and he had no qualms about airing his doubts in public. Writing three months after the *Report*'s release, Littman decried both Deschênes's conclusions on the Division and other aspects of the *Report* which he judged to be equally wrong-minded. But as for the Division, Littman remained convinced that those Ukrainians joining the Galicia Division knew full well the role of the ss generally in atrocities against Jews. That would make them technically guilty of war criminality, regardless of whether they had personally committed any war crimes.[39]

Littman's comments might still smart, but most Ukrainians were confident that in the wake of the *Report*, nobody was listening to him. In addition to the Commission's verdict on the Division, there was more for Ukrainians to cheer. The government's agreement with the recommendation not to set up a Canadian OSI was good news, even if they were not sure what would be created in its stead. Ukrainians were also relieved that the government had decided to play down the remedies of denaturalization, deportation and extradition. Canadians of east European origin would be spared traumas like the Demjanjuk trial in Israel or the April 22, 1987 deportation of Estonian Karl Linnas to the Soviet Union to face a possible death sentence. "I am very cheerful," said the CLC's John Gregorovich. "It is gratifying to see our position was one taken by the commission and the government. We are very happy."[40]

Notice that Canada would not set up an OSI and that trials rather than denaturalization hearings would occur in Canada was hailed by anti-OSI American groups which had followed events in Canada. Americans for Due Process representative Rasa Razagaitis reportedly called it "magnificent," while a spokesman for the American Latvian Association, perhaps with a tinge of jealousy, commented, "It's just what we've been asking for here."[41]

Indeed, only one outcome of the Commission *Report* seemed to aggrieve Ukrainian representatives. Deschênes had left open the door for the possible use of Soviet-supplied evidence in future war-crimes trials in Canada. That the Judge had reiterated the stringent conditions on its use did not mollify Ukrainian opposition. Their bedrock position was that *no* evidence gathered from Soviet bloc sources could be trusted. Gregorovich indicated that the UCC might still try to convince individual judges of that point as cases came up.[42]

Jewish communal reaction to the *Report* and to the government's response was one of general gratification tempered with caution. The *Report*, with its series of possible legal remedies, was seen as a vindication of years of Jewish prodding of government. Enthusiasm for the government's more narrow focusing on trial in Canada was more muted. But if the government moved with dispatch to amend the *Criminal Code* and proceed to trials, any doubts would be laid to rest. The Rodal study, once released, promised to substantiate Jewish allegations about lax screening and the resulting immigration of hundreds, if not thousands, of alleged war criminals into Canada after the war. Most important, the *Report* announced that twenty cases had been isolated where quick action was warranted. Congress's Cotler voiced his position succinctly. "The Deschênes Commission has given the government the remedies," he told a March 12 news conference. "It is now the responsibility of the government to exercise the requisite political will and to act upon the recommendations."[43]

David Matas of B'nai Brith also combined praise for the *Report* with apprehension about the government's single-remedy response. He, like Cotler, would have preferred to see the government accept all recommendations, including those of denaturalization and extradition. Matas had also advocated creation of an OSI-like unit, but he understood that the issue was not so much the name of the investigative unit or to which branch of government it reported. What was key, he told the press, was the unit's mandate, the drive and talent of the investigators and the resources at their disposal.

"To a certain extent it becomes a question of semantics as long as the people in the Justice Department and the RCMP are devoted to this task."[44]

Sol Littman sounded a strong discordant note amid the chorus of approval. Questioned by the *Canadian Jewish News*, he claimed that because of the time constraints imposed on the Commission, and the failure to consult evidence in eastern bloc countries, some allegations had been dismissed prematurely. This did not mean government should not act on the *Report*. On the contrary, Littman deeply regretted the failure of Deschênes to recommend creation of an OSI, fearing that "unless we streamline procedures, these people will die safely in their beds."[45] He insisted that action by the government be forthcoming within three to six months, "otherwise we'll know we've been given form but no substance."

Littman also felt that trial in Canada would prove a "limited remedy." He claimed that the first trials, if any, would be few in number, drawn out and with appeals following any convictions. And the first trial, a sort of test case, would leave all others on hold. "In all likelihood, Canada will try no more than two or three war criminals in the next ten years. By then most of those still alive will be able to claim with some justice that they are unfit to stand trial and the whole matter will be forgotten." Littman also questioned the Commission for failing to pursue war criminals far enough. According to Littman, ". . . if Eichmann had appeared on his list, the report would have described him as a minor bureaucrat in charge of a Jewish resettlement program. Since there would be no record that Eichmann had personally killed anyone, the case would, in all probability, be closed."[46]

Establishment Jewish leaders in Canada refrained — at least in public — from such harsh criticism of the *Report*, of which they generally approved, or the government's response which promised one line of concrete action. Some, like Cotler, wanted to prod government to move on the full array of options outlined by the

Judge. But most Congress leaders were willing to accept the government's position that trial in Canada would be a true remedy, not a judicial dead end. Only if the government failed to move on amending the *Criminal Code* should pressure be brought to bear. Congress National Executive Director Jack Silverstone set the tone. "Let's not kick down open doors."[47]

From a distance, some American Jewish communal activists were more critical. Eli Rosenbaum of the World Jewish Congress, and formerly of the OSI, lamented that the Commission did not have time to systematically cross-check lists of guards or members of "einsatzgruppen teams" which were available from OSI. Media reporting might help perpetuate the belief that only twenty war criminals were present in Canada. That, said Rosenbaum, was "absurd, a farce." In general, he felt that the *Report* was in many respects a "fraud" and the government's initial response, specifically the understaffed investigative unit, "a sham."[48]

American Nazi-hunters also expressed reservations. Allan Ryan, formerly a lawyer with the OSI, felt that Deschênes was wrong to recommend against setting up a Canadian version of the special Nazi-hunting unit. Judge Deschênes had argued that it would exacerbate relations between eastern Europeans and Jews. Ryan disagreed, and according to *The Ottawa Citizen*, issued a sober warning. "If the OSI were dissolved tomorrow," he contended, "and all its personnel transferred to the Federal Bureau of Investigation, Ukrainian opposition would not abate. No one in Canada should be fooled into thinking that placing investigators and prosecutors in the RCMP is going to mollify those who oppose Nazi prosecutions." At any rate, Canada had entered the Nazi-hunting game late, ten years after the Americans. "Hnatyshyn," he said, "had no time to lose."[49]

Even as the government began to move towards its promised amending of the *Criminal Code*, Ukrainian and Jewish leaders looked for ways to spin mutual approval of the *Report* into an opportunity for inter-ethnic fence-mending. For Ukrainians there was pride that, given the range of possible outcomes of the Deschênes process, they had achieved the best of all possible results, and as a community they had not shrunk from defence of their good name. Now they could seek *rapprochement* with the Jews, not as supplicants but as equals. For Jews, *rapprochement* would come only after concrete government action. Fence-mending, in turn, might reassure the government that trials in Canada need not lead to further inter-ethnic explosion.

The stage for renewed dialogue had been set several days before the *Report*'s release. Two *Globe and Mail* reporters, of Ukrainian and Jewish origin respectively, had published an article entitled "Ukrainians, Jews must try to bury the painful past." It recapitulated the basic themes of hostility and mutual resentment which resonated through Ukrainian-Jewish history. The writers, Victor Malarek and Sheldon E. Gordon, hoped that following the *Report*'s release, the two communities could "seek out common ground and build a more harmonious relationship." Indeed, they argued further, and perhaps optimistically, that the two groups "could yet provide a model for multicultural Canada."[50]

The peace offensives began with the release of the *Report*. Oddly, as the press called for reconciliation, there were those who blamed the media for the inter-ethnic hostilities in the first place. Media-bashing paved the way to reconciliation. Wasyl Veryha, spokesman for the Division brotherhood, claimed "All the hate came from the press." Michael Maryn, Vancouver Vice-President of the Ukrainian Canadian Professional and Business Club, followed suit. "I think we were put on the defensive unnecessarily as a community by persons like Sol Littman and various aspects of the media. . ."[51]

Like hesitant suitors, the two communities courted through the press. Division lawyer Yaroslaw Botiuk predicted that "relations between the Jewish and Ukrainian communities from now on will be much more harmonious." A member of the Manitoba UCC urged the groups to "lay all this aside and start rebuilding bridges." MP Andrew Witer, who had played a key role in Ukrainian mobilization efforts, likewise hoped that the *Report*'s release would ease tensions.[52]

Jewish community officials also welcomed the prospect of improved relations, especially since, as always, they had reason to reassure government that the hunt for war criminals was not an ethnic issue. Jewish officials in Winnipeg were particularly eager to see a return to the relative harmony of the past. One Winnipeg member of the National Congress Executive felt that Jews and Ukrainians could now begin to work together to solve problems. Another Winnipegger on the local Jewish Community Council also felt that the *Report* and government response would alleviate concerns felt in the two communities.[53]

Some Jewish spokesmen went even further. They claimed that the airing of tense feelings had ultimately been a positive experience for both communities, with perhaps therapeutic effects. Ellen Kachuck of B'nai Brith in Toronto felt that the Commission "brings together groups in discussions we hadn't had previously. I know the Jewish community now understand better the concerns of the Ukrainian community. I would hope the same could be said on the part of the Ukrainian community." Montrealer Frank Chalk, chairman of B'nai Brith's eastern region, had no doubts on that score. "The whole Deschênes process in fact improved relations between ethnic communities in Canada." When asked if the Ukrainian community shared that view, he replied, "In fact, I know they do."[54]

These calls for healing were highlighted by appropriate symbolic rituals. On the night of the *Report*'s release, CBC's "The Journal" featured a joint interview with Irwin Cotler and Lubomyr Luciuk, representing the two ethnic communities. Both speakers agreed that rifts between the two communities could now be healed. They joined in welcoming the government's pledge to amend the *Criminal Code* to facilitate prosecutions of war criminals in Canada. "The Journal" edited out a handshake between the two at the end of the interview, but the bipartisan symbolism had been established.

A few days later, CBC Radio's national open-line show "Cross Country Check-up" devoted itself to the Deschênes *Report*. The program featured Cotler as the studio guest and a pre-arranged phone interview with Luciuk. Luciuk exuberantly touted again all the areas of common agreement shared by the two communities.

The prospect of improved relations was also promoted in the ethnic press. The healing theme was expounded in an article by Luciuk and Ron Vastokas, anthropologist at Trent University. The authors asserted that the "Commission's recommendations will themselves serve to bridge over the rifts that emerged over the past two years between these various ethnic communities." They ended with a reference to the Luciuk-Cotler handshake which, they felt, symbolically sealed their communities' commitment to a healing process. The article, appropriately entitled "A Time for Healing," was reprinted in several Ukrainian journals.[55]

One would think the two adversaries were suddenly falling all over one another, the past forgotten. In late April 1987 Edmonton's *Ukrainian News* reprinted an editorial from *The Jewish Star* of Calgary entitled "Ukrainians, Jews Have Lived in Harmony Here." The *Star* article quoted the new thirty-three-year-old editor of the *Ukrainian News*, Brent Kostyniuk:

> What distresses me is that so many of these fights are left over from the old country. And there's really no reason for them to have any existence in Canada.

> There may have been scores to settle over the years, but that took place a long ways from here. . . Something that happened between Ukrainians and Jewish people 50 years ago and 10,000 miles away should be left alone.[56]

An editorial in the *Ukrainian News* offered an unusually strong call for an aggressive pursuit of war criminals: "Of course even one Nazi war criminal living free in Canada is one too many. . . It is now the task of the RCMP to track down these criminals and bring them to justice. And brought to justice they must be — whether they be German, Russian, or yes, even Ukrainian."[57]

Editorial reaction in the mainstream press was reassuring. Not surprisingly, newspapers like *The Globe and Mail*, *The Toronto Star*, *The Ottawa Citizen* and *The Gazette* (Montreal) which had staunchly supported the Commission's mandate, were supportive of its results. As if with one voice, their March 13 editorials endorsed the *Report* and the government's response and praised the steps towards inter-ethnic healing.

Yet amidst the chorus of hosannas, a few observers saw grey clouds on the horizon. *Toronto Sun* columnist Bob McDonald noted the problematic nature of the broad scope of the proposed amendments. War criminals past and present, from anywhere in the world, would be fair game for Canadian courts. Was that realistic?[58] As for trials in Canada of Nazi war criminals, would the Canadian government and the Canadian public have the stomach for trials of elderly pensioners accused of crimes committed forty-five years earlier and thousands of miles away?[59]

Trials more than four decades after the crimes were committed pose formidable problems to any prosecutor trying to establish a case beyond a reasonable doubt. Could one rely on elderly witnesses testifying on events which took place so long ago, even assuming witnesses could be found? These evidentiary problems for the lawyers might prove as formidable as the political problems for image-conscious governments. Judge Deschênes himself recognized these practical constraints. "Should prosecutions be launched against war criminals," he wrote, "a delay of some 45 years will have elapsed between the alleged crimes and the laying of charges. It shall belong to the executive and, eventually, to the judiciary to examine the effect, if any, of this delay on the prosecutions."[60]

Columnist Barbara Amiel, well known for her conservative views, added her reservations to the minority of sceptics. She thought war-crimes trials in Canada might further widen rifts between Jewish and eastern European groups. According to her, such trials would also prevent those groups from uniting against their common current oppressor, the "new Reich of the USSR." But some Jewish leaders, like the B'nai Brith's Frank Chalk, dismissed the notion that trials in Canada would fan the flames of anti-Semitism. Amiel was less confident. She also feared that the suspects to be tried in Canada would not be high-ranking criminals — no "big fish Nazis" as she called them. "Bringing some small time concentration camp guard or foot soldier of the Third Reich to trial," she reasoned, "would do nothing but make him a scapegoat."[61]

The government's proposed legislation promised to target *all* war criminals, past, present and future, even though Judge Deschênes had been mandated to examine only Nazi war criminals. But the government's commitment to move beyond Nazi war criminals to all war criminals or to all those who committed crimes against humanity was in harmony with a basic objective of Ukrainian briefs and public statements. The focus on Nazi war criminals alone, they had argued, was selective justice. Why not also go after the war criminals associated with Stalin and his henchmen? After all, were they not responsible for millions of innocent deaths?

Some Ukrainian Canadians wanted those who had victimized their brothers in Ukraine to be brought to account. They were particularly concerned with Soviet Secret Police agents who played a role in orchestrating the famine of 1932, or in persecuting Ukrainian nationalists during the Hitler-Stalin non-aggression pact of 1939–41. Soon after the release of the *Report*, John Gregorovich told the national convention of the Ukrainian Canadian Professional and Business Club that the UCC was preparing a list of such suspects.

Gregorovich further promised to unearth such suspects by sounding out the Ukrainian community through newspaper ads. Baltic groups apparently had a head start on the Ukrainians. According to *The Globe and Mail*, the Justice Department had received a list of 1,100 suspected Soviet war criminals who had victimized citizens of the Baltic states, but it was unclear how many, if any, of these people were in Canada.[62]

No case had yet been raised against a Jewish immigrant to North America alleged to have committed Soviet war crimes. But not so for the *Kapos*. The *Kapos* have played an important role in framing the debate about the degree of culpability of Ukrainian camp guards. Some have argued that Ukrainians who decided to serve as guards — like the Jewish *Kapos* — really did so under duress, to avoid the harsh conditions of Nazi slave labour camps for Soviet prisoners of war. If Jews can excuse the excesses of the Jewish *Kapos*, why not those of equally unfortunate Ukrainian guards?

As it happens, Jewish views of the *Kapos* have clustered around two poles. One emphasizes their callousness and brutality, often in excess of that demanded by their ss overseers. The other stresses the pressures under which they performed their duties, and cites instances of benevolent acts. The argument is that *Kapo* brutality may have shielded camp inmates from even greater suffering at the hands of the ss.

These debates have been more than theoretical. As far back as the 1950s, the American Immigration and Naturalization Service brought forward three cases against Jewish *Kapos*. One of the three was convicted, denaturalized and ordered deported to Poland. Poland refused to accept him, and he died years later in the United States.[63] While the issue lay dormant for some time afterwards, a new case has revived the painful debates about the *Kapos* and their guilt.

The recent case pitted the OSI against seventy-five-year-old Jacob Tannenbaum. The OSI moved to revoke his American citizenship because of accusations against him for the commission of war crimes. The case did not rest simply on the fact that Tannenbaum served as a *Kapo* in the Gorlitz labour camp, but on his specific actions there. "This was brought because he engaged in physical violence against inmates," said the OSI's Neal Sher. "It was based on a brutality that was unwarranted by any standard." Communal Jewish leaders may have empathized with his plight, and were aware of the wrenching moral dilemmas surrounding the *Kapo* issue. But they did not defend him against the specific allegations. Said Elan Steinberg of the World Jewish Congress, "We have complete faith and confidence in the integrity and professionalism of the OSI."

Canadian Jewish leaders might someday have to face the possibility that future war-crimes prosecutions might include a Jewish former NKVD agent, or a *Kapo*. The response would likely parallel that of their American counterparts. Canadian Jewish leader Alan Rose of Congress, when asked for his reaction to a hypothetical Jewish war criminal in Canada, said, "If that's the case, and they are found guilty, they should be punished."[64]

However Ukrainians and Jews might react to any eventual trials of their brethren in Canada, it is clear that the proposed *Criminal Code* amendments could cast a wide net. More than Nazi war criminals, more even than Soviet war criminals of the Stalin era, might be caught. It would be open season on all war criminals. Only time will tell if Canada will become the laundromat for the world's dirty laundry.

The notion that Canada might somehow undertake numerous prosecutions against former war criminals from around the globe now residents or citizens of Canada struck some observers as far-fetched indeed. "The idea of Canadian attorneys general trying to prosecute Argentine or Chilean army officers is absurd," wrote columnist W. A. Wilson. "The proposed amendment looks like a sop cynically tossed to concentration camp survivors and victims' relatives with no thought of ever employing it." Indeed a wave of such prosecutions might hopelessly complicate Canadian foreign policy. In developing countries with frequent, often violent changes of government, yesterday's war criminal might well be connected with today's "legitimate" regime.[65]

And yet, in the immediate aftermath of the *Report*'s release, the response of the mythical average Canadian was surprising. Nazis were not uppermost in their mind. Rather, the informed public seemed to welcome the possibility that contemporary war criminals — preferably from Central or South America, usually pro-American and right of centre — would be punished.

This view came through loud and clear on the CBC Radio open-line program, "Cross Country Check-up." The question posed was, "Should Canada prosecute war criminals?" Roughly a third of the callers were opposed or doubtful. But even the supportive callers were typically "yes — but" in their reactions. The "but" denoted their zeal in making sure that prosecutions should focus on the contemporary. War crimes in Indonesia, East Timor and the whole of Latin America were troubling listeners. Others hoped that Israel's Ariel Sharon or the perennial favourite, Henry Kissinger, might be prosecuted. Irwin Cotler, a guest on the show, was faced with a dilemma. As callers scrambled to name and vilify those they considered war criminals, Nazi war criminals were seemingly shunted aside. Cotler responded by reminding listeners of the singularity of the crimes of the Nazis: "If everything is a Holocaust, then nothing is a Holocaust." He argued further that the priority prosecutions must lie with the twenty suspects identified by the Commission. "If those war criminals are not prosecuted, then no war criminals will be prosecuted."[66]

Individual culpability was one thing, but the accusation of group culpability was quite another — and as unacceptable when applied to Jews as it was when applied to Ukrainians. All the worse when the charge against Jews is levelled by a member of parliament. Even as Jewish and Ukrainian leaders were, at long last, making conciliatory noises, Conservative William Lesick, an MP of Ukrainian origin representing Edmonton East, again raised the hoary issue of Jewish collaboration with the Nazis. "There were all peoples involved, including Jewish people," Lesick was quoted as saying in an interview with *The Edmonton Journal*'s Ottawa bureau chief. "Why should the Jewish people say 'they did it' and not point the fingers at themselves and say: 'Were we simon pure?' " According to *The Edmonton Journal*, Lesick also claimed that the Ukrainian holocaust was "a greater one" than the Jewish. Perhaps most grating for many Jews was Lesick's reference to the origins of Stalin's industry minister Lazar Kaganovich, allegedly responsible for orchestrating the famine. "And who did Stalin put in charge of the Ukrainian holocaust? It was a Jewish chap."

Lesick's comments sparked a sharp response. According to *The Gazette*, Irwin Cotler protested that it was that type of remark, not the Deschênes Commission itself, that raised tension between the two communities. "This is not an ethnic issue and can't be seen in that perspective." Sol Littman also minced few words. Calling the remarks "shameful and disgusting," *The Gazette* noted, he claimed, "It's essentially an anti-Semitic position that pits Ukrainians against Jews. . .Next he'll have us responsible for poisoning wells."[67]

Lesick, for his part, seemed surprised that his words should cause a furor. In a follow-up story *The Edmonton Journal* noted that he was eager to apologize if anyone could show how they had been wronged. "I want to have a dialogue with any group that feels I have slighted them." Rabbi Haim Kemelman of Edmonton's Beth Shalom synagogue reported that Lesick had personally expressed his remorse for having caused "hurt feelings" and seemed to be very eager "to mend fences."

Ukrainian spokesmen and Conservative politicians reportedly distanced themselves with varying degrees of vigour from Lesick's remarks. Myroslav Yurkevich of Alberta's UCC claimed Lesick "doesn't mean to say what he is misrepresented as saying." Archie Ewaskiw, president of the Edmonton East Progressive Conservative riding association, commented: "I don't directly support him at all." Fellow Alberta MP David Kilgour admitted that Lesick's comments didn't sit well with him, but would rather avoid "taking a shot" at a fellow politician. This was not enough for NDP justice critic Svend Robinson. "He should be asked to apologize in the House of Commons. If he refuses," argued Robinson, "Prime Minister Mulroney has no choice but to throw him out of the Tory caucus." Lesick did, on the other hand, have his outright defenders. Lawyer Doug Christie reportedly claimed Lesick was being victimized by a smear campaign.[68]

Equally dismaying was a letter to the editor by Ron Vastokas, which was published in the May 13 *Globe and Mail*. Vastokas objected to the United States government's decision in late April 1987 to put Austrian President Kurt Waldheim on its immigration "watch list" as a possible war-crimes suspect. Vastokas was the co-author with Lubomyr Luciuk of the "Time for Healing" article which had appeared in the Ukrainian press. But there was no suggestion of inter-ethnic healing in his letter to *The Globe and Mail* entitled "US Engages in Witch-hunt on Waldheim":

> The hypocrisy of the United States in putting Austrian President Kurt Waldheim on the "watch list". . .can only be explained by the witch-hunting mentality that periodically sweeps across that country. The undesirables and war criminals now in vogue are the Nazis. In times past, the list of U.S. enemies included the Red terrorists, the "black Papists,' the Orientals, the Jews and the Italians. In 1919, the anarchists Emma Goldman and Alexander Berkman, along with 200 other "traitors" were deported to the Soviet Union.
>
> For a country that has given haven to sundry murderous dictators running for their lives, and has recently accredited [Israeli] General Amos Yaron who was cited for negligence in not stopping the massacre of Palestinians at Sabra and Shatila refu-

gee camps, the barring of Mr. Waldheim has nothing to do with even-handed justice.

And for Prime Minister Brian Mulroney to at once
parrot the U.S. action, without at the same time
expelling from Ottawa Brig. Gen. Tissa Weera-
tunga, the Sri Lankan high commissioner in
Canada. . .shows that the lessons of the two-year-
long Deschênes exercise have completely escaped
him.[69]

This defence of Waldheim was bound to offend Jewish sensibilities. The implied double analogy — that
Waldheim was either as guilty as Israeli General Yaron
or as innocent as Jewish anarchist Emma Goldman —
was in the words of one Jewish leader, "abominable."[70]
What incidents like the Lesick comment or the Vastokas letter suggest is that clarion calls for restored ethnic
relations might not, by themselves, do the trick. Steps
forward were followed by steps back. Indeed, whatever
nice words now passed between Jewish and Ukrainian
leaders, there was an uneasy suspicion that any trial in
Canada of a suspected Nazi war criminal of eastern European origin, or where Soviet-supplied evidence was
involved, might serve to re-open old wounds. A pre-
view of those kinds of tensions was provided not only
by the Commission, but by the ongoing trial of John
Demjanjuk in Israel. Even as the Deschênes process
was working its way through the body politic in 1987,
Ukrainian-Canadian eyes were fixed on Jerusalem,
where Demjanjuk faced his accusers.
      Demjanjuk's defence rested on a claim of mistaken
identity. That in turn helped trigger the worries that the
Ukrainian briefs to the Commission had outlined. The
case featured conflicting evidence, based on ditfering
recollections of events that had happened forty-five
years earlier. Some survivors identified Dem injuk
without hesitation, in powerful and emotional scenes.
Yet others claimed that "Ivan the Terrible" had been
killed in a Treblinka uprising in 1943. More distressing

for Ukrainians was the role of Soviet evidence. The prosecution produced an identification card placing Demjanjuk at the SS training camp at Trawniki, complete with his 1942 photograph. The card, obtained from Soviet archives through the intercession of philo-Soviet industrialist Armand Hammer, was labelled a forgery by Demjanjuk's lawyers. Demjanjuk, they claimed, was never at Trawniki, and never at Treblinka. The card was a fake. Demjanjuk's lawyers claimed he had been framed by the Soviets to discredit all Ukrainians.[71]

The Demjanjuk trial in Israel served to sharpen Ukrainian vigilance in Canada, even after the *Report* and the government's response were made public. The link was strengthened when a Canadian lawyer of Ukrainian descent joined the Demjanjuk defence team in Israel. Any proposed new legislation on war criminals would have to be doubly scrutinized. Indeed, at the very time Ukrainian Canadians were awaiting the Commission's report, they were being canvassed for contributions to Demjanjuk's defence fund. Roughly $120,000 was raised as of early March 1987 in contributions from individuals, churches and other communal organizations. "Every person charged with a crime," said the CLC's Gregorovich, "is entitled to a proper defence." While Gregorovich reportedly conceded there was a chance that Demjanjuk was guilty, that view was apparently not universally shared. "The community as a whole feels he may very well be innocent." Edward Nishnic, Demjanjuk's son-in-law, went to Toronto to assist in the fundraising effort. He claimed his father-in-law had been a prisoner at the Chelm and Rovno camps during the time he was accused of being a guard at Treblinka. Convinced of his father-in-law's innocence, he swore that if he felt he were really Ivan the Terrible, "I'd push him up to the gallows myself."[72]

So concerned were many Ukrainian Canadians about the case that the CLC funded an informal group of observers to Jerusalem on a ten-day fact-finding mission to monitor the trial. A team of four Ukrainian Canadians

— academics and lawyers — studied the trial proceedings first hand. Their mission, organized with the help of Alex Epstein of Toronto, was intended in part as a goodwill gesture to try to alleviate Ukrainian concerns about the trial.

The tension and controversy surrounding the trial itself spilled over into conflicting accounts of their impressions and bitterly divided the Ukrainian community. First reports of their conclusions stressed the fairness of the trial and the respect which the observers had for the quality and integrity of the Israeli judicial system. Dr Yury Boshyk, leader of the group, went even further. Speaking on national radio, he argued that despite the shoddy practice of indiscriminate use of the term "Ukrainian" in media coverage, "it is an individual on trial and not a nation." The trial and the Israeli legal system, he insisted, were fair and impartial. He urged that those thinking of contributing to the Demjanjuk defence fund do so to support "an individual who they feel is innocent," rather than worry about the good name of the Ukrainian nation.

That was too much for many of Demjanjuk's supporters. Organizers of the Toronto-based Demjanjuk defence fund felt that Boshyk's remarks might undermine their campaign efforts. Indeed the remarks triggered an avalanche of legal criticism of the trial by Ukrainian lawyers and activists. Bohdan Onyschuk, who was also a member of the Canadian Ukrainian observer team, apparently took issue with Boshyk's remarks. Claiming that Boshyk may have been expressing his own personal views, Onyschuk found nothing wrong with Canadian Ukrainians contributing to the Demjanjuk defence fund. Moreover, he reported "very grave misgivings" about the conduct of the trial. Some of those reservations were shared by Boshyk himself. The attendance of members of the Israeli government at the trial, including Prime Minister Shamir, and the busing in of schoolchildren to a trial set in a converted Jerusalem theatre, added to a "show trial" atmosphere which in the view of most Ukrainians could compromise the fairness of the trial. Ukrainian lawyers from Canada and the United States joined in an open letter to the Israeli prime minister, outlining these and other reservations about the conduct of the trial, while avoiding any pronouncement on Demjanjuk's guilt or innocence. A disappointed Alex Epstein saw his peace-making shuttle turn sour. Barring an acquittal for Demjanjuk, no intercommunal bridges would be built through that Jerusalem courtroom.[73]

Thus, efforts at better Jewish-Ukrainian relations ran hot and cold; everyone saying they were for it, but few willing to push aside barriers to reach it. And even the government's response to Deschênes's recommendations was still not resolved. Jews and other committed Nazi-hunters hoped for swift implementation of the promised legislation. It was feared that some of the Canadian top twenty suspects might try to flee before proceedings could begin. Jewish communal leaders eyed with envy the rapid response of the Australian government to their own report on war criminals. It was released in November 1986, and by April of 1987, the Australians had established a Special Investigations Unit (War Crimes) assigned the task of investigating the seventy names listed in their report. Comprising investigators, historians, information analysts and lawyers, the SIU, which would report to the Attorney General, bore striking similarities to the OSI. Would Canada move as quickly?[74]

At first the outlook seemed dim. Time passed with no sign of legislation. Liberal MP Robert Kaplan, hoping to pressure the government, tabled his own private member's bill in early June based directly on Judge Deschênes's recommendations. "I don't know why they [the government] are taking so long," Kaplan wondered. Groups such as the Canadian veterans, mobilized as part of the Congress coalition strategy, were also urging the government to act.[75]

In fact, the government had begun to move, though much of its action was low key. Shortly after the release of the *Report*, the government announced the appointment of William Hobson to head the Justice Department's investigation of suspected war criminals. Hobson quietly pulled together a team of investigators, lawyers and historians. He walked a thin line between Jewish groups eager for action and eastern European groups still leery of witch-hunts. The Ukrainian community had early recognized the importance of the staffing of Hobson's unit. "When the government is looking for people to fill the positions, they should give a proper impression of fairness," claimed Orest Rudzik of the CLC. "They should have no links either to the Ukrainian community or the Jewish community."[76] Perhaps some Ukrainian officials may have been worried not only about Jewish biases but also about possible recruitment of Ukrainian researchers whose ties were to the left-wing Ukrainian community. While Hobson's recruiters might share that view, they were faced with their own dilemma: many applications for research positions came from Jewish and eastern European applicants. Hobson's unit set out a hiring policy that excluded no one on grounds such as ethnic origin. They were looking for recent Ph.D.s, preferably in history, with a knowledge of German. The staffers were to be historical technicians whose research would be guided from above. The unit received no formal directives to exclude Jewish or Ukrainian researchers.

Even before passage of the legislation, Hobson and his team began to work. Justice Minister Hnatyshyn, confirming the judgment of his department's professionals, admitted that additional evidence was needed before proceeding with any prosecutions. Part of the problem lay in the fact that the staffers working in the new unit included none of the researchers and investigators who had served the Commission. For those who had long struggled to see concrete action against Nazi war criminals in Canada, that seemed a terrible waste. Not even Judge Deschênes was consulted. "All the accumulated knowledge and experience of the Deschênes Commission is being duplicated," charged David Matas of B'nai Brith. "New people are having to learn what others have learned."[77] After two years of Commission work, still no case was ready to go.

Finally, on June 23, 1987, the government introduced its promised legislation, proposing to amend the *Criminal Code*, the *Immigration Act* and the *Citizenship Act*. Hnatyshyn hoped the package could become law within a week, but had "no idea when the first prosecution might be launched." Prospects for rapid passage of the amendments, *Bill C-71*, indeed looked good. Both the NDP's Robinson and the Liberals' Kaplan promised unanimous approval from their colleagues before the upcoming summer recess.[78]

But it was not to be. There had been an all-party agreement to support *Bill C-71*, and it could have been over in a day. But at the last minute, Tory backbenchers Alex Kindy and Andrew Witer denied the bill unanimous support and forced it into legislative committee for study. Witer argued that lawyers needed more time to review it; Kindy did not share the sense of time pressure felt by Jewish community representatives. "It's a major piece of legislation, so it should not be rammed down in five minutes. We have been waiting 40 years," he argued, "so if we wait a little bit longer and get a good piece of legislation, it is worthwhile." True to their word, and to their many eastern European constituents, they remained fixed in the Commons to prevent the bill from being passed in that form.[79]

Justice Minister Hnatyshyn had no choice but to withdraw the bill, and Parliament recessed for the summer. Indeed, on June 30, 1987, the last day before the summer recess, Witer proposed five amendments to the bill. Both Congress and B'nai Brith were disappointed. They feared it might take months for the bill to get through committee, despite reassurances by Hnatyshyn's chief of staff that it might only be a matter of weeks. Hnatyshyn, according to Congress's Jack Silverstone, did his best to move the two MPs. "In my opinion, Hnatyshyn made an extraordinary effort to try to get this legislation passed." When asked whether the government had used all its leverage on the recalcitrant

MPs, B'nai Brith's Matas replied, "I don't know if the government could have done more than it did."[80]

Cotler, commenting on the actions of Kindy and Witer, "refused to impugn the motives of anyone." But he was concerned with further delays and with a possibility of another round of hearings in committee. In proposing his amendments, Witer wanted the bill to allow for prosecution of all war criminals and not just those from countries "in armed conflict" with Canada; leave the power to authorize prosecution only with the federal attorney general; only permit deportations to countries with which Canada has extradition treaties; relax the *Immigration Act* so that only proven war criminals — not suspects — could be barred entry. Jewish officials allowed that these four amendments might have some merit or, at any rate, would not undermine the Bill. The fifth amendment, however, was strongly opposed by Congress and B'nai Brith. It would have prevented reporting about any trials until after a guilty verdict was delivered. This, the Jewish representatives felt, would have nullified any deterrent or educational effect of the trials. But amendments were not the issue. Congress and B'nai Brith wanted *Bill C-71* passed without the delay of a protracted amending process.[81]

The Witer and Kindy refusal to consent proved particularly galling to Congress President Dorothy Reitman. The previous June, she had met privately with the UCC's Dmytro Cipywnyk and Victor Goldbloom of the Canadian Council of Christians and Jews in what many hoped would become regular high-level meetings designed to promote dialogue. They had pledged to focus on academic and scholarly discussions as one avenue to improving relations and had had an amicable discussion.

When news of the Kindy-Witer action broke, Reitman wondered what was going on. Cipywnyk seemed not to have known of the pending Witer effort, or at least had not told Reitman. Witer reportedly claimed that regardless of any all-party agreement, no one from the Conservative leadership had talked to him. The episode again informed some Jewish leaders that UCC leaders were having trouble controlling a diverse community with a significant militant faction.[82]

But all was not lost for proponents of quick legislation. A boatload of Tamil refugees coming ashore off Nova Scotia paved the way. The hysteria that swept the country — or at least the media — that summer prompted the government to reconvene Parliament in emergency summer session. While the main objectives were passage of emergency refugee legislation and a controversial drug bill, Jewish leaders were promised that the government would use the session to push through *Bill C-71*. An eight-man legislative committee, comprising six Conservatives, one Liberal and one New Democrat (including Witer, Kaplan and Robinson) met for two sessions to discuss the legislation. Witer tried in vain to have representatives of the four groups with standing before the Deschênes Commission brought to testify before the committee, but the committee members were impatient. They heard from only one minister, Justice Minister Hnatyshyn, who, according to Congress's Jack Silverstone, "staunchly" defended the bill. All obstacles were removed, and *Bill C-71* received third and final reading on August 28. After Senate approval and Royal Assent, on September 16, 1987 it became the law of the land.[83]

What was the box score by the fall of 1987? It was something of a draw. The Jewish community saw a war-crimes law enacted — a law with enormous symbolic as well as legal importance. Justice, they hoped, would now be served. But the Jewish community did not get all it wanted. And, if the Jews got less than they wanted, the Ukrainians may have gotten more than they had originally hoped. Indeed, in spite of early fears, it appears that the Ukrainian polity had perhaps come out of the Deschênes experience escaping the worst. Although a team of forty people was at work under Hobson, no trials in Canada were yet pending. The legislation had just been passed, and further evidence would have to be gathered before any prosecution could be launched. Remedies like denaturalization or extradition, to Israel or elsewhere, were apparently not being pursued. The Rodal study had been released in heavily edited form. Public attention had been diverted by the "small" number of serious cases, or by the possibilities of war-crimes trials other than those for Nazis.

Ukrainian communal leaders were by and large happy. Judge Deschênes had seemingly exonerated the Division. Excessive claims as to the number of alleged war criminals in Canada had been whittled down from the thousands talked of earlier to twenty-odd hot cases. Soviet evidence remained a problem, but it could only be obtained under the most stringent conditions. In any event, there were likely no Ukrainians among the top twenty suspects. Perhaps most importantly, the Deschênes episode marked a coming of age for the Ukrainian polity. They had taken on the so-called "powerful" Jewish lobby and done rather well.

Epilogue

In the immediate post-war years, Toronto's College Street served as a gathering place — a town square — for immigrants from Europe. For Joseph, College Street was a far cry from the Displaced Persons camps of Europe from which he had recently come. But even on College Street, perhaps especially on College Street, the memories of Europe and the Holocaust refused to go away. The murder of his and his wife's parents and his two brothers was a pain too fresh to be put aside.

Joseph had been an instructor at an institute for post-graduate teacher education in Lvov when the 1941 Nazi invasion drove out the occupying Soviet forces. To Ukrainian nationalists, the Nazis at first appeared to be liberators, and a short-lived Ukrainian republic was soon declared. But to Jews, the Nazi arrival was cause for well-founded fears; they agonized over their fate.

One day a Ukrainian colleague at the institute came to warn Joseph that anti-Jewish action was planned to coincide with the anniversary of Petlura's assassination. He offered refuge to Joseph and his wife, an action which probably saved their lives. A pogrom swept the city, and many Jews, especially those in the white-collar professions — doctors, lawyers, teachers — and others, were dragged from their homes, taken to prisons and murdered. After the slaughter, with the help of other non-Jewish colleagues in Warsaw, Joseph and his wife escaped carrying papers identifying them as Poles. Joseph lost contact with his Ukrainian protector, but later learned that his friend had enlisted in the ss Galicia Division.

Years later, as Joseph strolled along College Street, a man suddenly darted out of the crowd and swept him up in an embrace. It was his colleague, the man who had saved his life. But the joy of recognition quickly gave way to resistance. As Joseph wrestled himself free of the encircling arms, he blurted out, "I am sorry, I

can never befriend a former member of the SS Halychyna [Galicia Division]. Our friendship is over." The
shocked Ukrainian began to explain that he was not an
anti-Semite, he just was fighting for his national cause,
but Joseph turned on his heels and walked away. They
never spoke again.[1]

Forty years after the war, relations between the Jewish and Ukrainian polities remain strained. And even
after the Deschênes Inquiry, the war-criminals issue is
not resolved. In the narrow sense, it will not be over
until the last war criminal and last survivor are dead.
But in another sense, memories of World War II and
the Holocaust may continue to disrupt inter-ethnic relations long after the last historical actor is gone. With
two communities so conscious of their own historical
narrative, the collisions of the past, including events of
World War II, are not likely to be forgotten.

The corrosive impact of the war-criminals issue on
Ukrainian-Jewish relations in Canada underscores the
critical role of historical understanding in the elabora-
tion of ethnic conflict. In the aftermath of the war the
larger public was satisfied that guilt for war crimes fell
on the Nazis. The war in Europe had been against Germany, and the Nuremberg trials focused responsibility
on Germany for the most monstrous crimes of modern
times.

But slowly, deliberate and painstaking historical research began to shake this certainty. Guilt and blame
diffused beyond the Germans. It was found that active
collaboration with the Nazis existed in all occupied
countries. For some adherents to Fascist or anti-Semitic
movements, the German occupation was an occasion
for the bonding of kindred spirits. In other cases, collaboration afforded some political elements an opening
to further parochial nationalist aims or allowed individual opportunists a chance to share in Nazi rule. In the
end, without the active participation of thousands, and
the passive acquiescence of millions throughout Europe,
it is now clear there would have been no Final Solution
as we know it. The Nazis are guilty. But they are not

alone. The discovery of this "hidden Holocaust" is reflected in the roster of names associated with the most recent war-crimes discussion: Barbie, Waldheim, Artukovic, Linnas, and of course Demjanjuk, all focusing on the collaboration of non-Germans.[2]

But questions about guilt do not stop with collaborators. Some historians now focus on Allied indifference. Why, it is asked, did the Allies not make the destruction of the death camps a greater military priority? Why didn't they raise a greater cry over the murder of Europe's Jews? And did the Jewish communities of North America do all they could to pressure their governments to save Jewish lives? Did the Zionist leadership of the *Yishuv* in Palestine, struggling against the oppressive British ban on immigration, do all it could? And finally, a most agonizing question — what of the Jewish victims themselves? Historians and essayists have addressed the role of the *Judenrate*, or Jewish Councils, and the *Kapos*, within the context of guilt and innocence.[3]

These questions also resonated in the arguments put forward by Ukrainian representatives during the course of the Deschênes Inquiry. If the net of guilt is spread so broadly, some ask, why are Ukrainians criticized and singled out for abuse? The very suggestion that if everyone is guilty, then no one is guilty outrages many Jewish spokesmen. They are only too aware that the next step could be an argument that if there were no war criminals, then perhaps there were no war crimes. Thus the failure to prosecute Nazi war criminals might have repercussions in the struggle with the Holocaust denial movement.

These historical debates feed into current ethnic sensitivities. Some Ukrainian Canadians are convinced they are under attack as a group while others — equally guilty — are spared, including Jews. The tragedy of World War II placed all Europeans in the most trying of conditions. How different, some ask, are eastern Europeans who served as concentration camp guards from Jewish *Kapos* who served the same master? The Jewish response — that all must be judged for their share of war criminality — does not allay the question.

Even as these questions are asked of history, history offers ethnic communities the source of the symbols which sustain a collective group memory and identity. Some might argue that there can be too much remembering, that history must be transcended lest it continue to nurture conflict and re-open old wounds. Some say that to remember the victims of the Holocaust, and the famine, is also to remember the perpetrators, and thus rekindle the fires of animosity even in the New World. Others disagree. For them there is the desperate hope that we may still learn from the horrors of our history.

The war-crimes debate has also raised thorny questions about the larger context of inter-ethnic relations in Canada and ethnic politics in particular. The architects of Canadian multicultural policy, past and present, have proven reluctant to grapple with the dark underbelly of multiculturalism. Folk-dancing and costumes are one thing, acrimony and conflict quite another. The passions unleashed within some segments of the Canadian Jewish and Ukrainian communities by Deschênes's war-criminals inquiry caught many Canadian politicians by surprise.

The events of World War II and the Holocaust do not weigh heavily on the minds of most Canadians with no personal ties to those events. Indeed, it is difficult for most Canadians to grasp the magnitude of the crimes and passions which flowed through continental Europe in the past century. How can they? Canadians have been sheltered and Canadian soil has not been drenched in blood.

This does not mean World War II and the Holocaust do not impact on the Canadian political system. These events, and their spillover into ethnic communities, shape identity and commitments. Our study has highlighted the importance of ethnic politicians in our democratic, plural, parliamentary system. Politicians of Jewish and Ukrainian origin played key roles in the lobbying efforts of their communities, brokering between the community and the political system. It was not easy. Some, no doubt, were caught between the sometimes conflicting tugs of party, country and community.

This is the product of an ever more open Canadian political process. Increasingly in the post-war period, Canadians of diverse origins have competed successfully for political office. The ramparts of Canada's political elite gradually fell to the aspiring children and grandchildren of immigrants. Many of these Canadians have ties, some stronger and some weaker, with their ethnic communities. On most political issues, ethnic origin is irrelevant to a policy maker, but it is unlikely that for Liberal Bob Kaplan or Conservative Andrew Witer their ethnic origin was completely irrelevant to their commitments and views on the war-criminals issue.

In earlier times, the charge of dual loyalty could be hurled at a citizen, and certainly a politician, whose ethnic ties might be seen as counter to his or her loyalties to the state. But democratic theory instructs that there is nothing wrong or illegitimate for ethnic politicians to represent concerns of their own communities, especially when these are represented in their constituencies. Certainly, francophone politicians throughout Canadian history have assumed the role of defenders of francophone interests. Others are now doing the same, and doing it openly. Despite the canards of racists, there is usually no conflict of interest between ethnic groups and the so-called national interest. From the standpoint of democratic, participatory politics, there may not be one ironclad national interest, defined as a singular identifiable, objective pattern of policies. Rather, the national interest is a whole defined as the sum of its parts. And ethnic interests, like those of consumers, union members, farmers, industrialists, fishermen and ecologists, are as legitimate in shaping policy as are the interests of any group of citizens.

Ethnic politicians, with one foot each in their communities and government, both articulate the ethnic interest and moderate it at the same time. For the most part they serve to limit, rather than exacerbate, any

ethnic conflicts. Even the crude notion of ethnic brokers delivering votes, or of ethnic groups making demands of politicians, or of politicians seeming to
"pander" to subgroups of citizens, be they ethnic or
otherwise, ought to be regarded with caution. Politicians pandering to citizens can be seen as one of the
best features of Canadian democracy — it reinforces
the notion of sovereignty of the citizens and the rule of
law. In dictatorships, whether of the left or the right,
political leaders pander to nobody, and certainly not to
citizens.

Our study has also stressed the role of ethnic organizations. The CLC, Congress, and B'nai Brith are now
comparable to other interest groups pressuring the political system on behalf of members or clients. They are
not alone. In the future can we expect to see other ethnic groups in Canada pitted against one another,
against other interests or against the state? They already are. We find Japanese Canadians demanding redress from the government for unjust internment during
World War II, as are Ukrainians regarding internment
during World War I; native peoples protest against industrial encroachment upon native lands and despoiling
of the ecological balance; Armenian, Sikh, Tamil and
Middle Eastern tensions spill over onto the Canadian
political landscape and touch ethnic groups in Canada.

But no ethnic group should be seen as monolithic.
For example, Jews and Ukrainians, through their organizations, reflect a broad spectrum of attitudes, including those on the war-criminals issue. In the Ukrainian
case, the Toronto-based and single-issue CLC coalesced
out of the passion of those most engaged by a perceived
threat to their community, bypassing the traditionalism
of the UCC. This was not the case for the Canadian Jewish Congress or B'nai Brith. Both are quintessentially
moderate, establishment organizations. B'nai Brith,
while regarding itself as more populist in approach than
Congress, is an organization of mainstream, traditional
leadership. Single-issue Jewish activists may have been
relegated to the margin, but one must not minimize

their importance. The Simon Wiesenthal Center and the stalwarts of the Holocaust Remembrance Association were able to garner media attention. Whether or not they relished their role as gadfly to the Jewish establishment, they undoubtedly quickened the pace of activity within the Jewish community in regard to war criminals. Most particularly, Sol Littman and the Simon Wiesenthal Center, through the Mengele letter and its attendant publicity, prodded the government towards establishing the Deschênes Commission. Similarly, Kenneth Narvey, acting for Network, brought his research and single-minded perseverance to the task. At times, establishment Jewish leaders may have found their zeal excessive or independence of action disruptive, but in fact, they complemented the conventional approaches of mainstream Jewish organizations. Taken all together, their efforts bore fruit.

But no matter how internally divided, even fractious, Jewish and Ukrainian communities might be, they tended to see each other in monolithic terms. For example, some Ukrainian militants remain unshaken in their belief that Sol Littman was but a stalking horse for the Jewish community whose views were shared, if not expressed, by establishment leaders. For their part, some Jewish leaders tended to discount the protestations of Ukrainian officials who claimed to share the objective of bringing criminals to justice but objected only to the means.

All this presented dilemmas for Canadian politicians and policy makers. How were they to judge who spoke for the ethnic groups? Both Judge Deschênes in the hearings as well as Senator Yuzyk in his negotiations felt that both Congress and B'nai Brith were needed to fully represent Canadian Jewry. But a fledgling Conservative government was apparently not nearly so well informed on communal Jewish organizations. As a result, the Prime Minister's office might have assumed that Sol Littman's affiliation with the Los Angeles-based Simon Wiesenthal Center gave him the cachet of the world-renowned Austrian Nazi-hunter, and might have over-

estimated his influence in the councils of Jewish establishment leadership.

Canadian governments, no less than the large Canadian civic culture, have had little previous need to deal
with such matters. Why should they? By and large, in
the past politically charged discussions of ethnicity have
focused on English-French differences, and the solidity
of French ties with the Liberals. Until recently there
had been little scholarly study of the "ethnic vote" in
Canada, nor had practising politicians moved far beyond ethnic fixers as a source of ethnic understanding.[4]

But all this is slowly changing. Ethnic organizations
continue to grow in importance as governments legitimate their roles, and particularly if they can be seen as
bringing tangible benefits to their constituencies. Ironically this is happening just as ethnic groups are assimilating culturally into mainstream Canadian society. For
some, membership in ethnic organizations can offer
prestige and even power, and can serve as a spring-
board to a career in public service or politics. More and
more, ethnic leaders are those who can combine attach-
ment to heritage with full participation in the larger Canadian society. What is more, a Canadian can be active
in ethnic organizations and support the ethnic cause,
without necessarily marrying within the group, speaking
or reading the ethnic language, living in the old ethnic
neighbourhood or going to the ethnic church every
week. A native-born Ukrainian Canadian active in the
local Ukrainian Canadian Professional and Business
Club is behaving like his Ukrainian or non-Ukrainian
neighbour active in the Shriners or the Boy Scouts.

Ethnic organizations are also vital to the structuring
of ethnic relations. In the old country, Jews and
Ukrainians often lived in adjacent neighbourhoods, rub-
bing shoulders in the market-place almost daily. But
Zalman no longer has the key to the church. The high
degree of voluntary ethnic segregation in Canada, especially in urban eastern Canada, has meant relatively little contact, economic as well as personal, between Jews
and Ukrainians. For better or worse, ethnic interactions

remain defined by the formalized exchanges between ethnic organizations and leaders.

Ethnic tensions over policy making also have important consequences for our understanding of the motivations and expressions of ethnic conflict. In earlier periods, tensions between groups were easily understood as resulting from prejudice or discrimination by one group against another. Things were clearer: Jews were Christ-killers and Bolsheviks, Ukrainians were pogromists or Fascists. But now the language of intergroup tensions has changed. There are very few manifestations of overt, unambiguous racism, and when they appear, they seem unusually vulgar and out of place. Today, conflict is more complex. If Ukrainian Canadians oppose the use of any Soviet evidence in war-crimes cases — which Jewish organizations support — are they anti-Semitic? If Jews urge aggressive prosecution of war criminals and support the use of Soviet evidence, are they Ukrainophobic or pro-Soviet?

The days of explicit oppression of racial or minority groups in Canada are, we trust, now over. All Canadians of goodwill agree there can be no more massacres, internments, pogroms. True, inter-ethnic tensions remain, but the new weapons of antagonism today are position papers, mailing lists and ballots.

This transformation is a strength of Canada's multicultural democracy. Integrating Canadian minorities into the fabric of Canadian plural politics will, one hopes, inevitably limit the scope of potential conflict. While the passions aroused by Deschênes were strong, their damage was controlled. Hostile feelings may simmer privately; publicly, they are usually muted, channelled into bureaucratic routine and formal procedures. Perhaps not the best of all worlds, but certainly not the worst.

* * *

In the wake of the Deschênes *Report* and the subsequent amendment to the *Criminal Code* allowing for the trial of alleged war criminals in Canada, there were signs of a thaw in Ukrainian-Jewish relations. If recent tensions were not forgotten, at least lines of communication were now open. It was mutually agreed that periodic meetings between the leadership of the Canadian Jewish Congress and the Ukrainian Canadian Committee were both possible and desirable to ensure relations continue to improve.

But this mood of reconciliation was soon to be tested. On April 18, 1988 the three-judge Israeli panel delivered its decision in the Jerusalem trial of accused Nazi war criminal John Demjanjuk. It took almost twelve hours for the judges to read their 450-page point-by-point rejection of defence arguments. They ruled there was no case of mistaken identity. The Ukrainian-born retired auto worker from Cleveland was mass murderer Ivan the Terrible who operated the gas chambers at Treblinka. The Soviet-supplied identity card placing Demjanjuk at Trawniki, a training camp for death-camp guards, was authentic. Eyewitness testimony of Treblinka survivors, even more than forty years after the war's end, was reliable. Demjanjuk, the judges pointed out, had offered neither documentary evidence nor eyewitnesses' substantiation of his claim to have been a prisoner of war during the period in question. Accordingly, they concluded that beyond a shadow of a doubt John Demjanjuk was guilty of war crimes, crimes against humanity, crimes against persecuted people and, under Israeli law, crimes against the Jewish people.

A few days later the Israeli panel of judges sentenced Demjanjuk. They held that fidelity to human dignity and the magnitude of Demjanjuk's crimes required he be punished to the full extent of the law. Demjanjuk was sentenced to hang — only the second person so sentenced in Israel's forty-year history. The other was Adolf Eichmann.

To some in the Ukrainian-Canadian community the conviction of Demjanjuk was a wound in the heart. Whatever the true facts of Demjanjuk's wartime experiences, they felt that the trial evidence had not established conclusively that he was Ivan the Terrible.[5] The Trawniki identity card, they charged, was a Soviet forgery designed to convict Demjanjuk and implicate the entire Ukrainian diaspora as Nazi collaborators. His Israeli trial, some protested, was a case of vengeance reaped by Holocaust victims on an innocent man. Demjanjuk may have been alone in the Jerusalem docket but for his Ukrainian-Canadian supporters the entire community stood accused. They eventually raised more than half a million dollars for the Demjanjuk defence.

The day of the Demjanjuk verdict, his supporters held a press conference in Toronto. The vice-president of the Demjanjuk defence fund lashed out against the guilty verdict. To the shock of some in the media covering the event, the vice-president of the Demjanjuk defence fund did more than protest the verdict. According to *The Toronto Star*, he reportedly equated Demjanjuk to Christ and the guilty verdict to the crucifixion.

"I do not want to believe that they would convict an innocent man to death because this will have the same results . . . as the conviction and crucifixion of Jesus Christ," he told the news conference.

"Through the 2,000 years, Jewish people paid for that — rightly or wrongly — but they did pay for that crucifixion.

"I believe this will have similar results in the future for this conviction today."[6]

Whether the comment was a poorly phrased slip of the tongue or indicative of deep-rooted anti-Semitism remains in doubt. There is no doubt that the comment hit a raw Jewish nerve. Here it seemed was an outrageous repetition of the age-old Christ killer canard that Canadian Jewry hoped they would never again hear from a public platform and certainly not in Canada. But the response from the Canadian Jewish Congress was controlled. Rather than dignify the outburst with a direct response, a Congress spokesman took the high road and called for restraint on all sides. Privately, the depth of Jewish anger was communicated to Ukrainian leadership.[7] It was likely hoped that in the glare of adverse publicity and with the future of better inter-ethnic relations at stake more moderate Ukrainian leaders would put a cap on any future provocations. Whether the ethnic leadership proves any more willing or able to either control or repudiate intemperate outbursts now any more than during the period of the Deschênes Inquiry remains to be seen. Hundreds of years of history and deeply ingrained attitudes on both sides are not easily set aside.

Even if mainstream Jewish and Ukrainian organizations reached a *modus vivendi*, relations in Canada are bound to be tested again. The still unresolved problem of Nazi war criminals in Canada, like an open sore, continues to fester. How could it be otherwise? The Deschênes process helped resolve the legal issues. It did not and could not eradicate lingering suspicion among some Jews that there still may be Nazi war criminals in the Ukrainian community. Nor could it eradicate concern by some that the government would stall any wholesale attack on the problem of Nazi war criminals in Canada until there were neither criminals nor victims still alive to see justice done. On the other hand, for some in the Ukrainian community the Deschênes Inquiry did not lessen the conviction that pressure to bring Nazi war criminals to justice merely masks a Soviet or Soviet-Jewish plot to undermine Ukrainian peoplehood.[8]

Will the arrest of Hungarian-born Imre Finta serve to light the fuse on another inter-ethnic confrontation? On December 9, 1987, 76-year-old Imre Finta was arrested by the RCMP in Hamilton, Ontario as he boarded a bus for Buffalo, New York. The retired Toronto restaurateur was charged with forcible confinement, kidnapping and manslaughter.[9]

None of these crimes took place in Canada. All are alleged to have taken place in Europe during World War II, more than forty years ago. During the war,

Finta served as a captain in the Hungarian *Gendarmerie* which stands accused of aiding the Nazis in the deportation of Jews to the death camps. According to recent press accounts, the Canadian government is in possession of documentary evidence and eyewitness testimony gathered in Austria, Hungary and Israel implicating Finta in acts of extreme cruelty, particularly against 8,612 Jews from Szeged, Hungary between April 11 and June 30, 1944. Much of this evidence may have been from the material made available to Deschênes following Finta's abortive legal action against CTV.[10]

Ironically, Finta may well have precipitated his own arrest. If one may assume that Finta was high on Deschênes's list of twenty hot files, it is also reasonable to assume that police authorities could not let him leave Canada. By boarding a Buffalo-bound bus, Finta likely forced the government's hand and accelerated the timetable for action against war criminals in Canada. As a result, Canada's and, indeed, North America's first war-crimes trial is now scheduled to begin in September 1988. More than forty years of government inaction has finally come to an end.

Notes on Primary Sources

In the preparation of this book we examined a wide array of primary documentation. Some of these data now rest in archival collections or with other public agencies. More do not. As a consequence we were dependent on the goodwill of private organizations and individuals: some opened up their private or institutional files to unrestricted access, while others offered a more limited appraisal of only a few relevant documents. In only two cases were we completely denied permission to examine documentation. In addition, every effort was made to interview persons who played a key role in events discussed.

We tried to be exhaustive but concede there will be collections of documentation we missed or individuals whom we somehow overlooked. This is unavoidable. Nevertheless, we did not suffer from any lack of research material and our book is testament to the cooperation we received in gathering it. The following lists collections or sources from which primary information was retrieved.

Manuscript Sources

i) Archival or Public
American Jewish Committee, New York
  Foreign Affairs Department
Canadian Institute of Ukrainian Studies, Edmonton
Commission of Inquiry on War Criminals, Ottawa
Canadian Jewish Congress Archives, Montreal
  Canadian Jewish Congress Papers
Canadian Jewish Congress Archives, Toronto
  Cateman Papers
  Hurwitz Papers
Multicultural History Society of Ontario, Toronto
Public Archives of Canada (National Archives of Canada), Ottawa

Citizenship and Immigration Papers
Immigration Department Papers
Labour Department Papers
Plaut (Gunther) Papers
Tarnopolsky (Walter) Papers
Ronson (Louis) Papers
Rosenberg (Imri) Papers
Toronto City Archives
Mayors' Office Records

ii) Institutional
B'nai Brith of Canada, Toronto
General Files
Deschênes Commission Files
Canadian Jewish Congress (National) Montreal
Kagedan (Ian) Papers
National Joint Community Relations Committee
Rose (Alan) Papers
Silverstone (Jack) Papers
Canadian Jewish Congress (Central Region), Toronto
Joint Community Relations Committee File
War Criminals — Press Clipping File
Civil Liberties Commission of the Ukrainian Canadian Committee,
Toronto
Office Files
Subject Files
(These files have been reorganized. As a result, some files have
been renamed or individual documents relocated.)
Simon Wiesenthal Center, Toronto
Ukrainian Canadian Committee, Winnipeg

iii) Personal Papers (often selected documents)
Boshyk (Yury) Papers
Botiuk (Yaroslaw) Papers
Diakun (Nadia) Papers
Epstein (Alex) Papers
Gregorovich (John) Papers
Harris (Milton) Papers
    War Criminals Files
Kaplan (Robert) Papers
Kayfetz (Ben) Papers
Krawchenko (Bohdan) Papers
Luciuk (Lubomyr) Papers
Matas (David) Papers
Rosenbaum (Eli) Papers
Narvey (Kenneth) Papers
Witer (Andrew) Papers
Witer Mailings

Interviews

Marika Bandera	February 9, 1988	Toronto
Monique Bégin	January 23, 1986	Montreal
Bishop Isidore Borecky	May 8, 1986	Toronto
Yury Boshyk	February 13, 1986	Toronto
	March 19, 1987	Toronto
	May 16, 1987	Toronto
Yaroslaw Botiuk	June 4, 1987	Toronto
Patrick Boyer	July 21, 1987	Toronto
Max Chirofsky	May 21, 1986	Toronto
Alex Chumak	August 6, 1987	Toronto
Sabina Citron	January 28, 1988	Toronto
Fred Clark	February 13, 1986	Toronto
Richard Cleroux	July 8, 1986	Ottawa
Stanley Cohen	February 11, 1987	Ottawa
Irwin Cotler	February 21, 1986	Montreal
	March 28, 1986	Montreal
	January 28, 1987	Montreal
	April 5, 1987	Montreal
	April 28, 1987	Montreal
	July 23, 1987	Montreal
Brian Derrah	February 14, 1988	Ottawa
Judge Jules Deschênes	November 12, 1987	Montreal
Nadia Diakun	March 20, 1986	Ottawa
Frank Dimant	January 28, 1988	Toronto
Alex Epstein	May 10, 1986	Toronto
B.J. Finestone	May 22, 1986	Montreal
Yves Fortier	April 21, 1986	Montreal
	April 21, 1987	Montreal
Victor Goldbloom	March 13, 1986	Toronto
Eddy Goldenberg	March 20, 1986	Ottawa
Douglas Goold	April 7, 1988	Toronto
Herb Gray	March 20, 1986	Ottawa
John Gregorovich	March 12, 1986	Toronto
	April 8, 1987	Toronto
Milton Harris	May 10, 1986	Toronto
	April 5, 1987	Montreal
Arthur Hiess	April 3, 1986	Montreal
	February 24, 1987	Montreal
Bob Hromadiuk	February 6, 1986	Calgary
Gershon Hundert	February 22, 1988	Montreal
Ellen Kachuck	April 21, 1986	Toronto
Ian Kagedan	February 20, 1986	Montreal
Robert Kaplan	March 19, 1986	Ottawa
Ben Kayfetz	April 27, 1987	Toronto
Joseph Klinghofer	May 9, 1986	Toronto

Audrey Kobayashi	April 10, 1986	Montreal
	March 17, 1987	Montreal
Bohdan Krawchenko	February 4, 1986	Edmonton
	March 15, 1987	Montreal
Peter Krawchuk	May 6, 1986	Toronto
Sol Littman	January 21, 1986	Toronto
	January 28, 1986	Toronto
	May 7, 1986	Toronto
	October 22, 1986	Toronto
	January 11, 1988	Toronto
	February 29, 1988	Toronto
Lubomyr Luciuk	January 27, 1986	Toronto
Manoly Lupul	February 5, 1986	Edmonton
Roderick Macdonald	February 19, 1987	Montreal
Paul Robert Magocsi	January 23, 1986	Toronto
Alex Malycky	February 6, 1986	Calgary
David Matas	March 29, 1986	Toronto
	January 20, 1987	Toronto
	March 29, 1987	Ottawa
	March 31, 1988	Winnipeg
Michael Meighen	May 15, 1987	Toronto
	June 10, 1987	Toronto
Ezra Mendelsohn	December 11, 1986	Jerusalem
Myron Momryk	July 9, 1986	Ottawa
Kenneth Narvey	February 23, 1988	Montreal
John Nicholls	March 20, 1986	Ottawa
Geoff Norquay	March 21, 1986	Ottawa
John Nowosad	May 30, 1986	Winnipeg
Phillip Perlmutter	May 14, 1987	Boston
D. Pivnicki	July 4, 1987	Montreal
Jack Porter	August 16, 1987	Montreal
Manuel Prutschi	March 19, 1987	Toronto
Susan Reid	May 4, 1988	Toronto
Susan Reisler	March 12, 1986	Toronto
Dorothy Reitman	April 8, 1987	Montreal
	August 14, 1987	Montreal
	May 3, 1988	Montreal
Alti Rodal	July 9, 1986	Ottawa
Alan Rose	February 19, 1986	Montreal
	May 13, 1986	Montreal
	April 5, 1987	Montreal
Eli Rosenbaum	May 11, 1987	Montreal
Orest Rudzik	March 31, 1987	Toronto
Allan Ryan Jr.	November 5, 1987	Toronto
David Satok	April 5, 1987	Montreal
Roman Serbyn	February 18, 1986	Montreal
	May 3, 1988	Montreal

Les Scheininger	March 25, 1987	Toronto
Neal Sher	December 31, 1986	Washington
Alan Shefman	February 19, 1987	Toronto
Jack Silverstone	February 19, 1986	Montreal
	April 9, 1987	Montreal
	May 4, 1987	Montreal
	May 3, 1988	Montreal
Ralph Snow	January 28, 1988	Toronto
John Sopinka	May 26, 1987	Toronto
Shmuel Spector	December 11, 1986	Jerusalem
Michael Stanislawski	April 13, 1987	New York
Father Myran Stasiw	April 14, 1988	Toronto
Roger Tassé	March 20, 1986	Ottawa
Father John Tataryn	May 7, 1986	Toronto
	May 27, 1986	Toronto
	December 21, 1987	Toronto
John Thompson	March 13, 1986	Montreal
Aharon Weiss	December 11, 1986	Jerusalem
Andrew Witer	March 20, 1986	Ottawa
Rose Wolfe	December 18, 1987	Toronto
Sharon Wolfe	February 15, 1986	Ottawa
Senator Paul Yuzyk	March 19, 1986	Ottawa
Jacques Zylberberg	February 1, 1986	Montreal

Notes

The following abbreviations have been used throughout the notes:

AJC	American Jewish Committee Inventory, New York
AWP	Andrew Witer, Office Papers
BBP	B'nai Brith Papers, Toronto
CIUS	Canadian Institute of Ukrainian Studies, Edmonton
CIWC	Commission of Inquiry on War Criminals
CJC	Canadian Jewish Congress Papers
CJC-R	Canadian Jewish Congress — Alan Rose Papers, Montreal
CJC-S	Canadian Jewish Congress — Jack Silverstone Papers, Montreal
CJC-T	Canadian Jewish Congress Archives, Toronto
CLC	Civil Liberties Commission of the Ukrainian Canadian Committee
CLC-MB	Civil Liberties Commission — Minute Books
CLCP	Civil Liberties Commission Papers, Toronto
DMP	David Matas Papers
JBG	John B. Gregorovich Papers
JCRC	Joint Community Relations Committee, Toronto
KNP	Kenneth Narvey Papers
MHP	Milton Harris Papers
NJCRC	National Joint Community Relations Committee, Montreal
PAC	Public Archives of Canada (National Archives of Canada), Ottawa
PYP	Paul Yuzyk Papers
SWC	Simon Wiesenthal Center, Toronto
TCA	Toronto City Archives
UCC	Ukrainian Canadian Committee
UCCP	Ukrainian Canadian Committee Papers, Winnipeg
YBP	Yury Boshyk Papers

Introduction: Zalman Is Coming with the Key

1   In these notes we have often combined several related issues or items into one note. We also refer to the Commission of Inquiry on War Criminals as the Deschênes Commission, or more briefly, as Deschênes, or the Commission. References to Judge Deschênes himself will be clearly specified. The major Ukrainian organizations, the Civil Liberties Commission and the Ukrainian Canadian Committee, will be denoted as CLC and UCC respectively. The Canadian Jewish Congress and the League of Human Rights of B'nai Brith are denoted in shorthand as Congress and B'nai Brith, respectively. To use the acronym CJC could lead to confusion with the CLC; to describe the CLC as the Commission would risk confusion with the Deschênes Commission itself.

2   *Winnipeg Free Press*, May 23, 1985; *The Winnipeg Sun*, May 23, 1985; *Western Jewish News*, May 31, 1985; *The Jewish Post*, May 31, 1985; Commission of Inquiry on War Criminals, *Proceedings*, XII, May 23, 1985, 1368–9; Commission of Inquiry on War Criminals, *Report, Part I Public*, Ottawa, 1986, 254. Interview with Judge Jules Deschênes, November 12, 1987, Montreal.

3   In preparing this study we encountered a problem in the use of the group designations Jews and Ukrainians generally, and Ukrainian Canadians and Canadian Jews in particular. At times in the text we will make general references to views or behaviours of Ukrainian Canadians or Canadian Jews. Of course, these may be overgeneralizations. We take this liberty, in parts, to relieve the monotony of the more precise designations, in part because we believe these designations have an elasticity of meaning which the reader will understand through the context and in part because of our intuitive sense that ethnic groups do share commonalities of spirit or destiny.

We have also chosen to use the terms "Ukrainian Canadians" and "Canadian Jews" from among the many variants, in the belief that these are the terms preferred by the communities themselves.

4   For a discussion of the components of ethnicity see Wsevolod W. Isajiw, "Definition of Ethnicity," *Ethnicity* 1 (1974), 111–24.

5   David M. Potter, "The Historian's Use of Nationalism and *Vice Versa*," in *Generalizations in Historical Writing*, Alexander V. Riasanovsky and Barnes Riznik, eds. (Philadelphia, 1963), 134.

6   Lester D. Stephens, *Probing the Past* (Boston, 1974), 19.

7   E.H. Carr, *What is History* (London, 2nd ed., 1986), 114.

8   Potter, "The Historian's Use of Nationalism and *Vice Versa*," 135.

9   Interview with Father John Tataryn, May 7, 1986, Toronto; the validity of the claim that specific Jews, acting for landlords, actually controlled and refused access to churches is still a matter of historical debate. Interview with Gershon Hundert, February 22, 1988, Montreal.

10   In 1596 a few Orthodox Ukrainian bishops, with the encouragement of the Polish rulers and the Roman Catholic Church, agreed to unite with Rome. The result was the creation of the Uniate Church, which recognized the authority of the Pope as head, but still was allowed to retain Orthodox liturgical traditions. The Uniates were based primarily in western Ukrainian lands ruled by Poland and later Austria; the Orthodox were in eastern Ukraine ruled by Muscovy and later the Russian Empire. After the onset of Austrian rule in 1772, the Uniates came to be called Greek Catholics, a term which in the twentieth century has gradually been replaced by Ukrainian Catholic. After its initial association with Poland and the Catholic west, the Greek Catholic Church, by the late nineteenth century, became a stronghold of Ukrainian national identity.

11   Interview with Michael Stanislawski, April 13, 1986, New York; Bernard D. Weinryb, *The Jews of Poland* (Philadelphia, 1972), 10.

12   Howard Aster and Peter Potichnyj, *Jewish-Ukrainian Relations: Two Solitudes* (Oakville, Ontario, 1983), 7.

13   For a discussion of the legal arguments relating to war criminals and to the Deschênes Commission, see David Matas and Susan Charendoff, *Justice Delayed: Nazi War Criminals in Canada* (Toronto, 1987); for a discussion of post-war immigration as it relates to war criminals, see Alti Rodal, "Nazi War Criminals in Canada: The Historical and Political Setting from the 1940s to the Present," prepared for the Commission of Inquiry on War Criminals (Ottawa, 1986).

14   Some additional comments on our research methods are in order. An important source of information we have used is the press. Press reports are part of the public record and help to shape the environment in which people act. To understand human behaviour, which we try to do, requires an appreciation of the opinions, beliefs and even prejudices and stereotypes which people hold regarding other people, groups or organizations. Much of the evidence we have gathered in our research involves the expressions of such opinions, at times passionate, as reported in both the ethnic and mainstream press, in interviews and in documents. These opinions or views may be incorrect, based not on fact but on emotion.

There is always a danger involved in repeating press reports of extreme views or comments, especially when they may border on fantasy or paranoia. To the extent that such comments are believed to be accurate, they may inform the reputation of individuals or groups. This is especially the case for figures whose high-profile involvement in our story has transformed them into public personalities.

For this reason we cannot omit them entirely. Our duty as scholars and our commitment to free inquiry and understanding preclude this. These extreme views are, in many ways, central to our story, in that they document our contentions about the old wounds of history being re-opened and about passions which still simmer. Contrary to some of the demonological views held by protagonists, we do not find arch-villains among either Jewish or Ukrainian personalities involved in our drama. Rather, our sense is of people tangled up in the web of history and community — as are we all.

The press is also sometimes criticized for misrepresenting facts or taking quotes out of context. This is not always their fault. The *ex post facto* recollections of participants in an event may also be incorrectly recalled by those involved. To avoid any particular bias, we have relied on a variety of reputable Canadian newspapers. In addition, in the case of the Deschênes Commission and related matters, we have, on occasion, referred back to Canadian Press wire copy, which removes a layer of selectivity from the reporting process. Where possible we have also cross-checked press reports of formal testimony before the Deschênes Commission with the official transcripts or other first-hand accounts.

15   Max Weber, *The Methodology of the Social Sciences*, Edward A. Shils and Henry A. Finch, eds. (New York, 1949), 60.

Chapter One: The Old World

1 Interview with Michael Stanislawski, April 13, 1986, New York.

2 Shmuel Ettinger, "Jewish Participation in the Settlement of Ukraine in the Sixteenth and Seventeenth Centuries," in Peter J. Potichnyj and Howard Aster (eds.), *Ukrainian-Jewish Relations in Historical Perspective* (Edmonton, 1988), 24.

3 Frank E. Sysyn, "The Jewish Factor in the Khmelnytsky Uprising," in Potichnyj and Aster (eds.), *Ukrainian-Jewish Relations*, 49.

4 Ms. cited in Stefan T. Possony, "The Ukrainian-Jewish Problem: A Historical Retrospective," *The Ukrainian Quarterly* 31 (1975), 141.

5 Bernard D. Weinryb, *The Jews of Poland* (Philadelphia, 1972), 181–205; Paul R. Magocsi, "Ukraine: An Introductory History" (unpublished manuscript), 159. We are especially grateful to Professor Magocsi for allowing us to read and cite this draft manuscript.

6 *Encyclopedia Judaica*, Vol. 5 (Jerusalem, 1971), 481.

7 Magocsi, "Ukraine," 193.

8 Possony, "The Ukrainian-Jewish Problem," 141. For a wider discussion of the historiography and reliability of sources on Khmelnytsky and the Jews see Bernard Weinryb, "Hebrew Chronicles of Bohdan Khmelnytski and the Cossack-Polish War," *Harvard Ukrainian Studies* 1 (1977), 153–77, and Sysyn, "The Jewish Factor," in Potichnyj and Aster (eds.), *Ukrainian-Jewish Relations*, 43–54.

9 An exceptionally fine thumbnail sketch of these events is offered in Magocsi, "Ukraine," 503–72g.

10 Jonathan Frankel, "The Dilemmas of Jewish Autonomism: The Case of Ukraine 1917–1920," in Potichnyj and Aster (eds.), *Ukrainian-Jewish Relations*, 263–79.

11 Simon Dubnow, *History of the Jews in Russia and Poland: From Earliest Times Until the Present Day*, Vol. V (Philadelphia, 1946), 841–46.

12 This historical debate continues. See Solomon Godelman, *Jewish National Autonomy in the Ukraine, 1917–1920* (Chicago, 1968), Zvi Gitelman, *Jewish Nationality and Soviet Policies* (Princeton, 1972), 155–76; John Reshetar, *The Ukrainian Revolution 1917–1920* (Princeton, 1952); Richard

Pipes, *The Formation of the Soviet Union: Communism and Nationalism, 1917–1923* (Cambridge, 1954). The debate about Petlura generated one particularly bitter scholarly exchange: Taras Hunczak, "A Reappraisal of Symon Petlura and Ukrainian-Jewish Relations, 1917–1921," *Jewish Social Studies* 31 (1969), 163–83; Zosa Szajkowski, " 'A Reappraisal of Symon Petlura and Ukrainian Jewish Relations, 1917–1921': A Rebuttal," *Jewish Social Studies* 31 (1969), 194–13; "Communications," *Jewish Social Studies* 32 (1970), 246–63. Much of the *Jewish Social Studies* debate with some accompanying documents was published in Taras Hunczak, *Symon Petlura and the Jews: A Reappraisal* (Toronto, 1985).

13 Arthur Adams, *Bolsheviks in the Ukraine: The Second Campaign, 1918–1919* (New Haven, 1963); Leonard Shapiro, "The Role of the Jews in the Russian Revolutionary Movement," *The Slavonic and East European Review* 40 (1961–62), 143–65; Gitelman, *Jewish Nationality and Soviet Politics.*

14 Robert Conquest, *The Harvest of Sorrow: Soviet Collectivization and the Terror Famine* (New York, 1986); Roman Serbyn and Bohdan Krawchenko (eds.), *Famine in Ukraine 1932–1933* (Edmonton, 1986).

15 Paul Magocsi, "Famine or Genocide?" *The World & I* (April 1987), 416–23.

16 Michael R. Marrus, *The Holocaust in History* (Toronto, 1987), 55–83.

17 Issues relating to the historiography of the *Kapos*, ghetto police and *Judenrate* are sensitively handled in Marrus, *The Holocaust in History*, 113–21, 129.

18 The calm of a scholarly conference on the history of Ukrainian-Jewish relations at McMaster University in 1983 was almost shattered when two separate papers laid out different Jewish and Ukrainian interpretations of events. The papers were edited and published. Yaroslav Bilinsky, "Methodological Problems and Philosophical Issues in the Study of Jewish-Ukrainian Relations During the Second World War," and Aharon Weiss, "Jewish-Ukrainian Relations in Western Ukraine during the Holocaust Period," in Potichnyj and Aster (eds.), *Ukrainian-Jewish Relations*, 409–20.

19 Orest Subtelny, "The Soviet Occupation of Western Ukraine, 1939–1941: An Overview," in Yury Boshyk, ed., *Ukraine During World War II: History and Its Aftermath* (Edmonton, 1986), 40–41.

20 John A. Armstrong, "Collaboration in World War II: The Integral Nationalist Variant in Eastern Europe," *Journal of Modern History* 40 (1968), 396–410.

21 OUN-B resolution as quoted in Philip Friedman, *Road to Extinction: Essays on the Holocaust* (New York, 1980), 170–80.

22 Taras Hunczak, "Ukrainian-Jewish Relations During the Soviet and Nazi Occupations," in Boshyk, *Ukraine During World War II*, 40–41; see also Richard C. Lukas, *The Forgotten Holocaust: The Poles Under German Occupation 1939–1944* (Lexington, Ky. 1986), 127–30.

23 Weiss, "Jewish-Ukrainian Relations," in Potichnyj and Aster (eds.), *Ukrainian-Jewish Relations*, 413; see also Friedman, *Road to Extinction*, 184; Lucy S. Dawidowicz, *The War Against the Jews, 1933–1945* (New York, 1975), 279; Raul Hilberg, *The Destruction of the European Jews* (New York, 1985), 309–12.

24 Ihor Kamenetsky, "The National Socialist Policy in Slovenia and Western Ukraine During World War II," *Annals of the Ukrainian Academy of Arts and Sciences in the United States* 14 (1978–1980), 48–49.

25 Bohdan Krawchenko, "Soviet Ukraine Under Nazi Occupation, 1941–4," in Boshyk, *Ukraine During World War II*, 25.

26 Hunczak, "Ukrainian-Jewish Relations," 46; John A. Armstrong, *Ukrainian Nationalism* (New York, 1963), 218; Bilinsky, "Jewish-Ukrainian Relations," 5–8. A special symposium on issues related to Ukraine during World War II with special focus on the problem of collaboration with the Nazis is found in "Ukrainians in World War II: Views and Points," *Nationalist Papers* 10 (1980), 1–39. The subject of Jewish councils is discussed in Isaiah Trunk, *Judenrat: The Jewish Councils in Eastern Europe Under Nazi Occupation* (New York, 1972).

27 Marrus, *The Holocaust in History*, 55–83.

28 Place names in eastern Europe usually have two or more different forms, depending on the language being used. In this book we could have opted to use the forms found in *Webster's New Geographical Dictionary* (Springfield, Mass., 1980) and the National Board of Geographic Names. For the administrative centre of eastern Galicia this would have required the form Lvov (Russian) rather than L'viv (Ukrainian), Lwów (Polish) or Lemberg (German and Yiddish). Instead, we opted for a more contextual usage, respecting,

where possible, the name most in keeping with persons or events under consideration.

29 Magocsi, "Ukraine," 681.

30 Magocsi, "Ukraine," 688.

31 Lev Shankovsky, "Ten Years of the UPA Struggle," *Ukrainian Review* 33 (1985), 20–30; Armstrong, *Ukrainian Nationalism*, 130–65.

32 Friedman, *Road to Extinction*, 188–89; Weiss, "Jewish-Ukrainian Relations," 8–10.

33 Leo Heiman, "We Fought for Ukraine! The Story of Jews with the UPA," *Ukrainian Quarterly* 20 (1964–65), 33–44.

34 See Sheptytsky to the Pope as quoted in Ryszard Torzecki, "Sheptyts'kyi and Polish Security," Paul Robert Magocsi (ed.), *Morality and Reality: The Life and Times of Metropolitan Andrei Sheptyts'kyi* (forthcoming). Kurt Lewin, "Andreas Count Sheptytsky, Archbishop of L'viv, Metropolitan of Halych, and the Jewish Community in Galicia During the Second World War," *The Annals of the Ukrainian Academy of Arts and Sciences in the United States* 7 (1959) 1656–67; Leo Heiman, "They Saved Jews," *Ukrainian Quarterly* 17 (1961), 320–32; Friedman, *Road to Extinction*, 191–92; Hunczak, "Ukrainian-Jewish Relations," 49–51; Shimon Redlich, "Sheptyts'kyi and the Jews During World War II," in Magocsi (ed.), *Morality and Reality*; Bohdan Budurowycz, "Sheptyts'kyi and the Ukrainian National Movement After 1914," in Magocsi (ed.), *Morality and Reality*.

35 George H. Stein, *The Waffen SS: Hitler's Elite Guard at War, 1939–1945* (Ithaca, 1966); Gerald Reitlinger, *The S.S.: Alibi of a Nation 1922–1945* (London, 1981 edition); Roger James Bender and Hugh Page Taylor, *Uniforms, Organization and History of Waffen-SS* (San Jose, 1975); Robert Koehl, *The Black Corps: The Structure and Power of the Nazi SS* (Madison, 1983); David Littlejohn, *The Patriotic Traitors: A History of Collaboration in German Occupied Europe, 1940–1945* (London,1972); Charles W. Sydnor Jr., *Soldiers of Destruction: The SS Death's Head Division, 1933–1945* (Princeton, 1977); Hansjakob Stehle, "Metropolitan Sheptyts'kyi and the German Regime," in Magocsi (ed.), *Morality and Reality*.

36 Myroslav Yurkevich, "Galician Ukrainians in German Military Formations and the German Administration," in Boshyk, *Ukraine During World War II*, 71–73, 77.

37 John Armstrong, *Ukrainian Nationalism*, 171–72.

38   Yurkevich, "Galician Ukrainians," 76–77.

39   Richard Landwehr, *Fighting for Freedom: The Ukrainian Volunteer Division of the Waffen-SS* (Silver Springs, 1985), 26–27; Bender and Taylor, *Uniforms, Organization and History*, 81–85.

40   Bender and Taylor, *Uniforms, Organization and History*, 88–89; Landwehr, *Fighting for Freedom*, 132–34.

41   Wolf Dietrich Heike, "History of the Ukrainian Division 'Galicia,'" Volodymyr Kubiiovych, ed. (unpublished manuscript, 1987), 97. The work was published in German, Wolf-Dietrich Heike, *Sie Wollten Die Freiheit: Die Geschichte der Ukrainischen Division, 1943–45* (Dorheim, Podzum-Verlag, [1973]).

42   Lubomyr Luciuk, "Searching for Place: Ukrainian Refugee Migration to Canada after World War II" (unpublished Ph.D. thesis, University of Alberta, 1984), 235–87.

43   Leonard Dinnerstein, *America and the Survivors of the Holocaust* (New York, 1982), 109; Howard Sachar, *Diaspora: An Inquiry into the Contemporary Jewish World* (New York, 1985), 325–29.

Chapter Two: In the New World

1   Myrna Kostash, *All of Baba's Children* (Edmonton, 1977), 214.

2   Erna Paris, *Jews: An Account of their Experience in Canada* (Toronto, 1980), 257–58.

3   For more favourable assessments of Ukrainian-Jewish relations in Manitoba, see Arthur A. Chiel, *The Jews in Manitoba* (Toronto, 1961), and O. Woycenko, *The Ukrainians in Canada* (Ottawa, 1967).

4   Paris, *Jews*, 153–54. Similar episodes of co-operation and conflict among Ukrainian and Jewish leftist groups are presented in Donald Avery, *Dangerous Foreigners: European Immigrant Workers and Labour Radicalism in Canada, 1896–1932* (Toronto, 1979), and John Kolasky, *The Shattered Illusion: The History of Ukrainian Pro-Communist Organizations in Canada* (Toronto, 1979).

5   The phrase "two solitudes" was aptly employed by Howard Aster and Peter J. Potichnyj as the subtitle for their path-

breaking essays on Ukrainian-Jewish relations. Howard Aster and Peter J. Potichnyj, *Jewish-Ukrainian Relations: Two Solitudes* (Oakville, Ont., 1983).

6   Two major sources on Ukrainian Canadians are William Darcovich and Paul Yuzyk, eds., *A Statistical Compendium on the Ukrainians in Canada, 1891–1976* (Ottawa, 1980) and M.H. Marunchak, *The Ukrainians in Canada: A History* (Winnipeg, 1970).

7   Darcovich and Yuzyk, *A Statistical Compendium*, 500–2; Marunchak, *The Ukrainians*, 64.

8   Darcovich and Yuzyk, *A Statistical Compendium*, 17–26.

9   Darcovich and Yuzyk, *A Statistical Compendium*, 517.

10   Marunchak, *The Ukrainians*, 161.

11   For a review of the Ukrainian internment during World War I, see F. Swyripa and J.H. Thompson, eds., *Loyalties in Conflict: Ukrainians in Canada during the Great War* (Edmonton, 1983); in December 1987 the Ukrainian Canadian Committee officially petitioned the federal government for redress. Lubomyr Luciuk submitted a brief to the government on behalf of the Civil Liberties Commission of the Ukrainian Canadian Committee. Lubomyr Luciuk, "A Time For Atonement: Canada's First National Internment Operations and the Ukrainian Canadians 1914–1920" (Toronto, December 7, 1987).

12   For a review of Jewish immigration to Canada, see Joseph Kage, *With Faith and Thanksgiving* (Montreal, 1962) and Simon Belkin, *Through Narrow Gates: A Review of Jewish Immigration, Colonization and Immigrant Aid in Canada* (Montreal, 1966).

13   Marunchak, *The Ukrainians*, 372.

14   A journalistic overview of the adjustment of Holocaust survivors in North America can be found in Dorothy Rabinowitz, *New Lives* (New York, 1976). While many survivor families did exhibit symptoms of psychological and social impairment, non-clinical studies have discovered that the majority of survivors, and their children, seem to have coped with their traumatic legacy. See Morton Weinfeld, John J. Sigal and William W. Eaton, "The long term effects of the Holocaust on selected social attitudes and behaviors of survivors: a cautionary note," *Social Forces* 60 (1981), 1–19, and John J. Sigal and Morton Weinfeld, "Control of Aggression in Adult

Children of Survivors of the Nazi Persecution," *Journal of Abnormal Psychology* 94 (1985), 556–64.

15   Apart from the Holocaust Committee of the Canadian Jewish Congress there are organizations such as the Association of Survivors of Nazi Oppression and the Canadian Holocaust Remembrance Association, as well as the Toronto branch of the Los Angeles-based Simon Wiesenthal Center. Indeed, the Congress Holocaust Committee, Quebec Region, lists thirty-one organizations (including six branches of the Workmen's Circle) as composing the complete list of "survivor organizations" in Montreal. Rosenfeld to Weinfeld, June 18, 1986, personal communication.

16   Marunchak, *The Ukrainians*, 579; Lubomyr Luciuk, "Searching for Place: Ukrainian Refugee Migration to Canada After World War II" (unpublished Ph.D. thesis, University of Alberta, 1984).

17   According to 1971 census data, nearly 50 percent of Ukrainian Canadians claimed non-traditional denominations, such as Anglican, Roman Catholic or United Church. Darcovich and Yuzyk, *A Statistical Compendium*, 175. Some of this may be due to conversion of first-wave settlers, but some reflect mixed marriages.

18   It might be noted that slightly more than 4 percent of Canadian Jews were born in the United States. Unless otherwise noted, the data in the following sections are taken from the 1981 Census, as reported in *Socio-economic Profiles of Selected Ethnic/visible Minority Groups* 1981 Census (Ottawa, March 1986).

19   Data from K.G. O'Bryan, J.G. Reitz and O. Kuplowska, *Les Langues non officielles* (Ottawa, 1975), 98, 119.

20   For Jewish enrolment estimates, see Y. Glickman, "Jewish Education: Success or Failure," in M. Weinfeld, W. Shaffir and I. Cotler, eds., *The Canadian Jewish Mosaic* (Rexdale, Ont, 1981), 113–28, and M. Weinfeld, *The System of Jewish Education in Montreal* (Montreal, 1985).

21   An estimated 15,000 students were enrolled in Ukrainian schools in Canada in 1980–81. V. Balan, "Ukrainian Language Education in Canada: Summary of Statistical Data 1980–81," in J. Rozumnyj, ed., *New Soil, Old Roots: The Ukrainian Experience in Canada* (Winnipeg, 1983), 277. The 1981 Census identifies 70,000 Ukrainian children, aged 15 and under, using only those claiming a single-Ukrainian-ethnic origin. Marunchak, *The Ukrainians*, 631, estimated that 30 per-

cent of Ukrainian-Canadian youth were receiving education from some formal Ukrainian institutions.

22 Darcovich and Yuzyk, *A Statistical Compendium*, 560, 567.

23 *Toronto Life*, May 1986; Interview with Yury Boshyk, May 16, 1987, Toronto.

24 See Peter S. Li, "Race and Ethnic Relations," in L. Tepperman and R. Jack Richardson, eds., *The Social World: An Introduction to Sociology* (Toronto, 1986), 335–60, and "Income Achievement and Adaptive Capacity: An Empirical Comparison of Chinese and Japanese in Canada," in K.V. Ujimoto and G. Hirabayashi, eds., *Visible Minorities and Multi-culturalism: Asians in Canada* (Toronto, 1980), 363–78.

25 For survey data on the extent of anti-Semitic prejudice among Canadians, see Gabriel Weimman and Conrad Winn, *Hate on Trial: The Zundel Affair, the Media and Public Opinion in Canada* (Oakville, Ont., 1986).

26 Li, "Race and Ethnic Relations," 355.

27 Raymond Breton, "The Ethnic Community as a Resource in Relation to Community Problems: Perceptions and Attitudes" (Toronto, 1981). Breton is currently completing a major volume on the sociology of ethnic politics in Canada.

28 Discussion of the Ukrainian historical self-understanding and image is still very much a part of internal Ukrainian community debate. See, for example, Martha Bohachevsky-Chomiak, "Ukrainians in Historical Perspective," *Ukrainian Weekly*, October 25, 1987.

29 This is illustrated by a passage from *Canada Made Me* by Norman Levine. "The hockey player was a Ukrainian, twenty-eight, blond straight hair, well built, a flat unintelligent face. He had been playing hockey since he left high school . . .," in Michael Czuboka, *Ukrainian Canadian, eh?: The Ukrainians of Canada and Elsewhere as Perceived by Themselves and Others* (Winnipeg, 1983), 66. Such passages perpetuate the stereotype of "the dumb Ukrainian jock," according to Czuboka. McGill historian John Thompson, reminiscing about fraternity life on Manitoba campuses in the early 1960s, recalls the prevailing stereotypes with which both groups had to contend: "The Ukrainians were the jocks, the Jews were the brains." Interview with John Thompson, March 13, 1986, Montreal.

30 Daniel J. Elazar, *Community and Polity: The Organizational Dynamics of American Jewry* (Philadelphia, 1976).

31   For a contemporary American review of these issues, see Steven M. Cohen, *American Modernity and Jewish Identity* (New York, 1983).

32   The idea of "institutional completeness" was first outlined in Raymond Breton, "Institutional Completeness of Ethnic Communities and the Personal Relations of Immigrants," *American Journal of Sociology* 70 (1964), 193–205.

33   The implications of this turning outward are explored in William Abrams, "The Covenantal Drama, Act Two Begins," *Judaism*, 36 (1987), 353–59.

34   See Darcovich and Yuzyk, *A Statistical Compendium*, 792–94, for national data for the 1960s and early 1970s. The Toronto figures are from Wsevolod W. Isajiw, "Identity retention among second and third-generation Ukrainians in Canada," in J. Rozumnyj, ed., *New Soil, Old Roots* (Winnipeg, 1983). In Western Canada, Jewish communities are served by a range of periodicals, either weeklies or bi-weeklies: *The Jewish Post* and *Western Jewish News* in Winnipeg, *The Jewish Star* serving Calgary and Edmonton, and the *Jewish Western Bulletin* serving Vancouver. All are written in English, which helps boost readership. The Ukrainian papers represent differing religious emphases (Catholic vs. Orthodox) and ideological orientations (e.g. Banderite vs. Melnykite). The major papers are *New Perspectives*, *Homin Ukrainy*, *Ukrainian Echo*, *Novy Shliakh* and *Nasha Meta* from Toronto; *Ukrainskyi Holos* from Winnipeg; and *Ukrainskyi Visti* and *Postup* from Edmonton. These papers are usually bilingual, or with specific English weekly supplements. In addition, the left-wing/Communist paper *Zyhttia i Slovo* and the related English-language *Ukrainian Canadian* are published in Toronto.

35   Part of the reason for higher readership among third-generation Jews may also lie in the distribution system. The *Canadian Jewish News (CJN)* is sent to anyone contributing a minimal amount to the Combined Jewish Appeal in Montreal or the United Jewish Appeal (UJA) in Toronto. There is no counterpart in the Ukrainian community to this fundraising connection. Readers of the Ukrainian press must make a special, deliberate effort to subscribe.

36   Harold Waller, "Power in the Jewish Community," in Weinfeld, et al., *The Canadian Jewish Mosaic*, 151–70.

37   For a brief discussion of the founding of the UCC, see Kolasky, *The Shattered Illusion*, 64–87, and Ol'ha Woycenko, *The Ukrainians in Canada* (Winnipeg, 1968), 203–15; interview

with Manoly Lupul, February 5, 1987, Edmonton; interview with John Nowosad, May 30, 1986, Winnipeg.

38 For example, see Paul Pross, *Pressure Group Behaviour in Canadian Politics* (Toronto, 1975) and Robert Presthus, *Elite Accommodation in Canadian Politics* (Cambridge, 1973).

39 More recent academic studies note the role of non-economic interest groups, of which ethnic groups are one major type. See H.G. Thorburn, *Interest Groups in the Canadian Federal System* (Toronto, 1985) and Robert J. Jackson, Doreen Jackson and Nicolas Baxter-Moore, *Politics in Canada* (Scarborough, Ont., 1986). For a cynical, more popular assessment of ethnic lobbies, see Paul Malvern, *Persuaders: Influence Peddling, Lobbying and Political Corruption in Canada* (Toronto, 1985), 156–96.

40 Irving Abella and Harold Troper, *None Is Too Many: Canada and the Jews of Europe*, 1933–1948 (Toronto, 1982).

41 David Taras, "Canada and the Arab-Israeli Conflict: A Study of the Yom Kippur War and the Domestic Political Climate" (unpublished Ph.D. thesis, University of Toronto, 1983).

42 Breton, "The Ethnic Community."

43 Isajiw, "Identity Retention."

44 These attitudes are confirmed by data on actual intermarriage patterns of Ukrainians and Jews. In 1971, for example, 91 percent of married Jews were married to other Jews; for Ukrainians, the corresponding percentage was 54 percent. Leo Driedger, "Ukrainian Identity in Canada," in J. Rozumnyj, *New Soil, Old Roots*, 196.

45 While Jewish philanthropy is second to none, there is growing discussion of how changing demographic trends will reshape the structure of Jewish giving. Of particular concern is the shift from business to the professions. See, for example, Steven M. Cohen, "Trends in Jewish Philanthropy," in *American Jewish Year Book* (New York, 1980), 29–51.

46 Vasyl Balan, "Cultural Vision and the Fulfillment of Visible Symbols," in Manoly Lupul, ed., *Visible Symbols: Cultural Expression Among Canada's Ukrainians* (Edmonton, 1984), 187.

47 Jacob Neusner, *Stranger at Home: "The Holocaust," Zionism and American Judaism* (Chicago, 1981).

48 See Lupul, *Visible Symbols*, for a discussion of symbols and Ukrainian identity.

49 Robert Conquest, *The Harvest of Sorrow: Soviet Collectiviza-tion and the Terror-Famine* (New York, 1986). The 55-minute Canadian documentary film on the famine, *Harvest of Despair*, won the 1985 gold medal in TV documentaries at the 28th International Film and TV Festival in New York. Follow-ing Conquest, we use the lower-case form for the famine.

50 Roman Onifrijchuk, "Ukrainian Canadian Cultural Experi-ence-As-Text: Toward a New Strategy," in Lupul, *Visible Symbols*, 154–55.

Chapter Three: Two Solitudes

1 For an examination of the Canadian Jewish postwar cam-paigns for admission of Jews from Europe, see Irving Abella and Harold Troper, *None Is Too Many: Canada and the Jews of Europe*, 1933–1948 (Toronto, 1982), 190–279. On Ukrain-ians, see Lubomyr Luciuk, "Searching for Place: Ukrainian Refugee Migration to Canada after World War II" (unpub-lished Ph.D. thesis, University of Alberta, 1984).

2 Canadian Institute of Public Opinion, Public Opinion News Release, October 30, 1946; Harold Troper, "Canadian Reset-tlement Policies" (unpublished paper, November 1983).

3 Myron Momryk, "Ukrainian Displaced Persons and the Ca-nadian Government 1946–1952" (unpublished paper, Septem-ber 1983), 5–6.

4 Luciuk, "Searching for Place," 318–23.

5 PAC, Department of Labour Records, Refugee Screening Commission, Vol. 147, File 3-43-1; D. Haldane Porter, "Re-port on Ukrainians in SEP Camp No. 374 Italy," February 21, 1947; Alti Rodal, "Nazi War Criminals in Canada: The Historical and Political Setting from the 1940s to the Present," prepared for the Commission of Inquiry on War Criminals (Ottawa, 1986), 366–408; For a discussion of Pan-chuk's key role, see Lubomyr Luciuk (ed.), *Heroes of Their Day: The Reminiscences of Bohdan Panchuk* (Toronto, 1983).

6 For an example of the process by which restrictive immigra-tion regulations were chipped away, see CIWC, Unclassified Public Exhibit, "An Outline of Recent Orders-in-Council. Broadening Canadian Immigration Holdings," in *Evolution of Policy and Procedures Security Screenings, 1945–1957*.

7   CIWC, Unclassified Public Exhibit, Memorandum Fortier to Jolliffe (Commissioner of Immigration), February 7, 1949.

8   Momryk, "Ukrainian Displaced Persons," 15–21.

9   House of Commons *Debates*, June 15, 1950, 3696. The Halychyna Division is the name commonly used for the military unit among Ukrainians. It is also commonly referred to by its German designation, Galicia Division, the term also used in this book.

10   *The Gazette* (Montreal), June 16, 1950.

11   CJC, CJCP, Ukrainian Galician Division, 1950–1951 Files, "Immigration," Memorandum Rosenberg to Hayes, June 19, 1950.

12   CJC, CJCP, Ukrainian Galician Division, 1950–1951 Files, Rosenberg to Segal, June 20, 1950; Rosenberg to Robinson, June 20, 1950.

13   CJC, CJCP, Ukrainian Galician Division, 1950–1951 Files, Segal to editor, *Daily Hebrew Journal*, June 30, 1950.

14   *Canadian Jewish Weekly*, June 29, 1950.

15   CJC, CJCP, Ukrainian Galician Division, 1950–1951 Files, Prokop to Harris, June 21, 1950.

16   CJC, CJCP, Ukrainian Galician Division, 1950–1951 Files, Robinson to Rosenberg, June 27, 1950.

17   CJC, CJCP, Ukrainian Galician Division, 1950-1951 Files, Memorandum Rosenberg to Hayes, June 30, 1950.

18   *JTA News*, July 7, 1950, 6.

19   CJC, CJCP, Ukrainian Galician Division, 1950–1951 Files, Telegram Bronfman to Harris, July 4, 1950.

20   CJC, CJCP, Ukrainian Galician Division, 1950–1951 Files, Harris to Bronfman, July 5, 1950.

21   CJC, CJCP, Ukrainian Galician Division, 1950–1951 Files, Telegram Hayes to *Israelite Post* (Winnipeg), *Daily Hebrew Journal* (Toronto), *Jewish Post* (Winnipeg), July 7, 1950; Hayes to Crestohl, July 10, 1950.

22   CJC, CJCP, Ukrainian Galician Division, 1950–1951 Files, Bronfman to Harris, July 12, 1950.

23   CJC, CJCP, Ukrainian Galician Division, 1950–1951 Files, Rosenberg to Easterman, July 14, 1950; Rosenberg to Robinson, July 14, 1950.

24 *The Forward* (New York), July 23, 1950. Translation in CJC, CJCP, Ukrainian Galician Division, 1950–1951 Files.

25 CJC, CJCP, Ukrainian Galician Division, 1950–1951 Files, Levine to JTA, July 10, 1950.

26 AJC, Foreign Affairs Department: Canada/Emigré Groups, FAD-1, Joseph Kellman to Rosenberg, July 13, 1950; CJC, CJCP, Ukrainian Galician Division, 1950–1951 Files, Kellman to Rosenberg, July 14, 1950; *Ukrainian Resistance: The Story of the Ukrainian National Liberation Movement in Modern Times* (New York, 1949), 98–103.

27 CJC, CJCP, Ukrainian Galician Division, 1950–1951 Files, Memorandum Rosenberg to Hayes, "Halychyna Division" July 26, 1950.

28 CJC, CJCP, Ukrainian Galician Division, 1950–1951 Files, Robinson to Rosenberg, August 1950; Hayes to Kellman, September 6, 1950; Kellman to Hayes, September 29, 1950; Hayes to Kellman, October 5, 1950; Rosenberg to Robinson, October 10, 1950; Robinson to Rosenberg, October 18, 1950; Memorandum of Rosenberg to Hayes, "Halychyna Division," October 23, 1950.

29 CJC, CJCP, Ukrainian Galician Division, 1950–1951 Files, Hayes to Harris, August 2, 1950; "Control Council Law No. 10," December 20, 1945 (a); Hayes to Harris, October 25, 1950, "Index of Materials Submitted to Honourable Walter Harris, Minister of Citizenship and Immigration," August 2, 1950; Affidavit, Bernard Berglas, Montreal, July 31, 1950; Affidavit, Jonas Freiman, Montreal, July 28, 1950.

30 CJC, CJCP, Ukrainian Galician Division, 1950–1951 Files, Harris to Bronfman, September 15, 1950. It has been argued that Canadian officials were not just under pressure from the Ukrainian community to proceed with the admissions. British authorities were also concerned to move the Division to Canada. Rodal, "Nazi War Criminals in Canada," 389–90.

31 CJC, CJCP, Ukrainian Galician Division, 1950–1951 Files, Hayes to Harris, October 5, 1950; Bronfman to Harris, September 25, 1950.

32 CJC, CJCP, Ukrainian Galician Division, 1950–1951 Files, Hayes to Bernstein, October 10, 1950.

33 CJC, CJCP, Ukrainian Galician Division, 1950–1951 Files, Wiesenthal to CJC, October 7, 1950.

34 AJC, Foreign Affairs Department: Canada/Emigré Groups, FAD-1, "The Galician Ukrainian Division (Preliminary Report)," December 1, 1950.

35 CJC, CJCP, Ukrainian Galician Division, 1950–1951 Files, Rosenberg to Hayes, October 23, 1950; Extract from pamphlet entitled "Trail of Terror."

36 CJC, CJCP, Ukrainian Galician Division, 1950–1951 Files, Harris to Hayes, November 6, 1950.

37 CJC, CJCP, Ukrainian Galician Division, 1950–1951 Files, Harris to Bronfman, November 7, 1950.

38 CJC, CJCP, Ukrainian Galician Division, 1950–1951 Files, Hayes, Memorandum, "Hour Meeting with Honourable Stewart Garson, Minister of Justice, on November 17, 1950."

39 CJC, CJCP, Ukrainian Galician Division, 1950–1951 Files, Rosenberg to Robinson, November 20, 1950; Rosenberg to Weiner, November 20, 1950, Rosenberg to Kellman, November 20, 1950; ACJ, Foreign Affairs Department: Canada/Emigré Groups, FAD-1, Edelman to Hexter, Segal, Faire and Cohen, November 30, 1950.

40 CJC, CJCP, Ukrainian Galician Division, 1950–1951 Files, Aronsfeld to Rosenberg, November 27, 1950; Aronsfeld to Rosenberg, December 10, 1950; Robinson to Rosenberg, December 27, 1950; Memorandum Rosenberg to Hayes re: "Halychyna Division," January 15, 1951; Rosenberg to Aronsfeld, January 26, 1951; *Chaz* as quoted in Rosenberg to Robinson, January 26, 1951.

41 CJC, CJCP, Ukrainian Galician Division, 1950–1951 Files, Memorandum of Hayes to National Executive, January 10, 1951.

42 CJC, CJCP, Ukrainian Galician Division, 1950–1951 Files, Karol to Hayes, July 25, 1950. The AUCC, incorporated in 1946, was the newest incarnation of the Ukrainian left, previously known as the Ukrainian Farmer Temple Association.

43 CJC, CJCP, Ukrainian Galician Division, 1950–1951 Files, Memorandum Rosenberg to Hayes re: "Immigration," June 19, 1950.

44 CJC, CJCP, Ukrainian Galician Divison, 1950–1951 Files, Kushnir and Syrnick to *The Israelite Press* and CJC/Winnipeg, August 26, 1950; Frank to Hayes, August 28, 1950.

45   CJC, CJCP, Ukrainian Galician Division, 1950–1951 Files, Hayes to Kushnir and Syrnick, September 6, 1950; Hayes to Frank, September 6, 1950; Zaharychuk to Hayes, September 15, 1950.

46   *Nasha Meta*, June 23, 1951, as quoted in translation in CJC, CJCP, Ukrainian Canadian Committee, 1963 File, Kayfetz to Hayes, June 29, 1951 (enclosure two).

47   *Jewish Post*, May 2, 1957.

48   CJC, CJCP, Melnyk, Andrii (Alleged War Criminals) File, British United Press dispatch, May 4, 1957.

49   CJC, CJCP, Melnyk, Andrii (Alleged War Criminals) File, Telegram Fenson to Hayes, May 8, 1957; Hayes to Fenson, May 9, 1957, Hayes to Wiesenthal, May 9, 1957; Hayes to Yad Vashem, May 9, 1957; Hayes to Kibbutz Mordei Haggettaot, May 9, 1957; (M) Fenson to Tennenbaum, May 4, 1957.

50   CJC, CJCP, Melnyk, Andrii (Alleged War Criminals) File, Frank to Hayes, May 8, 1957.

51   CJC-T, Catzman Papers, Hayes to Kayfetz, May 9, 1957; Among the secondary volumes examined were Joseph Tannenbaum, *Underground: Story of a People* (New York, 1952); CJC, CJCP, Melnyk, Andrii (Alleged War Criminals) File, Memorandum Kayfetz to Hayes, May 17, 1957.

52   CJC-T, Catzman Papers, Jacobs to Hayes, May 9, 1957; Wiesenthal to Hayes, May 13, 1957.

53   *Toronto Telegram*, May 9, 1957.

54   CJC-T, Catzman Papers. Ben Kayfetz, "Items for Administrative Committee," May 10, 1957; CJC, CJCP, Melnyk, Andrii (Alleged War Criminals) file. Memorandum Kayfetz to Hayes, re: "Melnyk" May 10, 1957.

55   CJC-T Catzman Papers. Memorandum Kayfetz to Harris, re: "Meeting with officers of Ukrainian National Federation," May 14, 1957.

56   CJC, CJCP, Melnyk, Andrii (Alleged War Criminals) File. Bilak to Kayfetz, May 14, 1957.

57   CJC, CJCP, Melnyk, Andrii (Alleged War Criminals) File. Frank to Hayes, May 16, 1957; Frank to Hayes, May 22, 1957; *Jewish Post*, May 23, 1957.

58   CJC, CJCP, Melnyk, Andrii (Allgeged War Criminals) File. Kochan to Fenson, May 31, 1957; Hayes to Jacobs, June 3, 1957; CJC-T, Catzman Papers, Frank to Hayes, June 4, 1957.

59   *Toronto Telegram*, May 29, 1957; For reactions to an earlier bombing in Toronto, see TCA, Mayor's Office Records, RG7A1 Box 59, File IIIB Skorokhid to McCallum, October 11, 1950; *The Toronto Star*, October 9, 1950; *The Globe and Mail*, October 9, 1950; *The Toronto Telegram*, October 9, 1950.

60   Much of the following discussion of the press is culled from *Press Digest*, the federal government's monthly review of the ethnic press. We quote their translations of non-English-language material. *Press Digest*, Vol. 16, no. 2, January, 1960, 5–7.

61   *Press Digest*, Vol. 16, no. 6, May 1960, 4.

62   *Press Digest*, Vol. 16, no. 7, June 1960, 3–5.

63   *Press Digest*, Vol. 16, no. 8, July 1960, 6–8. For a public airing of Ukrainian-Jewish relations during the 1960s see, for example, "Ukrainians and Jews: Must They Be Enemies," *Canadian Jewish News*, May 22, 1964; Zaharkevich to editor, Montreal *Gazette*, May 27, 1960. The discussion of Ukrainian-Jewish relations within the respective heritage press of both groups was often strident in its hostility. The *Kanadiysky Farmer* (Winnipeg) ran an eight-part series entitled "Ukrainians and Jews" by M. Trykhrest between August 22 and October 10, 1970. It seemingly blamed Jews for every evil that had befallen Christendom, and Ukrainians in particular, from the crucifixion of Christ to the subjugation of Ukraine by the Soviets. At one point the article simply listed the names of more than 400 prominent Jews claimed to have been at the "centre" of the Bolshevik Revolution. The author summed up the Jewish role in history:

      History supplies us with no evidence that the Jews, being the spiritual captives of aggressive materialism, have ever stood in defence of any enslaved nations, or have ever taken a neutral position. On the contrary, the Jews have always stood on the side of the stronger, the oppressor, so that they themselves could benefit.

      M. Trykhrest, "Ukrainians and Jews" *Canadian Farmer*, August 22–October 10, 1970, as translated by Department of

Secretary of State, Translation Bureau, November 3, 1970, 18.

64 *Press Digest*, Vol. 16, no. 8, July 1960, 6–8.

65 CJC, CJCP, Ukrainian Canadian Committee, 1963 File, Kushnir to CJC, September 16, 1963; Commemorative Committee, "The Western Free World in the Shadow of the Cruelty of Russian Imperialism over the Ukraine and Other Nations in the USSR," September 1963; Hayes to Kushnir, September 30, 1963.

66 Howard Stanislawski, "Canadian Jews and Foreign Policy in the Middle East," in *The Canadian Jewish Mosaic*, M. Weinfeld, et al., eds. (Rexdale, 1981), 397–483.

67 PAC, R. Louis Ronson Papers: NJCRC, Ukrainian-Jewish Relations 1971–1975, Vol. 4, File 20, "Note for Remarks by the Prime Minister to the Ukrainian-Canadian Congress, Winnipeg, Manitoba, October 9, 1971," October 9, 1971.

68 Peter Worthington, "A Jew Who Helps Ukrainians," *The Toronto Sun*, November 29, 1972; PAC, R. Louis Ronson Papers: NJCRC, Ukrainian-Jewish Relations 1971–1975, Vol. 4, File 20, Kayfetz to Pearlson, et al., November 30, 1972.

69 Peter Worthington, "A New Dialogue Against Soviet Oppression," *Toronto Telegram*, July 23, 1971; PAC, R. Louis Ronson Papers: NJCRC, Ukrainian-Jewish Relations 1971–1975, Vol. 4, File 20, Memorandum Levy to Korey, July 28, 1971; Memorandum Korey to Levy, August 2, 1971.

70 Harold Troper and Lee Palmer, *Issues in Cultural Diversity* (Toronto, 1976), 87–101; *Report of the Royal Commission of Inquiry in Relation to the Conduct of the Public and the Metropolitan Toronto Police* (Toronto, 1972).

71 PAC, R. Louis Ronson Papers: NJCRC, Ukrainian-Jewish Memorandum Levy to Ronson, "Ukrainian Contacts with JCRC," August 5, 1971.

72 Similar sentiment abounded in the American Jewish community. See Abraham Brumberg, "Poland and the Jews," *Tikkun* (July/August 1987), 15–20, 85–90.

73 CJC-T, J.C. Hurwitz Papers: File 1, File July–December, 1974, Memorandum Kayfetz to Horwitz re: Relations with Ukrainian Canadians, September 9, 1974; Minutes, JCRC, Toronto, September 11, 1974, 6–8.

74 CJC-T, J.C. Hurwitz Papers: File 1, File July–December 1974, Epstein to Kayfetz, November 5, 1974.

75   CJC-T, J.C. Hurwitz Papers: File 1, File January–June 1975, Memorandum Kayfetz to Pearlson and Hurwitz re: "Ukrainian-Canadians," February 4, 1975.

76   PAC, R. Louis Ronson Papers: NJCRC, Ukrainian-Jewish Relations 1971–1975, Vol. 4, File 20, Memorandum Kayfetz to Harris, et al., March 25, 1975.

77   CJC-T, J.C. Hurwitz Papers: File 1, File January–June 1975, Memorandum Kayfetz to Harris, et al., re: "Continuing Conversations with Ukrainian Leadership," April 15, 1975; Report of Ben Kayfetz, re: "Meeting with Ukrainians," June 3, 1975.

78   CJC-T, J.C. Hurwitz Papers: File 1. File July–December 1976, Kayfetz to Pearlson, October 17, 1976; Telegram of Pearlson to UCC, October 15, 1976. The 1977 invitation to Rabbi Gunther Plaut, President of Congress, to attend the CJC 12th National Congress in Winnipeg was delivered although representatives from the CJC in Winnipeg attended. PAC, Gunther Plaut Papers: CJC Ukrainian-Jewish Dialogue, 1977–78. Bardyn to Plaut, September 12, 1977; Plaut to Bardyn, September 28, 1977.

79   PAC, R. Louis Ronson Papers: NJCRC, Ukrainian-Jewish Relations 1971–1975, Vol. 4, File 20, Telegram Pearlson to Bezchlibnyk reported in *Ukrainian Echo*, June 20, 1979; Sokolsky to Kayfetz, May 11, 1979; Memorandum Kayfetz to Pearlson, July 16, 1974 re: Ukrainians/Moroz.

80   PAC, Gunther Plaut Papers: CJC Ukrainian-Jewish Dialogue, 1977–78, Bardyn to Plaut, January 31, 1978; Kayfetz to Plaut, February 15, 1978; Plaut to Bardyn, February 17, 1978; Plaut to Bardyn, March 7, 1978.

81   *Canadian Jewish News*, April 28, 1970; PAC, Gunther Plaut Papers: CJC Ukrainian-Jewish Dialogue, 1977–78, Summary of an address to Ukrainian Professional and Business Club of Toronto, April 20, 1978; *The Globe and Mail*, April 22, 1978.

82   PAC, Gunther Plaut Papers: CJC Ukrainian-Jewish Dialogue, 1977–78, Memorandum of Plaut re: "Visit of Rabbi Plaut and Address to Ukrainian Professional and Business Club of Toronto, April 26, 1978," April 24, 1978.

83   PAC, R. Louis Ronson Papers: NJCRC, Ukrainian-Jewish Relations 1971–1975, Vol. 4, File 20, Memorandum Schachter to Kayfetz, May 30, 1978; Report by Schachter, "Meeting Between Representatives of W.J.C.C. and Ukrainian-Canadian Committee," May 29, 1978.

84 PAC, R. Louis Ronson Papers: NJCRC, Ukrainian-Jewish Relations 1971–1975, Vol. 4, File 20, Shymko to Epstein, December 2, 1977.

85 PAC, R. Louis Ronson Papers: NJCRC, Ukrainian-Jewish Relations 1971–1975, Vol. 4, File 20, Epstein to Ronson, December 16, 1977.

86 PAC, Gunther Plaut Papers: CJC, NJCRC, Memoranda (Pt. 1), 1977, Memorandum Kayfetz to Plaut et al. re: "Ukrainians," August 18, 1977.

87 PAC, R. Louis Ronson Papers: NJCRC, Ukrainian-Jewish Relations 1971–1975, Vol. 4, File 20, Relations 1971–1975, Vol. 4, File 20, Flyer entitled "Nazi Crimes in Przemysl (Poland)," n.d.

88 PAC, Gunther Plaut Papers: CJC, NJCRC, Memoranda (Pt. 1), 1977, Shymko to Kayfetz, August 8, 1977.

89 PAC, Gunther Plaut Papers: CJC, NJCRC, Memoranda (Pt. 1), 1977, Memorandum Kayfetz to Plaut et al. re: "Ukrainians," August 18, 1977.

90 For a comprehensive analysis of the concept of "war criminals" in the Canadian legal context, see Commission of Inquiry on War Criminals, *Report, Part I: Public* (Ottawa, 1986), 37–44.

91 See for example CJC-T, Catzman Papers, Memorandum Kayfetz to Catzman, et al., September 5, 1958; Kayfetz to Finestone, September 23, 1958.
Beyond passing on chance information on alleged war criminals in Canada to authorities and making repeated representations, there seemed little the Canadian Jewish Congress or Jews could do to arouse government or public. The case of Alexander Laak is a case in point. At a 1960 Congress National Executive meeting, discussion of federal immigration policy turned to the recent suicide of Alexander Laak, a naturalized Canadian citizen. Before coming to Canada Laak was accused of being the commandant of a Nazi concentration camp in Estonia. How, it was asked, could immigration authorities who reportedly knew of the accusations have allowed Laak and his sort into Canada unless the government decided to "intentionally allow these people in"?

But, if the position of the federal authorities was troubling, several Jewish leaders felt the view of some in the press was even worse. They were shocked when a *Globe and Mail* editorial, rather than demanding to know how an accused war criminal like Laak could gain Canadian entry and citizenship in Canada, seemed to condemn those who denounced Laak and might have pushed him to suicide. Reflecting the temper of the time, the paper suggested it was time for the victims to put bitter memories behind them even if forgiveness in this case meant that mass murderers would never face justice.

Did the federal government and Canadian people quietly endorse *The Globe and Mail*'s position? Perhaps so. The government "had whitewashed the whole affair," a Congress executive member lamented, "and the public was left with the impression that the man had been persecuted." It was obvious that fifteen years after the Holocaust ended most Canadians knew next to nothing of the genocidal crimes of the Nazis and cared less. CJC-T, Catzman Papers, Minutes of CJC National Executive Meeting, Montreal, September 11, 1960.

92   Hanna Arendt, *Eichmann in Jerusalem: A Report on the Banality of Evil* (New York, 1964) and Gideon Hausner, *Justice in Jerusalem* (London, 1967).

93   CJC, CJCP, Submissions to L.B. Pearson file, Memorandum Saalheimer to Garber, March 27, 1964; Prinz to Rusk, March 2, 1964; Garber to Martin, April 13, 1964.

94   CJC, CJCP, Submissions to L.B. Pearson file, Hayes to Coutts, October 1, 1964; Bronfman to Pearson, October 14, 1964.

95   Interview with Ben Kayfetz, August 9, 1986, Toronto; Stanley R. Barrett, *Is God A Racist: The Right Wing in Canada* (Toronto, 1987).

It was not long before these survivor groups were welcomed under Congress's umbrella. Survivor spokesmen were appointed to Congress committees, their voices increasingly heard, their priorities given special attention. Few questioned their moral authority.

But not all newly organized Jewish groups fit neatly into the Congress structure. In Toronto and Montreal the most important self-defence group remained for a time outside Congress. After first battling the neo-Nazis in the parks, N-3, named for Newton's Third Law — for every action there is an equal and opposite reaction — formalized their structure. They began self-defence training for members and eventually often provided security service at Jewish community meetings and gatherings. As the 1965 neo-Nazi scare subsided, N-3 turned its attention to unmasking war criminals living in Canada. Rumour had it that the group was gathering material for the Wiesenthal Documentation Center in Vienna.

Eventually absorbed into Congress, the N-3 spokesmen joined the survivors in pressuring Congress for a more militant and, at times, more confrontational response to any and all manifestations of anti-Semitism in Canadian society. They also demanded active lobbying of government to take legal action against alleged Nazi war criminals in Canada. Interview with Max Chirofsky, May 21, 1986, Toronto.

96 Past experience with naming had been none too successful. In 1962, for example, the editor of the then privately owned *Canadian Jewish News* made allegations about the wartime record of a central European newspaper editor in Canada. It was widely accepted within the Jewish community that the editor had been a Nazi activist and party organizer in his homeland. When the Nazis took power, he is alleged to have surfaced as a senior official in the Nazi puppet government and actively supported the implementation of the anti-Semitic Nuremberg-type laws against Jews in the new political jurisdiction. But the paper went further. It accused the editor of collaborating in Eichmann's wartime deportation of Jews to death in concentration camps.

The editor sued for libel. The case dragged on until the *CJN*, unable to produce solid evidence of its more damning charges, surrendered. The *CJN* was forced to recant and offer up a public apology. The lawsuit was dropped. Interview with Ben Kayfetz, August 9, 1986, Toronto; PAC, Imri Rosenberg Papers, Rosenberg to "Sir," August 3, 1962; Gasner to Rosenberg, August 8, 1962; Kayfetz to Rosenberg, August 20, 1962; Rosenberg to Gasner, August 13, 1962; Rosenberg to Kayfetz, August 21, 1962; Kayfetz to Rosenberg, October 27, 1962.

Nor was the larger public press immune to dangers inherent in naming. Almost ten years after the *CJN* incident, in the spring of 1971, *The London Free Press* ran a follow-up story about a Galicia Division member and previous resident of London then working as a janitor in Vancouver. He was reportedly accused of war crimes by Simon Wiesenthal. The story was picked up by the Vancouver *Sun*. In several articles over three days, the janitor was identified as having been chief of a Ukrainian Auxiliary Police unit which, Wiesenthal was said to have explained, took part in the murder of 10,000 Jews. A letter from Wiesenthal listing charges and containing the Nazi-hunter's evidence was allegedly on the way to Ottawa with a demand for legal action.

The janitor denied all and sued the Vancouver *Sun*. Under investigation, the Wiesenthal story began to crumble for lack of hard evidence. In a telephone interview with the *Sun*,

Wiesenthal reportedly named several witnesses who, he claimed, would corroborate his charges. They failed to do so. The janitor's counter-story held up.

With a lawsuit pending the *Sun* argued that the public's right to know, its right to place detailed information about the Wiesenthal accusation before the public, was paramount. The case never went to court. The paper had not, it claimed, intended to defame the janitor. The *Sun*, perhaps concluding its case was weak and the publicity from a lawsuit unwelcome, offered an out-of-court settlement. The janitor, content to avoid a costly trial and wishing only to be exonerated, dropped his suit. In addition to compensation, he received a letter from the *Sun*'s solicitor stating "the allegations that were made . . . were untrue."

The end of the janitor affair did not pass without comment from the UCC in London, Ontario, where the episode began. In a sharp rebuke to Wiesenthal, copied to local Jewish organizations and the Ukrainian press, a UCC spokesman attacked the Nazi-hunter. The letter allowed that the Nazis had indeed made use of Ukrainian collaborators. But, it claimed, Nazis also found willing Jews ready to serve their ends, just as the Soviets have since found both Ukrainians and Jews willing to serve their cause in Ukraine. Collaborators, both Ukrainian and Jewish, both pro-Nazi and pro-Soviet, had "committed heinous crimes against our people and against humanity in general . . . We feel therefore that every effort should be made to bring them to trial." But the letter warned against making a war criminal a case study in mass ethnic collaboration. "Since Nazi collaborators were in no way representative of either the Ukrainian or the Jewish people, but because members of the Auxiliary Police acted as individuals and served the interests of a foreign power, you will readily understand that Ukrainians are sensitive about being linked with activities of these criminals." Vancouver *Sun*, March 9, 10, 11, 12, 1971; Legal documentation and other materials pertaining to the incident are assembled as a package in CLC. Subject files: Legal Matters File. The package has been widely circulated through the Ukrainian community as an example of the false accusations of war criminality made periodically against Ukrainians; CIUS, UCC Civil Liberties Commission, 1985 File, Butler to Chrabatyn, May 10, 1972; UCC/Winnipeg Papers, Roslycky to Wiesenthal, April 5, 1971; PAC, R. Louis Ronson Papers: NJCRC, Ukrainian-Jewish Relations 1971–1975, Vol. 4, File 20, Roslychy to Kayfetz, April 5, 1971.

97 Interview with Monique Bégin, January 23, 1986, Montreal; commenting on her study for the Deschênes Commission, Alti Rodal noted that Pierre Trudeau's negative attitude towards action against war criminals in Canada was "politically motivated" and widely understood as such in Cabinet. *The Globe and Mail*, August 8, 1987; *The Gazette* (Montreal), August 12, 1987; *The Gazette* (Montreal), August 13, 1987; *The Gazette* (Montreal), August 19, 1987. In a luncheon talk at a conference in Montreal marking the fortieth anniversary of the Nuremberg trials, Trudeau spoke of his reluctance while prime minister to address the issue. It was, he said, just not a priority of his government. It was a problem "of previous times." He mused that the opening of the war-crimes issue could dredge up war-crimes allegations against the Allies and wondered where one could draw the line in trying to redress the past. Author's notes on Trudeau lecture, November 4, 1987, Montreal; *The Globe and Mail*, November 9, 1987.

98 PAC, Gunther Plaut Papers: CJC, JCRC 1966–67 (Pt. 1), Minutes of the National JCRC, Toronto, June 8, 1966.

99 PAC, Gunther Plaut Papers: CJC; War Criminals, Correspondence, 1977–80, Confidential Memorandum Rose to National Officers, October 7, 1974.

100 PAC, Gunther Plaut Papers: CJC, JCRC 1965–66, Minutes of National JCRC, Montreal, January 16, 1974.

101 See Allan A. Ryan, Jr., *Quiet Neighbors: Prosecuting Nazi War Criminals in America* (New York, 1984), 46–52.

102 CJC-T, J.C. Hurwitz Papers: File 1, File Jan.–June, 1975, Members of JCRC/Toronto, January 29, 1975; PAC, Gunther Plaut Papers: CJC Executive Committee Meetings, 1975–78, Memorandum Rose to National Executive, January 12, 1975; Memorandum Rose to National Executive, February 24, 1975; CJC-T, J.C. Hurwitz Papers: File 1, File Jan.–June, 1977, Minutes of JRCT/T March 30, 1977.

103 Ryan, *Quiet Neighbors*, 60–62, 66.

104 CJC-T, J.C. Hurwitz Papers: File 1, File Jan.–June 1977, Minutes of JCRC/T, March 30, 1977; Memorandum Cooper to Legal Committee, May, 26, 1977; Memorandum Cooper to Legal Committee re: Geneva Convention," June 1, 1977.

105 CJC-T, J.C. Hurwitz Papers: File 1, File July–Dec. 1977, Memorandum Kayfetz to Rose re: "War Crimes," July 19, 1977; interview with Kenneth Narvey, February 23, 1988, Montreal.

Chapter Four: The Stage Is Set

1   CJC-S, War Criminal Correspondence, 1977–78–79, Memorandum Weiss to Rose, June 2, 1977; PAC, Gunther Plaut Papers, CJC War Crimes, Roberts to Rose, September 16, 1977; Memorandum Rose to Satok, September 29, 1977; Rose to Roberts, November 4, 1977; Rose to Roberts, November 29, 1977.

2   CJC-S, War Crimes, Analysis of Legislation, Memorandum Hayes to Rose, April 11, 1978.

3   PAC, Gunther Plaut Papers, CJC War Crimes Project, Kenneth N. Narvey, Correspondence, Report, 1978, Rose to Narvey, May 1, 1978; Carr to Narvey, September 5, 1978; PAC, Gunther Plaut Papers, CJC War Crimes Project Correspondence, Report 1979, Rose to Narvey, November 21, 1978; CJC-S, War Crimes, Analysis of Legislation, Hayes to Rose, November 27, 1978; PAC, Gunther Plaut Papers, CJC War Crimes Project Correspondence, Report 1979, Carr to Rose, December 4, 1978; PAC, Gunther Plaut Papers, CJC War Crimes Project, Kenneth Narvey Correspondence, Report, 1978, Memorandum Rose to Brass re: "Kenneth Narvey," December 5, 1978; Narvey to Hayes, December 7, 1978; PAC, Gunther Plaut Papers, CJC War Crimes Project Correspondence, Report 1979, Minutes of the National Officers, Montreal, December 11, 1978; Carr to Rose, January 2, 1979; Rose to Narvey, January 24, 1979; Narvey to Plaut, January 19, 1979; *The Globe and Mail*, March 31, 1982; interview with Kenneth Narvey, February 23, 1988, Montreal.

4   Interview with Sabina Citron, January 28, 1988, Toronto; interview with Ben Kayfetz, September 10, 1986, Toronto.

5   Interview with Robert Kaplan, March 19, 1986, Ottawa.

6   House of Commons, Bill C-215, *An Act Respecting War Criminals in Canada*, October 30, 1978.

7   CJC-S, War Criminal Correspondence, 1977–78–79, Memorandum Hayes to Rose re: "War Criminals," February 28, 1979.

8   PAC, Gunther Plaut Papers, CJC Executive Committee Meetings, 1975–78, Memorandum to National Executive, Toronto, January 28, 1979; PAC, Gunther Plaut Papers, CJC War Criminals Correspondence, 1977–80, Rose to Roberts, December 28, 1978; PAC, Gunther Plaut Papers, CJC War Crimes Project Correspondence, Report 1979, Rose to Roberts, February 23, 1979.

9   *The Gazette* (Montreal), March 29, 1979.

10   CJC-S, War Criminal Correspondence, 1977–78–79, Schacter to Kayfetz, November 2, 1977; Kayfetz to Schacter, November 9, 1977; *Winnipeg Free Press*, November 2, 1977; PAC, Gunther Plaut Papers, CJC War Crimes Project, Kenneth Narvey, Correspondence, 1977, Memorandum Rose to Kayfetz, November 14, 1977.

11   *The Gazette* (Montreal), March 24, 1979; *The Toronto Star*, April 1, 1979.

12   PAC, Gunther Plaut Papers, CJC, Federal Republic of Germany, Statute of Limitations, Correspondence, Telegrams, "Statute of Limitations on Nazi War Crimes — Progress Report," January 22, 1979.

13   PAC, Gunther Plaut Papers, CJC, Federal Republic of Germany, Statute of Limitations, Correspondence, Telegrams, Telegram Jamieson to Plaut, Satok, Rose, March 9, 1979; Montreal *Star*, March 14, 1979; *The Toronto Sun*, March 14, 1979.

14   Nor was the statute of limitations debate without its Canadian spillover. If it again highlighted Jewish community concern for rooting out Nazi war criminals, it also served to educate some parliamentarians about the unfinished business of the Holocaust. One MP, noting that 1979 had been declared the United Nations' International Year of the Child, tied this special year and the Holocaust together in a personal appeal to German Chancellor Schmidt.
The passage of time has not dulled or mitigated in any way the cruelty and horror of these [Holocaust] acts; if the race of man is to ensure that such crimes are not repeated, I would respectfully suggest that those who committed them should not be offered, even inadvertently, what amounts to amnesty . . . When we consider that of the millions of victims of the Second World War, hundreds of thousands of them were innocent children, surely there is no more basic tribute to their memory from individuals and nations than a refusal to allow their murderers to rest.
PAC, Gunther Plaut Papers, CJC, Federal Republic of Germany, Statute of Limitations, Correspondence, Telegrams, Telegram Plaut, Rose, Beer to Schmidt, July 5, 1979.

15   PAC, Gunther Plaut Papers, CJC War Crimes Project Correspondence, Report 1979, "Questions re: War Crimes posed to Candidates by North American Jewish Students' Network, April 30, 1979 with answers by Mr Ed Broadbent and Mr Joe

Clark"; *The Globe and Mail*, May 19, 1979; *Canadian Jewish News*, May 17, 1979.

This poll was not the only sample of partisan opinion on the issue of war criminals. A Congress questionnaire prepared by Kenneth Narvey and addressed to all Toronto-area candidates asked each about the German statute of limitations and Nazi war criminals in Canada. The results seemed heartening, although Congress leaders were only too aware of the difference between election-time promises and post-election delivery. Liberal candidates made the best of their government's long record of inaction. They boasted of government intervention with German authorities on the statute of limitations, and individual candidates declared themselves in favour of RCMP investigation of specified allegations against individuals.

The Conservatives were still more assertive. They promised that should they form the next government they would take immediate action to root out Nazi war criminals. The Conservative candidate for the heavily Jewish Toronto riding of St Paul's, lawyer Ron Atkey, went still further. He sent Congress a copy of a letter previously sent to the federal Solicitor General voicing concern about Nazi war criminals in Canada and offering his assistance to federal "officials in pursuing this matter and bringing war criminals to justice under Canadian law." PAC, Gunther Plaut Papers, CJC War Crimes Project Correspondence, Report 1979, Atkey to Lalonde, March 19, 1979; "Materials on Progressive Conservative Policy with Respect to Alleged War Criminals Resident in Canada," August 15, 1979; *Canadian Jewish News*, May 10, 1979; interview with Kenneth Narvey, February 23, 1988, Montreal.

16 PAC, Gunther Plaut Papers, CJC War Crimes Project Correspondence, Report 1979, Narvey to Hayes, June 7, 1979.

17 PAC, Gunther Plaut Papers, CJC Executive Committee Meetings, 1975–78, Minutes of CJC National Officers, Toronto, September 5, 1979; PAC, Gunther Plaut Papers, CJC War Crimes Project Correspondence, Report 1979, Plaut to Rose, August 16, 1979.

18 Interview with Eddy Goldenberg, March 20, 1986, Ottawa.

19 David Taras, "Canada and the Arab-Israeli Conflict: A Study of the Yom Kippur War and the Domestic Political Climate" (unpublished Ph.D. thesis, University of Toronto, 1983); David DeWitt, *Canada as a Principal Power* (Toronto, 1983), 389–93, 396–400; Howard J. Stanislawski, "Elites, Domestic Interest Groups, and International Interests in the Canadian

Foreign Decision Making Process (unpublished Ph.D. thesis, Brandeis University, 1981), 324–53.

20 PAC, Gunther Plaut Papers, CJC, NCRC, Memoranda (Pt. 3), 1979, Memorandum Kayfetz to Wolfe re: "Sabina Citron," November 16, 1979.

21 PAC, Gunther Plaut Papers, CJC, NCRC, Memoranda (Pt. 3), 1979, Memorandum of Kayfetz to Plaut, re "Wiesenthal," November 20, 1979.

22 CJC-S, War Criminal Correspondence, 1977–78–79, Plaut to Wiesenthal, February 8, 1980.

23 CIWC, Memorandum Bissonnette to Kaplan re: War Crimes, March 6, 1980.

24 Interview with Monique Bégin, January 23, 1986, Montreal; interview with Robert Kaplan, March 19, 1986, Ottawa; interview with Irwin Cotler, March 28, 1986, Montreal.

25 CIWC, Memorandum Bissonette to Kaplan, re: War Crimes, March 6, 1980.

26 CIWC, Memorandum Director, Security Policy Division to file re: war criminals, March 10, 1980; Memo Senior ADM, Police and Jury Branch, from Deputy Solicitor General re: war criminals, March 17, 1980; Bissonette to Simmonds, April 9, 1980.

27 "Kaplan Reacts to Photos," *Images* 1:6 (April 15, 1980); interview with Eddy Goldenberg, March 20, 1986, Ottawa.

28 Interview with Roger Tassé, March 20, 1986, Ottawa; interview with Eddy Goldenberg, March 20, 1988, Ottawa.

29 Interview with Robert Kaplan, March 19, 1986, Ottawa; *The Jewish Post* (Winnipeg), October 16, 1980; *The Ottawa Citizen*, January 29, 1981; interview with Kenneth Narvey, February 23, 1988, Montreal.

30 Discussion Paper (Ministry of Justice), "Alleged War Criminals in Canada," March 1981. For a critique of the Report see David Matas and Susan Charendoff, *Justice Delayed: Nazi War Criminals in Canada* (Toronto, 1987), 117–38.

31 CIWC, Kaplan to Arsano, March 8, 1982; Kaplan to Simmonds, October 10, 1981.

32 Interview with Robert Kaplan, March 19, 1986, Ottawa.

33 Interview with Robert Kaplan, March 19, 1986, Ottawa.

34 *Canadian Jewish News*, April 23, 1981.

35   PAC, Louis Ronson Papers: NJCRC, War Criminals Issue, 1961–82, Vol. 4, File 7, Cotler to Kaplan June 30, 1981; Memorandum Araf to Leadership, October 6, 1981.

36   Interview with Irwin Cotler, March 28, 1986, Montreal,

37   CIWC, Cotler to Kaplan, January 22, 1981; interview with David Matas, December 10, 1986.

38   CJC-S, War Criminal Correspondence, 1982, Smolach to Trudeau, June 17, 1982; Karstadt to Kayfetz, June 17, 1982; Memorandum Kayfetz to Cotler, June 25, 1982; Urman to Smolach, June 26, 1982.

39   Interview with Irwin Cotler, February 21, 1986, Montreal; interview with Kenneth Narvey, February 23, 1988, Montreal.

40   Interview with David Matas, March 29, 1986, Toronto.

41   Interview with David Matas, March 29, 1986, Toronto. For a study of the Rauca case, see Sol Littman, *War Criminal on Trial: The Rauca Case* (Toronto, 1983). The tumult of the Rauca proceedings raised concerns that other wanted Nazi war criminals might be living comfortably in Canada. In late August 1982 *Today* magazine published an article about Harold Puntulis who, like Rauca, had lived quietly in suburban Toronto for many years and who, also like Rauca, had reportedly participated in the murder of thousands of Jews in the Baltic countries during World War II. But Puntulis escaped justice forever; he died peacefully only a few weeks before the magazine article was published. Jeff Ansell and Paul Appleby, "The War Criminal," *Today* magazine, August 28, 1982.

42   Irving Abella and Harold Troper, *None Is Too Many: Canada and the Jews of Europe, 1933–1948* (Toronto, 1982). Indicative of the controversy generated by the book, *None Is Too Many* was on Canadian best-seller lists for almost a year.

43   CJC-S, War Criminal Correspondence, 1982, Cotler to MacGuigan, December 22, 1982; interview with Irwin Cotler, March 28, 1986, Montreal.

44   Interview with Les Scheininger, March 25, 1987, Toronto.

45   MHP, Memorandum Diamon and Narvey to Urman, re: "CJC continuing role in the Rauca case," March 21, 1983.

46   Interview with Milton Harris, May 10, 1986, Toronto.

47   MHP, War Crimes Files, Cotler to Harris, February 2, 1983; CJC-S, War Crimes — Cross Canada Campaign, Aide Memoire "Proposed Cross-Can of National Organizations, Febru-

ary 10, 1983"; CJC-S, War Criminal Correspondence, 1977–78–79, Cotler to Matas, February 7, 1983; CJC-S War Crimes Correspondence, 1983, Cotler to Zablow, February 7, 1983.

48 MHP, War Crimes Files, Raphael to Matas, July 28, 1983.

49 CIWC, Kaplan to Simmonds, March 30, 1983; Kaplan to Simmonds, April 12, 1983; *The Gazette* (Montreal), March 23, 1983.

50 CJC-S, War Crimes Correspondence, 1983, Memorandum Archibald to Sternberg, re: "War Criminals Petition," March 22, 1983; MHP, War Crimes Files, "War Criminals: Draft Mobilization Plan" (n.d.); MacIsaac to Kayfetz, April 21, 1983; Kayfetz to Silverberg, April 29, 1983; *The Toronto Star*, April 14, 1983.

51 MHP, War Crimes Files Rose to Kaplan, March 4, 1983; Kaplan to Rose, March 17, 1983; *Canadian Jewish News*, May 19, 1983.

52 MHP, War Crimes Files, Memorandum Amerasinghe to Christie and Rutherford re: "Opinion — Nazi War Criminals Revocation of Citizenship," May 27, 1983.

53 CIWC, Kaplan to MacGuigan, July 7, 1983.

54 Interview with Milton Harris, May 10, 1986, Toronto.

55 MHP, War Crimes Files, Report of the Legal Committee on War Crimes, (Supplementary) Canadian Jewish Congress, September 1983; interview with David Matas, March 29, 1986, Toronto; interview with Milton Harris, May 10, 1986, Toronto. Much of the brief Matas took to the B'nai Brith was published. League for Human Rights of B'nai Brith, *One Is Too Many: Nazi War Criminals in Canada* (Toronto, 1984).

56 CIWC, MacGuigan to Kaplan, December 8, 1983; interview with Milton Harris, May 10, 1986, Toronto.

57 CIWC, Kaplan to Jensen, December 12, 1983.

58 MHP, War Crimes Files, Raphael to Harris, March 13, 1984.

59 MHP, War Crimes Files, "War Criminals in Canada," (n.d.).

60 CIWC, Simmons to Kaplan, Arpil 30, 1984.

61 MHP, War Crimes Files, Raphael to Harris, March 23, 1984.

62 MHP, War Crimes Files, Kaplan to Harris, March 29, 1984.

63 MHP, War Crimes Files, Harris to Granovsky, January 8, 1985; at the same time, Narvey and Network were also pressing MacGuigan to try the option of trial in Canada to deal with Nazi war criminals in Canada. MacGuigan was not persuaded. Interview with Kenneth Narvey, February 23, 1988, Montreal; KNP, MacGuigan to Narvey, June 28, 1984.

64 MHP, War Crimes Files, Harris to Johnson, July 5, 1984.

65 Harold Waller and Morton Weinfeld, "A *Viewpoints* Survey of Canadian Jewish Leadership Opinion," *Viewpoints* 15 (Supplement to *Canadian Jewish News*, October 8, 1987), 1–3; during the election efforts were made by the B'nai Brith to sensitize candidates on items of Jewish concern, including the problem of Nazi war criminals in Canada. Meetings were held with approximately one hundred candidates, but not with the leadership candidates. Interview with Frank Dimant, January 28, 1988, Toronto; Network and Kenneth Narvey polled the three party leaders. Each indicated concern for the issue but offered no concrete plan of action. Interview with Kenneth Narvey, February 23, 1988, Montreal.

66 MHP, War Crimes Files, MacKay to Raphael, November 13, 1984; Crosbie to Raphael, November 19, 1984; Raphael to Harris, November 21, 1984.

67 MHP, War Crimes Files, Harris to Granovsky, January 8, 1985.

68 Littman, *War Criminal on Trial*.

69 In 1980 Littman ran afoul of the Galicia Division after writing an article on the search for Nazi war criminals in Canada for *The Sunday Star*. *The Sunday Star* (Toronto), August 8, 1980.

70 Interview with Sol Littman, January 2, 1986, Toronto; interview with Sol Littman, May 7, 1986, Toronto; interview with Sol Littman, February 29, 1988, Toronto.

71 Sol Littman, "Agent of the Holocaust, The Secret Life of Helmut Rauca," *Saturday Night*, July 1983, 11–23; Littman, *War Criminals on Trial*, iv.

72 Interview with Robert Kaplan, March 19, 1986, Ottawa.

73 Interview with Sol Littman, January 28, 1986, Toronto; while Littman met with MacKay, Narvey joined Congress and other Jewish leaders in inviting Justice officials. KNP, Narvey to Crosbie, November 19, 1984; Good to Narvey, January 5, 1985.

74   CIWC, Littman to Mulroney, December 20, 1984.

75   Interview with Sol Littman, May 7, 1986, Toronto.

76   Interview with Michael Meighen, May 15, 1987, Toronto.

77   Interview with Sol Littman, October 22, 1986, Toronto; *The Toronto Star*, January 23, 1985; *The New York Times*, January 23, 1985.

78   Interview with Bernard J. Finestone, May 22, 1986, Montreal; interview with Michael Meighen, May 15, 1987, Toronto.

79   Interview with Michael Meighen, May 15, 1987, Toronto; interview with Dr. D. Pivnicki, July 4, 1987, Montreal.

80   Interview with Geoff Norquay, March 21, 1986, Ottawa; Interview with Richard Cleroux, July 8, 1986, Ottawa.

81   Interview with Milton Harris, May, 10, 1986, Toronto.

82   Interview with Geoff Norquay, March 21, 1986, Ottawa; Interview with Frank Dimant, January 28, 1988, Toronto.

83   Interview with Geoff Norquay, March 21, 1986, Ottawa.

84   Interview with Michael Meighen, May 15, 1987, Toronto.

85   Interview with Geoff Norquay, March 21, 1986, Ottawa.

86   Interview with Les Scheininger, March 26, 1987, Toronto.

87   Interview with Milton Harris, May 10, 1986, Toronto; MHP, War Crimes Files, P.C. 1985–348, Minutes of a Meeting of the Committee of the Privy Council, February 7, 1985.

88   CJC-S, Deschênes Commission, Press Releases, Newspaper Clippings, CJC Press Release, "Canadian Jewish Congress President Says War Criminal Commission Not Enough," February 7, 1985.

89   *The Sunday Sun* (Toronto), February 10, 1985; Documentation Center, *Bulletin of Information No. 25*, Vienna, January 21, 1985; *The Globe and Mail*, February 11, 1985; Ironically, Littman publicly eschewed the label of "Nazi-hunger." "I've never been a hunter. I've never hunted anything or anyone. I've never played policeman and I don't choose to do so," Littman later explained. "I'm essentially an investigative reporter, a sociologist and historian trying to bring out the facts about certain historical situations." The Ukrainian community, of course, thought otherwise. *Ukrainian Canadian*, March 1986. For a discussion of the numbers game, see Com-

mission of Inquiry on War Criminals, *Report, Part I: Public* (Ottawa, 1986), 243–48.

90   Interview with Bohdan Krawchenko, March 15, 1987, Ottawa.

91   Interview with Father John Tataryn, May 27, 1986, Toronto; Interview with Andrew Witer, March 20, 1986, Ottawa; Boris Zayachkowski, "On Target, Deschênes Commission" *Student*, December 1985, 3, 10.

92   *Winnipeg Free Press*, February 12, 1985.

93   Interview with John Nowosad, May 30, 1986, Winnipeg.

94   CIUS, UCC Civil Liberties Commission, 1985 File, "Press Release, February 13, 1985, 1:30 p.m.," Ukrainian Canadian Committee, Alberta Provincial Council, Edmonton.

95   Interview with John Gregorovich, March 12, 1986, Toronto; BBP, Deschênes Commission File, "Press Release, Ukrainian Canadian Committee National Executive, February 14, 1985"; *The Bulletin* (UCC), Vol. 33 (January-March, 1985), 2–4; interview with Yaroslaw Botiuk, June 4, 1987, Toronto; interview with Roman Serbyn, February 18, 1986, Montreal; interview with Andrew Witer, May 20, 1986, Ottawa; interview with Father John Tataryn, May 20, 1986, Toronto.

96   *The Sunday Star* (Toronto), August 8, 1980; *The Sunday Star* (Toronto), June 8, 1980.

97   *The Globe and Mail*, February 15, 1985; CIUS, UCC Civil Liberties Commission, 1985 File, "Historical Note on the Ukrainian Division, Ukrainian Canadian Committee Press Conference in Toronto, February 14, 1985."

98   JCRC Papers, Ukrainian File, Epstein to Satok, February 11, 1985; Interview with Alex Epstein, May 10, 1986, Toronto.

99   JCRC Papers, Ukrainian File, Satok to Epstein, February 13, 1985.

100 Interview with John Gregorovich, April 8, 1987, Toronto.

101 SWC, "Radio Commentary – February, 1985." A manuscript of Father Stasiw's broadcast in English translation and a copy of the transcript in Ukrainian were given to Sol Littman by the attorneys for CHIN radio. SWC, Eddenberg to Rabinowitz, April 22, 1985; Rabinowitz to Littman, April 22, 1985. Interview with Father Myran Stasiw, April 14, 1988, Toronto. For a lengthy recent articulation of similar views, see Yurij Chumatskyj, *Why Is One Holocaust Worth More Than Others?* (Baulkham Hills, NSW, Australia, 1986).

102 *New Perspectives*, May 1985.

103 Paul Evans, "A Blind Eye to Murder: National Socialist War Criminals in Canada," *The New Edition* 6 (February 5, 1985), 8–9, 16.

104 Interview with Yury Boshyk, February 3, 1986 and March 4, 1987, Toronto.

105 YBP, "A Public Appeal for Funds," Memorandum of the Organizing Committee (n.d.); "Press Release: By Journal of Ukrainian Studies Re: Conference on Ukraine and Ukrainians During World War II" (n.d.); BBP, UCC File, Letter Boshyk to Shefman (n.d.).

106 JCRC Papers, Ukrainian File, Kayfetz to Wolfe, Memorandum, "Seminar on Ukrainians in World War II," March 4, 1985; Most of the symposium papers were assembled, copy-edited and published: Yury Boshyk, ed., *Ukraine During World War II: History and Its Aftermath* (Edmonton, 1986).

107 YBP, Czich to Boshyk, March 3, 1985; Taras Hunczak, "Ukrainian-Jewish Relations During the Soviet and Nazi Occupations," in Boshyk, *Ukraine During World War II*, 39–57.

108 Lubomyr Luciuk, "A Proposal Concerning the Formation of a Research and Documentation Group by the Ukrainian Canadian Committee," February 23, 1985.

109 Interview with Yury Boshyk, March 4, 1986, Toronto.

110 Interview with John Gregorovich, March 12, 1986, Toronto; interview with John Nowosad, May 30, 1986, Winnipeg.

111 Ukrainians thought the name well chosen. But the name was not greeted with pleasure by the Canadian Civil Liberties Association. The Association worried that the public might confuse the two organizations; in early 1987 the two organizations would clash on exactly that point.

112 Interview with John Gregorovich, March 12, 1986, Toronto; CIUS, UCC Civil Liberties Commission, 1985 File, J.B. Gregorovich, Résumé (1985).

113 Interview with Bohdan Krawchenko, March 15, 1987, Ottawa.

114 JGP, "Civil Liberties Commission of the Ukrainian Committee" (n.d.), (CANCO 2.5).

115 JGP, Memorandum of UCC, Toronto Branch, to Members of the Ukrainian Community (n.d.).

116   CLCP, Community Action Group File, "Local Political Action — Visitation to Your Local M.P." (n.d.); "Sample Letters for *Guidelines* Only" (n.d.); CIUS, UCC Civil Liberties Commission, 1985 File, postcard.

117   YBP, L.Y. Luciuk, "The Ukrainian Canadian Committee's Civil Liberties Commission: Its Research Groups Members and Budgetary Requirements," April 21, 1985; interview with Orest Rudzik, March 31, 1987, Toronto.

118   YBP, Discussion Paper by JBG, "Coping with Anti-Ukrainianism" (n.d.), (CANCO 1.15).

119   Phone conversation with Yaroslaw Botiuk, March 19, 1987, Toronto.

120   YBP, JBG "Coping with Anti-Ukrainianism," (n.d.), (CANCO 1.15).

121   Interview with Irwin Cotler, February 21, 1986, Montreal; interview with David Matas, March 29, 1986, Toronto.

122   Interview with Milton Harris, May 10, 1985, Toronto.

Chapter Five: One is Too Many

1   CIWC, Submission by Marika Bandera, May 1, 1985; interview with Marika Bandera, February 10, 1988, Toronto; *The Globe and Mail*, May 2, 1985.

2   CIWC, "Report on the Presence of War Criminals in Canada," by Sol Littman, Canadian Representative of Simon Wiesenthal Center, April 24, 1985, 10–11; Commission of Inquiry on War Criminals, *Proceedings* 3 (1985), 366.

3   CIWC, Unclassified Public Exhibit, Littman to Deschênes, May 2, 1985.

4   Cited in Petro Mirchuk, *In the German Mills of Death* (New York, 1976); CIWC, Submission by Bandera, May 1, 1985; interview with Marika Bandera, February 10, 1988, Toronto.

5   CIWC, Littman, "Report on the Presence of War Criminals in Canada," 4; Commission of Inquiry, *Proceedings* 3 (1985), 359–61.

6   Interview with Sol Littman, May 7, 1986, Toronto.

7   CIWC, Submission by Bandera, May 1, 1985.

8   Commission of Inquiry on War Criminals, *Report, Part I: Public* (Ottawa, 1986), 17–19.

9   Interview with David Matas, March 29, 1987, Ottawa; interview with Milton Harris, May 10, 1986, Toronto; interview with Les Scheininger, March 25, 1987, Toronto; interview with Frank Dimant, January 28, 1988, Toronto; interview with Kenneth Narvey, February 23, 1988, Montreal.

10 Interview with Les Scheininger, March 25, 1987, Toronto.

11 Interview with David Matas, March 29, 1987, Ottawa.

12 *The Globe and Mail*, April 25, 1985; interview with John Gregorovich, March 12, 1986, Toronto.

13 Interview with Yaroslaw Botiuk, March 17, 1987, Toronto.

14 Interview with Orest Rudzik, March 31, 1987, Toronto.

15 Interview with Yves Fortier, April 21, 1987, Montreal; interview with John Gregorovich, March 12, 1986, Toronto.

16 Biographical data on Deschênes, Fortier and Meighen from *Who's Who in Canada*, Heather Kerrigan (ed.), (Agincourt, 1987).

17 "Proposal concerning a definition of the term 'minority,'" submitted by Judge Jules Deschênes, United Nations Economic and Social Council, Commission on Human Rights, Sub-Commission on Prevention of Discrimination and Protection of Minorities, 38th session, Item 16 of the provisional agenda, E/CN. 4Sub2/1985/31, May 14, 1985.

18 United Nations Economic and Social Council, E/CN.4/Sub.2/1985/SR.16 20 August, 1985.

19 CJC-S, Commission of Inquiry, Correspondence, 1985, Silverstone to Harris, September 4, 1985.

20 *The Sword and the Scales* (Toronto, 1979), 187.

21 *The Globe and Mail*, November 12, 1985.

22 Interview with Bernard Finestone, May 22, 1986, Montreal.

23 *The Globe and Mail*, November 12, 1985.

24 Interview with Michael Meighen, May 15, 1987, Toronto. Even after the Commission was completed, Deschênes refrained from public comment on this issue. Interview with Judge Jules Deschênes, November 12, 1987, Montreal.

25 Interview with Yves Fortier, April 21, 1987, Montreal; interview with Michael Meighen, May 15, 1987, Toronto.

26   Interview with Judge Jules Deschênes, November 12, 1987, Montreal; interview with Geoff Norquay, March 21, 1986, Ottawa.

27   Gordon R. Bohdan Panchuk, *Heroes of Their Day: The Reminiscences of Bohdan Panchuk*, Lubomyr Luciuk, ed. (Toronto, 1983).

28   CLCP, CLC-Internal, Luciuk to Sopinka, September 9, 1985.

29   Interview with Yves Fortier, April 21, 1987, Montreal; interview with Alti Rodal, July 9, 1986, Ottawa; interview with Paula Draper, May 9, 1986, Toronto; interview with Michael Meighen, May 15, 1987, Toronto.

30   Interview with Yaroslaw Botiuk, June 4, 1987, Toronto.

31   Commission of Inquiry, *Proceedings* 19 (1985), 2428–2437; interview with Yaroslaw Botiuk, June 4, 1987, Toronto.

32   Interview with Milton Harris, May 10, 1986, Toronto; interview with Les Scheininger, March 25, 1987, Toronto; interview with Irwin Cotler, February 21, 1986, Montreal; interview with David Matas, March 29, 1986, Toronto.

33   Interview with John Gregorovich, March 31, 1987, Toronto.

34   Interview with Orest Rudzik, March 31, 1987, Toronto; interview with John Gregorovich, April 8, 1987, Toronto; interview with John Sopinka, May 27, 1987, Toronto.

35   Interview with John Sopinka, May 27, 1987, Toronto.

36   Interview with Yves Fortier, April 21, 1985, Montreal; interview with Michael Meighen, May 15, 1987, Toronto; interview with John Sopinka, May 26, 1987, Toronto.

37   Commission of Inquiry, *Report*, 851.

38   *The Globe and Mail*, May 3, 1985.

39   CIWC, Unclassified Public Exhibits, Littman to Mulroney, March 25, 1985.

40   CIWC, Littman, "Report on the Presence of War Criminals in Canada," April 24, 1985; interview with Sol Littman, June 21, 1986, Toronto; Commission of Inquiry, *Proceedings* 3 (1985), 369–70.

41   *Maclean's*, March 11, 1985, 47–48.

42   Commission of Inquiry, *Report*, 246–47.

43   PYP, John Sopinka, Submission of the Ukrainian Canadian Committee, May 5, 1985; League of Human Rights of B'nai

Brith, *One Is Too Many: Nazi War Criminals in Canada* (Toronto, 1984).

44   CIWC, Littman, "Report on the Presence of War Criminals in Canada," 15; Commission of Inquiry, *Proceedings* 3 (1985), 370.

45   Canadian Press 1639 ES 25-04-85. For a listing of who supplied names to the Commission and how many, see Commission of Inquiry, *Report*, 47–52.

46   Interview with Michael Meighen, May 15, 1987, Toronto; Commission of Inquiry, *Report*, 58.

47   Commission of Inquiry, *Report*, 67–82; Canadian Press 2137 ED 01-05-85; Commission of Inquiry, *Proceedings* 5 (1985), 529–585, 618–626.

48   Not all such cases involved people who were household names. German scientists and technicians admitted to Canada after the war were also investigated by the Deschênes Commission. See Commission of Inquiry, *Report*, 776–826.

49   Canadian Press 1833 ED 03-05-85; Commission of Inquiry, *Proceedings* 6 (1985), 670–777, 778–834; Canadian Press 1940 ED 03-05-85.

50   Commission of Inquiry, *Proceedings* 7 (1985), 891–972; Canadian Press 1953 ED 08-05-85.

51   Commission of Inquiry, *Proceedings* 8 (1985), 985–1079; Canadian Press 1515 ED 09-05-85.

52   Memoranda as quoted in *The Toronto Star*, November 6, 1985.

53   *The Gazette* (Montreal), June 2, 1986. A detailed review of the government's actions on war criminals can be found in the study produced by Commission researcher Alti Rodal, entitled "Nazi War Criminals in Canada: The Historical and Policy Setting from the 1940s to the Present," (unpublished Paper) Ottawa, 1986.

54   CIWC, *Report*, 26–27; *Winnipeg Free Press*, October 3, 1985.

55   *The Gazette* (Montreal), October 3, 1985.

56   *The Toronto Star*, October 10, 1985; Commission of Inquiry, *Proceedings* 20 (1985), 2610, 2613.

57   *Winnipeg Free Press*, October 12, 1985; *The Ottawa Citizen*, October 11, 1985; David Matas and Susan Charendoff, *Justice Delayed: Nazi War Criminals in Canada* (Toronto, 1987), 84–88.

58   *The Toronto Sun*, October 27, 1985; Press Release, Employment and Immigration Canada, October 24, 1985.

59   *The Gazette* (Montreal), November 9, 1985.

60   *The Ottawa Citizen*, December 4, 1985. The media reports of possible bungling on the part of Canadian archivists cast a cloud over the profession. The charge rankled, and Terry Cook, chief of Social Affairs and National Resources Records at the Public Archives of Canada, tried to set the record straight. In an August 11, 1986 *Globe and Mail* article, he pointed out that immigration files were normally destroyed after a two- to five-year retention period. Thus the vast majority of pre-1950 files would have been destroyed by 1960. Moreover, keeping all five million immigrant files would "triple the Government's entire archival holdings for all departments." Retaining a sample of files was the only option.

61   *The Toronto Star*, December 26, 1985. For a review of the Bernonville story see Sol Littman, "Barbie's Buddy in Canada," *Canadian Dimension* (October 1987), 13–15.

62   *The Gazette* (Montreal) December 6, 1985; Commission of Inquiry, *Proceedings* 24 (1985), 3336.

63   *The Toronto Star*, Friday, December 6, 1985; Commission of Inquiry, *Proceedings* 24 (1985), 3363–64.

64   *Kitchener-Waterloo Record*, December 7, 1985.

65   For a list of the scholars and their studies, see Commission of Inquiry, *Report, Part I*, 859; interview with Irwin Cotler, March 28, 1986, Montreal; interview with David Matas, March 29, 1986, Toronto; Matas and Charendoff, *Justice Delayed*, 240–45.

66   *The Globe and Mail*, January 30, 1986.

67   Interview with Irwin Cotler, March 6, 1987, Montreal.

68   *The Ottawa Citizen*, February 13, 1986.

69   Interview with Irwin Cotler, March 6, 1987, Montreal.

70   *Winnipeg Free Press*, May 14, 1986; Commission of Inquiry on War Criminals, *Report*, 917–25.

71   *The Gazette* (Montreal), June 17, 1986; Matas and Charendoff, *Justice Delayed*, 245.

72   *The Ottawa Citizen*, April 25, 1986.

73   *The Ottawa Citizen*, May 10, 1986.

74   *The Ottawa Citizen*, May 8, 1986.

75 *The Ottawa Citizen*, May 9, 1986.

76 *The Globe and Mail*, May 29, 1986.

77 *The Globe and Mail*, May 31, 1986.

78 *The Toronto Sun*, June 1, 1986; interview with Jack Silverstone, January 14, 1987, Montreal. For a more critical view of the decision not to take evidence in the Soviet Union, see Matas and Charendoff, *Justice Delayed*, 201–208.

79 *Canadian Jewish News*, June 12, 1986; *The Toronto Star*, June 5, 1987.

80 The UCC submission was published and distributed widely as part of the CLC's ongoing lobbying effort. *Ukrainian Canadian Committee Submission to the Commission of Inquiry on War Criminals* (Toronto, 1986).

81 CIWC, Littman, "Report on the Presence of War Criminals in Canada," April 24, 1985. Commission of Inquiry, *Proceedings* 3 (1985), 356, 360–361. In making this claim, Littman was not out in left field. The identical point of view — that Jews accused of war crimes should likewise be prosecuted — was stressed by Alan Rose of Congress and by Neal Sher, director of the American OSI, Interview with Alan Rose, February 19, 1986, Montreal; interview with Neal Sher, December 31, 1986, Washington.

82 BBP, Deschênes Commission File, Matas, "Submission of the League for Human Rights of B'nai Brith Canada to the Commission of Inquiry on Nazi War Criminals in Canada," May 22, 1985. Commission of Inquiry, *Proceedings* 12 (1985), 1456–60.

83 CIWC, "Government Inaction in the Matter of Bringing Suspected Nazi War Criminals to Justice, Submission and Reply by the Canadian Jewish Congress to the Commission of Inquiry on War Criminals," Submitted by Irwin Cotler, December 4, 1985, 8–10; Commission of Inquiry, *Proceedings* 24 (1985), 3397–401.

84 For a detailed discussion of the Low Report and the rebuttal of that report, see Matas and Charendoff, *Justice Delayed*, 117–38.

85 CIWC, Irwin Cotler "Government Inaction," December 4, 1985. See note 87; Commission of Inquiry, *Proceedings* 24 (1985), 3402–8.

86 CJC-J, Commission of Inquiry Correspondence, 1985, September 7, 1985, Matas speech at Shaare Zedek in Montreal.

87 Congress submitted four key briefs, all over the signature of Irwin Cotler, Congress counsel. These were: CWIC, "Submissions and Recommendations of the Canadian Jewish Congress to the Commission of Inquiry on War Criminals," July 10, 1985; "Government Inaction in the Matter of Bringing Suspected Nazi War Criminals to Justice, Submission and Reply by the Canadian Jewish Congress to the Commission of Inquiry on War Criminals," December 4, 1985; "Dossier: A Documentary Record in the Matter of Bringing Suspected Nazi War Criminals in Canada to Justice, Forty Years of Government Inaction — Raising a Reasonable Apprehension of Obstruction of Justice," December 11, 1985; "Closing Submission and Recommendations of the Canadian Jewish Congress to the Commission Inquiry," July 29, 1986. The latter is summarized in Commission of Inquiry, *Proceedings* 27 (1985), 3644–725. The major B'nai Brith brief was "Submission of the League for Human Rights of B'nai Brith Canada to the Commission of Inquiry on Nazi War Criminals in Canada," by Frank Dimant, David Matas, Bert Raphael, May 22, 1985. BBP, Deschênes Commission File, Matas "Submission of B'nai Brith." See Commission of Inquiry, *Proceedings* 12 (1985), 1448–1507; *Proceedings* 26 (1985), 3508–90. In addition, three major briefs were submitted by Kenneth Narvey, representing North America Jewish Students Network-Canada. CIWC, "Notes for a Submission to be Made in Person before the Commission of Inquiry on War Criminals," June 10, 1985; "Some Comments on the Presently Available Views of Mr. Martin Low and on Some Matters Arising Therefrom," September 20, 1985; "Some Comments on and Research Inspired by the Reports of the Commission's Work Group of Legal Experts," August 22, 1986. For a detailed review of the thrust of legal arguments developed by Congress and B'nai Brith, see Matas and Charendoff, *Justice Delayed*, 94–116.

88 CIWC, Cotler, "Submissions and Recommendations," July 10, 1985, 31.

89 Found in Section 6 of the Canadian *Criminal Code*. See Commission of Inquiry, *Report*, 157–68.

90 CIWC, Irwin Cotler, "Government Inaction," December 4, 1985, 19–20. See also Commission of Inquiry, *Report*, 134.

91 CIWC, Cotler "Submissions and Recommendations," 29–34.

92 BBP, Deschênes Commission File, Matas, "Submission of B'nai Brith," May 22, 1985, 35; Commission of Inquiry, *Proceedings* 12 (1985), 1501.

93 BBP, Deschênes Commission File, Matas, "Submission of B'nai Brith," May 22, 1985, 31; Commission of Inquiry, *Proceedings* 12 (1985), 1462–1508.

94 Allan A. Ryan, Jr., *Quiet Neighbors: Prosecuting Nazi War Criminals in America* (New York, 1984), 65–93; interview with Neal Sher, Dec. 31, 1986, Washington.

95 The official Ukrainian views are best reflected in the following briefs: PYP, John Sopinka, "Commission of Inquiry on War Criminals Submission of the Ukrainian Canadian Committee," May 5, 1986; Commission of Inquiry, *Proceedings* 26 (1985), 3477–507; PYP, Y.R. Botiuk, "Submissions and Recommendations of the Veterans of the First Division of the Ukrainian National Army to the Commission of Inquiry on War Criminals," May 5, 1986; Commission of Inquiry, *Proceedings* 27 (1985), 3592–3643; CIWC, Roman Serbyn, "Soumission à la commission d'enquête sur les criminels de guerre," for La commission d'information et contre la diffamation du comité Ukrainien du Canada (section de Montréal), May 6, 1985.

96 PYP, Sopinka, "Commission of Inquiry," May 5, 1986, 9–17; Commission of Inquiry, *Proceedings* 26 (1985), 3480.

97 PYP, Sopinka, "Commission of Inquiry," May 5, 1986, 12–13.

98 PYP, Sopinka, "Commission of Inquiry," May 5, 1986, 16.

99 PYP, Sopinka, "Commission of Inquiry," May 5, 1986, 31, 35–47.

100 PYP, Sopinka, "Commission of Inquiry," May 5, 1986, 47.

101 *The Globe and Mail*, January 31, 1987.

Chapter Six: The Perils of Ethnic Politics

1 Interview with Orest Rudzik, March 31, 1987, Toronto.

2 *New Perspective*, May 1985.

3 Bohdan Krawchenko Papers, Minister, Ukrainian Community Development Committee — Prairie Region, June 21–22, 1985, Winnipeg; CLCP, Mail out — CLC Executive File, Gregorovich to Rozumna, June 21, 1985; Report to the National Executive of the Ukrainian Canadian Committee by the Executive Committee of the Civil Liberties Commission,

June 21, 1985; CLCP, Conference CLC File, Gregorovich to Nowosad, July 10, 1985.

4   CIUS, UCC Civil Liberties Commission, 1985 File, CLC, *Bulletin*, August 12, 1985.

5   Bohdan Krawchenko Papers, Simon Wiesenthal Center, Press Release, "Ukrainian and Baltic Organizations Seek $1,000,000 to Thwart War Crimes Enquiry," July 25, 1985.

6   *The Toronto Star*, July 26, 1985; CIUS, UCC Civil Liberties Commission, 1985 File, CLC Press Release, August 8, 1985, Toronto; JCRC Papers, Ukrainian File, Simon Wiesenthal Center, Press Kit, July 25, 1985.

7   JTA Daily News Bulletin (New York), August 14, 1985; *Jewish Western Bulletin* (Vancouver), August 29, 1985.

8   Interview with Rose Wolfe, December 17, 1987, Toronto.

9   Interview with Sol Littman, January 21, 1986, Toronto. Littman's relations with B'nai Brith were somewhat warmer and he maintained a good working relationship with both Cotler and Matas at the Deschênes hearings. Interview with Frank Dimant, January 28, 1988.

10   Interview with Milton Harris, May 10, 1986, Toronto.

11   CJC-S, Deschênes-Littman Material, Littman to "Member of Parliament," October 15, 1985; MHP, War Crimes Files, Harris to "Members of Parliament," October 29, 1985; *Echo*, November 27, 1985.

12   SWC, Littman to Rose, November 15, 1985.

13   Witer Mailing, Littman to "Members of Parliament" November 7, 1985.

14   CJC-S, War Crimes-Cross Canada Campaign file, Harris to Littman, December 13, 1985.

15   Interview with Sol Littman, January 11, 1988, Toronto.

16   Interview with Andrew Witer, March 20, 1986, Ottawa.

17   YBP, "A Brief Discussion Paper, June 12, 1985, Commission of Inquiry on War Criminals, Jules Deschênes, Commissioner, 1985." An almost identical "Discussion Paper" is dated June 26, 1985.

18   *Ukrainian Echo*, September 4, 1985; *Homin Ukrainy*, July 11, 1985; *Homin Ukrainy*, September 11, 1985. The demonstration did not go unnoticed on Parliament Hill. Several MPs delivered personal greetings, but, to the chagrin of the

demonstrators, there was no official greeting from the government itself. Nevertheless, among the speakers was Mississauga Conservative MP Patrick Boyer, who denounced any use of "Soviet evidence in Canada." Boyer, a fervent anti-Communist, was sufficiently concerned by the arguments swirling about the Deschênes Inquiry that he determined to set up a Parliamentary Study Group among interested MPs and Senators. But July in Ottawa was not a time for parliamentary study groups. Although Boyer could do the preparatory work, the study group would not formally meet until mid-autumn. Interview with Richard Cleroux, July 8, 1986, Ottawa; interview with Nadia Diakun, March 20, 1986, Ottawa; interview with Patrick Boyer, July 21, 1987, Toronto.

19 Interview with Andrew Witer, March 20, 1986, Ottawa; interview with Paul Yuzyk, March 19, 1986, Ottawa.

20 BBP, Deschênes Commission File, Office of the Prime Minister, "Notes for an Address by Prime Minister Brian Mulroney, Israel Bond Dinner, Montreal, June 5, 1985."

21 Interview with Geoff Norquay, March 21, 1986, Ottawa; interview with John Nicholls, March 20, 1986, Ottawa.

22 Interview with Bohdan Krawchenko, March 15, 1987, Ottawa; interview with John Nowosad, May 30, 1986, Winnipeg; interview with John Gregorovich, April 8, 1987, Toronto.

23 Interview with Orest Rudzik, March 31, 1987, Toronto.

24 CLCP, CLC-Other Organizations File, Gregorovich to Angus, November 20, 1985.

25 Interview with John Nicholls, March 20, 1986, Ottawa.

26 Secretary of State for Multiculturalism, Memorandum to Minister of State — Multiculturalism from Under Secretary of State — Multiculturalism, September 17, 1985; Memorandum to Minister of State — Multiculturalism from Assistant Under Secretary of State — Multiculturalism, re: "Possible Intervention Relating to the Deschênes Commission," September 23, 1985; Memorandum of Bisson to Bowie re: "Deschênes Commission," September 19, 1986; interview with Geoff Norquay, March 21, 1986, Ottawa; interview with John Nicholls, March 20, 1986, Ottawa.

27 CLCP, Other Government File, Witer to Deschênes, September 18, 1985; Logan to Witer, September 20, 1985.

28 *The Globe and Mail*, September 25, 1985; *The Toronto Star*, September 25, 1985; *Winnipeg Free Press*, September 25,

1985; *The Ottawa Citizen*, September 25, 1985; *Kitchener-Waterloo Record*, September 25, 1985; interview with Patrick Boyer, July 21, 1987, Toronto.

29 CLCP, Other Government File, Boudria to Mulroney, September 25, 1985; House of Commons *Debates*, September 27, 1985, 7090; *The Globe and Mail*, September 28, 1985; House of Commons *Debates*, October 1, 1985, 7199–7200; CLCP, Other Government File, McCrossan to Lysenko, October 10, 1985.

30 BBP, Deschênes Commission File, Kilgour to Deschênes, September 18, 1985; Kilgour to Rose, October 2, 1985; *The Gazette* (Montreal), September 25, 1985.

31 CLCP, CLC-UCC File, Gregorovich to Dmytryshyn, March 23, 1986.

32 *The Globe and Mail*, September 25, 1985. A French-language version of the same advertisement appeared in *L'Actualité*, December 1985, 149. The combined cost of the English and French ads came to approximately $46,000. Interview with John Gregorovich, March 12, 1985, Toronto; interview with Yury Boshyk, February 13, 1986, Toronto.

33 *Canadian Jewish News*, October 10, 1985.

34 *Canadian Jewish News*, October 10, 1985; BBP, Deschênes Commission File, Memorandum to Toronto Regional Council Executive and Toronto Lodge Presidents from Dimant re: "The Use of Soviet Evidence in Prosecuting Nazi War Criminals in Canada," September 26, 1985.

35 Toronto JCRC Papers, Ukrainian File, Minutes, JCRC Ad Hoc Sub-committee re: "Issues Arising Out of the Campaign by Certain East European Interest Groups, October 4, 1985.

36 MHP, War Crimes Files, Minutes, JCRC Meeting, October Region, Toronto, October 10, 1985 JCRC; JCRC Ontario Meeting with MPs and MPPs re: "Deschênes Commission," October–November, 1985," n.d.

37 *The Globe and Mail*, November 6, 1985.

38 YBP, Grossman to Shymko, October 21, 1985; Shymko to "Friends and Fellow Conservatives," November 6, 1985; Timbrell to Shymko, October 30, 1985; Pope to Friends, November 4, 1985.

39 *Vilne Slovo*, December 14, 1985; *The Globe and Mail*, November 6, 1985.

40 MHP, War Crimes Files, Report, JCRC Ontario Meetings with MPs and MPPs re: Deschênes Commission, October–November, 1985.

41 CJC-S, Deschênes Commission, Press Releases, Newspaper Clippings, Statement by Milton Harris re: "Suspected Nazi Mass Murderers in Canada," February 27, 1985.

42 Interview with Les Scheininger, March 25, 1987, Toronto.

43 JCRC, Minutes, Central Region, CJRC, Toronto, June 26, 1985; NJCRC, Minutes, National JCRC, September 9, 1985, Montreal.

44 Interview with Ben Kayfetz, June 17, 1987, Toronto.

45 Interview with Roman Serbyn, February 18, 1986, Montreal; CJC-R, Ukrainians, Memorandum Rose to Harris re: "Proposed CJC/CCCJ dialogue with Ukrainian leadership," May 14, 1985; Memorandum Rose to Harris, May 16, 1985; NJCRC, Minutes of National JCRC, September 9, 1985, Montreal.

46 YBP, Kotick to Tataryn, February 20, 1985; Tataryn to Kotick, February 26, 1985; Kotick to Boshyk, March 4, 1985; JCRC, Minutes, Central Region JCRC, June 26, 1985, Toronto; interview with Victor Goldbloom, March 13, 1986, Toronto; interview with Father John Tataryn, May 27, 1986, Toronto.

47 JCRC Papers, Ukrainian File, Bartkiw to National Executive, May 21, 1985. Enclosed with the letter was a partial transcript of Littman's remarks; a similar letter was sent to the B'nai Brith. BBP, UCC File, Bartkiw to B'nai Brith Canada, May 28, 1985.

48 CJC-R, Ukrainians, Rose to Bartkiw, May 30, 1985; JCRC Papers, Ukrainian File, Bartkiw to Rose, June 5, 1985; DMP, Matas to Bartkiw, June 21, 1985.

49 CLCP, Conference CLC File, Minutes, CLC National Executive Meeting, July 13, 1985.

50 Interview with Ian Kagedan, February 20, 1986, Montreal.

51 CJC-R, Ukrainians, Kagedan to Rose, June 25, 1985.

52 CIUS, Simon Wiesenthal File, Rose to Nowosad, July 26, 1985; interview with Alan Rose, February 19, 1986, Montreal.

53 CJC-R, Ukrainians, Nowosad to Rose, August 27, 1985; JCRC Papers, Ukrainian File, Rose to Kondra, September 3,

1985, CJC-R, Ukrainians, Weretelynk to Rose, October 8, 1985. Interview with John Nowosad, May 30, 1986, Winnipeg.

54   CLCP, Conference CLC File, Minutes, National Executive, CLC, June 13, 1985.

55   CJC-R, Ukrainians, Rose to Weretelnyk, October 8, 1985.

56   CJC-S, Ukrainian Canadian Committee re: Deschênes File, Weretelnyk to Rose, December 2, 1985; CJC-R, Ukrainians, Telegram Rose to Weretelnyk, December 6, 1986; BBP, UCC File, Memorandum of Dimant to Kachuck re: "Deschênes Commission — Ukrainian National Committee, December 12, 1985.

57   Interview with Ellen Kachuck, April 21, 1986, Toronto; interview with Paul Yuzyk, March 19, 1986, Ottawa; interview with Alan Rose, February 16, 1986, Montreal; interview with Jack Silverstone, February 29, 1986, Montreal; interview with Arthur Hiess, April 3, 1986, Montreal.

58   Interview with Senator Paul Yuzyk, March 19, 1986, Ottawa.

59   *The Ottawa Citizen*, December 7, 1985.

60   *The Globe and Mail*, December 10, 1985.

61   *Ukrainian News*, December 11, 1985; *Ukrainian Echo*, December, 1985.

62   CLCP, CLC-General File, Christie to Hyrhouych [sic], n.d.; Gregorovich to Christie, November 26, 1985.

63   CLC-MB, Minutes of the Meeting of the Executive Committee of the Civil Liberties Association of the Ukrainian Canadian Committee, March 12, 1986; March 29, 1986. Henceforth meetings of the CLC executive will be cited as Minutes, CLC Executive Committee, with appropriate date.

64   CLC-MB, Minutes, CLC Executive Committee, March 12, 1986.

65   CLC-MB, Minutes of CLC Executive Committee, Dec. 10, 1986.

66   CLCP, Report File, Executive Report of the Civil Liberties Commission to the Fifteenth Congress, Ukrainian Canadian Committee, October 10–13, 1986.

67   J. Rozumnyj, ed. *New Soil, Old Roots* (Winnipeg), 1983.

68   Nikolai Tolstoy, *Trial and Error: Canada's Commission of Inquiry on War Criminals and the Soviets* (Toronto, 1986).

69   Peter Paluch, "Spiking the Ukrainian Famine, Again," *The National Review* (April 11, 1986), 33–38.

70   CLCP, CLC — Other Organizations File, Witer to Gregorovich, December 22, 1985; Gregorovich to Witer, March 2, 1986.

71   Interview with Ian Kagedan, Feb. 20, 1986, Montreal; *The Globe and Mail* Nov. 18, 1986; interview with Alex Chumak, August 6, 1987, Toronto.

72   Interview with Paul R. Magocsi, January 26, 1986, Toronto.

73   Paluch, "Spiking the Ukrainian Famine, Again"; see also Paul R. Magocsi, "Famine or Genocide," *The World and I* (April 1987), 416–423.

74   CLCP, Reports File, Executive Report of the Civil Liberties Commission to the Fifteenth Congress of the Ukrainian Canadian Committee, October 10–13, 1986, 13.

75   CLCP, Reports File, Executive Report of the Civil Liberties Commission, October 10–13, 1986, 16.

76   CLCP, CLC — General File, Gregorovich to Artemenko, Jan. 5, 1986.

77   CLCP, CLC-Legal File, Christie to Gregorovich to Christie, April 21, 1986. The reference in the letter is to Holocaust historian Raul Hilberg of the University of Vermont, author of *The Destruction of the European Jews*, 3 vol., rev. ed. (New York, 1985). Hilberg was one of the expert witnesses brought in by the Crown to testify for the prosecution in the Zundel trial.

78   CLCP, CLC-Legal File, Christie to Gregorovich, May 17, 1986.

79   CLCP, CLC-Legal File, Gregorovich, July 4, 1986; CLCP, Press Release File, Minutes, Executive Committee of the CLC, Feb 12, 1986.

80   *The Globe and Mail*, February 6, 1987.

81   *Ukrainian Weekly*, December 1, 1985, 6.

82   CLCP, Ukr. Orgs., Gregorovich to Moravski, December 17, 1986.

83   *The Gazette* (Montreal) January 23, 1986; *The Globe and Mail*, May 9, 1986; *The Ottawa Citizen*, May 31, 1986; *The Toronto Star*, June 3, 1986 and June 14, 1986.

84 Gregorovich to Jelinek, Jan 24, 1986; Jelinek to Gregorovich, March 10, 1986; CLCP, Government File. Dickson to Gregorovich, March 5, 1986; Gregorovich to Jelinek, April 22, 1986; McInnes to Gregorovich, May 16, 1986; Labrie to Gregorovich, April 22, 1986.

85 UCCP, Hladkyj to Crosbie, Jan. 9, 1986; *Western Jewish News*, December 5, 1985.

86 DMP, Ontario Press Council, Advance for Release, Monday June 23, 1986.

87 DMP, Matas to Ontario Press Council, July 10, 1986.

88 *The Globe and Mail*, March 18, 1986.

89 JCRC, JCRC Press Release, March 19, 1986.

90 JCRC, Minutes of the JCRC, March 26, 1986.

91 *The Edmonton Journal*, January 20, 1987; Letter in possession of authors, Rosenbaum to Weinfeld, May 27, 1987; Choloc to CBS, March 18, 1987; Lebedin to CBS Programming Division, March 9, 1987.

92 Eli Rosenbaum papers, Rosenbaum to CBS Programming Division, April 8, 1987.

93 Correspondence from Rosenbaum, *The Ukrainian Weekly*, May 10, 1987, June 28, 1987.

94 *The Gazette* (Montreal), Oct. 16, 1986; *The Financial Post*, April 12, 1986.

95 CLCP, Others-government, Members of the Skovoroda seniors group, Ukrainian Welfare Services Inc. to Mulroney, April 3, 1986; Pattison to Minister of Justice, reprinted in *Ukrainian Echo*, December 25, 1986; CCCP, Others-government, Balaban to Mulroney, February 25, 1987; Boyer to Mulroney, February 2, 1987.

96 Interview with John Gregorovich, April 8, 1987, Toronto.

97 *Canadian Jewish News*, January 16, 1986; interview with Patrick Boyer, July 21, 1987, Toronto.

98 *Novy Shliakh*, February 22, 1986, 4. Much of the Ukrainian-language press material used in this chapter was summarized and translated by Joe Forster and Associates; interview with David Matas, March 31, 1988, Winnipeg.

99 Shymko to Deschênes, February 12, 1986; Diakun to Deschênes, February 26, 1986; SWC, Littman to Shymko, March 5, 1986.

100 *Canadian Jewish News*, January 16, 1986.

101 CLCP, CLC-Other Organization Files, Gregorovich to Angus, February 23, 1986.

102 *Ukrainian Echo*, September 18, 1986; interview with Andrew Witer, March 20, 1986, Ottawa.

103 As mentioned earlier, data on voting patterns in the 1984 federal elections did show movement, at least among "young leaders" of the Jewish community, to the Conservatives. See Harold Waller and Morton Weinfeld, "A *Viewpoints* Survey of Canadian Jewish Leadership Opinion," *Viewpoints* 15 (Supplement to *Canadian Jewish News*, October 8, 1987), 1–3.

104 BBP, Deschênes Commission File, Memorandum from Ellen Kachuck to B'nai Brith Toronto Regional Council Executive and Toronto Lodge Presidents, January 6 1986.

105 CJC-S, Commission of Inquiry, Correspondence, 1986, Silverstone, general letter Dear Friend, December 18, 1985.

106 *The Ottawa Citizen*, November 20, 1985; interview with Roman Serbyn, February 18, 1986, Montreal.

107 Interview with Irwin Cotler, July 23, 1987, Montreal.

108 *Maariv*, March 14, 1986.

109 JC-S, Commission of Inquiry, Correspondence, 1986, Harris to Silverstone, "re: Meeting with the Solicitor General," January 17, 1986.

110 CJC-R, Ukrainian File, Rose to Silverstone, Aug. 12, 1986.

111 CJC-R, Ukrainian File, Memorandum Silverstone to National Officers Committee, "Commission of Inquiry on War Criminals, Congress Post Report Action Plan," September 7, 1987.

112 *Canadian Jewish News*, February 13, 1986.

113 *The Globe and Mail*, March 1, 1986; interview with Andrew Witer, MP, March 20, 1986, Ottawa; interview with Father John Tataryn, May 7, 1986, Toronto.

114 CLCP, untagged file, John Gregorovich, Memorandum: "Report on Meeting with Eli M. Rosenbaum," January 12, 1986; interview with Eli Rosenbaum, May 11, 1987, New York.

115 CJC-S, Commission of Inquiry, Correspondence, 1986, Silverstone to Yuzyk, January 22, 1986.

116 Interview with Senator Paul Yuzyk, March 19, 1986, Ottawa.

117 BBP, UCC File, Draft, Statement by Canadian Jewish Congress, B'nai Brith of Canada, and the Ukrainian Canadian Committee, prepared by Canadian Jewish Congress.

118 Interview with Alan Rose, February 19, 1986, Montreal.

119 BBP, Deschênes Commission File, Draft, Statement by Canadian Jewish Congress, B'nai Brith of Canada, and the Ukrainian Canadian Committee, prepared by Paul Yuzyk.

120 BBP, UCC File, Kachuck, Rosenbluth to Silverstone, February 26, 1986; Rose to Dimant, Feb. 28, 1986.

121 Interview with Jack Silverstone, May 11, 1987, Montreal; interview with Alan Rose, May 13, 1986. Montreal.

122 *Canadian Jewish News*, April 23, 1986; interview with Dorothy Reitman, April, 8 1987; BBP, UCC File, Nowosad to Bick, July 2, 1986.

123 JCRC, Flyer, "Let My People Go," n.d.

124 UCCP, News Release, "The Ukrainian Canadian Committee condemns attacks on the Jewish Canadian community," March 13, 1986; *Canadian Jewish News*, March 20, 1986. This disavowal did not, however, stop broadsides attacking Jews for their alleged persecution of Ukrainians. In April the Ukrainian Anti-Defamation League distributed flyers, taking over where the Ukrainian Defence League left off. Those flyers, in the form of open letters to Toronto residents, attacked both Congress and Sol Littman for implying that "the great Ukrainian nation is comprised of nazi war criminals. These are the same types of attacks which have been launched against Mr. Kurt Waldheim . . ." BBP, General File, Flyer of UA-DL.

125 *Ukrainian News* April 9, 1986.

126 *Ukrainian News*, March 19, 1986; interview with Bohdan Krawchenko, March 15, 1987, Ottawa.

127 *The Globe and Mail*, Feb. 25, 1986.

128 CLC-MB, Minutes, CLC Executive Committee, March 1, 1986; *The Globe and Mail*, May 16, 1986. Canadian Jewish leaders, forever concerned lest the Deschênes exercise slide into open ethnic warfare, also exercised restraint. An Israeli scholar, taking part in a Ukrainian-Jewish academic symposium at McMaster University in Hamilton, recalls being approached by two self-declared representatives of the Toronto Jewish community. They told him that relations between Jews and Ukrainians were very tense as a result of the Des-

chênes Commission. Ukrainians in Canada outnumbered Jews, and they were very powerful. The scholar, a historian of eastern Europe, was urged to "take that into consideration" when delivering his remarks. It was hoped he could thereby avoid antagonizing the Ukrainians present. Interview with Aharon Weiss, December 11, 1986, Jerusalem.

129 See Randolph Braham, *The Politics of Genocide: The Holocaust in Hungary* (New York, 1981).

130 *The Globe and Mail*, April 30, 1986.

131 *The Globe and Mail*, September 3, 1986; interview with John Sopinka, May 26, 1987, Toronto. Sopinka explained there was no contradiction between his gathering communist evidence for CTV against Finta, and his opposition to Soviet evidence for the UCC. In the Finta case, they had the cooperation of the Hungarian government, and proceeded "as if in a Canadian court." Moreover, Finta's counsel was present and active in Hungary during the video-taped examination of witnesses.

132 *Ukrainian Weekly*, January 19, 1986; UCCP, Press Release, "Ukrainian Canadians Express Outrage," April 11, 1986.

133 *Ukrainian News*, March 19, 1986.

134 At first glance, it would seem that Ukrainians are severely under-represented among the righteous gentiles of Yad Vashem. There are 79 Ukrainians compared to more than 2,000 Poles. But, according to a Yad Vashem official, these differences may, in part, reflect reporting discrepancies. Many of those listed as Poles may have been Ukrainians by ethnic origin. Of greater importance is the relative encouragement given to discovery and publicity of righteous gentiles in the two areas. In Poland there are two national institutions which research the area of non-Jewish rescue of Jews and communicate findings to Yad Vashem. No such institutions operate within Ukraine or the USSR. Personal correspondence to the authors, Paldiel to Weinfeld, March 22, 1987.

135 The role of the Catholic Church and the Vatican during the Holocaust remains a topic of heated historical debate. See Michael Marrus, *The Holocaust in History* (Toronto, 1987), 179–83.

136 Interview with Aharon Weiss, December 11, 1986, Jerusalem.

137 CLCP, Demjanjuk File, Olshaniwsky to the Knesset, September 18, 1986.

138 CLCP, Demjanjuk File, Ben Meir to the President, Americans for Human Rights in Ukraine, October, 1986.

139 CLCP, Demjanjuk File, Olshaniwsky to Ben Meir, December 15, 1986.

140 *The Globe and Mail*, January 14, 1987; *Canadian Jewish News*, January 22, 1987.

141 In the United States, when faced with a 1984 electoral choice between right-wing Republicans or a Democratic party that had tolerated Jesse Jackson's ambivalent posture on Jews and Israel, Jews remained strongly attached to their Democratic, liberal roots. Steven M. Cohen, *American Modernity and Jewish Identity* (New York, 1983), 134–53. The problem is that some of the bedfellows of the radical right, of the leading anti-Soviet groups in North America, are thought by some to be either closet or outspoken anti-Semites. This makes Jewish participation in any broadly based anti-Soviet coalition improbable. For example, according to a 1985 *New York Times* editorial, the Anti-Defamation League of the B'nai Brith had expressed concern that an anti-Semitic fringe existed within the right–wing World Anti-Communist League. The League's president, the *Times* noted, declared that this was "no longer so, that former Nazi SS officers and other extremists had been purged" from the League's ranks.

Canadian Jewish leaders might wonder at the kind of contact Canadian parliamentarians had with the League. According to one radical right–wing Canadian publication, at the 1987 World Anti-Communist League annual conference meeting in Taipei a resolution was passed "against the Canadian Deschênes Report, and all so called 'Nazi-hunting' activities were condemned. This action was supported by everyone of the 23 Canadian delegates present, including both federal and provincial parliamentarians, leaders of ethnic groups, and others." *New York Times*, August 30, 1985; *The Gazette* (Montreal), December 18, 1986; Ron Gostick, "From Week To Week", *On Target*, September 7, 1987, 2; interview with Alan Shefman, February 19, 1987, Toronto.

142 *The Toronto Star*, November 23, 1986 and November 29, 1986.

143 A.C. Menzies, *Review of Material Relating to the Entry of Suspected War Criminals into Australia* (Canberra, 1986).

144 *The Gazette* (Montreal), February 17, 1987; *Canadian Jewish News*, January 13, 1987.

145 Interview with John Sopinka, May 26, 1987, Toronto; *The Calgary Sun* January 16, 1987; *The Toronto Star*, January 21, 1987.

146 *Ukrainian Echo*, February 25, 1987.

147 Interview with John Gregorovich, April 8, 1987, Toronto; interview with David Matas, January 20, 1987, Toronto.

148 *The Globe and Mail*, February 2, 1987.

149 *Kanadai Magyarsag*, February 14, 1987; interview with Audrey Kobayashi, March 17, 1987, Montreal. Another group absent from the list was the Poles. With regard to World War II, Poles would tend to emphasize their resistance to the Nazis, as well as the existence of a large anti-Nazi underground. Even William Styron chose as the heroine/victim of his Holocaust novel, *Sophie's Choice*, a Polish Gentile woman. In addition, one secret organization of Poles, the *Zagota*, was devoted to the rescue of Jews. Roughly 2,000 of the righteous gentiles identified by Yad Vashem are Poles.
It was thus not without some pleasure that Ukrainian leaders must have greeted the film *Shoah*. The film offers a portrayal not only of Polish (and Ukrainian) anti-Semitism during the war, but also demonstrates, in interviews with Poles today, a still lingering hatred of Jews. The ensuing scholarly debates about the Polish track record during the war were followed by Ukrainian-Canadian leaders. CLCP, CLC-Ukr. Orgs., Yurkevich to Gregorovich, March 4, 1986.

150 *Canadian Jewish News*, March 5, 1987; interview with Arthur Hiess, February 24, 1987.

151 DMP, David Matas, "Protect the Innocent," remarks prepared for delivery to the National Congress of Italian Canadians, Montreal, February 21, 1987. Recent literature on Italy during the Holocaust would tend to reinforce Matas's argument. See Meir Michaelis, *Mussolini and the Jews: German-Italian Relations and the Jewish Question in Italy, 1922–1945* (Oxford, 1978) and Susan Zuccotti, *The Italians and the Holocaust: Persecution, Rescue and Survival* (New York, 1987).

152 CLCP, Other Organizations, Rose to the President, Canadian Coalition for Vietnamese Human Rights, March 5, 1987. David Matas and Susan Charendoff, *Justice Delayed: Nazi War Criminals in Canada* (Toronto, 1987), 183–86.

153 Interview with Alan Rose, August 12, 1987, Montreal.

154 *The Globe and Mail*, February 4, 1987.

155 *The Globe and Mail*, February 13, 1987; CLCP, Legal File, Johnston, per Patricia Rose, to CLC, February 19, 1987. Sopinka to Rose, c/o Johnston, March 23, 1987.

156 CLCP, Media File, Gregorovich per Michael Kulyk to *The Globe and Mail*, Feb. 13, 1987.

Chapter Seven: The Report and its Aftermath

1 Interview with David Matas, March 29, 1987, Ottawa; interview with John Gregorovich, April 8, 1987, Toronto; interview with Ellen Kachuck, March 29, 1987, Ottawa.

2 Cited in Sol Littman, "Report on the Deschênes Commission," *The Canadian Forum* (June/July, 1987), 7.

3 Commission of Inquiry on War Criminals. *Report, Part I: Public* (Ottawa, 1986).

4 Commission of Inquiry, *Report*, 262, 827–28.

5 Commission of Inquiry, *Report*, 268–72.

6 Commission of Inquiry, *Report*, 47–48. Among those contributing names were: Joseph Riwash of Montreal who supplied 707 names culled from Yad Vashem in Israel; Simon Wiesenthal of Vienna, 219; the Canadian Jewish Congress and Irwin Cotler, 209; Sol Littman, 171; B'nai Brith of Canada, 100; The Department of Justice of Canada, 81; the Simon Wiesenthal Center of Los Angeles, 63; the Canadian Holocaust Remembrance Association, 54; Israeli police, 54; the Jewish Federation of North Jersey, 49; the government of the USSR, 43; and Ephraim Zuroff, formerly of OSI, 29. There was substantial overlap among the lists.

7 Commission of Inquiry, *Report*, 55–58.

8 Commission of Inquiry, *Report*, 59.

9 Commission of Inquiry, *Report*, 59–61.

10 Commission of Inquiry, *Report*, 62.

11 Commission of Inquiry, *Report*, 249–61; interview with Michael Meighen, May 15, 1987, Toronto.

12 Commission of Inquiry, *Report*, 258, 249; interview with Michael Meighen, May 15, 1987, Toronto.

13 Commission of Inquiry, *Report*, 373, 391, 623, 444–45.

14 Commission of Inquiry, *Report*, 759–60, 501–2.

15 Commission of Inquiry, *Report*, 734, 330–31.

16 Commission of Inquiry, *Report*, 447–48, 474–75, 522, 724.

17 Commission of Inquiry, *Report*, 262. Such cases are almost certainly not ones referring to eastern Europe, since deportation there might not be countenanced. In eighteen cases the assistance of a foreign government is required to support criminal prosecution in Canada. Four require assistance from western governments, and fourteen from eastern bloc countries, including eight from the Soviet Union.

18 Canadian Press 1944 ES 16-03 87; *The Ottawa Citizen*, March 13, 1987; Alti Rodal, "Nazi War Criminals in Canada: The Historical and Policy Setting from the 1940s to the Present" (Prepared for the Commission of Inquiry on War Criminals, September 1986), 343–65; Sol Littman, "Barbie's Buddy in Canada," *Canadian Dimension* (October 1987), 13–15.

19 *The Toronto Star*, March 14, 1987; *The Globe and Mail*, March 18, 1987; Rodal, "Nazi War Criminals in Canada," 446–81.

20 Canadian Press 1856 ES 16-03-87; *The Toronto Star*, March 14, 1987; *The Globe and Mail*, March 18, 1987; Rodal, "Nazi War Criminals in Canada," 409–45.

21 Commission of Inquiry, *Report*, 833; *The Ottawa Citizen*, March 13, 1987; *The Globe and Mail*, March 18, 1987.

22 *The Ottawa Citizen*, March 13, 1987; Canadian Press Ottawa 17-03 0446.

23 *The Globe and Mail*, March 17, 1987. *The Gazette* (Montreal), March 18, 1987.

24 *The Globe and Mail*, March 18, 1987; interview with Alti Rodal, July 3, 1987, Ottawa.

25 Interview with Irwin Cotler, July 23, 1987, Montreal.

26 *The Globe and Mail*, Aug. 8, 1987; *The Gazette* (Montreal) August 12, 1987, August 13, 1987, August 14, 1987; *The Globe and Mail*, November 9, 1987; Rodal, "Nazi War Criminals in Canada," 324–26B.

27 *The Globe and Mail*, August 22, 1987; Rodal, "Nazi War Criminals in Canada," 326A–26B.

28 *The Globe and Mail*, August 7, 1987.

29   Commission of Inquiry, *Report*, 167–242, 91, 96, 105, 225, 239. Deschênes offered his own draft amendment to the *Criminal Code* and acknowledged his reliance on the wording prepared earlier by Kenneth Narvey. Commission of Inquiry, *Report*, 159.

30   Commission of Inquiry, *Report*, 869–92.

31   Commission of Inquiry, *Report*, 829; recommendation 81, 830.

32   *Ukrainian Weekly*, March 22, 1987.

33   House of Commons, *Debates*, March 12, 1987, 4076.

34   House of Commons, *Debates*, March 12, 1987, 4084.

35   House of Commons, *Debates*, Hansard, March 12, 1987, 4078, 4083.

36   House of Commons, *Debates*, March 12,1987, 4082–83.

37   Centre for Communications, Culture, and Society, Carleton University, Ottawa, "The Impact of the Deschênes Commission: Part 2: The Reaction of the Public. Attitudes Towards War Crime Issues. Report of Western Canada Survey," January 29, 1987; interestingly, polls carried out for the government *after* the release of the Deschênes *Report* and the attendant publicity show essentially no change in the pattern of attitudes. There was only a slight increase in support for war-criminals investigations, no apparent linkage of Ukrainians to war criminality and only minimal public awareness of the recent Deschênes Commission itself. Centre for Communications, Culture, and Society, Carleton University, "Highlights of Interim Report #5," June 30, 1987.

38   *The Gazette* (Montreal) March 13, 1987; *The Ottawa Citizen*, March 13 1987; *The Globe and Mail*, March 13, 1987; Commission of Inquiry *Report*, 261.

39   Sol Littman, "Report on the Deschênes Commission," 8.

40   *The Globe and Mail*, March 13, 1987; *Winnipeg Free Press*, March 13, 1987.

41   *The Toronto Star*, March 16, 1987.

42   *Winnipeg Free Press*, March 13, 1987.

43   Canadian Press 1759ES, 12-03-87.

44   *Winnipeg Free Press*, March 13, 1987.

45   Canadian Press 1922 ES 12-03-87; *Canadian Jewish News*, March 19, 1987.

46   Sol Littman, "Report on Deschênes Commission," 7–8.

47   Author's notes, Meeting of the Canadian Jewish Congress National Executive, March 5, 1987, Montreal.

48   Interview with Eli Rosenbaum, May 11, 1987, New York; correspondence with authors, Rosenbaum to Weinfeld, July 9, 1987.

49   *The Ottawa Citizen*, March 19, 1987.

50   *The Globe and Mail*, March 10, 1987.

51   *The Globe and Mail*, March 13, 1987.

52   *The Toronto Star*, March 13, 1987; *The Winnipeg Sun*, March 13, 1987; *The Globe and Mail*, March 13, 1987.

53   *The Toronto Sun*, March 13, 1987; *Winnipeg Free Press*, March 13, 1987.

54   *The Toronto Star*, March 13, 1987.

55   *Ukrainian Echo*, March 25, 1987. Reprinted in *Ukrainian News*, Edmonton, April 15, 1987 and *Ukrainian Weekly*, March 29, 1987.

56   *Ukrainian News*, April 29, 1987, 14.

57   *Ukrainian News*, March 18, 1987. *Rapprochement* was in the air on other fronts as well. For some time Poles and Jews had sensed the need for a clearing of the air about the murkier aspects of their relations. Polish and Jewish scholars in the diaspora, as well as in Poland and Israel, had begun meeting in international exchanges. Closer to home, leaders of the two communities had begun to make tentative efforts at dialogue. Perhaps the impact of Claude Lanzmann's *Shoah*, with its focus on Polish involvement in the destruction of Polish Jewry, made such encounters more timely. But there were also practical considerations.
     Polish organizations in both Canada and the United States were generally more sympathetic to the hunt for Nazi war criminals (interview with Neal Sher, December 31, 1987, Washington). Poles and Ukrainians, moreover, had been at odds historically, and relations were at times uneasy in the New World as well. Against the backdrop of the impending release of the *Report*, a meeting of Congress officials and the Quebec region of the Canadian Polish Congress took place on March 6. Alan Rose of the Canadian Jewish Congress asked for support in the campaign to prod the government to act on recommendations of the forthcoming Deschênes *Report*.

The Poles obliged. In a March 13 letter to Justice Minister Hnatyshyn, the Polish Congress expressed support for Deschênes's major recommendations and urged the minister to "expedite the passage of the necessary amendments to the law, in order that it may have some effect before all of the alleged offenders are dead." JCRC, Czarnocki and Rawicz to Hnatyshyn, March 13, 1987.

58 *The Toronto Sun*, March 13, 1987.

59 *The Edmonton Sun*, March 16, 1987; *The Toronto Sun*, March 13, 1987.

60 Commission of Inquiry, *Report*, 6.

61 *The Gazette* (Montreal), March 13, 1987; *The Toronto Sun*, March 17, 1987.

62 *The Globe and Mail*, May 18, 1987.

63 Allan A. Ryan, Jr., *Quiet Neighbors: Prosecuting Nazi War Criminals in America* (New York, 1984), 32–35.

64 *The New York Times*, May 26, 1987; interview with Alan Rose, February 19, 1986, Montreal; Jacob Tannenbaum eventually confessed to the charges of brutalizing fellow prisoners and was stripped of his American citizenship. Because of his failing health, confirmed by defence and government doctors, the Justice Department agreed he would not be deported. *The New York Times*, February 5, 1988.

65 *Winnipeg Free Press*, March 19, 1987.

66 Tape, "Cross Country Check-up," CBC Radio, March 15, 1987.

67 Interview with Douglas Gold, April 7, 1988, Toronto *The Edmonton Journal*, March 13, 1987; *The Globe and Mail*, March 14, 1987; *The Gazette* (Montreal) March 14, 1987; *The Edmonton Journal*, March 14, 1987.

68 Canadian Press 1547 ES 14-03-87; *The Gazette* (Montreal), March 16, 1987.

69 *The Globe and Mail*, May 13, 1987.

70 Interview with Alan Rose, May 13, 1987, Montreal.

71 *The Gazette* (Montreal), February 17, 1987; *The Gazette* (Montreal), April 9, 1987.

72 *Canadian Jewish News* March 12, 1987; *The Globe and Mail*, March 9, 1987.

73   *Ukrainian Weekly*, April 5, 1987; *Ukrainian Weekly*, April 19, 1987; *Canadian Jewish News*, April 16, 1987. *Ukrainian Echo*, April 25, 1987, *Ukrainian Voice*, May 11, 1987.

74   *Canadian Jewish News*, April 23, 1987.

75   *Canadian Jewish News*, May 28, 1987 and June 18, 1987; Prutschi to Dunkelman, March 25, 1987; Stacey to Hnatyshyn, March 19, 1987.

76   *The Globe and Mail*, May 18, 1987.

77   Interview with Judge Jules Deschênes, November 12, 1987, Montreal; *The Gazette* (Montreal), March 13, 1987; *The Globe and Mail*, March 18, 1987 and October 6, 1987.

78   *The Globe and Mail*, June 24, 1987.

79   *The Globe and Mail*, June 27, 1987.

80   *Canadian Jewish News*, July 9, 1987.

81   *Interview with Irwin Cotler*, July 13, 1987; *Canadian Jewish News*, July 9, 1987; David Matas and Susan Charendoff, *Justice Delayed: Nazi War Criminals in Canada* (Toronto, 1987), 220–22.

82   Interview with Dorothy Reitman, August 14, 1987, Montreal.

83   *Canadian Jewish News*, August 30, August 27, and September 3, 1987; *The Globe and Mail, August 29, 1987*, and October 6, 1987. For a discussion of legal issues on *Bill C-71* see Matas and Charendoff, *Justice Delayed*, Chapter 12.

Epilogue

1   Interview with Joseph Klinghofer, May 9, 1986, Toronto. Years later Klinghofer vividly recalled the episode and wished there had been some other way he could have responded.

2   Theodore S. Hamerow, "The Hidden Holocaust," *Commentary* (March 1985), 32–42; David Engel, "The Western Allies and the Holocaust," *Polin* 1 (1987), 300–15; Deborah Lipstadt, *Beyond Belief: The American Press and the Coming of the Holocaust* (New York, 1986).

3   Henry Feingold, "Who Shall Bear Guilt for the Holocaust: The Human Dilemma," *American Jewish History* 68 (1979), 261–82; Ben Hecht, *Perfidy* (New York, 1961); Yehuda

Bauer, *Flight and Rescue* (New York, 1970); Yehuda Bauer, "The Mission of Joel Brand," *The Holocaust in Historical Perspective* (Seattle, 1978); Isaiah Trunk, *Judenrat: The Jewish Councils of Eastern Europe under Nazi Occupation* (New York, 1972); Maurice Friedberg, "The Question of the Judenrate," *Commentary* 41 (July 1973), 61–63; Aharon Weiss, "Jewish Leadership in Occupied Europe — Postures and Attitudes," *Yad Vashem Studies* 2 (1977), 335–65; Yisrael Gutman and Cynthia J. Haft (eds.), *Patterns of Jewish Leadership in Nazi Europe, 1933–1945* (Jerusalem, 1979); Michael Marrus, *The Holocaust in History* (Toronto, 1987), 55–107.

4   This can be contrasted with the American case. Studies of the black vote, the Italian vote, the Jewish vote, the Hispanic vote and the ethnic vote, sometimes called the Catholic vote, abound. For example, see Edgar Litt, *Ethnic Politics in America: Beyond Pluralism* (Glenview, Ill., 1970).

5   Interview with Roman Serbyn, May 3, 1988, Montreal; *Winnipeg Free Press*, April 26, 1988.

6   *The Toronto Star*, April 19, 1988. This comment was quoted in Alan Dershowitz, "Hour of Truth for 'Ivan the Terrible'," *Chicago Sun Times*, April 27, 1988; interview with Susan Reid, May 4, 1988, Toronto; The authors are in possession of an audio tape of the April 18, 1988 press conference.

7   Interview with Dorothy Reitman, May 3, 1988, Montreal; interview with Jack Silverstone, May 3, 1988, Montreal; *The Toronto Star*, April 19, 1988.

8   *Canadian Jewish News*, November 12, 1987; *Canadian Jewish News*, November 19, 1987; *The Globe and Mail*, April 22, 1988. There would doubtless be disagreement as to the pace, method and intent of Canadian negotiations with other countries to allow Canadian investigators to collect evidence in accord with Canadian rules of evidence. *The Globe and Mail*, December 9, 1987; *Canadian Jewish News*, February 18, 1988; *Canadian Jewish News*, March 3, 1988. Jews and Ukrainians are also aware that other jurisdictions, including Britain, Australia, Sweden and Italy, are now initiating legal action against alleged Nazi war criminals, in some cases, with seemingly more speed than Canada. *The Globe and Mail*, February 4, 1988; *Canadian Jewish News*, February 18, 1988.

9   Canada. Province of Ontario, Judicial District of York (College Park Provincial Court). Consent of Minister of Justice regarding Her Majesty the Queen vs. Imre Finta, Ottawa,

Dec. 9, 1987; Information of Sgt. Wayne Frederick Yetter, Dec. 9, 1987.

10 Interview with John Sopinka, May 26, 1987, Toronto; *The Toronto Star*, December 19, 1987; *The Gazette* (Montreal), January 15, 1988.

The lawyer acting for CTV was, of course, John Sopinka who also acted for the Ukranian-Canadian committee before the Deschênes commission. John Sopinka has now been appointed a Justice of the Supreme Court of Canada.

Index

422